The Very Best of the Red Lodge LOCAL RAG

by Gary D. Robson

Proseyr Publishing
Red Lodge, MT U.S.A

Copyright ©2015 Gary D. Robson and the Local Rag
Portions of this book that came from the Local Rag newspaper
are copyrighted the date they were printed.
All rights reserved.

Scanning, uploading, and distribution of this book via the Internet or via any other means without the permission of the publisher is illegal and punishable by law. Please purchase only authorized electronic editions, and do not participate in or encourage electronic piracy of copyrighted materials. Your support of the author's rights is greatly appreciated.

For information about permissions to reprint sections of this book,
email info@proseyr.com.

The Very Best of the Red Lodge Local Rag
By Gary D. Robson

First edition, December 2015
ISBN 978-0-9659609-7-7

Proseyr Publishing
PO Box 1630, Red Lodge, MT 59068
www.proseyr.com

This book is dedicated to all of the people who have contributed to the Local Rag over the years, both those who were paid and those who did it out of love for Red Lodge and the Rag. Thank you!

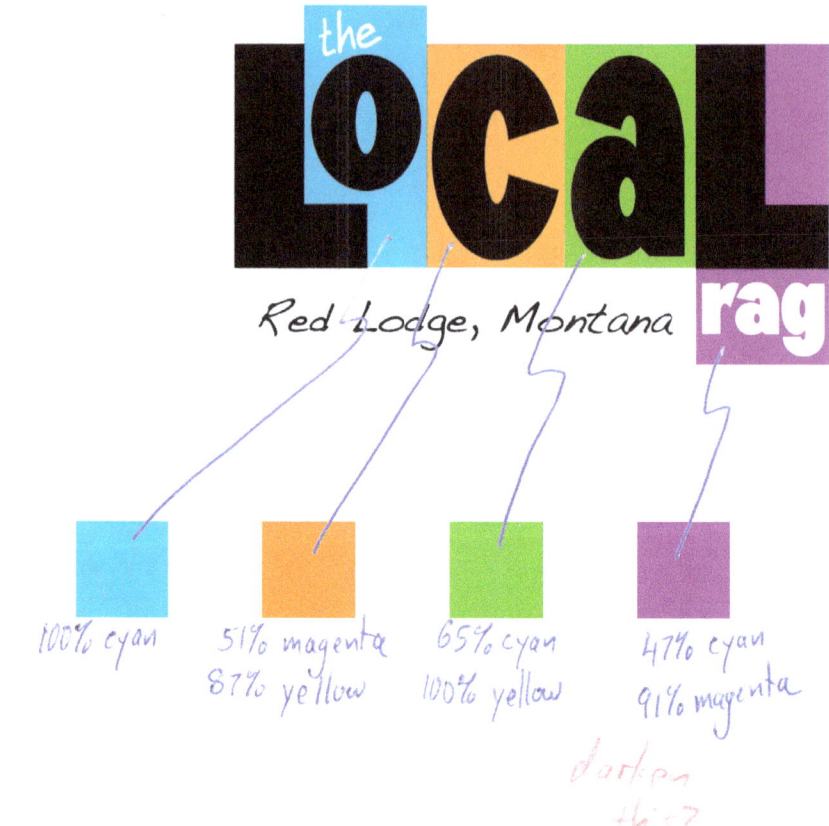

Put the date in this corner, and don't screw it up this time!

100% cyan

51% magenta
87% yellow

65% cyan
100% yellow

47% cyan
91% magenta

darken this?

What can we use as a cover picture this time?

I don't know. A duck?

This is BORING! Can we put "Awesome Rag Reader" instead?

NO!

We're going to use the actual permit number, right?

duh

BOXHOLDER

Please recycle your Rag

PRSRT-STD
U.S. Postage
PAID
Red Lodge, MT
Permit No.

Contents

Introduction by Gary Robson 1

What *is* this Local Rag thing? .5

Where do you read *your* Local Rag? 29

If we may be serious for a moment 71

People & Profiles 95

Bathroom humor 113

Food & Drink 119

Columns & Regular Features 131

Red Lodge Believe it or NOT! 153

Christmas in Red Lodge 163

That strange *Local Rag* sense of humor 173

The Cody Quarterline Saga .183

Red Lodge Major Events 207

Local Rag Election Coverage 213

The Best of Red Lodge 223

Index 239

Introduction
by Gary Robson

The Local Rag is one of the reasons that my family and I moved to Red Lodge. We were just passing through on our way to a family reunion. We set up camp outside of town, and then came in the next morning for breakfast at the Red Lodge Café. Sitting in the restaurant, we saw a copy of this little local newspaper. The cover said "free," so we picked one up and started flipping through it.

Let me tell you, that paper really made us want to learn more about the town! We wandered around and shopped for a while before we left, and just couldn't get Red Lodge out of our heads.

After we got home, we kept thinking about Red Lodge, and eventually we called the Chamber of Commerce to ask for some information about the town. They sent out a packet of information, which included a copy of — are you ready for this? — The Local Rag. Specifically, the August 2001 issue, which contained an article by editor Lou Ward called "Things I Most Love About Red Lodge." We loved it. It's not the only reason we moved here, but it certainly contributed.

In late 2001, we bought the bookstore in Red Lodge and a nearby ranch. The following year, I started writing for the Rag. In 2007 my wife, Kathy, and I bought the paper.

I called my brother to tell him and he said, "So you now have a bookstore and a newspaper? What's next? A buggy whip factory?"

Over the following years, I wrote content, edited other people's content, chased down columnists, designed and laid out each issue, and took them to the post office to mail them.

I was lucky enough to have help. Kathy handled the finances, my daughter Heather did ad sales in the beginning and later took over as editor. I had several other ad sales people and ad designers (although I did both of those jobs for a while as well).

Eventually, it just got to be too much. I published my last issue of the Local Rag in December of 2014.

This book is my way of bringing back some of what I have always loved about the Rag.

Most of the old content appears here exactly as it was first published, warts and all. I haven't re-edited any of the stories, but I'm sure I've managed to introduce some errors along the way. Don't blame Lou, Jean, Kari, Anne or Heather. That part's all on me.

THINGS I MOST LOVE ABOUT RED LODGE:

During heavy traffic, locals will let sidestreet traffic onto mainstreet and...

Local pedestrians will step in the crosswalk to stop traffic on mainstreet so cars on the sidestreets can move.

Locals wave when they drive by, even if they've already passed by a couple of times before.

Everbody watches over each other's kids at the park and downtown with being asked to do so.

Locals band together when tourists are being assholes, even if the locals don't always get along.

We let someone cut in line ahead of us at the store if they look like they're in a hurry or if they've only a few items.

Most locals will tell you when you have something stuck in between your teeth or hanging out of your nose.

Local shops will usually trust locals to pay for goods without a credit check or application.

Local merchants will barter for goods or services when you're low on cash but rich in effort.

Locals are always quick to empathize, support, console and help out whenever tragedy hits one of us or we lose a loved one.

Red Lodge lets anyone who moves here be as weird as they want to be without holding it against them. Everyone gets a fair chance unless they start screwing people over, then they're history.

Locals call a spade a spade and will most often verify rumors instead of spreading them.

We respect the older people in our town and give them the credit they deserve for all they've done and seen and contributed to this town. We listen to them and learn from them.

We support and encourage those who are physically and mentally challenged or less fortunate than we are.

We protect each other's property and keep an eye on each other's homes.

Locals can sit down, argue vehemenantly over any issue (resort tax, ski hill, religion, politics) and leave each other's company still as friends.

Most local merchants support each other with the patronage to keep the money in Red Lodge instead of giving it to another town... good for you! Shame on those of you who don't!

Red Lodge is the most tolerent place I've ever seen... nobody cares about the color of your skin, what your political party affiliation is, what your religious denomination is or what your sexual preference is! This is undoubtedly my favorite thing about this town.

We have a fashion of our own, consisting of a combination of any of the following: Carhartt's, Birkenstocks, polar fleece, Indonesian imports and a multitude of Levi's, flannel plaids and leathers!

There isn't a bad infidelity problem. Most of us respect other people's relationships and avoid other people's partners.

We offer each other rides when one of us too drunk to drive or can't afford to get a DUI.

Most of the people who read this little newspaper don't even know the name of it. The real name is The Red Lodge Local News. I nicknamed it "The Local Rag" myself some years back to spite Kathy Plumb for calling it that in her rag. Most of you call it "Lou's little paper."

There seems (outside of the peer pressure in the schools at times) to be no real class distinction that divides residents here into No Class, Lower Class, Middle Class or Fat-Ass High Class standards. There also seems to be very few hypocrits here. Give your selves and pat on the back for that, Red Lodge.

Lou Ward's 2001 article was one of the things that brought our family to Red Lodge!

There's a secret pride we locals feel when tourists come here and rave about the rodeo (Home of Champions and Iron Horse), ski-joring, the Festival of Nations or any of the fun events we host. They all think we do it for them... they've no clue that we do it for ourselves!

We have great friendly competition between merchants, like the annual football game between the Pizza Company and Bridge Creek. Yeah, like nobody takes that game serious! Not! But for the most part, local merchants compliment each other. Good on ya!

We're very proud of Crazy Creek Products and King's Cupboard Chocolate Sauces and everyone who is exporting goods from here out into the world.

This town loves dogs and it shows. Dogs are welcome in most businesses and are treated with the respect they deserve. Now, if we could just get everyone to keep the dogs safe inside fenced yards so they'll quit roaming, digging in trash cans and getting in fights or hit by cars.

This town has an incredible support system, be it AA, Al-Anon, Codependence, whatever. If there isn't a meeting for it, somebody has a book they'll loan you on it or advice to share about it.

We call bullshit on our teenagers when we see them screwing up or we tell their parents to. If we know they're doing drugs or drinking, we try to help them or we tell their parents to get help for them.

The merchants in this town foot the bill for most of the charitable events hosted here, they sponsor just about everything that goes on, pay for the printed programs that we have available to us with their advertising, plus keeping two newspapers and a radio station in business, paying for school yearbooks and so much more. They do it out of kindness, not because they need the advertising.

If two cars are stopped in the middle of the street so the driver's can chat, everyone just goes around them without a bother.

Continued on page 9 (blah, blah, blah)...

...continued from page 2

There is an inner-library loan system that goes well beyond anything a real library could ever do... it's the one that happens when we loan each other books, then pass them on to someone else who pass them on, and so on, until eventually someone returns it to us. It never fails. I love this honesty.

The American flags that fly downtown during the Fourth of July belong to the Festival of Nations. The Festival Flag Committee put them out early just to make the town look patriotic during the Fourth, then they come out again at the end of the month and hang the foreign flags before the Festival begins. It's this kind of consideration that makes this town special.

The beautiful flowers in Pride Park and those in wooden planter boxes in front of most businesses downtown are there for our pleasure only, not because they generate more business.

The foods given away during the Christmas Stroll are better on the first night of the Stroll because it's "local night" and we care more about our friends and neighbors than we do about those we've not met.

Continued on page 10 (will she ever stop?)...

There is a serious drive to learn here, to further our intelligence, to succeed at whatever we choose to do by better educating ourselves instead of letting a lack of knowledge hold us back. I respect the people in this town who are constantly learning and taking responsibility for their own destiny.

There aren't very many lazy, habitually unemployed or system-sucking leeches here who aren't happy to earn an honest dollar. We'd rather work and have dignity than get a free ride and lose our pride.

There are a thousand other things that I love about Red Lodge, but these stand out today. I'll send the rest of them to Jean once I'm all settled in at Doolin and have time to write them down. If you think of things I forgot to mention, things that you most love about Red Lodge, sure she'd like to hear from you, too. I'm not the only one who spouts off about how awesome this town is... I hear many of you doing the same thing often. How about sharing it with the rest of us? You guys have been reading my rave reviews about Red Lodge long enough... now it's time for you to start sharing your views with me. I'm going to be sitting there 7,000 miles away in serious need of news from Red Lodge by the time this issue arrives each month... make it worth my wait, people. Tell me.

Well, I guess I'm just about done, nearly got it all out of my system until the next big fit of sentiment hits me... which will no doubt happen in the middle of my yard sale this weekend when I suddenly can't part with any of the crap I desperately need to get rid of! "Hey, gimme that back! I didn't mean to put it on the sale table."

The Very Best of the Red Lodge Local Rag

As you look through this book, you are probably going to remember certain favorite things from the Local Rag that aren't here. I understand. Some of my favorite things aren't here, either.

I went through over 20 years of Local Rags to come up with what is in this book. I could have filled the book using only one page per issue! It was inevitable that some of the good stuff got left out.

Perhaps we're saving that stuff for volume 2?

CHAPTER 1

What *is* this Local Rag thing?

by Gary Robson

This article appeared in February 2008.

History of the Local Rag, part I
Lou Ward and the "Local News"

In September of last year, my wife Kathy and I purchased a 16-year-old newspaper called the *Local Rag*. It's fun, it's challenging, and it makes one stop and think: how did my predecessors do this? Where did the *Local Rag* really come from and how does it work? To answer these questions for our readers, we're pleased to present part one of this multi-part saga: History of the Local Rag.

Our story starts almost two decades ago. A woman named Lou Ward, who owned a newspaper in New Mexico called the *Jemez Valley Voice*, wanted to take some time off from work and focus on just being a mom. She sold the paper, and calculated that it would provide enough money to live for a year in her favorite place: Red Lodge, Montana.

Unfortunately for Lou (but, in the long run, fortunately for Red Lodge), her buyers defaulted on the loan and Lou found herself looking for work. She took a part-time job tending bar at the Snow Creek, but that didn't provide enough income to live on, so she got a full-time job at the Bierstube on Red Lodge Mountain. The stage was set.

"The more people I got to know thru the Snow Creek and Bierstube," Lou told me, "the more I learned about what was going on around town and how many interesting people there were. No disrespect to the *Carbon County News* but there seemed to be a whole 'nother civilization in Red Lodge that I never read about in it. I was only there ten months before I couldn't stand it and had to start a local paper." Thus, the *Red Lodge Local News* was born.

Then, as now, the newspaper was free, funded by advertising. Bringing in advertisers in the beginning wasn't easy. For one thing, Lou wasn't your typical business-suit-wearing ad salesman. She was a devout headbanger, and walked into businesses with a nose ring, blonde and black-dyed hair, tattoos, ratty Levi's, and a heavy metal shirt trying to sell ads. Nonetheless, she got their business. Ads were just $10 per column inch, which helped.

"It took a lot of faith for the merchants to trust me that first time," Lou said, "but they did, fair play to them all."

Pulling together content wasn't particularly easy, either. Lou really wanted her new *Red Lodge Local News* to appeal to everyone in town. She didn't have many contributors back then, so she spent a lot of time talking to people in the bars for news, digging through books, and surfing the Web. She drove around town with her camera looking for photo opportunities.

Deliveries were a lot of fun back then, too. "I delivered a paper to every house in town on foot," she said, "during which time I got chased by every dog in town (three times bitten) and I left a handful into each business... and there weren't many businesses operating at that time—downtown nearly looked like a ghost town at night. I was a stress case the last week of every month, usually pulling a 72-hour straight shift to get it to the printer on time."

A lot has changed since those days. *The Local Rag* uses the U.S. Post Office to handle most of the deliveries these days (more expensive, but a whole lot easier), but we're also covering a whole lot more ground. Lou covered all of the houses in Red Lodge. Today, the *Rag* is distributed to every P.O. Box, mailbox, and rural route address in Red Lodge, Bearcreek, Belfry, Bridger, Fox, Luther, Roberts, Roscoe, and Washoe.

Lou's original vision was to have a paper that appealed to everyone in town, but it was clearly her baby from the start. "I needed it as a vehicle to express myself," she told me. "It was my very own soap

Lou and Frankie

"For one thing, Lou wasn't your typical business-suit-wearing ad salesman."

box, bulletin board, bragger's book and information exchange. My mind never shuts down and the only way I can quiet it down is to put its thoughts, dreams, ideas, tips and stories on paper! It wasn't always fun either, it was a lot of work doing it all by myself."

Since she always had another job going (tending bar in the beginning, working at Yellowstone Printing later), the profitability of the paper wasn't a big issue for her. She envisioned a free publication—which it still is today—and kept the ads as cheap as she could. "I always felt sort of guilty getting paid for something I loved doing," she said. It wasn't always fun, because putting out a paper like this by yourself is an immense amount of work. Overall, though, she loved what she did.

Lou had little tolerance for bitching and moaning. The disclaimer on the back page of the paper each month said, "If you notice mistakes in this publication, please consider that they are there for a reason... We try to print something for everyone and some people are just looking for mistakes."

Red Lodge has a very eclectic mix of people, with a broad range of interests. Every editor has tended to provide their favorite places and favorite events with a lot of free press (e.g., the two-page article last month about Robert Burns Night in Red Lodge). Lou's favorites were snowboarding, ski-joring, and the Beartooth Rally (the big Harley event in the summer). Under her management, the *Rag* wasn't impressed with rich people nor was it disgusted by poor. Everyone was equal in importance, although she did give short shrift at times to what she referred to as the "trust fund babies."

"Two of my favorite people in town were Don Coutts and Mike Farley," she said, "both as different as day and night, but both so real and genuine. I loved seeing them sitting together at the Red Lodge Café at lunch because it symbolized what makes Red Lodge so unique: an open-minded place where people are just people and this awesome little town lets them live their lives the way they want without judgment or prejudice."

Some of the questions I asked in the interview got pretty calm answers. One that really got a reaction from Lou was when I asked what the single most important characteristic of a paper like the Rag is that distinguishes it from papers like the *Carbon County News* or *Billings Gazette*.

"I don't know how to say it nicely so I'll just say it the way I feel it," she responded. "Because a local rag doesn't give a fiddler's fart about hard news, controversial issues, political bickering and scandal that embarrasses locals. Leave that crap to the 'real' newspapers. A local rag should be something locals read to feel good about their town, something that reminds them why they live there. Man, I don't want to know the dirt on other people; it makes me feel sorry for them or angry at them and it's just none of my beeswax who's shagging who or who got busted for dope or who has a drinking problem... I DON'T WANT TO KNOW! And I sure as hell don't want to print it."

All newspaper editors make mistakes, and Lou was no exception. Dates seem to be a common bugaboo. She'd mix up the dates on the masthead frequently (as your current editor did last November), and often mixed up the words "bizarre" and "bazaar," which she said mortified

Lou in 2006

"I needed it as a vehicle to express myself. It was my very own soap box, bulletin board, bragger's book and information exchange. My mind never shuts down and the only way I can quiet it down is to put its thoughts, dreams, ideas, tips and stories on paper!"

Lou with her best friend and editorial assistant, Isis. Note her beloved Macintosh computer equipment. Lou was very pleased to hear that the Local Rag is once again being produced on a Mac.

The Very Best of the Red Lodge Local Rag

FREE — Volume III May 1993 Issue 5

Red Lodge Local

HELLO, Red Lodge! "LOVE ... your front teeth down your throat with a hot grounder! I don't care if you can't breathe... your boobies will hang to your knees if you don't wear a

---

please recycle this newspaper — 50¢ if you got it... FREE if you don't! — Volume 6 · March 1996 · Issue 3

Red Lodge Local

Éiréann Go Bragh! • Ireland for Ever!

please recycle this newspaper — 50¢ if you got it... FREE if you don't! — Volume 10 · March 2000 · Issue 3

Red Lodge Local Rag

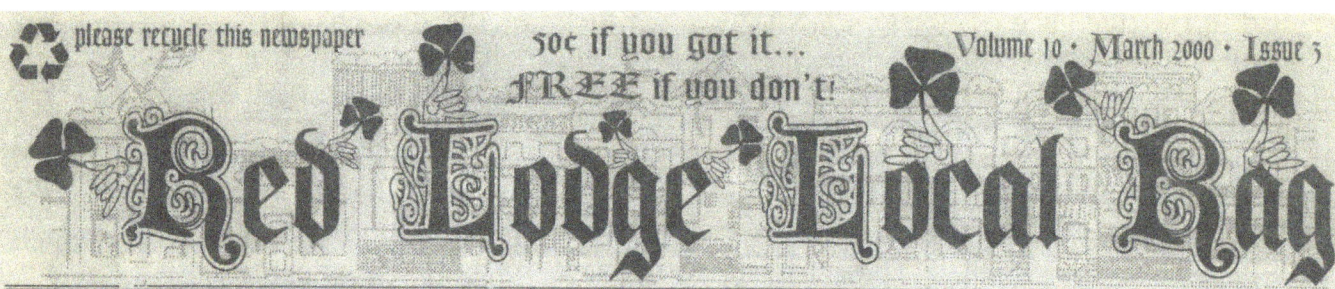

please recycle this newspaper — 50¢ if you got it... FREE if you don't! — Volume 11 · June 2001 · Issue 6

The Local Rag

please recycle this newspaper — 50 cents if you have it, FREE if you don't! — Volume 12 · October 2001 · Issue 10

THE LOCAL RAG

---

please recycle this newspaper — Volume 13 · November 2001 · Issue 11

The Local Rag

FREE!! And well worth every penny!

the church ladies. Probably her most embarrassing day was when she walked all over town selling ads with a huge rip across the back of her skirt that exposed her "sexy boxer shorts," and nobody mentioned it to her.

Despite Lou's stated goal of avoiding the big controversial issues, she did manage to annoy a few people around town. When she was pouring beers on Red Lodge Mountain during a particularly bad ski season, she used the term "Rock Dodge" instead of "Red Lodge," which didn't make her bosses very happy. For the most part, she avoided offending people intentionally, but there was one particular incident that led to the paper getting a name change.

Lou remembers it well: "That woman who had the *Northern Lights* newspaper was so offended by my Christmas issue jokes that she went to every one of my advertisers and asked them to boycott that 'local rag' for being so paganistic." It wasn't a big financial hit to the paper, although Lou did lose one advertiser over it. "Then I changed the name of the paper from *The Red Lodge Local News* to *The Local Rag* just to piss her off. Twenty years later, I'm the good Catholic girl who's appalled at the way young girls dress these days and wondering whatever happened to decency... who'da thunk it."

From the moment she and her son arrived in Red Lodge, they loved the town. "My son said it best," she told us. "We'd been there a week or so and he came home, dressed like his then-hero Ozzy Osbourne, and said, 'Mom, the people in this town are awesome. They don't look at me like I'm a scumbag when I'm dressed like this—they say hello! Is that cool or what'? That's the incredible thing about Red Lodge. People will give you a chance to better yourself and they'll support you with their friendship and trust as long as you're making an effort to walk on your own two feet."

It wasn't always wine and roses in town though. During time living here, her father committed suicide, she divorced her husband when she found he was cheating on her, the love of her life turned out to be gay, and her son developed a meth adiction. Her friends in town were patient with her during the hard times, and her son's meth addiction led to what she still feels is the best article she ever wrote.

"I wrote it because the shame of keeping that hell secret was making me sick with depression and I was hoping the truth would set me free," she said. "It did set me free, and it helped him accept his situation (once he came out of rehab in MCDC). But the most amazing thing was that it filled my mailbox with letters and my answering machine with messages from so many family members in town who were going through the same thing—I had no idea, thought it was just my screwed-up family. I still get requests for it from people in Red Lodge."

The rough times just made her love Red Lodge more, though. "I was fat and hated my body, I drank too much and smoked like a freight train, I was crazy with codependence, and every man I dated either dumped me, cheated on me, used me or was too lost in alcohol or drugs to be available to me. I was a mess. But this precious town stood behind me while I figured out what I really wanted to do with my life. I owe a huge debt of gratitude to Red Lodge for the contentment I have in my world now."

Throughout the process, she stuck (for the most part) with her policy of not printing bad news, sad news, gossip, police reports, obituaries, politics, and religion. To quote from the front page of a 1993 issue, "As usual, we invite readers to make suggestions and comments about what they'd like to see in our pages. We aim to please... no sleaze." 🐾

> "She went to every one of my advertisers and asked them to boycott that 'local rag' for being so paganistic.
>
> Then I changed the name of the paper from 'The Red Lodge Local News' to 'The Local Rag' just to piss her off."

Lou Ward, the founding editor/publisher of the Local Rag, would like everyone to know that yes, Frankie really does exist, and they have finally gotten married. This is the happy couple at home in Doolin, Ireland last month. Well, we don't mean to imply that their "home" is the pub, but it's close enough!

This announcement was in the personals section in August 2008

The Very Best of the Red Lodge Local Rag

A CLOSER LOOK AT THE TWELVE DAYS OF CHRISTMAS

by Randy Tracy

How romantic: get a gift every day for the twelve days of Christmas. In fact, get lots of gifts. What could be nicer? Let's take a look at the gifts:

 12 Drummers Drumming
 11 Lords a' Leaping
 10 Ladies Dancing
 9 Pipers Piping
 8 Maids a' Milking
 7 Swans a' swimming
 6 Geese a' Laying
 5 Gold Rings
 4 Calling Birds
 3 French Hens
 2 Turtle Doves
 1 Partridge in a Pear Tree

On the 12th day alone, you get 23 birds, 50 house guests, a herd of cows, a lot of noise and a big mess. But remember, on each successive day, you get all the gifts from all the previous days as well as the new gifts. On the first day of Christmas, you get one bird. On the second day, you get 3 birds, and you already had one from the day before, giving you 4 birds. On the third day of Christmas, you will have 10 birds. And so on. If you add all twelve days together, you get:

 12 Drummers Drumming
 22 Lords a' Leaping
 30 Ladies Dancing
 36 Pipers Piping
 40 Maids a' Milking
 42 Swans a' swimming
 42 Geese a' Laying
 40 Gold Rings
 36 Calling Birds
 30 French Hens
 22 Turtle Doves
 12 Partridges in 12 Pear Trees

This comes out to 376 items, including 184 birds, 128 people, enough livestock to start a small ranch, a fair orchard, the makings of a jumbo omelet, and a class-action suit from the neighbors. You'll have to sell all 40 gold rings to retain an attorney.

Christmas humor in the Local Rag? Yep, right along with Halloween humor and St. Paddy's Day humor and all of the other holiday humor that the Rag printed over the years. As "History of the Local Rag, Part I" explains, Christmas jokes were responsible for the name of the paper changing from "The Red Lodge Local" to "The Local Rag."

Randy Tracy's article ran in December of 1996.

The other two items on this page were part of the "Find the Fake Ad" series that ran while I was the editor. The Classy Girl Salon ad ran in December of 2009, and Harold's Certified Pre-Owned Christmas Trees ran in January 2008.

BACK BY POPULAR DEMAND...
The Twelve Days of Christmas

On The First Day of Christmas:
Tom Sweetness, You sweet, sentimental fool, you. I can't tell you how surprised I was when they delivered the partridge in a pear tree! I rushed right out and bought the best cage I could find. I just hope the tree lives until Spring. All my love, Aggie

On The Second Day of Christmas:
My Dear Tom, Today the two turtle doves arrived, and Tom, they are ADORABLE. I had to go out and buy another cage ($27) but they're worth it. I'm SURE I'll get used to the cooing.
With love, Agnes

On The Third Day of Christmas
Dear Tom; Sweetheart, you're truly generous. Three French Hens! I just bought the last bird cage in town and I think the last bag of bird feed. (Had to use my MasterCard, but now I have 3 months to pay it off). Tom, they're just great but don't you think six birds are just a little much for my four-room house? Love, Agnes

On The Fourth Day of Christmas
Dear Tom; They delivered the four calling birds today. I have to admit they're beautiful to LOOK at but do you know how much NOISE they make? Now, really, Tom. Enough is enough.
Affectionately, Ag

On The Fifth Day of Christmas
Dearest Tom; What a surprise! Five golden rings; one for each finger! I would be so happy if only those birds would stop squawking - they're beginning to get on my nerves.
Love, Agnes

On The Sixth Day of Christmas
Dear Tom; So, we're back to those damn birds again, are we? When I got home, those six geese were laying all over my porch. Those things are HUGE! Where the hell am I going to keep them? I can't sleep and the neighbors are complaining, so please stop. Cordially, Agnes

On The Seventh Day of Christmas
Tom! What the hell is with you and these friggin' birds? Seven swans a swimming? My whole house now looks like the bottom of a dirty bird cage and the NOISE!!! Knock it off, smartass!
Agnes

On The Eighth Day of Christmas
Mr. Tom Acker: I think I prefer the birds. What the hell did I do to deserve eight maids a milking? And in a four-room house with 23 birds! My backyard is 40'x30'. Do you know what eight cows can do to a yard like that? Lay off it!
Agnes

On The Ninth Day of Christmas
Tom - you bastard: What are you - some kind of sadist? Now there are nine pipers piping while chasing those maids around the house... the birds are squawking their heads off and I'm going nuts! The cows trampled the neighbor's yard into a mud hole and they're getting up a petition to have me evicted.
You'll get yours, Agnes

On The Tenth Day of Christmas
You S.O.B., you! Ten ladies dancing... I don't know why I call them LADIES! They've been doing those pipers all night long. The cows are trampling the birds and those damn geese are laying eggs in my bed! The Commissioner of Buildings subpoenaed me to give cause why my place shouldn't be condemned. I'm sending the cops to see you!
Agnes

On The Eleventh Day of Christmas
Listen, asshole! What's with the eleven lads a leaping on those maids and ladies? Some of those broads will never walk again! All 23 of the birds are dead - thank God! They've been trampled to death in the orgy! I hope you're satisfied, you rotten fleck of phlegm! I hate your guts! A. Mc.

On The Twelfth Day of Christmas
That does it, XXXXhead! Twelve drummers drumming. This house sounds like half time at a football game. I just got picked up for running a whore house and the neighbors are trying to set my place on fire. The cops were here and hauled all 51 of us to jail; and the cows have been stampeded to the butcher shop. If I ever get out of this XXXXXXX mess, I am going to come looking for you, you no good mother-XXXXXX, and I'm going to whack your XXXXs off and stuff them up your XXX with a hot poker!   A. McHolstein
#59372489, (censored by Beaver Valley Police Dept.)

A little censored Christmas humor from December of 2005.

I forgot to mention this in the introduction, but we decided to include a bunch of the old ads for businesses that aren't around any more.

August 2004

Only In Red Lodge...

Now, we've heard of people pulling some serious publicity stunts for keeping customers in your business, but The Snag Bar has taken this cake to the extreme.

One morning in mid-March, Snag owner, Greg Zyler, called the Red Lodge Police Department to report an overnight break-in. After inspecting the splintered door, Police Chief Tony Krumheuer had to inform Greg that no one had broken in. They had, in fact, broken out!

The cash registers and all the liquor bottles hadn't been touched. The poor guy didn't even borrow a quarter to use the pay phone and call for help!

The new door cost $127 to fix. And Greg says, "This time there's no breaking out!"

This "Only in Red Lodge" is from April 1993.

GIVE 'EM HELL, JEAN!

Jean, Jean, Jean...
And to think I was worried that you might be one of those uptight anal rententive people who wouldn't find my biker friends interesting! I'm not worried anymore, lady. I have complete faith in you and your ability to keep this little newspaper traveling on a path worthy of a "local" rag. Have fun with it... you've the best subjects in the world to write about and they'll never let you down by failing to give you something "newsworthy."

Locals, Please be nice to Jean! Weird women are hard to find and I'm not here to beat you up for giving her a hard time!
Love,
Lou

In April 2001, Lou showed her approval of the people Jean was hanging out with.

> "I'm not exactly Emily Post as far as manners go, but I do discourage excessive slurping, burping, and farting at the dinner table."

The Local Rag
ramblin

Well, you know how when you're growing up and there are people who have an influence on your life but maybe at the time you just don't realize it?? Well, I just had one of those epiphanical moments. See when I was growing up, we lived next door to this really nice family and the mom was Florence. She was best friends with my mom and served as my second mom. When my parents left on trips I would often stay at Florence's house. I remember she had a really loud wind-up alarm clock in the room I stayed in and it was hard for me to fall asleep. And she made me drink my milk even though I really hated milk. But I did it without arguing because, well, I wanted to please Florence.

So when Florence told me that I was a very funny person and a great writer, I listened. So I became a great writer. The easiest way to become a great writer is to write a bunch of stuff. If nobody really reads it, it doesn't matter if it's good or not. So I wrote a bunch of stuff. And she told me once that she had always wanted to be a dancer. Now being a writer is easy, everyone has the equipment for that one. You just need a working brain and a pen, pencil or (in this age) a computer. But to be a dancer, now that is something else again. And since Florence had a leg brace since childhood, well that one kind of stuck with me. I remember her there on her couch slapping her brace saying "If it weren't for this damn thing, I would have been a dancer." But she wasn't bitter, just stating a fact. So, anyway, when I turned 40, I took a look at my life. My parents were dead, (and still are, to the best of my knowledge), and I thought hmmm. Maybe it's time to decide what I want to be when I grow up. Well, I want to be a dancer. So I started to dance with the Scandinavian group here in Red Lodge. Sure, it's not exactly Fred Astaire quality, but, know what? It's loads of fun. And I'm fulfilling one of those dreams that Florence and I shared.

And I want to be a writer. So suddenly there was this job opening at the Local Rag. So I became editor of this monthly paper. That was a funny thing. One of those "God's got a dream for you" sort of deals. So, I became the Rag, and kept thinking, "Gee, I need to send Florence a copy of the Rag so she knows that I'm finally doing what she said I could do." But, as things sometimes happen, that didn't happen in time. Florence died before I could get a copy sent. So I'll just have to think she would appreciate what I'm doing. Thanks, Flo, for your influence. And thanks to mom and dad, thanks for the dancing gene. I'll try to use it wisely although I do tend to abuse it with that nasty rock and roll stuff from time to time.

Something else I remember about Florence was she once sent me a quote while I was in college. It was "You can't teach a pig to sing, it wastes your time and annoys the pig." She sent me that because one day we'd sat there on her couch laughing till tears came talking about a pig with a wooden leg. I don't remember that whole story, but I just know we had fun.

So to people reading this, it's March. So march out there and tell people who have made a difference in your life that they've made a difference. Guess what? Otherwise they might end up like Florence and just never know what a difference they've made.

OK and speaking of making a difference, what a difference having kids make. So back when I was a stay-at-home-mom, I was always busy. But now that I'm a working mom, I'm still busy. When I was at home, I had little kids and those rugrats kept me running. I often thought how much easier it would have been to just go get a job so I didn't have to deal with the day-to-day kid stuff. And well, maybe doing it when the kids were young would have been easier, but then I would have missed out on all those firsts. You know, the first time you crack a beer at noon because your morning was so crazy, or the first time you actually go to the bathroom ALONE!

Don't get me wrong. I love my kids more than anything, but sometimes I wonder if maybe there should have been another person here instead of me in those "formative years". I'm not exactly Emily Post as far as manners go, but I do discourage excessive slurping, burping and farting at the dinner table. And what's that guy's name who is always so gentle with the children? Dr. Brazelton? Nope. I wasn't him. My kids know that you just don't talk to mom before she's had her coffee. We just sit there on the couch, all snuggled together, and no words are spoken. Once Ev started singing during snuggle time and we politely asked him to leave the area. Well, "politely" might be a stretch, but we did ask him to leave.

And what about that language thing? My kids have picked up some really bad language from those other kids at school. Man, if I can find the little bastard who taught my kids those damn words, well I'll kick their ass.

It's starting to feel like spring. Usually I love that feeling, but I feel like I missed out on winter. I rarely had time to whine about the cold weather. What's up with that?? Hey, have a great March; there is plenty of fun to be had here.... WAHOO!!

Here's some "Ramblin'" from Jean in her March 2002 editorial.

History of the Local Rag, part II
The Jean Years

by Gary Robson

This article appeared in March 2008.

Last month, in the first installment of the History of *The Local Rag*, we met Lou Ward, who started the paper in Red Lodge in 1991. She had both good times and bad times, and put in a lot of hard work producing the paper, but it's in her blood. Before *The Local Rag*, she owned a newspaper in New Mexico called the *Jemez Valley Voice*.

When we ended Part I, Lou had established the *Red Lodge Local News*, changed its name to *The Local Rag*, got divorced, and settled into running the paper and printing business.

What happened next was love. Double love, in fact, with both a man and a place. The place, as it turns out, was Ireland. After running *The Local Rag* for ten years, she decided it was time to move on. The June 2001 issue had a front-page story entitled "Local Rag Changing Hands." It started like this:

"Okay, now this is the REAL story. I know I told you last month I had it all figured out so that *The Local Rag* would keep showing up on newsstands every month and *that* was the truth. However, there's been a change of plans regarding *who'll* be putting it there.

"Jean Atherly will be your new editor of *The Local Rag* and will be taking care of your printing needs once I've moved to Ireland in August. Trust me, you'll be comfortable with her... she has that same twisted sense of humor you're used to, except I don't think she has quite the potty-mouth that I have, so if you miss the foul language in print, just add the dirty words in where you think I'd swear."

She then went on to say that "A group of local investors who felt that Local News & Design should remain a locally-owned business are buying my company." The investors, who she didn't name in the article, were the Dillons, a Red Lodge family with several business interests in town.

Jean Atherly

Jean had contacted Lou about buying the paper in response to an article Lou ran about moving to Ireland. Jean had worked at newspapers (doing everything except writing and editing) since high school, and felt up to the job. The only thing she'd ever had published was a poem in the 2nd grade, but she knew she was the one to keep the paper going.

From the beginning, Jean felt that she and Lou had a lot in common. They both shared a love for the Festival of Nations (your current editor was also president of the Festival for two years), and were meticulous about similar things. Jean was concerned, though, that Lou thought she had too many "yuppie scum" friends.

"My friend Candis Thompson persuaded me to attend the street dance during the Beartooth Rally," Jean told me. "I was reluctant, but had spent the week working with Leo, Joan and Tim Brockman trying to get all their printing stuff done. I figured they'd protect me if the bikers got too rowdy. I showed up in a tie-dyed t-shirt, shorts and Tevas. Yeah, I blended, but I had been working all day trying to get the paper done. After a few beers, I decided I'd do something to make Lou proud, so I picked out two of the gnarliest looking bikers and asked them to pose for a picture with me."

Alastair Baker from the *Carbon County News* was there to snap the shot. The following Monday, Lou told Jean that "Alastair sent me a picture over the weekend that set my mind at ease." And Lou printed the picture in the *Rag*.

Just like Lou before her, Jean started out by doing everything herself: all the writing, all the ad sales, all the layout, all the ad building, and the print shop work, all the page building and paste up plus taking it to Powell to have it printed, then

> "I don't think she has quite the potty-mouth that I have, so if you miss the foul language in print, just add the dirty words in where you think I'd swear."

That all changed after the Halloween issue where Jean's face was printed on the front cover as a "do-it-yourself editor costume."

Please recycle this newspaper

bringing it back and distributing it. The Dillons hired Cheryl Tower to help out, but it was still an overwhelming task.

Jean did end up staying on with the paper, but the Dillons didn't. They owned *The Local Rag* and the printing business for a few months and found that it just wasn't working for them—especially the printing part. They had no prior printing experience, and they were having a difficult time keeping the printer working. Jean understood their decision (she told me she always admired them for giving it a shot), but she was very upset. She knew the Rag could make it, but she knew she couldn't do it by herself.

Jean said, "One day I was at the post office when Tim Weamer and Jenny Zimmerman of Creative Design Works were walking across the parking lot. I burst into tears and told them that the Rag was done. Jenny asked me to come in and visit with them. They asked a lot about the paper and if I actually thought it could work, what changes would have to be made to keep it, etc. I don't remember exactly how everything fell into place after that, but they asked me if I'd be willing to keep working there if it were somehow able to keep going. I said I would and shortly after that, they bought the company from Lou."

The newspaper and printing operation fit with what they were already doing, and their skills allowed them to provide Jean with a little bit of backup help.

Soon, some articles began appearing under Tim's byline, and they started lining up volunteers to write columns, many of whom are still writing for the *Rag*. Tim and Jenny came up with a lot of good article ideas, but Jean still did the majority of the writing. Any article that didn't carry a byline was written by Jean.

Jenny's artistic skills showed up in the *Rag* very soon, too. She was doing all of the ad design and she changed the look of the paper significantly.

It had been Lou's practice to change the masthead on a regular basis. The fonts, look, and phrasing changed, although there were certain elements that stayed the same. Lou always had "Please recycle this newspaper" on the front page, which Jean kept, but she replaced the phrase "50¢ if you got it...FREE if you don't!" with "Free! And well worth every penny."

Jenny designed a logo to replace the constantly changing phrase "The Local Rag" and that logo (with slight modifications) appeared on every front page from early 2002 until the end of 2007.

On the inside pages, Jenny created new headline blocks and produced a generally more consistent look.

The next addition to the paper was a section called "Around Town." They printed more copies of "Around Town" than they did of the *Rag* itself, and distributed copies around other parts of Carbon County. Since it as printed separately, they had to manually insert the "Around Town" section into *The Local Rag* before sending it out.

There were some difficult times for Jean as editor of *The Local Rag*, but overall, she enjoyed it. She told me that, "One thing I love about Red Lodge is that a person can just decide they want to be editor of a monthly newspaper and just go do it. No experience, no journalism degree, just the desire to see it done. This is a cool town."

In the beginning, not too many people

knew Jean, and she enjoyed sitting in local bars and restaurants watching people read the *Rag* to see their reactions. That all changed after the Halloween issue where Jean's face was printed on the front cover as a "do-it-yourself editor costume."

I moved to Red Lodge shortly before Jean took over as editor of *The Local Rag*. One of the things my wife and I noticed about town was that wherever we went, we saw Jean with a camera. Meetings, parties, concerts, and other community events always featured the intrepid editor taking pictures.

Jean's favorite of all the articles she wrote was one about when she was in first grade, and she had to buy a present for a girl named Caroline. Jean absolutely hated having to buy something for this dirty, poor girl, until she found out that hers was the only present Caroline got. "Every time I think of that story, I still get teary-eyed," said Jean. "Like right now."

Another favorite of hers is the one she wrote about her son's snake escaping from its cage. "To answer the questions, no, we still haven't found it but at least we don't have a mouse problem anymore. Dead serious. I hear a mouse one night, then never again. One day that snake is gonna pop out of the heater vent and I'm gonna have a heart attack right there in the kitchen!"

Jean and Lou both put in their time delivering papers, but that came to an end thanks to Jean's friend, Candis. The *Montana Free Press* used to be delivered to every mailbox in town, and when they stopped doing it, Candis suggested to Jean that the *Rag* should be mailed that way. They started doing it, and advertising skyrocketed. Jean put Candis on the "free drinks for life" program for that suggestion.

Another thing Jean added was "Where Do You Read Your Local Rag?" She got the idea from the *Triangle Review* in Fort Collins, Colorado. The idea really caught on. I had so many submissions for this month that we had to set most of them aside for April and May!

Putting out a newspaper means working no matter what is going on in your life at the time. The day came in 2005 when Jean was suffering through a case of mono and running a temperature of 105°. She was scheduled to do an interview on Red Lodge Mountain, and headed out to do it despite being sick.

"I don't even remember who they were or what the article was about," Jean told me. "But I remember driving up to the ski area, looking at the steps to the Bierstube—where we were meeting for the interview—and just sitting down by my car and almost crying because it looked like such a long climb."

She did make the climb, though. "I could barely focus or stay awake during the interview," she said, "But I did it, went back to the office and typed it up (we were at deadline) went home, crashed, and the next day I wrote my letter of resignation."

There's a high burnout rate for newspaper editors. Jean went on to add, "People were pissed that I quit but they had no idea what kind of stress that job was. I mean, it was fun, but it was stressful. But I kept doing it because I thought nobody else would do it. Then God sent His next victim... Kari." ❄

We had intended to continue this series with an article about the other Rag editors (Kari Clayton, Anne Rood, me, and Heather Robson), but it never happened. We can let them tell their stories through editorials and letters...

"One thing I love about Red Lodge is that a person can just decide they want to be editor of a monthly newspaper and just go do it. No experience, no journalism degree, just the desire to see it done. This is a cool town."

This logo was introduced in early 2002, shortly after Creative Design Works bought the Local Rag. Variants of this logo were used until Jan '08. After several other logos, the paper went back to a variation of this one in Dec '13.

Once the covers went color, the look of the Local Rag changed from newspaper to magazine style. A variety of photographers and designers left their marks through cover design, interior layout, and ad design.

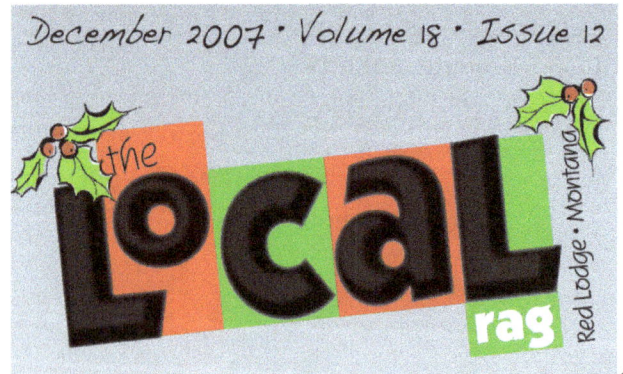

Logos and mastheads had a tendancy to change colors around Christmastime.

The Local Rag logo went briefly oval for use on some swag like t-shirts.

In 2008-2009, the Rag went back to a masthead design on the cover instead of a logo, but eventually returned to a version of the logo from the early 2000's.

The Very Best of the Red Lodge Local Rag

The exchange that resulted in changing The Local Rag's name was neither the first nor the last volley fired in the ongoing battle between the Local Rag and the Northern Lights.

Here's an August 1993 example of Lou firing back at Kathy Plumb.

Lou had a soapbox and she wasn't afraid to use it. The Rag later went through periods of both happy positivism and angry activism, sometimes in the very same issue!

Another NORTHERN sLIGHT

Once again I was forced to open a copy of The Northern Light, having learned that the editor, Kathy Plumb, had launched yet another attack on The Red Lodge Local and, again, I was at odds with myself about whether or not to rebut this witch-burning self-appointed judge of sinners. Excuse me for a moment... ah, there it is, I found it.

Now that I've located my soapbox and stepped upon it (nice view from up here), I'm ready to joust.

Dear Northern sLight editor;

At the risk of sounding like the venomous and spiteful person that I can be when pushed too far, I find that I no longer have any tolerance for the likes of you. If you learned to read at the same home-school that you publicize so highly, I think your school is failing in the art of interpretation. How you manage to twist things that I write so far out of proportion amazes me. Have you ever considered employment with The National Enquirer?

I won't address all the points in your article but I will say this in defense of my advertisers that you slammed, and my advertisers are all but a few Red Lodge merchants. They know and I know that you're just pissed off because they will no longer advertise with you or let you leave your paper in their stores because it's offensive to their customers. How dare you say that my "advertisers support the persecution of Christians and hatred of their values." How dare you! Who made you God? Who gave you the right to judge anyone? Just because other people don't subscribe to the same lifestyle as you do, doesn't mean their lifestyle is wrong. Personally, I find it very frightening to learn that such an extremely condescending lifestyle and beliefs such as yours exist in this twentieth century. Your condemnation of everything and everyone who is different from you is horrid.

Your paper is one of the most offensive pieces of literature (bad use of a good word) I have ever laid my hands on. Don't you ever find anything NICE to write about? Do you just walk around looking for things to be offended by so you can write about them? You're so negative... don't you think people would rather hear about all the wonderful things God has done, rather than only hearing about all the bad things other people do that offend you?

By the way, who the hell do you think you are to say that you had one of the only two decent entries in the Fourth of July parade? Don't break your arm patting yourself on the back because you are so WRONG.

Since when do *"Condoms symbolize illicit sex (premarital, extramarital and deviant) because they are primarily advocated as a disease deterrent for teens, singles and homosexuals - and not needed by faithfully married couples or those who abstain from sex."*? Where do you dig this garbage up? Are you aware that there is an overpopulation problem on this planet? Just because you don't need condoms doesn't mean the rest of the world doesn't, and I don't care what the Pope or anybody else says about birth control or the prevention of sexually transmitted diseases.

Your constant jamming of your abortion opinions in other people's faces is abhorrent. What any woman does with her own body is none of your business. When I worked at the Carbon County News, an employee at an abortion clinic in Billings called and asked if we knew who you were and said that you had called their clinic and asked for the names of all Red Lodge women who had gotten an abortion there so you could expose them in your paper. That's sick.

Another article in your July issue states that, *"In a praiseworthy ruling June 11th, the Supreme Court struck down laws designed to ban the sacrifice of animals for religious purposes. Our right of freedom to practice religion was protected. No constitutional rights exist for animals, but the right to hunt and kill animals is implicit in our Second Amendment right to bear firearms."* I've read that amendment and I can't see where it says anywhere that you have the right to kill animals just because you can bear firearms. As a matter of fact, I recall that your paper recently attempted to do a rude article about Mark Kotar because of your dislike for his hunting ethics. Isn't that a bit hypocritical of you? Besides, other than Dark Ages paganism and satanic cults, what religions use the blood sacrifice of animals these days?

I think it's probably in your best interest to quit reading The Local and critiquing it in your paper. I'm not the kind of person who will be swayed by your ranting or intimidated by your false sense of power. You are wasting precious trees that make the paper you print on if you're trying to change me or my beliefs. Stay out of my face and please keep your self-righteous comments to yourself. Get a life.

--Lou Ward Steinmasel

Hot dog standin'

You can't help but have noticed Gary Kisthard's as-yet-unnamed hot dog vending stand on Broadway this past month. Gary moved to town this spring and is happy to finally be running his own business, with the occasional ketchup-and-mustard help from his brother Jim. He says he isn't going to name the business yet, but instead is "just going to wait to see what Red Lodge names me." So help him out—names, anyone?

The town ended up naming him G-Dawg, and so everyone called the hotdog stand G-Dawg's.

This article appeared in August of 2004.

The Very Best of the Red Lodge Local Rag

May 2007

fare well

Kari's Top Ten

By Kari Clayton

Well, this is it, friends. It almost makes me teary to say it, but this is where I get off. Anne has decided, after these past few trial months, that she likes this whole *Rag*-business, and so she's taking it on. And I'm thrilled for her, and happy to be moving on to other things, myself. I look forward to the things Anne will bring to the Local Rag.

As I look back on the past four years, however—the opportunities the Local Rag has offered me, and the headaches it has insisted upon—I feel the need to assess my time here. To…review, and…memorialize my years in this office. To offer you a…Top Ten list. (How else do we assess these things?)

But before I go on, I have to thank the person who has kept me sane in the office, kept me laughing right up to our deadlines, and the person I have loved working with more than I could ever have imagined. Robyn Rivers, you are an angel. Let's do (something like) this again soon.

And so, without further ado, a list you won't see on Letterman. The Top Ten things I learned from the Local Rag, in no particular order:

#10. The period goes inside the quotation marks.

#9. There's nothing too difficult, too random, or too obscure, for Google. Long live Sergey Brin and Larry Page!!

#8. There's always more to a person than you think you know. We've all got our stories, from what brought us here, to what keeps us from leaving. Who we are, and who we want to be. My greatest joy with this little Rag has been getting to know so many amazing, interesting, unlikely stories from all of you.

#7. It's usually those who refuse to blow their own horn who most deserve thanks. This town is so full of people who contribute in quiet ways.

#6. People love to be asked up-front if a rumor about them is true. The Local Rag has always had a bit of a "gossip-sheet" vibe to it, a quality I've fully embraced. But I like to think we're more than a small-town Page Six (Google it!), so I've attempted to find out if there's any truth to the rumors I'm intending to print each month. And along the way, I've found that people are rarely offended by being given a chance to set the record straight.

#5. And speaking of Page Six, after four years of what—for me—has been horrifyingly public, I've learned that I would never desire real celebrity. I'm basically a hermit by nature and one of the most difficult things has been *being* the Local Rag. I look forward to the day I can say, "great idea – call Anne." As much as I've worked it over the years, I am happy to pass that mantle on.

#4. I've learned—reluctantly—that it's okay to suck at some things. I've always preferred to make my mistakes in private. But over the past four years, my mistakes have been out there—in print, all month long—for everyone to see. That nearly drove me out of my mind the first several months. But I've come to realize that nobody expects perfection out of any of us. (..and they don't notice on those rare occasions in which we *are* perfect!!)

#3. And, while I screw up all the time, I've realized there are some things I'm pretty good at. This job has shown me strengths I never imagined I had. And it's given me the courage to put my thoughts out there, for all of you to see, and appreciate or not.

#2. I've learned that sometimes you have to go *waaaaaay* out of your comfort zone to catch a glimpse your potential.

#1. And finally: Dogs. I can't say it enough. In this town, you cannot go wrong writing about dogs.

You can see the rest of Kari's farewell a couple of pages from now.

> "And finally: Dogs. I can't say it enough. In this town, you cannot go wrong writing about dogs."

Paul Otsu is an ad designer that's willing to drop everything to get a job done, as he demonstrated in this January 2011 S&T ad.

BAR DOGS
Of Red Lodge

Intimidating, isn't he? It's only an illusion... Zeus is one of the more docile bar dogs around, and sticks to Dad's, Alladin Butler, ankles waiting for ear rubs.

Sugar, who used to hang out at the Front Bar of Natali's, is now a Snow Creek babe. She loves all the big strong guy-dogs that hang out there. Her companions are Bobbie Peterson and Nat Erckenbrack.

Sweetie Pie, a regular at the Blue Ribbon Bar, is Steve Coss' sidekick. Her favorite form of entertainment is shredding socks left in the laundromat.

The Red Lodge Local • page 9

This handsome devil is Maxx, the maxiumum overdog who's been a Snow Creek regular for many years. Here we see him assuming his usual position by the woodstove, waiting for someone to give him a cherry. Maxx is *Chums* with Dan Seymour.

Trip is our token blonde bar dog (like father, like son). Fortunately he's so big the other dogs won't mess with him, or else they might find out what a sweetheart he is, sorta like his pretend-owner, Bruce Bondo.

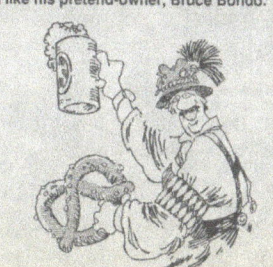

Oõtek the Goo Head, is Mike Holmes buddy, and has talents reach far beyond your average dog... a gymnast in his own right, he can perform on handrails like Cathy Rigby on a balance beam!

Meet McFly (name may change), the newest bardog in town. He has to go piddle often and chews on ears, but he has good taste... "7&7 for me and my buddy, Shark!"

Zilla, the lap dog, is a bit shy and a lot cute, hangs out with Tera Reynolds and Kerry Jetmore most of the time, unless they try to take a ride in the car... don't like cars.

Red Lodge is definitely a dog-loving town, and the Local Rag editors have run with the theme.

These days, unlike May of 1993 when this article ran, you can't take your dog in the bar with you. You can, however, walk down the street and tell which of your friends are in which bar by the dogs tied up in front!

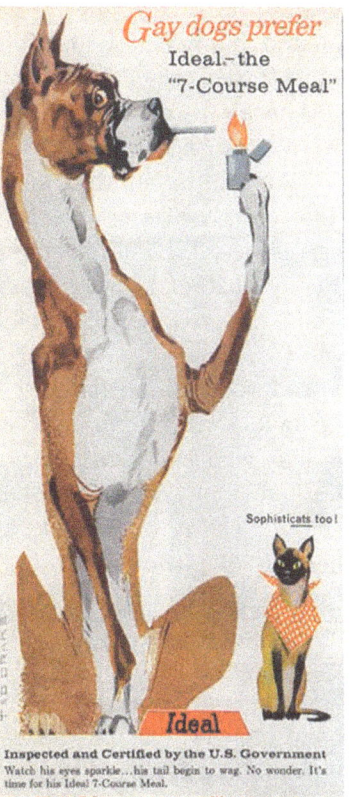
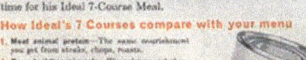

The Local Rag logo recreated in the Minecraft video game as the stone & wool floor of a castle keep.

The version of the logo used on Local Rag covers starting in 2013.

The Very Best of the Red Lodge Local Rag

The Anne Rood Era

The Local Rag reflections

Anne's first issue as editor was April of 2007. Her tenure as editor was far too short. She did a great job, despite having an annoying tendency to put two spaces after a period.

The time has come, the walrus said, to do some other things. Other things which, for me, include mounting a publicity tour for my husband's new book. *["The Cowboy Girl: The Life of Caroline Lockhart," available now at fine bookstores near you! And don't miss our Book release party April 13 at Café Regis, see pgs. 11 & 16 for details!]*

As a result, I am thrilled to announce that I've hired Anne Rood to take over as your Local Rag editor, starting with this very issue. I'll still be hanging around, selling ads and whatnot. Mostly whatnot, if I have anything to say about it. But in hiring Anne, this becomes my final editorial. My Swan Song, if you will.

So I won't be able to tell you about how, coming home from Costa Rica last month, John and I had been unable to confirm exactly who might be at the airport to pick us up, and how we hadn't taken our cell phones with us on vacation so we couldn't check with anyone, and how we were two hours late because of a snowstorm in Minneapolis, and were worrying that we might be overnighting in Billings when we finally did arrive, and how lo and behold, as we walked up to our gate for the Mpls-Blgs leg of our flight, there sat three people from Red Lodge, all of whom could have given us a ride home that night; none of which became necessary because Jerry and Tressa were waiting for us at baggage claim. I really love this goofy little town.

Or about how the other day walking out of the grocery store, I got into my red 4Runner, wondering vaguely why the back seats were flipped up instead of flat, and then half-thinking that the front seat was awfully neat as I dug for my keys, and then being SO embarrassed to realize I'd just climbed into Annie Rice's vehicle! ...And then of course there was the surreptitious looking-over-my-shoulder, hoping-noone-saw-me as I climbed back out of it, when of course Annie happened to be walking out of the store just then, not even surprised by my mistake. I love this goofy little town.

I won't even tell you about becoming a white Subaru stalker, due to this month's cover. Because Anne will tell you all about that. And I have no doubts that Anne will take the best possible care of you as I slip into my diminished role here. So adieu, my friends, and be good to Anne. She's a keeper.

Kari Clayton
owner, editor, etc.

First you spend two or three months looking at Thrifty Nickel and eBay dreaming of replacing your 12-year-old truck with a seven-year-old version. Then combine that with your own personal habit of never waving at white Subaru station wagons because you have no idea who is behind the wheel and voila, you have the April cover of the Local Rag.

There are way too many of these cars in town. Owners should lobby City Council for an official "Town Car" designation, receive a tax break and then unite for the 4th of July parade, driving three abreast down Broadway, culminating at a rally in Sam's Taproom parking lot.

When the idea was hatched, searching for white Subaru wagons was akin to first love. The heart races following one home, your palms sweat when you eye one on a parallel street -- will it be at the next intersection? And then when you eventually lose sight of your white prey, your heart falls. Will I ever see one again?

Well, that lasted for about a day. They travel in threes down Ski Hill Road, parked on Broadway, the post office, in downtown alleys, the Regis, and always at Beartooth Market. Ho, hum. It's you again.

And you are certain everyone in town knows what you are up to. Loitering around a white car with a camera -- what else would it be but a spoof of white Subaru wagons? The only person I know who saw me clicking away was Terri Holt at the P.O. "Oh, are you taking a picture of me?" she asks. There happened to be a cute dog in the bed of the truck next to her so I quickly, and easily, distracted her with canine conversation.

So I hope you enjoy the April issue. It's fun to have a place to put all the ideas swirling in my brain to, hopefully, good use. Of course, all the thanks goes to Kari for first knocking on my door in January and asking for help with the Rag that I am so happy to provide. But she learned early on that I can only Google expertly and send attachments. What's the right button on the Mouse for? Thanks for your incredible patience.

And Robyn, you have to actually do the work that we dream up and laugh about. You are terrific. I am LOVING Photo Shop.

Thanks to everyone for your interest and support.

Anne Rood
editor

Nifty Trickel WANT ADS

YOUR FREE PAPER

www.niftytrickel.com   April 2007

NICE
AWD Subaru wagon, PS, PB, PL, PBJ, One owner, non-smoker, new brakes, great mpg. 446-0000

VERY NICE
AWD Subaru wagon, PS, PB, PL, PBJ, One owner, non-smoker, new brakes, great mpg. 446-0000

SUPER NICE
AWD Subaru wagon, PS, PB, PL, PBJ, One owner, non-smoker, new brakes, great mpg. 446-0000

NONE NICER
AWD Subaru wagon, PS, PB, PL, PBJ, One owner, non-smoker, new brakes, great mpg. 446-0000

HARD TO FIND
AWD Subaru wagon, PS, PB, PL, PBJ, One owner, non-smoker, new brakes, great mpg. 446-0000

TAKE ME HOME
AWD Subaru wagon, PS, PB, PL, PBJ, One owner, non-smoker, new brakes, great mpg. 446-0000

FAMILY OWNED
AWD Subaru wagon, PS, PB, PL, PBJ, One owner, non-smoker, new brakes, great mpg. 446-0000

NO DOG HAIR!
AWD Subaru wagon, PS, PB, PL, PBJ, One owner, non-smoker, new brakes, great mpg. 446-0000

TO CHURCH ON SUNDAY
AWD Subaru wagon, PS, PB, PL, PBJ, One owner, non-smoker, new brakes, great mpg. 446-0000

REAR ENTERTAINMENT
AWD Subaru wagon, PS, PB, PL, PBJ, One owner, non-smoker, new brakes, great mpg. 446-0000

GAS SIPPER
AWD Subaru wagon, PS, PB, PL, PBJ, One owner, non-smoker, new brakes, great mpg. 446-0000

MECHANIC'S DREAM
AWD Subaru wagon, PS, PB, PL, PBJ, One owner, non-smoker, new brakes, great mpg. 446-0000

GOT TO SEE
AWD Subaru wagon, PS, PB, PL, PBJ, One owner, non-smoker, new brakes, great mpg. 446-0000

HIGHLY SOUGHT AFTER
AWD Subaru wagon, PS, PB, PL, One owner, non-smoker, new brakes, great mpg. 446-0000

NEW TRANNY
AWD Subaru wagon, PS, PB, PL, PBJ, One owner, non-smoker, new brakes, great mpg. 446-0000

the Local rag

PRSRT-STD U.S. Postage PAID Red Lodge, MT Permit No. 75

BOXHOLDER

Of all of the April Fool covers in the Rag, this was the first one that really fooled me. I called Anne to see why I hadn't gotten a Rag that month, and she said, "Did you throw away a Nifty Trickle?" It took a moment, but I finally realized what had happened. Well played, Anne. Well played.

The Very Best of the Red Lodge Local Rag

reflections

We have two new staff persons to introduce to you this month. First, **John Overton** has taken on the role of Ombudsman. We liked the word "om-BUDS-man" and its long tradition in newspapers as a reader representative, so we searched high and low and asked the first person who came along. John's first task is researching what "Ombudsman" means. After that he plans on joining the Organization of Newspaper Ombudsmen (ONO!) – our emphasis – and traveling to conferences with Shirley. When in town, we see him as our ear-to-the-ground, man-on-the-street, problem solver, rumor confirmer, and chief investigator, all the while assuring our readers of accuracy and balance. We have set up an email address for John for you to send in story ideas, queries, letters and grievances. Please don't make this a thankless job, compliments are appreciated. You can reach John at `ombudsman@localrag.com`.

… **and Nicole Lohof**

A Red Lodge native, Nicole came back after a few years of doing this and that, here and there mostly in Billings. One day in April while visiting her friend Amari Mitzkus at the Sheriff's Office, discussing her lack of worthwhile employment, the clouds parted and an angel appeared in the form of Anne Rood. (Nicole's words. Discussion point for the ombudsman) Anne was working her second job as a Sheriff's Office dispatcher and knew she needed an ads sales person, so then and there the pitch was made. Ever since, Nicole's been running the Local Rag staff ragged with her ideas and energy. (Yeah, another Gemini in the office.) When not pounding the pavement slinging ads for the Rag you can find Nicole digging for worms with her 4 year old son, Isaac. After reading John's introduction, Nicole asked us to note that she doesn't mind this job being thankless as long as you're advertising. After all, folks, Isaac's sick and tired of Ramen. You can reach Nicole at `ads@localrag.com`.

So we have lots of changes and additions at the Rag beginning this month. All these changes are spread out in stories and ads all over the paper like a scavenger hunt.

I'd like to thank Madame Zora who stopped by the office to make a few predictions for us. She was in a hurry to get back to Toledo so she won't be here on May 25th to see if her predictions came true. She's always fun to visit with and we hope she'll stop in again.

And for those of you who recycled your paper before you caught on that it was our April Fools issue, we still have a few copies here at the office. Boy, that was fun fooling everyone. Just ask us!

April 2007

March 2002

What I Like About Red Lodge

By Gary Robson, October 2006

The first time I visited Red Lodge with my family, we picked up a copy of a little newspaper called the Red Lodge Local Rag. In it was an article by then-editor Lou Ward called "Things I Most Love About Red Lodge." One that really stood out was, "local pedestrians will step into the crosswalk to stop traffic so that cars on the side streets can move." I got a chuckle out of it then. Now, I catch myself doing it.

Driving home the other night, I got to thinking about that article and was inspired to write one of my own. Let me caution you, though. It's more editorial than article, and reflects my own personal opinions of the town. If you disagree, let's chat about it sometime. That's another of the things I like about this town! So without further ado, let me present Gary's favorite things about Red Lodge:

For the most part, Red Lodge is completely unpretentious. We have a newspaper called the Local Rag, for goodness' sake. I love it!

The town is full of places that make your dog welcome, and people who teach their dogs proper manners before taking them around town.

Parades! Red Lodge will put on a parade at the drop of a hat, whether it's a two-hour parade with the Budweiser Clydesdales or the whole parade is just one car, one horse, one flag, and one bagpiper (probably Brad Logan).

Numerous businesses in town have discounts or other incentives for locals—in many cases you have to ask, but there are a lot of "frequent buyer" or "loyalty reward" programs in town.

Red Lodge is a literate community. The experts say it takes a town of 60,000 people to keep a bookstore going. I say hah! Nobody will ever get rich running a bookstore in Red Lodge, but we've had one here for 20 years. We also have a great library and a host of book clubs.

This town puts together more benefits and fundraisers for good causes than any place I've seen, and it's not for the publicity. Most of the good things done by individuals and groups like the Elks, Lions, Rotary (and dozens of others) never show up in press releases (more on this later).

It's easy to be a part of Red Lodge. If you want to pitch in, there are approximately 6,493,201 committees, clubs, charities, foundations, and other groups for you to join.

People willing to help out when you have animal problems, like the Red Lodge police officer that caught my escaped horse last month and kept

him at his own house until he found out who he (the horse) belonged to.

I love all the diverse backgrounds of the people in town, and the fact that they tend to unite rather than separate. Cowboys & hippies, farmers & rocket scientists, vegans & hunters, bikers & yuppies can all sit and have a drink together.

Locals value Red Lodge's history and work to preserve the look and feel of the town. It's great to see historic lighting, roundabouts, and restaurants with personality instead of modern 40-foot light poles, traffic lights, and McDonald's.

A special note to people who keep the Red Lodge economy going by shopping locally instead of driving to Billings or Cody to shop: Thank you! You keep our town alive!

I love the pride people take in the town. The flags and flowers on Broadway in the summertime, the flowers in the parks, the garbage cans downtown, and all of the other little things the volunteers and merchants do in town. And graffiti is rare because residents have no tolerance for it.

We have business owners that "get it." As an example, the first time I walked into Foster & Logan's, Tom Doddy introduced himself and asked what I thought of his selection of beers on draught. I said he needed a Scottish Ale. Next time I walked in, he greeted me by name and poured me a Scottish Ale.

If you accidentally leave your coat [or wallet!] in a bar or restaurant (not that I would ever do such a thing), you don't have to worry about whether it'll be there the next day. In fact, they'll probably call and tell you they have it.

It's the little things that make you feel at home: the couches at the theater; the free popcorn at several stores & clubs; the personal notes on the first page of the Local Rag…

If someone's walking, it's generally because they want to. Rides are easy to come by. If you don't believe me, pull your car off to the side of the road and stand next to it. See how many people stop to see if you have a problem?

Last names are generally superfluous. If you have a common first name, a short descriptor is enough (e.g., Kari at the Rag or Gary at the bookstore).

The biggest thing I love about Red Lodge is how most residents do things because it's the right thing to do, not because they want publicity or kudos. People quietly help their neighbors in need. Stores quietly offer discounts to ship gifts to friends and family serving overseas in the military. Service organizations quietly pitch in when families are in trouble.

Anne Rood was doing a good job as editor, but Kari was really looking for somebody to sell the Rag to. It went into a short publishing hiatus until Speak Like A Pirate Day in 2007 (look it up), when Kathy and I bought the Rag from Kari.

For my first issue, designer Robyn Rivers created this lovely cover with Kari handing over the keys to Local Rag NCC-1701-D. I created my first typo by getting the date wrong on the front cover. It was supposed to say November 2007.

The Local Rag
Editor's Page

A New and (Hopefully) Improved Local Rag

The dust has settled. The negotiations are complete. The Local Rag has new owners.

The process of buying the paper wasn't as complex as we feared. Kari told us it would be billions of dollars, and we counter-offered four cheese sandwiches and a sixpack of Glacier Ale. Eventually, we agreed upon the terms, and set to work creating our first issue.

For those of you who don't know us, my name is Gary Robson, and my partner-slash-Chief Financial Officer is my wife, Kathy. You've probably encountered us before at Red Lodge Books, and you're probably wondering now what we're planning to do to your beloved newspaper.

First off, don't worry. We aren't changing the things that count. We're keeping the irreverent tone, the strong local focus, the strange ads, and the editorial policy of not printing the boring stuff.

We're keeping most of your favorite contributors, including Viv Beam (gardening), Craig Beam (fishing), Marci Dye (outdoors and equipment), John and Shirley Overton (cooking), and Dr. Dan Upton (Health). We're also keeping designer Robyn Rivers. I have no idea what we'd do without her.

We are adding quite a few new writers, and some new features, too:

- The "**Stop and Think**" column (page 14) is your chance to talk back to us. Each month, we'll throw out a controversial topic. If you have an opinion, shoot us an email, and we'll print the ones we like.

- We'll be putting in more coverage of **the arts**, starting in this issue with a series of Nancy DeRosiers' bird art and a photo tip column by Gene Rodman.

- We'll be keeping your favorite **music** correspondent, Stylus T. Table, but also adding guest columnists talking about different music genres, starting with Tré Eyden's feature on punk rock.

- Somewhere in each issue of the Local Rag, there will be a **fake ad**. See if you can find it. There's a free Local Rag T-shirt for the first person who finds the fake ad and emails me at Gary@LocalRag.com.

- In our new **crossword puzzle** (page 35), all of the answers can be found in the articles and ads in this month's paper.

We also have some other new contributors, cartoons, poetry, and more. And, of course, since this is the November issue, we're including ballots for the **Best of Red Lodge** awards and coverage of the **2007 election** season.

Kathy and I hope that you'll like the new (and hopefully improved) Red Lodge Local Rag. Please give us a call or email and let us know what you think. We'd love to hear from you.

Gary Robson, Editor-in-Chief

> "We counter-offered four cheese sandwiches and a sixpack of Glacier Ale."

December Crossword Puzzle — All answers can be found in this issue of the Local Rag

Across
1. Trans-Siberian Orchestra's best-known song.
2. They do custom concrete countertops
4. A great new place to hike.
5. Nana Inga's Christmas Gingersnaps
6. Cover artist for this month's Local Rag.
7. The shoes Jean Petersen is writing about
8. Cody Q's latest love interest
9. What Rhonda inoculates her hogs against

Down
3. Maker of glasses (and even shades)
10. She'll fix up your aching muscles.
11. Your eggnog needs brandy, milk, eggs, and what?
12. The king that made December the 12th month
13. He doesn't want Hannah Nyquist to beat him this year!
14. Mix with aquamarine blue paint to get black.
15. What SADD needs for DSVS.

The idea behind the Local Rag crossword puzzles was that you shouldn't have to grab an encyclopedia (or Google) to help with a tough answer. All of the answers could be found right in your hands, spread throughout the ads and editorial content in the paper.

A little over three years later, I found myself ready to sell the Rag, just as my predecessors had. As much fun as I was having, I just had too much else — oh, I'll just let myself tell the story. Here:

"The Pauls" mentioned in the editorial are these two entertaining characters that took care of designing ads and covers for the Rag (see September 2009 article below).

The other folks mentioned are graphic designers Robyn Rivers and Jesse Reko, website designer Doug Robson, ad salesman Craig Conlee, and intern Bethany George.

A Few Words from the outgoing editor

Thirty-seven months ago, I wrote my first editorial in the Local Rag. Today, I write my last. Oh, I had written articles for the Rag before then (book reviews for Jean, fiction for Kari), and I will hopefully write more. But this is the last time I'll write as your editor-in-chief.

When we moved to Red Lodge almost ten years ago, I was escaping from the rat-race of the microelectronics industry and hoping to slow down and relax with a nice, quiet bookstore. Since then, I've written 18 books, served on four nonprofit boards, kept the bookstore, and bought this newspaper. So much for slowing down.

I bought the Local Rag for pretty much the same reasons that all of my predecessors bought the Local Rag: I love this paper and I didn't want to see it go away. Jean changed it and made it her own when she took over from Lou. Kari did the same when she took over from Jean. And I did it when I took over from Kari.

I believe, at age 52, that I'm the oldest editor the Rag has ever had. And now I'm turning it over to a pair of 20-somethings. I expect things will probably change again.

There's no possible way I could have kept the Rag going by myself. My wife, Kathy, thought I was nuts for buying it, but she's been the best Chief Financial Officer I could ever hope for (not to mention all the time she spent on things like the calendar). And I am a writer/editor; not a salesman. Without Heather for the first two years and Craig for the last year, we wouldn't have had any income. I've done quite a bit of ad design, but Robyn, Jesse, and the Pauls have carried the bulk of that load. And we haven't had our intern, Bethany, for long, but she's been a big help, and she's taken over a lot of the website work Doug did before going off to college.

All of those people had their names on the masthead. The Rag was a job for them. The main reason you all picked up the paper every month wasn't the staff, though. It was the volunteers. The columnists. They write all this stuff for free! When you see them, tell them they rock.

When you get to the bottom line, it costs money to produce a newspaper. Unlike the Billings Gazette or Carbon County News, we don't make our money from paid subscriptions. The Local Rag is free, delivered to your mailbox or P.O. Box every month. Why? Because of our advertisers. It's the money that they spend every month on ads that funds the printing and distribution of the Local Rag. I implore you all, if you like getting the Rag for free, thank the advertisers. Stop by and do some business with them.

But now it's time for me to do some of that slowing down I talked about at the beginning of this editorial. It's time to step away from the Local Rag and turn it over to my daughter, Heather, and her partner, Melissa. I hope you'll be as good to them as you have been to me.

So long, and thank you all!

—*Gary Robson, editor-in-chief*

GOOD-BYE, PAUL

Local Rag Graphic Designer Paul Johnson is saying farewell to the Local Rag, and farewell to Red Lodge. Most of the ads you've been reading in the Rag have been Paul's doing, as have two of the covers.

We'll let him explain in his own words what's going on:

"Feeling a need for an adventure and some cross culteral perspective and experience, I'll be heading to Ghana, Africa in mid September for a 20 week volunteer placement. I'll be working as a graphic designer, handling the visual output for an Art and Culture Foundation based in the capital city, Accra. The Foundation collects and displays art and other items of Ghanaian heritage and also provides a support system for the creation of contemporary art in Ghana. The only concern now is ajusting to the equitorial heat and humidity after living in the comfortable and bug-free Red Lodge climate!"

We'll miss Paul, but have no fear—we've found someone to take over designing your ads!

HELLO, PAUL

Hi, I'm the new Paul: Paul Otsu, to be precise. Just a few days ago, I stumbled out of the mountains and into Red Lodge Books looking for a new read to get me thru the long winter. Gary took one look at me and just knew that I was an artistic gent, and hired me on at the Local Rag (but I honestly think that he just hired me because he didn't want to remember another name). I truthfully know nothing about computers and art, I spend most of my time in a cave. But when I'm out and about I'm riding bikes, catching fish, skiing and just causing general havoc.

This isn't the first time that I've popped up in the Red Lodge media scene, you've heard me on the Red Lodge Mountain Snow Phone, on FM99.3 the Mountain, and my art has been catching your eye in many different publications. This doesn't include police reports or rumors that I look like Brad Pitt. I'm very exited about my future time spent at the Local Rag, Gary and the crew have promised me some food, and little shelter for all the work that they make me do. I like food. This should be good.

The Very Best of the Red Lodge Local Rag

A chat with the new owners of the Local Rag

Gary: Who are you guys, anyway?

Melissa: I'm Melissa Cross. I grew up in western Montana and moved to Red Lodge about 8 years ago from Missoula. I have family from Red Lodge, so I visited often as a kid. I use my degree in interpersonal communication (with focus in argumentation and rhetoric) at work, as a bartender at the Snag. I live in Red Lodge with my kitty, Earl.

Heather: I'm Heather Robson. I've lived in Red Lodge on and off since I was 14, and just moved back a couple years ago from Colorado. I live in a tiny house with my three cats, two dogs, boyfriend Steve, and my three-year-old son, Brodie.

Gary: So why the Local Rag?

Heather: I worked for the Local Rag for a couple of years as the ad sales person, and really enjoyed being tapped into the community and the occasional writing projects I got to do. I like investigating, keeping people informed, and getting paid to hang out at the bar and talk to people!

Melissa: I think it's really good for small communities to have a local paper that's aimed more at local interest than "news".

Gary: Do you have any big changes planned for the Rag?

Heather: I've got some new contributors lined up, and we're really excited about bringing in some new content. We'll have a lot more focus on outdoor activities, local interest, and what's going on in the community.

Melissa: I think our main goal is to make the Rag more well-rounded and bring in some new readers.

Gary: What are your favorite things to do around town?

Melissa: I love camping, snowboarding, and just enjoying the people I see every day. With our locals, there's always some entertainment happening!

Heather: Other than getting paid to sit at the bar? I like pretty much anything that involves being outside, as long as it doesn't also involve standing on slippery bits of wood and careening down mountains. My favorite thing about Red Lodge is that I can drive for 10 minutes and be in the middle of nowhere.

Gary: What fun fact about you would our readers find entertaining?

Melissa: I LOVE baby cows! I even have a baby cow picture on my fridge. And the best part is at the end of the year, they turn into beef. Then you get to get a new baby cow.

Heather: My favorite thing to do is read outside. Any day I'm not at work, and the weather is warm enough, you can usually find me sitting on a big rock by a river somewhere with a book in my hand.

Melissa with her cat, Earl

Gary: What's your favorite Red Lodge Ales beer?

Heather: Definitely the Chocolate Stout! But since it's only seasonal, I usually drink the Scottish Ale.

Melissa: PBR in a can! But if I'm at Sam's I'm drinking a Scottish Ale.

Gary: Tell us your best Red Lodge wildlife story.

Melissa: I had to miss 2 days of work when a momma and baby moose bedded down at the foot of my front stairs. There was no other way out of the house, and they weren't moving!

Heather: Having to sit in my car in front of my house while I waited for the black bear to get out of the way was a good time. He sat there nibbling on my dogwood trees and staring at me for a good 20 minutes before he took off.

Gary: What is the airspeed velocity of an unladen swallow?

Heather: What do you mean? African or European swallow?

Gary: Huh? I don't know that. Ahhhhhh!

Melissa: How do you know so much about swallows?

Heather: Well, you have to know these things when you're a Local Rag editor, you know.

Heather with her son, Brodie

Unfortunately, the sale fell through, and the Rag ended up going into a publishing hiatus again until late 2013.

When the Rag came back, I continued as publisher, with Heather as editor. Our last issue came out in December of 2014.

CHAPTER 2

Where do you read your Local Rag?

Where do you read *your* Local Rag?

In September 2004, editor Jean Atherly implemented an idea she got from the *Triangle Review* in Fort Collins, Colorado: "Where do you read your Local Rag?" She kicked off the new feature with this picture of Aaron Kampfe in Rome.

In the following years, people took their favorite reading material all over the world, from boats to airplanes, South Africa to Alaska, beaches to mountaintops.
This became the most popular feature in the Local Rag, and one of the most fun for the editors as well!

Susan Bury in Arizona

Jodie & Judy Christensen in London

Kari at the Metropolitan Opera

The Very Best of the Red Lodge Local Rag

Where do you read *your* Local Rag?

Joan Cline, Richard Gessling, Janal Martin, Shelly Kennen & Erika Binando in San Francisco

Dave Beach in Kuala Lumpur, Malaysia.

This is the first of what would become a long list of pictures of Tory Host Hanson in exotic locations, both in and out of his airplane cockpit.

David Heinzen in Louisville, KY

Mike Cardoza in Malta

The Very Best of the Red Lodge Local Rag

March 2005

Where do you read your rag?
In Central Park, checking out "The Gates" ~Jean Albus

June 2005

Where do you read your rag?
On the Pass with the snowplow ~Dan Upton

May 2005

Where do you read your rag?
Gregg Hodges, **Lou Ward**, & Frankie Davis in Doolin, County Clare, Ireland

September 2005

Where do you read your rag?
At Ha Long Bay, Vietnam ~a very shy Don Hamilton

April 2005

Where do you read your rag?
In Tucson, Arizona ~Sue Bury

At Aspen ski resort ~Robert Drake

March 1996

Where do you read your rag?

March 2005

In NYC's Times Square ~Charla Carter, Tom Manuel, Lila Poore, & David Beach

June 2006

In Moscow, Russia ~Richard & Jean Anne Bullock

July 2005

In Patagonia, Argentina ~Doug & Liza McClelland

August 2005

In Sayulita, Mexico ~ Robby Ringer, Abbi Dayton, Kylie Chupp, Angela Schilz, Stephen Sommerfeld, Adam Lynn

October 2005

In Rome ~Paula & George Clow

November 2005

In Prague, Czech Republic ~Tonya Kosorok

The Very Best of the Red Lodge Local Rag

Where do you read your rag?

At Notre Dame, the Leaning Tower of Pisa, the Eiffel Tower, & the Colosseum
~Anita & Laure Sandretto

November 2005

February 2004

Where do you read your rag?

On Kauai, Hawaii ~Craig Beam

December 2005

Getting married in New York City
(to Heather, not each other!)
~Robert & Jacob Drake

January 2006

At Palm Cove, Queensland, Australia
~Mike Cardoza, Scott Martin, & Anner Marble

January 2006

At Taktshang Monastery, Paro, Bhutan
~Aaron Kampfe

April 2006

July 2006

Where do you read your rag?

Skiing in Portillo, Chile
~Pat & Gregg Hodges

May 2006

Where do you read your rag?

At Lambeau Field in Green Bay, Wisconsin
~Taylor Upton

Where do you read your rag?

Mountain climbing in Peru,
& Bruxella, Belguim
~Tore Host-Hanson

December 2005

CAUGHT IN THE ACT
That tired old stereotype about cops and donuts? There's not a bit of truth to it. Just ask Sgt. Scott Cope of the RLPD!
(photo from 2010)

The Very Best of the Red Lodge Local Rag

Where do you read your rag?

May 2006

In Timbuktu
~Ruth Sheller & Paula Priest

June 2006

At Auckland & Cardrona, New Zealand
~Richard & Gretchen Nolan
(Ask Richard about the bras!!)

July 2006

David & Donna Ritter with Martha Sobral & Phil Robertson on top of "80 Mountain" and at Mogollon Ghost Town, New Mexico

February 2006

At Pawleys Island, South Carolina
~The Buckaroo

Can you spot the fake RAG readers?
(They're not the ones on the right)

Where do you read your rag?

At the summit of Ecuador's Mt. Cotopaxi, 19,347'

~Tore Host-Hansen with unidentified friends & sherpas

At the Winter Olympics in Torino, Italy

~Shari Whiteside, Frank Pirtz, Snowboarding Bronze medalist Toby Dawson & Karen Saint

April 2006

August 2006

Where do you read your rag?

In Belize
~Dave Malin & Terry Perkins

August 2006

Where do you read your rag?

At Kittery Point, Maine
~Pat Tate

September 2006

Where do you read your rag?

In Arizona ~Jason & Cathy Magida

The Very Best of the Red Lodge Local Rag

Where do you read your rag?

Buried in the sand in Mazatlan, Mexico
~Jon Trapp

August 2006

At Maachu Picchu
~Rand Herzberg & Janet Gale

September 2006

During monks' debate hour at the Sera Monastery in Lhasa, Tibet
~Marlene Tetrault

September 2006

October 2006

In Dubai, UAE & Accra, Ghana
~Tore Host-Hansen
(The guy gets around!)

December 2006

At Kleine Scheidegg, Switzerland
~Barb Beck

October 2006

In Istanbul
~Kit Richards

Where do you read your rag?

In Fernie, British Columbia
~Susan Lyall

November 2006

We all tried to hold back a few "Where do you read your Local Rag?" submissions in case we didn't get any one month, but sometimes we really started falling behind.

In November 2006, Kari caught up with her backlog by running these six all in one issue.

Where do you read your rag?

In America's Northernmost city: Barrow, Alaska
~Bryan Romeijn

Where do you read your rag?

On the dock of Swiftcurrent Lake in Glacier Park
~Audrey Clark, Kris Thomas & Bobbie Sacks

Where do you read your rag?

In a blackhawk helicopter in Kabul, Afghanistan
~Edmund McCafferty

Where do you read your rag?

With a mime in Venice, Italy
~Dennis Christ & John Overton
(Were the girls out shopping?)

Where do you read your rag?

At Exit Glacier, Alaska
~Ernie & Marge Strum

The Very Best of the Red Lodge Local Rag

Where do you read your rag?

At Folly Beach, South Carolina
~Molly Hardy & Clare Witcomb

October 2006

Where do you read your rag?

In Lake Mary Ronan
(as the dock is collapsing beneath us!)
~Bridgett Tucker (with the Rag), Dianne & Kent Young, Scott & Pam Tucker, Tracy Young, Mark Tucker, Dan Cross, Linda Tucker, Matt Young, Emma Evenson, Eileen & Harvey Roemmich.

December 2006

Where do you read your rag?

At Lake Louise, Banff Canada
~John & Kari Clayton

January 2007

Where do you read your rag?

At the 1924 base camp for Mt. Everest, Tibet
~Carrie Culp & Debbie Goldberg

December 2006

THE EDGE OF RED LODGE

**Ski & Snowboard Repair & Tuning
Custom Boot Fitting & Footbeds**

Open every day 8 am - 5:30 pm
Check out our new location
24 S. Broadway
(behind Water's Dept. Store)

446-4023 • 861-7011

January 2002

Where do you read your rag?

At the pyramids of Giza, Egypt
~Barb Ostrum & Norma Scheidecker

January 2007

Where do you read your rag?

In Antarctica ~David Lehnherr

February 2007

Where do you read your rag?

Jumping off the world's highest bungee in Tsitsikamma National Park, South Africa
~Aaron Kampfe

January 2007

Where do you read your rag?

In the Local Rag office
~John Clayton, honorary copy editor

April 2007

Where do you read your rag?

April 2007

In Pride Park
~Shelly Link

Where do you read your rag?

May 2007

In Cabo San Lucas ~ Don & Janis Williams

Where do you read your rag?

May 2007

In Ireland ~ Skip & Kandy Aleksich

July 2003

Horny Toad · Royal Robbins Rugged Outdoor Clothing · The North Face · patagonia

Come in and check out our new spring arrivals!

MOUNTAIN PEOPLE
446-1542
123 S. Broadway • Red Lodge

Where do you read *your* Local Rag?

Stockholm, Sweden
Buster, Clay, Laurie & Carly Haugen enjoy a little "Ragtime" at the harbor.

January 2008

Where do you read *your* Local Rag?

Paris, France (in front of the Louvre)
–Cobe Chatwood and Susan Hovde

December 2007

Where do you read *your* Local Rag?

Glacier Lake
Andrea, Gretchen, Cara, Deb, Wanda, and Kelly celebrate a couple of birthdays at Glacier Lake and do a little bit of summer swimming (they put their clothes back on just for this picture)

November 2006

January 2008

Where do you read *your* Local Rag?

Reykjavic, Iceland
Marco Restani shared his Local Rag with some rather scary guys outside of the Saga Museum last May.

November 2007

Where do you read *your* Local Rag?

Windy Mountain, Wyoming
–Thomas Ehlers (who was hopefully only *reading* the Rag)

Where do you read your Local Rag?

March 2008

Luxor, Egypt
Marguerite Storm reading her Rag in front of a colossal statue of Rameses II in the temple of Karnak.

March 2003

Where do you read your Local Rag?

Eastern Caribbean
Don & Janis Williams; Lee & Teresa Hauge; and Jim & Mary Beth Noe reading their Rag aboard the Mariner of the Seas.

February 2008

Where do you read your Local Rag?

Bergen, Norway
Clay, Laurie & Carly Haugen share their Rag with some underdressed Norwegians.

February 2008

Where do you read your Local Rag?

Johannesburg, South Africa
Tory Host Hansen reads his Rag in Nelson Mandela Square

Where do you read your Local Rag?

March 2008

Preikestolen, Norway
Kirsten Arthun (RLHS Class of 1998) Wilson and her husband Jarl Wilson

Ad from March 1996

Montana Chinook
6 South Broadway
Downtown Red Lodge
446-1810
Open 7 Days A Week
Shopper's Paradise!

February 2008

Costa Rica
Nancy Kriner, Evelyn Rolshouen, Shirlee Quin, and Rosemary McAlpine remembered to take their March Local Rag along to a Costa Rica hot springs.

April 2008

Amsterdam, the Netherlands
Peggy and Erik Arthun enjoying a bit of relaxing Local Rag time before entering the Amsterdam Museum of Torture.

May 2008

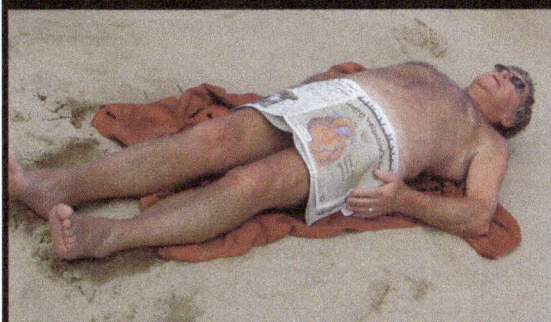

On a Nude Beach
Our tireless ombudsman, John Overton, relaxes with his Local Rag. Okay, maybe he's not so tireless. And remind us not to borrow a newspaper at his house.

Where do you read your Local Rag?

Balad, Iraq

U.S. Air Force Captain Curt Prudden, grandson of Harry and Lillian Sibary and nephew of Lola Ashby, reads his Local Rag on the wing of a C-130 "Hercules" transport.

May 2008

July 2008

Where do you read your Local Rag?

Machu Picchu, Peru

Bob Jorgenson enjoys his April Fools edition of the Local Rag in the Lost City of the Incas.

The Very Best of the Red Lodge Local Rag

Where do you read *your* Local Rag?

Melbourne, Australia
Marek Rosin demonstrates his ability to read his Rag in the dark. Maybe that's how they do it down under!

June 2008 ↕   December 2008 →

Where do you read *your* Local Rag?

Don't forget to take a copy of the Local Rag when you travel! Email your pics to gary@LocalRag.com or drop them off at our office.

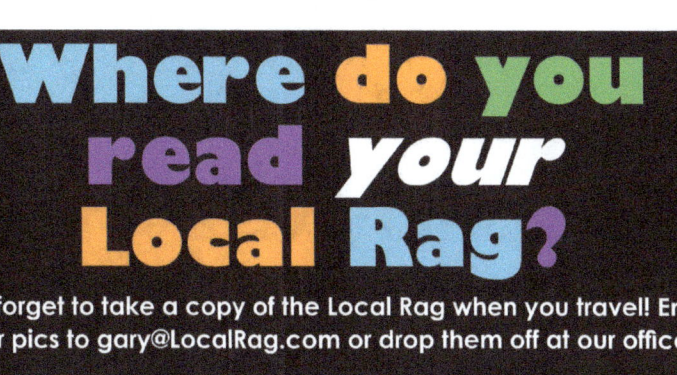

Santorini, Greece
Rosemary McAlpine (left) and Nancy Kriner make an island visit.

Florence, Italy
Evelyn Rolshoven reads her Rag by one of Florence's many statues.

Budapest, Hungary
Kathy Davidson on a trip with her husband, Chuck Shenk.

The Grand Canyon
MaryEllen Mangus, Wanda Kennicott, and Dick & Gretchen Nolan.

The Very Best of the Red Lodge Local Rag

Where do you read your Local Rag?

October 2008

Machu Picchu, Peru
Becky Hill and Don Hardy of Red Lodge join Art & Bonnie Daniel of Fishtail at the "Lost City of the Incas."

September 2008

Where do you read your Local Rag?

Nairobi, Kenya
Tory Host Hansen reads his Rag at a bus stop in Kenya.

August 2008

Where do you read your Local Rag?

Doolin, County Clare, Ireland
Local Rag founding editor Lou Ward catches up on what's happening in Red Lodge as current *Rag* editor Gary Robson reads Lou's new paper, the *North Clare Local*.

Where do you read your Local Rag?

In Mommy's Lap
Brodie Eyden shows a decided lack of respect for the Local Rag's community calendar. Brodie is the son of Ad Saleswoman Extraordinaire Heather Eyden (he's also the grandson of Rag owners Gary & Kathy Robson)

May 2008

Where do you read your Local Rag?

A British Isles double-header
Don't forget to take a copy of the Rag with you when you travel! Email your pics to gary@LocalRag.com or drop them off at our office.

Doolin, Ireland
Robin & Jerry Doherty bring Local Rag founder Lou Ward Davis up to speed on what's happening back in Red Lodge.

Robin Hood's Bay, England
JoAnn Eder and Marlene Tetrault catch up on news from home at the end of their coast-to-coast walk all the way across England.

November 2008

San Francisco, CA
Lola Ashby relaxes with her Local Rag after completing a 60-mile fundraising walk in 3 days.

October 2008

The Very Best of the Red Lodge Local Rag

Where do you read *your* Local Rag?

Tulum, Mexico
Lew and Diny Gumper pause to read their Local Rag while touring Mayan ruins on the Yucatan Peninsula in Mexico.

April 2009

Where do you read *your* Local Rag?

Helena, Montana
Paul Beck, Montana State Representative for House District #59, takes a few moments out of his busy day to read the Local Rag on the House Floor Rostrum in the state capitol building in Helena with a group of 7th graders from Luther school.

The picture below from the September 2009 issue isn't the only one that Kimberly LeFore tried to get in Athens reading the Local Rag. She also had someone take a picture of her in front of the Parthenon up on the Acropolis. Two security people rushed in and took her camera, insisting that the picture be deleted in front of them or they wouldn't give the camera back.

It appears that people aren't allowed to take pictures of the Parthenon with a newspaper in your hand, because the shot could be used "for commercial purposes."

Not that we'd ever do that, of course!

Where do you read *your* Local Rag?

Athens, Greece
Kimberly LeFore in front of a temple in the ancient Agora (marketplace) below the Acropolis.

Where do you read *your* Local Rag?

February 2009

At Barack Obama's Inauguration
Allison Smith-Estelle, and Graham & Steve Estelle take a break from the inauguration ceremonies to catch up on news from home by the Washington Memorial.

The fake telemarketer ad was in the November 2007 issue.

TELEMARKETERS WANTED

Must be able to work during dinnertime

Heavy accent a plus

Call 555-2736 to change your future career

Where do you read *your* Local Rag?

November 2009

Iceland
Jay Mennenga reads his Local Rag in Iceland, where he gained the inspiration to write this month's *Green Scene* article.

The Very Best of the Red Lodge Local Rag

Where do you read *your* Local Rag?
Special Brazil segment

Manaus, Brazil
Theresa & Steve Morgan reading their Rag in the city square with the statue dedicated to the opening of Manaus' large Amazonian port.

Pantanal, Brazil
Ruth Sheller and Paula Priest, carefully not reading the funny part of the Rag so they won't fall off their horses laughing in the Wild West of Brazil.

Agua Boa River, Brazil
Chuck Mattraw of Luther takes a break from fishing for Peacock Bass.

February 2009

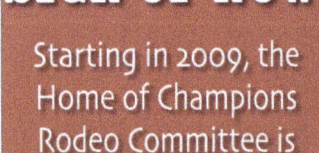

SIGN UP NOW! Starting in 2009, the Home of Champions Rodeo Committee is proud to bring you **Gnome Roping!**

No gnomes were harmed in making this ad

This fake ad appeared in the December 2008 issue of the Rag.

Page 52 — *The Very Best of the Red Lodge Local Rag*

Where do you read your Local Rag?

Puerto Quetzal, Guatemala
Keith Robson, big brother to your humble Local Rag Editor, catches up on Red Lodge news at one of the stops on a cruise with his wife, Sharon.

Rotorua, New Zealand
Terry and Bonnie McKown of Red Lodge and Don and Anita Shiver of Roscoe in front of the Rotorua Museum of Art and History on the North Island in New Zealand.

Blarney, Ireland
Kerry Burns reads a slightly damp Local Rag on the battlements of Blarney Castle. We're not sure if he kissed the blarney stone, as he had the gift already!

Haleakala Crater, Hawaii
Jodee Hogg, Mike Taylor, Roberta and Peter Kaiser trying to see in a lava tube cavern in Haleakala Crater, Haleakala National Park, East Maui, Hawaii.

Where? Local Rag — May 2009

The Very Best of the Red Lodge Local Rag

Where do you read *your* Local Rag?

Don't forget to take a copy of the Local Rag when you travel! Email your pics to gary@LocalRag.com or drop them off at our office.

Meddelin, Colombia

Tory Host Hansen sent us two this month. A busy (or perhaps not-so-busy) man!

Addis Ababa, Ethiopia

Chobe National Park, Botswana
Bill Stratton relaxes with his Local Rag at the Chobe Game Lodge, where Elizabeth Taylor and Richard Burton honeymooned.

Rotorua, New Zealand
Bonnie McKown (Red Lodge) and Anita Shiver (Roscoe) attempt to explain the Local Rag to a Maori lady named Mere Ana.

March 2009

August 2004

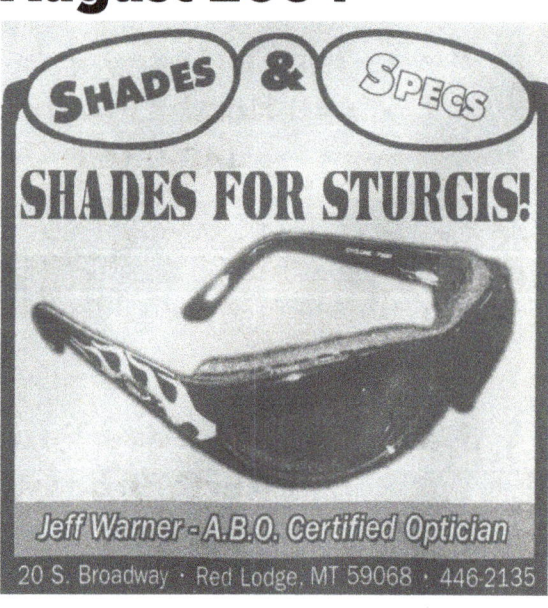

Where do you read *your* Local Rag?

December 2009

Tanzania
Tory Host Hansen takes a break near the summit of Mount Kilimanjaro to catch up on news from back home.

Where do you read *your* Local Rag?

Denali, Alaska
David Kallenbach, who took a summer job as an interpretive ranger in Denali National Park, catches up on news of home with Local Rag owners Kathy & Gary Robson

Pointe Noviar, Congo
Tory Host Hansen enchants the locals on the coast of Congo-Brazzaville (a.k.a. Republic of the Congo) on the Western coast of Africa.

Where?

Local Rag

June 2009

Sailing Up the Nile
Evelyn Rolshoven sent us this Local Rag picture from her visit to ancient Egypt and sailing trip up the Nile River. A shame we couldn't get her the special heiroglyphic edition!

Sydney, Australia
Shirlee Quinn and Marlene Tetrault read their Local Rag with the Sydney Opera House and the Sydney Harbor Bridge in the background.

The Very Best of the Red Lodge Local Rag — Page 55

Where do you read your Local Rag?

July 2009

Philadelphia, Pennsylvania
Ken Adams gets in a patriotic mood for Independence Day in front of Independence Hall.

Mombasa, Kenya
Tory Host Hansen settles into the shade on the Indian Ocean for a little R&R with his Local Rag.

Where?

Fallujah, Iraq
This picture was taken in Fallujah, Iraq with Battalion Commander LtCol Scott Fosdal, USMC (1st Battalion, 7th Marines) sharing the Local Rag as he hands the city back over to the Iraqis. Scott is a resident of Red Lodge when the Marine Corps doesn't send him elsewhere.

Where do you read your Local Rag?

Fossil Lake
We really wish we could tell which page the Gildehaus family was reading in this Fossil Lake picture!

Auckland, New Zealand
Bonnie McKown and Anita Shiver check up on news from Red Lodge in front of the newly-docked Queen Victoria.

Drimoleague, Ireland
Mike Taylor, Tim Simpson, and Jack Lynch with Harry and Eileen Deane at "Harry Deane's Pub"

Glacier Bay, Alaska
As others scrambled for coats and gloves, Kathy Robson put on a swimsuit and climbed in the jacuzzi when the cruise ship entered Glacier Bay.

August 2009

The Very Best of the Red Lodge Local Rag

Where do you read your Local Rag?

Right Here in Red Lodge
Katelyn Trapp "reads" the Local Rag before Mom gets to it. What's black & white & red all over? The Rag!

Sacred Valley, Peru
Dan Seymour and Mom (Martha) floating the Urubamba River in Sacred Valley, Peru.

Where? Local Rag — September 2009

At the Nature Center...
Levi the coyote says, "Special cow issue? Where's the cow? Ooooh! A picture of a cow! Or is it a real cow that got flattened? Doesn't smell like a cow..."

...in his cage.
"...Maybe there's a cow underneath it. I could dig, right? Or just chew my way in. There's got to be a cow around here somewhere! It says it's a cow issue."

Where do you read your Local Rag?

Northern Ireland
Jim & Carol Erkens trying to stay warm at Giant's Causeway.

Rag Where?

Sea of Galilee, Israel
Jim & Betsy Richards off the coast of Israel.

November 2009

September 2014

Where do you read your Local Rag?

Southern Ethiopia
Tory Host Hanson introduces the Local Rag to Ethiopian natives, 75 miles from the nearest road.

Napa Valley, CA
Pam & Troy Trammel enjoy a bottle of wine and the Local Rag on a restaurant patio in wine country.

The Very Best of the Red Lodge Local Rag

December 2009

Where do you read your Local Rag?

Seward, Alaska
Beverly, Bruce and April Lubbers try to keep warm while reading their Rag in Seward.

Rag Where?

Red Lodge, Montana
Rose Filkin, Anne Rood, Joan Cline, and Karen Chupp enjoy their Local Rag at Beartooth Elks Lodge #534 in downtown Red Lodge.

Where do you read your Local Rag?

Pikes Peak, Colorado
Barbara and Sid Herbert read their Rag at the summit of Pikes Peak.

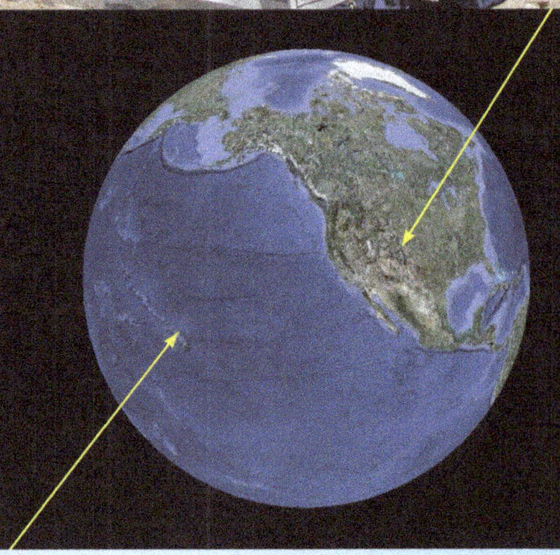

Honolulu, Hawaii
Don and Anita Shiver at the top of Diamond Head Crater in Honolulu.

August 2010

Where do you read *your* Local Rag?

Patagonia, Argentina
Marian Collar and Bobbie Sacks read their Rag in Argentina's Lanín National Park in Patagonia, with the Lanín Volcano in the background.

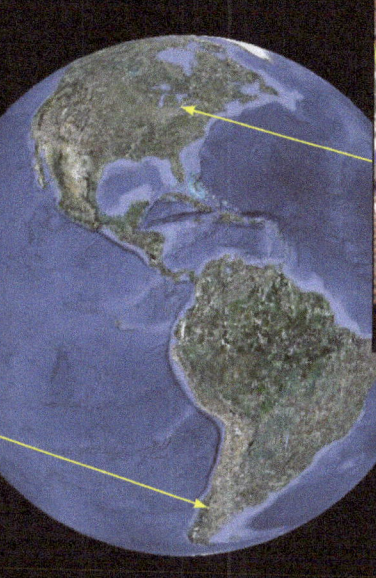

Cleveland, Ohio
Jeff Ewelt realizes he'd have been a lot warmer if he just watched the Cleveland Browns game on TV. Oh, well. At least he brought his Rag so there's something fun to do.

January 2010

February 2010

Where do you read *your* Local Rag?

BEFORE reading the Rag

Ormond by the Sea
In our first-ever "before & after" edition, we see the soporific effects of the Local Rag on Eliza Seifert at Ormond by the Sea, just north of Daytona Beach, Florida.

AFTER reading the Rag

Montréal, Québec
Gerry Khatchikian reads his Local Rag at the Kondiaronk Belvedere atop Mount Royal (from which Montréal gets its name) overlooking downtown Montreal.

The Very Best of the Red Lodge Local Rag

Where do you read *your* Local Rag?

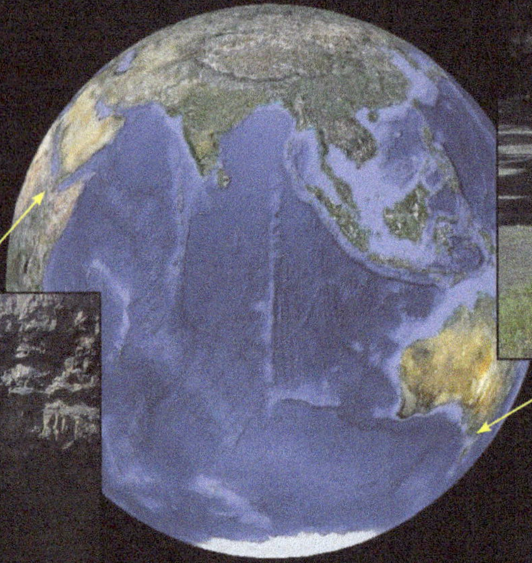

Ethiopian Highlands
Tory Host Hansen checks out the Local Rag at the Blue Niles Falls near Lake Tana (the source of the Blue Nile river) in northern Ethiopia.

Gippsland, Australia
Charles & Virginia Stanhope of Joliet enjoy their Local Rag by a "Kangaroo Crossing" sign near Wahalla, Victoria.

February 2010

April 2010

Where do you read *your* Local Rag?

Multnomah Falls, OR
Tracy Shaw poses with daughter Kandiss and granddaughter Bella in front of Multnomah Falls near Portland, Oregon.

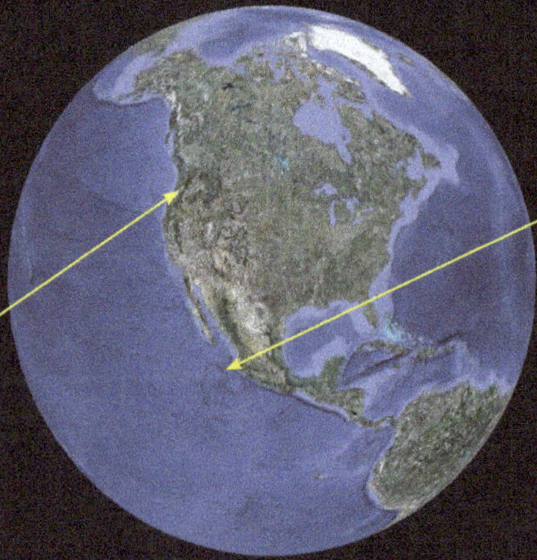

Mexican Riviera
The Hauges, Williams, and Noes share their Local Rag with the staff aboard the ship "Carnival Sprit" in the Mexican Riviera.

Where do you read *your* Local Rag?

San Pancho, Mexico
Sandy Brajcich, Karen Chupp, Julie Lindgren, Beverly Parker, Barb Kramsky, and Nancy Stevens decide that a cold drink and a copy of the Local Rag is better than getting sand in your swimsuit.

Liberty Island, NY
Roberts High School Seniors on their senior trip. Left to right: Monja Boyer, Kasi Miller, Macy Ropp, Wyatt DeVries, Taylor Nelson, Emma Green, and advisor Mary Allen. Seniors not pictured: Becky Ayre and Alyssa Carter.

May 2010

June 2010

Where do you read *your* Local Rag?

Huntington Beach, CA
Roberts BPA (Zane Holbrook, Jacob Miller, Kasi Miller, Monja Boyer, Wyatt DeVries, McKenzie Ropp, Macy Ropp, and Becky Ayre) take a break from the Anaheim competition.

Baja California, Mexico
Andy Reed & Joe Reseland relax with a Local Rag in San Jose del Cabo, at the tip of Baja.

Eklutna Lake, Alaska
Stan and Gina Farnham read their Rag in front of the old Russian Orthodox Church at Eklutna Lake.

The Very Best of the Red Lodge Local Rag

Where do you read your Local Rag?

The Dead Sea, Jordan
Laurie Jorgenson dries out after a mud bath.

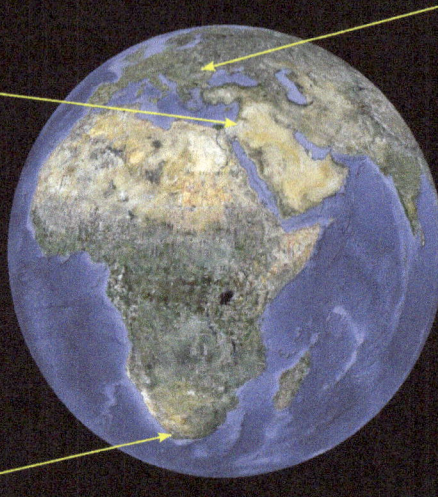
Transylvania, Romania
Barb Ostrum and Marlene Tetrault read that spooky Valentine issue of the Local Rag at Bran Castle in Transylvania, haunt of Vlad the Impaler, otherwise known as Dracula.

Cape of Good Hope
Chuck Shenk & Kathy Davidson fight to keep their Local Rag from blowing away in the wind.

May 2010

July 2010

Where do you read your Local Rag?

Hanoi, Vietnam
Jamie and Dennis Stevens in Hanoi last November.

Red Lodge, MT
This isn't so much where Bill Barnes reads his Rag, it's where he stashed his Rag so that somebody, someday, will find it — along with a model '57 Chevy — inside his walls. We presume they'll read it here in Red Lodge. And they darned well better have flying cars by then!

Where do you read *your* Local Rag?

Giza, Egypt
Bob Jorgenson stands before the great pyramids of Giza, reading his Local Rag from back home.

Zanzibar, Tanzania
Tory Host Hansen catches up on news from Red Lodge with some of the locals on Zanzibar Island in the South Indian ocean.

June 2010

April 2005

Where do you read your rag?

Jumping off the Duck Creek Bridge ~Mr. Bill

February 2014

Where do you read your Local Rag?

Seattle, Washington
Jim Manderscheid reads last month's Local Rag at a Seattle restaurant, with the Great Wheel (Seattle's 175-foot ferris wheel) visible in the background.

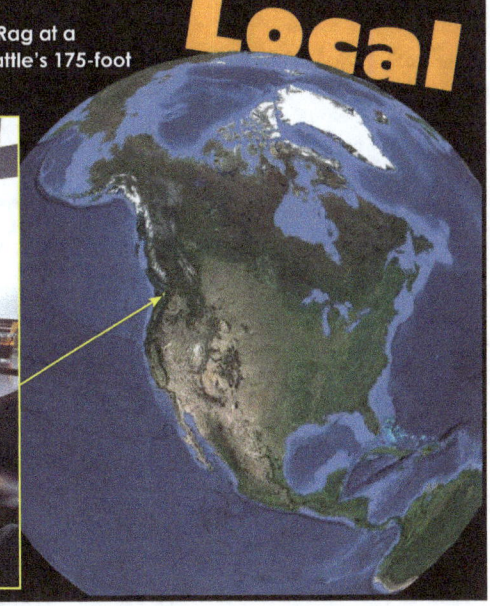

The Very Best of the Red Lodge Local Rag

Where do you read *your* Local Rag?

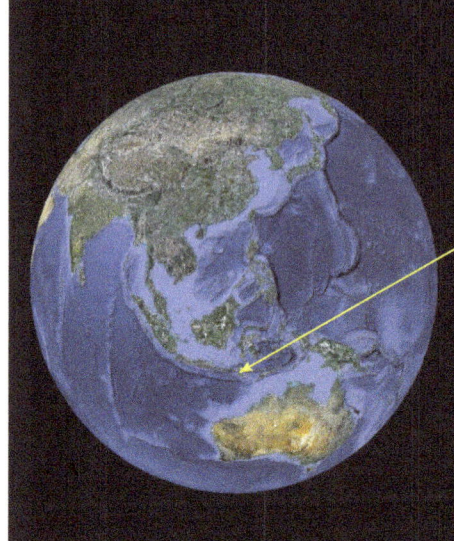

Loh Buaya — Komodo National Park
We made sure that Bill Caporali made it safely back from Komodo Island before printing this. We wouldn't to caption this photo, "the last picture of Bill Caporali before being eaten by a Komodo Dragon."

September 2010

October 2010

Where do you read *your* Local Rag?

60 Feet Underwater in Hawaii
Brent Oliphant actually went to the trouble of laminating a Local Rag and taking it down with him on a dive. The picture shows him sharing the Rag with a new friend from Canada.

12,807 Feet High on Granite Peak
Instead of heading down, Frank Annighofer headed up with his Local Rag, to the highest point in the state of Montana.

Where do you read *your* Local Rag?

Kigio Wildlife Camp in Kenya
A group of 23 ladies, including Linda Sokoloski of Roberts, just got back from a trip to Kenya last month. They are part of a travel group called the Global Grannies. They are reading the rag at Kigio Wildlife Camp in Kenya.

January 2011

November 2010

Where do you read *your* Local Rag?

Mont Blanc (France/Italy)
David Lehnherr takes a rather chilly break at 15,781 feet above sea level at the summit of Mont Blanc, at the border between France and Italy.

Persepolis, Iran
Don & Nancy Hamilton of Red Lodge and Alan Schulyer (on right) of Roberts spent three weeks traversing Iran. They remembered to bring along a Local Rag so they'd have something to do!

The Very Best of the Red Lodge Local Rag

Where do you read your Local Rag?

Hendy Woods State Park, CA
This Steller's Jay thinks that the *Local Rag* might make more sense upside-down. He just might be right!

Tacoma, WA
Ted Olczak of *Publisher's Weekly* peruses a *Local Rag* at the Pacific Northwest Bestsellers Association 2014 fall conference opening reception.

October 2014

With over 165 photos printed, "Where do you read your Local Rag" was definitely the most popular feature in the paper.

There were pictures on top of mountains, underwater, in the middle of cities, and far out in the wilderness. Various animals enjoyed the Rag in the pictures along with the people.

There were more countries represented in the photos than there were U.S. states. We suspect that people just didn't consider pictures in the U.S. as exciting as pics from foreign countries, but we enjoyed every picture we received, including these 17 states and one district:

- Alaska
- Arizona
- California
- Colorado
- Florida
- Hawaii
- Kentucky
- Maine
- Montana
- New Mexico
- New York
- Oregon
- Pennsylvania
- South Carolina
- Washington
- Washington, DC
- Wisconsin
- Wyoming

During the time the "Where do you read your Local Rag" feature ran, readers of the Rag provided photos of them enjoying the paper in 50 different countries, spanning every continent. We even have a picture from Antarctica!

THANK YOU to everybody who took a Local Rag with you when you traveled and went to the trouble to take a picture!

The Very Best of the Red Lodge Local Rag

- Afghanistan
- Argentina
- Australia
- Belgium
- Belize
- Bhutan
- Botswana
- Brazil
- Canada
- Chile
- Colombia
- Congo
- Costa Rica
- Czech Republic
- Egypt
- England
- Ethiopia
- France
- Ghana
- Greece
- Guatemala
- Hungary
- Iceland
- Indonesia
- Iran
- Iraq
- Ireland
- Israel
- Italy
- Jordan
- Kenya
- Malaysia
- Mali
- Malta
- Mexico
- The Netherlands
- New Zealand
- Norway
- Peru
- Romania
- Russia
- South Africa
- Sweden
- Switzerland
- Tanzania
- Tibet
- Turkey
- United Arab Emirates
- United States
- Vietnam

Where do you read your Local Rag?

December 2014

Yosemite National Park
Priscilla Neff, Jeremy Battles, Jenn Fusaro, Jessica Jelley, and David Neff ponder their Local Rag at Lembert Dome in Yosemite National Park.

The Very Best of the Red Lodge Local Rag

Where do you read *your* Local Rag?

The Beartooth Wilderness
Jeff and Liam Gildehaus read the Local Rag on Sundance Pass.

Killarney, Ireland
Al and Carol Bloomer stop for directions and spend a moment with their Local Rag.

December 2010

December 2014

Where do you read *your* Local Rag?

New York City
Kimberly LeFore enjoys her Local Rag on a boat with the New York City skyline in the background.

The Very Best of the Red Lodge Local Rag

CHAPTER 3

If we may be serious for a moment

Anna's Story
by Becky Hardy

This article first appeared as a two part series in the July and August 2010 issues.

She was not yet called Anna when I first met her, and she was so beautiful she took my breath away. Her greasy hair was in a topknot, and her filthy toes poked from her flipflops onto the dirt floor of the squatters' kitchen. Fresh evidence of a runny nose belied her recently washed face and hands, and her intense brown eyes seemed somehow bigger than her face. Even through thick smoke churning from the open fire, I could clearly see fear in her eyes. She was trying to be strong.

So was I.

She had surely seen white foreigners before, as she had lived on the popular Himalayan trekking route known as the Annapurna Circuit for at least half her short life. I gave her a smile and sat awkwardly on a rock in the dirt, tucking my dusty hiking boots beneath my long Tibetan skirt, realizing that I was likely the first foreigner inside the family's humble quarters. Anna's mother must have told her that we would be important visitors, so she must be quiet and behave.

My Tibetan friend, Sandoop Lama, and I looked closely at Anna and, in English, discussed her fate. She was very small; I guessed around three years old. But her mother, Meera, insisted she was four. Meera knew that if her daughter were younger than four, we wouldn't take her down the mountains to live in Kathmandu.

Anna was uneasy with the attention of two strangers sitting so near, while her mother smiled nervously and made tea for her guests. We asked Anna to stand up and walk around and, indeed, she did seem perfectly mobile and healthy. Sandoop asked her some friendly questions in Nepali, gauging her language skills and trying to assess her age. The tension was briefly broken when she quietly answered, "Mother," to the question, "What is your favorite animal?"

We asked Meera to describe their family's daily life and, as expected, it was grim. Her husband was fiercely drunk most days, but often slept and drank in the woods. Destitute and alone with her daughter and infant son in an impoverished Nepali village, she was forced to beg for food among already poor, displaced Tibetan villagers. She often left her children alone with reluctant neighbors, or left them completely unattended, while she ran the trail to more remote villages where begging might be more productive.

Her description matched those we had heard from more than a dozen villagers, including the "village elders," who told us they sometimes gave Meera food or odd jobs, though they knew she often went to sleep with hunger pains. They said she is a simple, illiterate, low-caste woman with a terrifying and violent husband, yet she's trying to help her children all she can.

In her home, Meera pleaded with us, begging us to save her daughter by taking her to the faraway city, where she could join Sandoop's fast-growing and blended family. For two years, she had begged Sandoop, his parents, and his acquaintances to take the girl. She had even begged strangers to take her daughter, knowing that almost certainly her life with them would be better than her current prospects.

As chickens pecked at my boots, elbows, and the dirt floor of the kitchen, I noted familiar features of extreme poverty I'd seen before, many times. This lowest-caste

The first picture ever taken of Anna

family was the "poorest in a poor community" and their neighbors were embarrassed that they had settled here. The elders agreed that the head of this family was a shameful transient and they wanted to boot him from town.

Anna's situation was bad, and I knew it, yet I doubted it was the worst in Nepal. Over the past few years, my husband and I had spent months around this country, hearing some appalling firsthand stories of abandonment of children, including Sandoop, who grew up homeless on gangland streets of Kathmandu while his parents served time in city prison for smuggling.

Now, I couldn't stop thinking, "What would this family do if I weren't here? I don't even know these people! What right do I have to decide the fate of a fellow human being? What if I hadn't asked Sandoop to guide me on a weeklong trek to his mountain village, and I had never come here? What if Sandoop had agreed to bring me here simply for my self-centered 'bucket list' aspiration, and not to consider removing a child from her family?"

Days earlier, as we made final preparations for this trek, Sandoop reluctantly revealed his ulterior purpose. My husband, Don, and I were shocked and angry that our friend had kept this important secret. Sandoop visits his home village very rarely, and when I asked him to take me there because the Maoist and political environment would be safer, I did not know anything about Meera and Anna's situation. Even before this trek, we had serious concerns that Sandoop and his wife, Furpoo, were expanding their family too quickly. His five adopted daughters had foreign sponsors, including Don and myself, but we feared that bringing more children so quickly into his family would bring stress.

Before beginning the trek, I was strongly biased to do everything possible to keep Anna with her family, if she would be reasonably safe. I figured we could secretly have money delivered to Meera on a fairly regular basis, up the trail, which might provide the relief she needed to care for her children. Maybe only $10 a month, without her husband knowing, would make the difference in keeping this fragile little family intact. I would not consider taking Anna from her mother unless this and every other avenue had been exhausted.

Meera and Anna

We knew Meera wanted nothing more in the world than to see her daughter leave with us, but we asked to meet Anna's father. I wanted to meet the man who was locally known for representing pure evil, and to see for myself if he was perhaps misunderstood, or if this was some sort of scam, so common in Third World countries.

In response to our request, Meera jumped up, left us alone with her children, and ran into the forest in search of her husband, hoping he was passed out in his favorite cave. While she was gone, I snapped some photos of Anna, certainly the first photos in which she'd been a subject.

Less than an hour later, Meera appeared with an angry, silent little man with a dark and fearsome demeanor. He had been drinking, and listened irritably while Meera pleaded her case to all of us.

Finally he mumbled his declaration: He didn't want anyone else taking care of his miserable little girl, and he would never

"What would this family do if I weren't here? I don't even know these people! What right do I have to decide the fate of a fellow human being?"

Anna with her parents outside their shelter. Behind them is the Annapurna Trail where trekkers remained unaware of the family's drama.

The Very Best of the Red Lodge Local Rag

let his wife have her dream of giving her away. With lip curled, he proclaimed he did not like Sandoop and me. At all.

To his wife, he quietly said that he was going to really beat her as soon as Sandoop and I leave.

Instantly, Meera shrieked and wailed in tears, while wide-eyed Anna innocently looked on, trying to avoid being noticed. She had evidently seen a lot of this in her young life, and was smart enough to know how to increase her chances of remaining unharmed.

Anna's mother was at the end of her rope, and could take no more. Easing to a blood-chilling calm, Meera played her final card.

She proclaimed that if Sandoop and I don't take away her daughter, then she will abandon her family, right here and now. She will leave this girl and her good-for-nothing father, and run away. She would be happy to never see them again.

Meera reasoned that if Sandoop and I won't take her daughter, then there's no question that the child will grow up as abused and illiterate as she is, with nothing to live for. If the girl stays in this family, she'll surely be prostituted out "on loan" to drinking friends of her father, if she hasn't already, and will get married too young to a low-caste loser who will abuse her, continuing her mother's path of poverty, hunger, and begging for subsistence.

> "Webster's defines 'epiphany' as a sudden and intuitive leap of certain understanding. I was experiencing one."

The possibility that Sandoop would someday take away her daughter was the only hope she had clung to for two years.

Webster's defines "epiphany" as a sudden and intuitive leap of certain understanding. I was experiencing one.

My life had followed an extremely unlikely, serpentine path and I did not understand why or how fate brought me here, at this moment, for the purpose of altering the destiny of a tiny, foreign stranger. Yet I didn't need to understand, and this was not about me. This was much bigger than me.

Sandoop, with tears in his eyes from the struggle to restrain himself from pummeling Anna's father, said, "This woman is desperate, and I really believe she will do this. Bauju, what should we do? We will do whatever you say."

My decision was sudden, intuitive, and certain. I would lead this innocent little girl to safety in a new life. Or I would die trying.

PART 2

Before sunrise, I woke to the smell of burned yak butter lamps. My eyes slowly focused on yellowed photographs of the Dalai Lama, then through the window to a looming monastery amid snowcapped peaks. I was waking in the Lama family's prayer room, where honored guests sleep. I was grateful this day had come, the "turn around" point on my trek. It could also mark the beginning of a new life for a helpless four year old Nepali girl.

Like my Himalayan hosts, before daylight I peed on the narrow pedestrian main street of the two-toilet village (both were clogged), and then joined Sandoop Lama's parents and elderly family members in the smoke-filled kitchen overlooking the raging river and Annapurna Circuit Trail. Before sitting cross-legged on the floor for a breakfast of instant noodles, I presented Sandoop's mother with gifts carried from Kathmandu. My porter would appreciate the weight reduction in the pack he toted for me, especially the 22 pounds of yak butter.

Breakfast conversation was about Anna and her parents, who lived in a nearby village. Everyone present knew that Anna's destitute mother, Meera, had begged villagers and strangers to take away her

Anna with Sandoop (standing), Don (sitting) and Becky

daughter, so the girl might escape her violent family life. Today, Sandoop and I would try to make Meera's wish come true.

As I packed to leave the Lama's home, in the hallway of the communal building, a neighbor was holding a tiny newborn baby. The child had been born during the night, which explained some of the strange noises I'd heard. This was the third newborn Nepali I had seen on my ten-day trek.

Sandoop's female relatives offered tearful goodbyes and blessings, and prayerfully placed "kata" scarves around our necks to protect us on our journey to Anna's village and then down the mountains to Kathmandu. His mother blessed our trip repeatedly, and rubbed a clump of yak butter on top of our heads as she chanted in Tibetan. Always a helpful translator, Sandoop advised me not to touch it, because the full effect of the blessing would come later in the day, when the sun melted the yak butter and it ran down my head.

As we walked toward the footbridge to join the Annapurna Trail, Sandoop spoke of a ritual necessary to protect me from evil spirits that haunt first-time visitors when leaving this Tibetan settlement. As instructed, I stepped over a small wall that Sandoop's father, father-in-law and other village elders had just built on the foot of the bridge. Then they waved a wickedly thorny branch over my head. When I crossed the bridge to the far side of the river, I turned to spit three times, as instructed. Sandoop congratulated me on successfully completing the ritual and said that evil spirits would probably leave me alone for the rest of our trek. I welcomed the news.

We walked to the next village, where we joined Anna, her mother and father, and the village elders in the family's tiny, lean-to kitchen. Meera spent the previous evening visiting each elder, begging for help in giving away her daughter. Grim revelations of the previous day led to our decision that Sandoop and I would permanently remove the girl from her family, and relocate her to Kathmandu where she would live with Sandoop, his wife, and their blended family of ten.

The elders were gathered on the floor to serve as witnesses, to force Meera's indigent and violent husband to agree

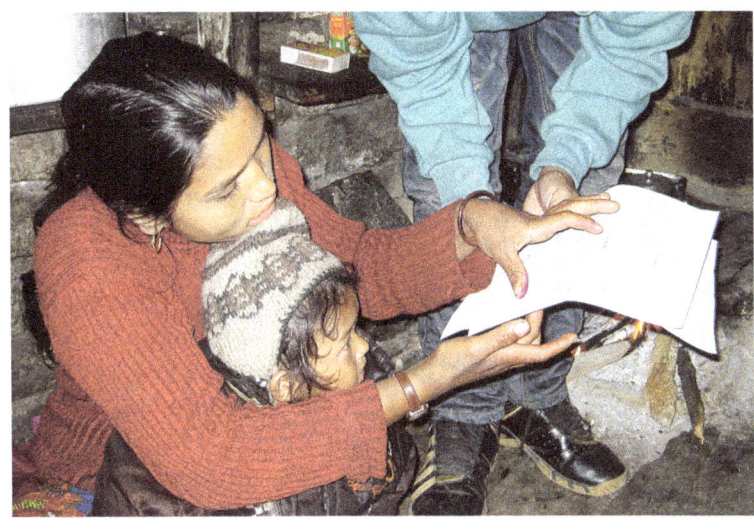

Meera's thumbprint gives away her daughter, Anna.

to the adoption, and to protect Sandoop from any future accusations that he had kidnapped the girl. The contract prohibited the father from contacting the girl until after she marries. If he should return her to the village before then, he will be considered a kidnapper.

One condition of the adoption regarded the girl's name. Low-caste peasants in Nepal often choose names for their children that reflect their lowly social and educational status, and this had been the case here. Sandoop and Furpoo had changed the names of each of their adopted daughters, removing the low-caste indicators to offer the girls better opportunity for success in their new lives. This girl, too, would have a new name.

Earlier, Sandoop had said he would prefer a western name for this newest daughter. I suggested my mother's first name: Anna. Sandoop loved it, and later asked Meera what she thought. She lit up, repeated it several times with a smile, and gave her approval.

So Samikcha Basnet became Anna Lama.

When the contract — in English — was clearly understood by all, each of the village elders signed their names as witnesses, using my diary as a clipboard on their knees. I took photos to record the agreement. Sandoop had asked me to be a witness and I was proud to have won my struggle against crying while signing the life-altering document. No one else showed any emotion, except annoyance at the girl's father.

Illiterate, Anna's mother and father pressed their fingertips into an inkpad, and made their mark on the agreement, giving away their daughter. Meera beamed

"His mother blessed our trip repeatedly, and rubbed a clump of yak butter on top of our heads as she chanted in Tibetan."

The Very Best of the Red Lodge Local Rag

Page 75

> "Low-caste peasants in Nepal often choose names for their children that reflect their lowly social and educational status."

with happiness, evidence that a heavy weight had been lifted off her shoulders.

However, I remained concerned that in the coming years she may give birth to more children who would face hunger, destitution and abandonment. I cautioned that we will never take any more of her children, and spoke with her about the importance of birth control, which was available — free of charge — at a mountain clinic in a nearby village. Earlier, she had told me that she regularly received injections providing three months of birth control protection against her drunken husband's assaults. Suspicious, I sought out the lone medical worker who, upon my request, examined the clinic's records. Meera had never been there.

When I confronted her, she quickly admitted that she had lied to me, in part because she was afraid we wouldn't take her daughter. She seemed sincere when she promised to immediately start getting birth control. Doubtful, I told a fib of my own, saying that I would stay in close contact with the "doctor" who would report whether Meera received the injections. When translating my words to her, Sandoop repeatedly added that I — a complete outsider — would be furious if I ever returned and found that she had more unwanted children. I wasn't sure why a threat from me would be more menacing, but Sandoop used this technique throughout the trek.

At Sandoop's request, the local leader of the Maoist rebel group soon arrived, escorted by his teenage bodyguards. They looked like hipster Himalayan gangsters. Maoists are self-styled, uneducated, rural militants who, over the previous decade, had essentially held citizens of Nepal hostage and created a civil war that ultimately led to the collapse of Nepal's centuries-old, godlike monarchy and the deaths of thousands of civilians. They had raided communities in the mountains, taking possession of all privately owned guns in Nepal. During the war, Sandoop had been on the Maoists' "list" because, rather than risk being forcibly recruited, he escaped to the relative safety of Kathmandu.

Today, we were asking a favor of the Maoist leader: Would he let us take Anna away? Sandoop has skills of a street-wise hustler, and I'll never know exactly what he said to the gun-toting young rebels. My only job was to attest to his good intentions, while acting uninterested in the girl so they would not force me to pay extortion money. Ultimately, they approved her release, plus granted Sandoop free passage with his family anytime he wanted to return.

We had been concerned about how to get tiny Anna down the challenging mountain trails, and the ingenious village elders forced her father to escort us down the mountain, carrying her when necessary. They lectured him as if he were a child, insisting that he remain sober by avoiding "rakshi," a homemade Himalayan whiskey. They commanded that he take good care of his daughter, and give us no trouble.

When it came time to leave, villagers assembled to wish Anna a safe journey and good fortune in her new life. They placed prayer "katas" around her neck for protection during her trek, and even gave her a few rupees. I had expected the occasion to have a funeral atmosphere. Instead, it was more like a party. Bright-eyed Anna could not fully understand what was about to happen, but she enjoyed the attention of neighbors who were usually not happy to see her.

As Anna walked with us to the edge of the village, Meera carried her infant son on her back. When she instructed Anna to go with her father, the little girl, aware of her father's mean spirit, screamed and cried. Meera said her final goodbye and stepped behind a small tree, so Anna wouldn't see her cry.

We departed, and Anna's mood changed quickly. She became curious when we stopped at the foot of a nearby bridge and her father performed the "evil spirits protection ceremony," waving a thorny branch over Anna's head, and briefly over Sandoop's and mine. It was a "safe journey" gesture I appreciated, since our

Anna's father carries her down a steep trail

ragtag troop needed all the help we could get.

As we made our way down the Himalayas over the next four days, Anna didn't cry again. In fact, she was enjoying the positive attention of adults. She grew to trust Sandoop and me, and let me hold her hand on steep and cliffside passes of the trail. Interestingly, we watched her father transform into a sensitive, sober, and attentive parent. Sandoop and I gave him pep talks, encouraging him to be a better father to his son, and a better husband and provider. Sandoop threatened that I would be angry if I returned to the village to find that he hadn't significantly improved his life.

We finally reached the trailhead and the van that my husband, Don, had brought for our drive to Pokhara. Anna's father tied katas around her neck and quietly offered prayers. With tears in his eyes, he turned and began his long trek back to his life in the mountains. He did not ask us for another chance at being better father to Anna or ask if he could take her back home.

A week later, in Kathmandu, Anna finally received good results on her medical tests (HIV, hepatitis, etc.) and was allowed to start school mid-semester. Don and I were in the Lama family's apartment when she came home from her first day of school, and we had never seen her so happy. She loved her new life, her new family, and the chance to go to school.

Today, months later, Anna continues to adapt smoothly, in large part due to Furpoo's wonderful mothering skills. Anna learns infinite lessons from her loving, adopted sisters who have gone through similar experiences. We are especially proud of Meena Lama, whom Don and I sponsor, as she's really taken Anna under her wing. Already, little Anna has had more schooling than either of her parents, and shows indications of being especially bright.

If she is like other Nepali kids I know, Anna will never look back on the life she previously led, and won't be curious about her birth parents or little brother or the life she would have led in her impoverished village. She may never ponder why she was born Hindu, and is now Buddhist. Or that she used to speak Nepali at home, and now speaks Tibetan and learns English in school. She may never wonder how her birthday was chosen, or her name.

Still, my life will forever be tied to hers. How could it not, when I shared her wonder as she saw and rode in her first vehicle, and ate the first banana she ever saw?

Don and I daydream that Anna will grow up to have a fulfilling and bountiful life, and someday go to college, maybe even in the U.S. Perhaps she'll move to Red Lodge and take care of us in our old age! One sure thing is that I will love her no matter who she grows up to be. And I'll never forget the precious little girl in the mountains, who became Anna Lama. ❧

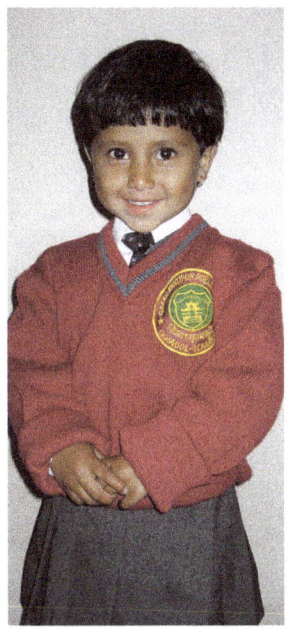

Anna was so tiny and undernourished that her school uniform had to be custom made. She was very excited about her first day of school!

There were many great Pat's Plumbing ads in the Rag over the years. This one is from May of 2005.

The Local Rag
hangin' out

The way I see it...
By: Tim Weamer

The Visitor's Center is the most underrated tourism asset in Red Lodge. Located at the North Entrance to Red Lodge and staffed and funded entirely by the Red Lodge Area Chamber of Commerce, many people seem to think that it is just the office for the Chamber but it is much more. To a visitor it is a virtual oasis, with information about every event, business and amenity in the Red Lodge area. Is this important to area businesses and event promoters and locals? Hell yes!

The phone rings non-stop. Don't believe me? Go out for a visit in the summer. This last summer I somehow got stuck there for about an hour answering phones, it sucked. I was answering 2 phones at once and all while trying to keep a customer satisfied at the counter. Without the Visitor's Center, someone needing information would have to open up the phone book and pick one of us for information or maybe they could just call City Hall. I bet that would go over big. Even worse, they might pick another town that has a Visitor's Center. The walk-ins are equally high volume. Approximately 10,000 people walked through the doors last year. They always have questions about where to stay, where to eat, how to get to the Park, etc. Is a service such as this important in a tourist town? I say we can't live without it.

Think about what would happen if the Visitor's Center didn't exist. Virtually every event in town uses it as an info center. Without them the already overworked event chairman would have to put their personal or business phone number on the event poster as contact information. Some already do, but unless your business benefits directly from the event, use the Visitor's Center.

The Visitor's Center does not come without a price. The operating budget for a year is $60,000 and they have 4 full and part time employees. The phone bill is astronomical, and when you add in postage and utilities along with all the other expenses the Center is like any other business in town – expensive to operate. Is it worth it? I think so, and every year I write my check to the Chamber for dues knowing that I am doing my part to keep the doors to the Visitor's Center open. I know of some businesses in Red Lodge who do not pay dues to the Chamber and I know that some of them are not paying because they are mad at the Chamber for one reason or another. First of all let me say I think they should join the damn Chamber and try to fix whatever it is they consider broken. Maybe those businesses would rather not be part of the Chamber so they can sit back and bitch about it from the outside. I myself would rather pay my dues and become part of a solution instead of staying part of the problem. As a member they have to listen to my crap. Whether you think the Chamber of Commerce is an effective organization or not is your business. The Visitor's Center is Red Lodge's business office and should be thought of and funded that way. I think you should just pay your damn dues. You'll feel better about yourself.

But that's just my opinion, pass the beernuts…

> [The Visitor's Center] is a virtual oasis of information…

Volume IV • June 1994 • Issue 6

Hello Red Lodge!

Guess what? I made it! The sun has been making regular visits and I'm feeling fine! Hope I didn't depress or offend or kill anyone during the cold, wet, gray spell last month.

Like most local merchants I've been holding my breathe (and my bills) waiting for business to pick up. Thought I'd choke in poverty before Memorial Weekend got here. But it came and went just in time to bring a few dollars to town that were much needed.

As a resident of this beautiful little tourist-oriented town, it is (contrary to popular belief) our community obligation to be nice, friendly and welcoming to tourists. While you may not make your living directly from visitors, you can bet that most of your friends and neighbors do! Many of us rely on tourist dollars to survive and to continue to provide a functional service year round (even though we need tourist income during Summer and Ski Season).

I would never suggest that any of you become boot-licking brown-nosers or anything like that, but is it really necessary to give them the finger for driving too slow or looking a little lost?

In my hometown up in the mountains of Northern New Mexico, tourists were fairly unwelcome. The locals wore t-shirts that said "NO! I don't know where the Hot Springs are. The hunting sucks here. There's no land for sale" and bumper stickers on their trucks stated "As A Matter of Fact, I Do Own The Whole Road!" Tourist season was called The Mighty Maggot Invasion.

Because visitors felt spited, they developed a bad attitude about the town. They responded with poor behavior, littered and defaced the mountains. Because they had no respect for the people, they had no respect for their property. Vandalism was extremely high, especially toward the Indian ruins and burial grounds.

Eventually, quality tourists with money to spend quit coming. But the bad element of tourists came in droves to the mean and wild town - it was their kind of place. Call it Karma, but the unfriendly town was crawling with unfriendly visitors.

You get what you play for. If we want our visitors to respect our beautiful town and mountains, we must take the first step by treating them with respect.

I don't know about you, but I like to see my friends prosper and I don't care who they earn their money from, be it locals or tourists. Besides, we all get to stare at each other during Spring and Autumn when tourist flow is down… it's nice to have some new faces in town! New faces, new money… bring it on!

These articles show a generally pro-business feeling, which carried through all of the editors and owners of the Local Rag.

Everyone may have joked about the tourists, but we all know they're the ones who help Red Lodge pay the bills.

---

fun... SCHEDULED DAILY
Yellowstone Park • This Exit
RED LODGE
www.redlodge.com

Red Lodge's new Pin-up girl

Red Lodge area businesses are excited to unveil a 12' x 48' billboard advertising Red Lodge on I-90 just east of the Laurel exit. The billboard project is the result of a cooperative marketing effort between Red Lodge Mountain Resort and local business associations, including Red Lodge Area Chamber of Commerce, Merchants' Association, Lodging Association and others. The billboard has been contracted for three years and will change every six months featuring Summer and Winter activities. The Summer billboard was designed by Creative Design Works and made possible by the cooperative talents of Tom Egenes, Merv Coleman and Liza Kuntz.

"Hello Red Lodge" by Lou Ward appeared in June 1994.

"The way I see it" by Tim Weamer appeared in December 2002.

The billboard story appeared in March 2004.

A Summer in Yellowstone
by Patty Mills

With the Yellowstone Association employment application filled out and mailed, the next step for me was to wait and see if someone would call, or if I'd receive a nice "thanks, but no thanks" letter. This was one of those adventures that I thought about many times. I had no control over its ending now, with the application being filed away in a metal cabinet or shredded, or someone reading it and thinking, hey, let's give this woman a call.

Working in Yellowstone Park for a summer has always appealed to me. I have a special bond with Yellowstone that started when I was a kid from Kansas. Those were the days when the bears were all over the road and begging cars for food. As fortunate as it is for bears and people that this situation has been corrected, it was a thrill at that time to see such a sight. As we drove through the park I remember thinking what a wondrous place it was. To me, at the age of nine or ten, I imagined it must be like walking on the moon or some other mysterious planet with rainbow colored thermal pools and erupting geysers. I rapid-fired on Old Faithful, shooting a whole roll of film, thinking each eruption was the "big one." It wasn't and I was out of film when the big one came.

My bond for the park grew deeper after taking several Yellowstone Association courses, one on wolves, one on grizzly bears, and most recently "Writing the Wild" with local author Gary Ferguson. The courses the association offers, from any type of wildlife watching to fish bones and scat piles, put you right in the Yellowstone landscape. With a lot of their courses you stay in a cabin at the Buffalo Ranch in the Lamar Valley, which is wildlife viewing heaven. After a bit of classroom education from top experts in the field, you head out to observe wildlife in their natural habitat from a respectable distance. Spotting scopes are amazing. If you're heading to the park and want to see wildlife, buy, rent, or borrow a spotting scope.

Among our many scope observations were a female wolf feeding her pups near their den, a courting pair of grizzly bears frolicking on a snow bank, two coyotes chasing a lone wolf away from their territory, and several wolves challenging a grizzly for the rights to a carcass. After watching wildlife the class might take a nature hike, return to the ranch for more classroom education, or gather in the ranch kitchen to talk over the glorious events of the day.

After my first three-day course I no longer felt like I was *in* the park, I felt like I was *part of* the park. As I drove away from the ranch I felt like this wasn't just Yellowstone National Park, this was *my* park. As I watched other visitors to my park I felt a great sense of pride that they were also here to see this wondrous place. I hoped that they would bond with it as I had and learn to respect it and all its creatures. I was so filled with park and wildlife knowledge that I wanted to greet each person and welcome them to my Yellowstone National Park. I grew further enchanted with Yellowstone after several winter visits. The park is a glorious wonderland in the winter. The wildlife is active and seems to enjoy getting their park back for a few months, and you pretty much have the place to yourself.

My desire for this new adventure grew stronger when I moved to Red Lodge and this special place was just over the pass. The timing fit in with my vagabond ways, which I think started as a kid traveling back

This article first appeared as a four part series in the summer of 2010.

"The landscape reflects the harsh reality of life for the wild residents of Yellowstone, but at the same time it offers serenity to visitors who take the time to seek it."

and forth between divorced parents, one in Kansas, one in Montana. Plus I totally buy into "life is short, live every day like it's your last." I was always okay with this theory but most of us have to work for several years until we're in a position to practice it. Once that happened, my mind was a kid in the adventure candy store. I didn't actually make a list of adventures that I wanted to accomplish. Most began hovering around in the back of my mind

Buffalo Ranch Cabin

Photo by Patty Mills

as life hurled opportunities my way.

Motorcycling in the Swiss Alps: done and checked off my list of great adventures but added to the list of I'd do it again in a heartbeat. Bungee jumping in New Zealand: I don't need to do this again because the three-day high from this jump will always be remembered. Kissing the Blarney Stone in Ireland: I wasn't real sure what the significance was of kissing the Blarney Stone but as they say, "When in Blarney," or is that Rome? You know, I've never been to Rome but it's hovering in my mind along with Paris, the Greek Isles, and Poughkeepsie (I just like the sound of that place, where is Poughkeepsie anyway?) Sailing and scuba driving in the Virgin Islands: Really great. How much closer can you get to serenity then bobbing around the Caribbean and living in swimwear for a week (well, that was in my younger, slimmer days). Motorcycle racing school was pretty awesome, especially when I rode around the track with a professional racer and felt the pavement brush the side of my boot. Our instructor said "See the tread on the side of that tire? It's there for a reason".

I did neglect to list a few adventures that I have no desire to experience but they involve being on the wrong side of a bear, moose, buffalo, any four legged animal, mad eagle (bald or otherwise), flying squirrels, bats, and just about anything I can't outrun or that I have to play dead with.

Several weeks after sending in my application to the Yellowstone Association I got a call to do an interview. Two weeks later the District Manager called and offered me a position in their Mammoth Hot Springs bookstore.

From May to early October I'll be waking up each morning in a place that's full of wonder and adventure. The landscape reflects the harsh reality of life for the wild residents of Yellowstone but at the same time it offers serenity to all visitors who take the time to seek it. I look forward to exploring trails, learning more about the park, meeting lots of people and reading a bundle of great books. At times it will be hectic as thousands of visitors roll through the gates but my wish for each will be to find the magic that is Yellowstone National Park.

Follow me on this journey as I keep you updated on how it's going and if you are in Yellowstone this summer—as you should be—stop by and I'll introduce you to my park and help you make it yours.

PART 2

The hills are alive with the sound of music; the same could be said for Yellowstone National Park except the hills were alive with the sights and sounds of life. Beginning in early spring, the landscape faded from black and white to the full spectrum of a rainbow including the gold in the black pot. Thanks to spring showers, green had returned to the landscape along with red, purple, yellow, and blue, while the white of snow slowly melted away, exposing the yawning grasses and wildflowers as they peeked above ground.

"The Yellowstone is a wildflower garden. Wander where you will, you have the ever new charm, the finishing touch, the ever refreshing radiance of the wild flowers."
—Enos Mills, *Your National Parks*, 1917.
No relation I know of, but a beautiful enduring statement.

March and April found bears ambling

out of hibernation in search of food to quiet their growling and empty bellies. Mother bears and their cubs began their challenging season with pre-school as she taught survival skills to her new offspring. Grizzly bears could be seen in open areas turning over rocks or feeding on winterkill while black bears meandered and hunted along the edges of trees. The bears were so active this spring that many wide-eyed visitors came to the Albright Visitor Center in Mammoth to report amazing viewing opportunities. On one of my excursions around the park we witnessed a mother grizzly bear chasing away a male who was threatening her cub of the year. The speed of her reaction was amazing as she tucked her cub away in a safe place to begin her challenge of the large male, eventually running him off then returning to her cub to await the next challenge. Her season of challenges had just begun.

Early excitement around the park came with the first report of a female grizzly with four cubs. Many visitors were able to witness this rare sight as mother and cubs seemed to enjoy hanging out in the same area. The runt of the litter could most often be seen riding on momma bear's back. When seeing the female for the first time it looked as though she had a hiking pack on, only to realize the pack was moving and had a tiny light brown face. Since she stayed some distance away from the road I was envying the array of humongous camera lenses but was glad she and her cubs were not disturbed by the mass of people hovering on the roadside.

The bald eagles began nesting in February so from March through April the eaglets were being born in their nests, elevated from view. In late June the fledglings began to leave their high-rise homes and soar with the magnificent splendor beholding of eagles. An abundance of bird life could be seen throughout the park, at every turn in the road it seemed as though new life was taking flight.

May was the time that bison calves could be seen clinging to their rather large mothers. Bison calves fare somewhat better from predators due to the size of their protectors and the fact that in no time they will grow to a rather intimidating size themselves. Most visitors to the park underestimate the speed of these huge animals and despite all the warnings several visitors a year are injured. A few bison are hanging around in Mammoth, so this might be an interesting summer of bison versus tourist watching.

Wolf pups were beginning to romp and play out of their dens in late May. Some could be viewed with spotting scopes if one waited long enough. The once strong Druid Peak Pack was reported as non-existent primarily due to mange. Some reported a few stray members still alive but no one seemed to know for sure so time will write the final story about this once great pack. Mollie's Pack, Blacktail Plateau Pack, and the Quadrant Peak Pack are the three leading packs in size according to the 2010 Northern Yellowstone Wolves chart published by A

Yellowstone photos by Patty Mills

Naturalist's World.

In the following month hundreds of elk calves appeared to be standing on ground that was shaking from an earthquake as they acquired their land legs. They seemed tiny and fragile but could weigh 25-40 lbs. Nature has given them the extra protection of having almost no scent when born so they can hunker down in tall grass and hide from predators. When visitors enter the park through Mammoth their first wildlife sighting is likely to be elk as there are many around town; some think they are deer, or moose, or I'm told that one unconvinced visitor argued that they were camels.

> "The runt of the litter could most often be seen riding on momma bear's back. When seeing the female for the first time it looked as though she had a hiking pack on, only to realize the pack was moving and had a tiny light brown face."

The number one question from visitors seems to be where to view wildlife. A great way to tour the park, whether you want to see wildlife or geysers, is to pick up a copy of *Yellowstone: The Official Guide*, bring your binoculars, and a spotting scope. As I learned from the experts, when looking for wildlife (unless it's standing in the road), get up early, drive along your selected area and scan the landscape for movement. Once you spot something, grab the binoculars and check out what it is, then set up the spotting scope and enjoy the gift you've just been given. Of course you can also drive around until you come upon a people jam and check out what they have spotted!

Two-legged life also returned to the sleeping giant after what many called a mild winter. The park employs over 3,200 people for the summer season and they streamed in from every direction. Some were first-timers, like me, but the majority were seasoned workers returning for yet another summer. In either case they all had great stories to tell about why they were drawn to Yellowstone. It was a flurry of activity as people arrived to check in, move in, start training, or go immediately to work. My workdays are spent in the Yellowstone Association park store at the Albright Visitor Center in Mammoth. The park store is a collection of games and books devoted to education, from history to wildlife to field guides to *Who Pooped in the Park*. Before the summer ends I hope to have read many of those great books. It somehow feels sacred to walk among all those written words.

As I stopped at the park entrance gate in early spring I flashed my brand new employee card and said to the park ranger, "This is the first time that I'm entering the park as an employee," she replied with a big smile, "This is my first summer and my first day and welcome to Yellowstone."

PART 3

Oh how I love my days off! While workdays in the park can be filled with interesting happenings, and a flurry of activity, days off can be whatever I imagined them to be in this wonderland of adventure. I get to join the thousands of visitors who travel the 466 miles of park roads and let Yellowstone determine what the day will hold. While that might not sound fun to some, it's like showing off my backyard to family and friends. Before working in the park my short visits were concentrated in the northeast and wildlife watching. Now that I am living in the park for the summer I can explore more of the hydrothermal areas and recall my first impressions as a youngster. I still get the feeling that I'm walking on some other mysterious planet.

The National Park Service and Yellowstone Association have available trail guides for the thermal areas that divide Yellowstone into seven distinct sections. The guides are most helpful in assisting visitors in planning their day, especially for those with limited time. Along with visiting these popular areas and wildlife watching, there are 92 trailheads, 15 miles of boardwalks, 52 picnic areas, and about 1,000 miles of backcountry trails to explore. Who needs TV — which I don't have and surprisingly don't miss? I will admit to having Season 1 and 2 of The Big Bang Theory which I've watched over and over and...

At Mammoth Hot Springs visitors can walk along the Fort Yellowstone Historic District and view the first buildings, which were finished in late 1891. The U.S. Army arrived in 1886 and for 32 years men from Company M, First United States Cavalry, acted as caretakers for Yellowstone National Park. By 1910 there were 324 soldiers living in the park. The

Albright Visitor's Center, where I spend my workdays, was originally the bachelor officers' quarters and was built in 1909. Most of the other buildings now serve as housing for park service employees but a walk along the historic stone buildings give visitors a glimpse of this fascinating past.

Traveling up the road from Fort Yellowstone visitors get the first view of what is called one of the park's most dynamic hydrothermal areas. Water temperature in the Mammoth Terraces are reported at 165 degrees F. Visitors can walk the maze of boardwalks to view all the terrace structures or go on a ranger walk for an in-depth tour. The trail guide also indicates that "this area is one of the world's best examples of travertine-depositing hot springs." Because the terraces are constantly changing due to the volume of water that cuts through the sloping ground, they are considered a "living sculpture."

Heading south past the terraces, the world's tallest active geyser, Steamboat Geyser, can be found at Norris Geyser Basin. Years can pass before this unpredictable geyser erupts to over 300 feet. The last eruption was May 23, 2005 and I understand it was quite an event. Norris Geyser Basin is known to be one of the most active earthquake areas in the park as it sits on three major faults. Norris was named after P.W. Norris, superintendent of Yellowstone from 1877-1882. Two miles of boardwalks take you along the geysers, hot springs, fumaroles and mudpots. Some great geyser names in this area; Whirligig, Pinwheels, Porkchop, and Puff 'n Stuff.

South of Madison lays the Fountain Paint Pot area, which is in the Lower Geyser Basin. This area also provides viewing of four types of hydrothermal features. It's possible to see half a dozen geysers erupting at the same time as you walk along this half-mile loop boardwalk with geysers galore. Looking to the north from this area you see the volcanic tableland, "a panorama of the major events of Yellowstone's geologic past." A short drive from the paint pot area is Firehole Lake, the largest hot spring in this area, and more geysers. Great Fountain Geyser can erupt up to 200 feet and last 45 to 60 minutes while White Dome Geyser might last a couple of minutes and can shoot up to 30 feet.

Naturally the most popular area in the park is the Upper Geyser Basin where Old Faithful dominates the attention of most visitors. This is also where the majority of the world's active geysers are located. There are five geysers in this area that are predicted by the rangers. Old Faithful is erupting approximately every 90 minutes, can last 1½ to 5 minutes, and can reach from 106 to 184 feet high. When going to see Old Faithful make sure to check the next estimated eruption time FIRST and then look around the area. I made the mistake of shopping first and missed the eruption. Oh well, I'll just have to go back again.

Traveling southeast from Old Faithful is the West Thumb Geyser Basin, which overlooks beautiful big blue Yellowstone Lake. The boardwalk travels along Lakeside

Yellowstone photos by Patty Mills

The Very Best of the Red Lodge Local Rag

Spring, Percolating Spring, Thumb Paint Pots, Collapsing Pool, and Lakeshore Geyser, just to name a few. According to the trail guide, Native Americans used this area for hunting bison and gathering medicinal herbs.

Heading back north on the Grand Loop is Mud Volcano. The trail guide tells me this is one of the most acidic features with many faults converging here, making earthquakes common. The two-thirds mile walking loop travels along pools of hot muddy water that smells like rotten eggs from the hydrogen sulfide gas. Speaking of earthquakes, I'm told there are 1,000 to 3,000 minor earthquakes annually in the Yellowstone area. Wait a minute…that wasn't in the employee manual!

The second "place you gotta see" in Yellowstone is the Grand Canyon of the Yellowstone River. It's located in the appropriately named, Canyon, which is a hop, skip, and a jump northwest of Mud Volcano. The canyon is 1,000 feet deep and 20 miles long. Both Upper and Lower Falls can be viewed from here, the latter being the most popular, cascading down 308 feet. Steam can be seen rising from the hydrothermal features in the canyon. Several north or south rim overlooks, trails and walkways meander along the rim and into the canyon. Uncle Tom's Trail leads about 500 feet down into the canyon for a powerful view of Lower Falls. Ospreys are common in this area and can be seen fishing the river.

All of these fascinating areas and much more make up the Grand Loop of Yellowstone. In mileage the loop (actually made up of two large circles) isn't that far but it does take time to see all there is to see. If the loop isn't enough, each road that connects to one of the five park entrances has its own interesting places and breathtaking views. Every week on my days off I think I'll stay in, do laundry, clean my room, cook something, or take a nap, but forces greater than me draw me back to the Grand Loop and how grand it is!

PART 4

As September sweeps across Yellowstone National Park it will be like watching a flower slowly close. In early spring the landscape gradually opened to reveal new colors, new life, and the beginning of a whirlwind of summer activity. Now the leaves will begin to change, turning the once-green forests orange and gold. Many of the birds will prepare to head south. Mating season for the elk will begin and the circle of life will continue. Bears will spend all their time eating to prepare for hibernation. The wolves will be one month closer to the winter season when they rule the kingdom. The record number of summer visitors will travel on and many of the park employees will head out. The curtain will begin to close on the summer season, only to reopen again for the start of the park's winter season. For me it's nearing the end of a great adventure and my summer in Yellowstone.

In May I jotted down my goals for working in the park for a summer and I'm grateful to have met all of them, not that they would have been hard to achieve…after all, this is Yellowstone. I knew I'd meet some great people and that began with my roommates who made the summer such a joy with their warmth, friendliness, enthusiasm and great cooking (lamb burgers, blueberry pancakes, and homemade pizza)…yum! The Yellowstone Association staff proved to be hard working, fun, full of energy, and have a genuine love for what they do. The park rangers are obviously a great bunch of dedicated individuals. They devote their skills, their summers, and their love for Yellowstone to making the park experience the best it can be for all who pass through it.

Most of the visitors were friendly and full of excitement. Not too many nasty tourists, except the ones who tried to navigate the park using GPS, which can cause you to drive in circles. I did feel sorry for one fellow who thought he was in Canyon, only to find out he was in Mammoth (33 miles away). He and his wife were heading to Jackson, it was very late in the day, and I think he would have fared

> "The park employs over 3,200 people for the summer season and they streamed in from every direction. Some were first-timers, like me, but the majority were seasoned workers returning for yet another summer."

better with a grizzly bear in the car then to make that long drive to the Tetons with his furious wife who swore up and down there were no road signs.

My favorite visitors were the thousands of foreigners. They were in awe of the park and the United States and loved to share that excitement, even if it wasn't in a language I understood. Many told me how beautiful my county was and how it had exceeded their expectations. It made me proud to be an American and live in one of our nation's most beautiful places.

We were asked some pretty funny questions or we were asked many of the same questions over the past four months: can we swim in the hot springs, where are the bathrooms, we're running late can they hold Old Faithful until we get there, where are the bathrooms, what's the difference between a female elk and a female moose, where are the presidents, where are we, how do we put the bell on the bear, do we spray it first (I was told about this one but surely they were kidding), what should I see, did they pose the elk in the yard, where are the bathrooms, what national park is this, where is El Capitan, at what elevation does an elk become a moose, where are the bathrooms! One of the rangers summed it up best by saying a summer assisting visitors in Yellowstone should make us all better tourists.

With 92 trailheads, hiking is a major attraction in the park and was another one of my goals. I took several great hikes, one being a ranger hike to Snow Pass and the Hoodoos, which is an area with masses of huge limestone boulders that tumbled down the mountain. A park visitor in 1927 described this area as a playground for giants. Hiking into the backcountry of Yellowstone is a super way to see the park from a different angle and get to know it better.

My number one goal was to see as much wildlife as possible and take some great photos with my new digital camera. "Great" didn't have to be great by professional standards, just great to me, so I'm thrilled with the photos I got and with all the wildlife I was able to observe. I plan to devote a wall in my house with photos and mementos of my summer in Yellowstone.

The second best thing about being in Yellowstone all summer was being able to travel the whole park. I drove out all five entrances and I'm pretty sure part of my motivation was the kick I got out of showing my employee pass upon re-entering. I also wanted to stay in areas I hadn't spent much time in so I traveled to the beautiful Yellowstone Lake area and the Lake Hotel, which opened in 1891, and is touted as the oldest building in Yellowstone today. I rented one of their comfortable, quaint cabins and splurged on a scrumptious surf and turf dinner in the Lake Hotel dining room. The old-world elegance of this place intrigued me, as well as how remote the location would have been before the automobile. Until 1917 people were arriving here by boat or stagecoach. Back then, the wealthy were the only ones who could afford to travel to these places, making elegance and comfortable a requirement if travelers were to endure the dusty roads or the long lake crossing.

Much less elegant—but more fitting of the outdoor rustic western feel—is Roosevelt Lodge. This area was once called Camp Roosevelt and all the lodging and dining structures were candy-striped tents. Around 1919 the lodge was build and all the lodging tents were replaced with cabins. The greatest thing about Roosevelt Lodge is the long porch, which runs across the front of the lodge and is lined with wicker rockers. After having a delicious dinner in the dining room, which feels and looks like someone's log cabin, it's a must to sit on the porch with a nice glass of wine. I enjoyed watching an evening thunderstorm roll in, leaving behind a brilliant rainbow. I then took a stroll to my cozy one-room cabin and drifted off to sleep to the sound of raindrops spattering on the roof. It doesn't get much better than that!

There were so many great trips around the Grand Loop of Yellowstone that I now know the park much better, which makes the bond even stronger. When asked if there were any negatives, I can only think of one and that was being away from my cats, my house, my family, my friends and Red Lodge for five months but I'm so grateful to have had this adventure. From now on when I travel back to Yellowstone; I'll never feel like I'm just visiting the park, I'll feel like I'm returning home to the greatest place on Earth. ☘

> "Until 1917 people were arriving here by boat or stagecoach. Back then, the wealthy were the only ones who could afford to travel to these places, making elegance and comfortable a requirement if travelers were to endure the dusty roads or the long lake crossing."

Kari wrote this editorial in June of 2005. Ten years later, we're still groaning about the pun in the last sentence.

It's like watching a train wreck. You can't stop yourself from wanting to know more, but everything you hear and see makes you sick. Trees on the blacktop, rivers of mud washing underneath. Guardrail, the least of the problems. I can't help but want to cry. If a road could have cancer, this is what it would look like: Beartooth Highway, May 20, 2005.

As with any catastrophe, in the void of information, the talk that circulates is all over the map: from *it'll never open again*, to *maybe mid-June*. To *2009*. It's human nature, I suppose, not that that helps much. Part of our need to control things. Like, maybe if we knew more, we'd be able to do something about it. Like maybe we could rationalize our way out of thousands of tons of rock slumped over our playground. Like knowing can make it go away.

I had just arrived in Russia when the Willie fire hit. I'd just hiked Sundance Pass, exhilarating in the knowledge that that wilderness I loved so much was mine. In a strange country with strange ideas, I felt like a part of me was dying as I scrounged for news about home. About my mountains. As if my knowing would bring on the rain, stop the winds.

The past few days have reminded me a lot of that painful week, spent wheedling information off websites through antiquated phone lines half a world away. That road means so many things to each of us. Economic, historic, scenic. Is it possible that we can love this inanimate thing? Can you love a crazy-assed, haphazard, take-no-prisoners ribbon of tar? And, if so, who do you blame when it falls apart?

As in the very best of cases, there is no one to blame. Mother Nature wins once again, and we are left doing hasty patchwork. But that's so much a part of why we live here. We've chosen to have our lives ruled by Mother Nature: skiers, ranchers, shopkeepers, bicyclists. If we weren't so enchanted, we'd live more removed from her. We'd live somewhere safe, pasteurized.

But we don't. We're Montanans, like it or not, and we pluck ourselves up. This is a life we've chosen, and with the drought and the cold comes weird stuff, like spring floods and catastrophic mudslides. In Miles City, it was always the hailstorm of '78. Nothing compared to the hailstorm of '78. Within a few years, we were almost proud of that storm that tore the roofs off of houses, downed 100-year-old cottonwoods, and took years off quite a few farmers' lives. Anything that came up after that, got an "Ah, hell—it ain't nothing compared to '78."

So this month I raise my glass to the Highway Department. They've got a job ahead of them that nobody wants, and everyone's going to complain about. This could be a tough summer for them. It will definitely be for many of us. But maybe it's time we see what we're made of. What our tourists are made of. I believe there comes a time–in any relationship–when you just have to find out: do they really like us for who we are, or do they just think we've got a nice Pass?

Kari Clayton—editor, etc.

Tourist Season Appears to be Over...

...but we just spotted this sign down at Hank's Place, so there must still be a few tourists running around!

Red Lodge, Montana

MARCH 2014 FREE
& WORTH EVERY PENNY

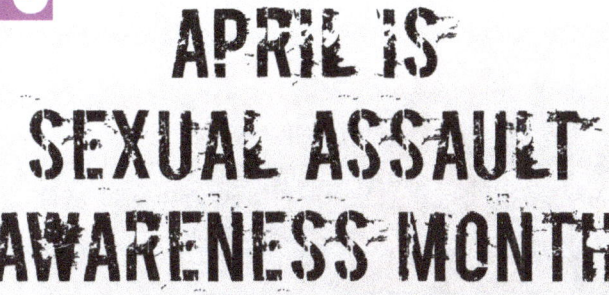

APRIL IS SEXUAL ASSAULT AWARENESS MONTH

STAND WITH US AGAINST VIOLENCE AND END THE SILENCE

April is Sexual Assault Awareness Month. I know what you're thinking -- this is going to be another article filled with national statistics that make me feel hopeless, sad, and uncomfortable (sigh). Your emotional response may remain the same, but sexual assault is a real problem – and it's right in our backyards. According to the Montana Incident Based Reporting System, sexual offenses (sexual assault, sexual abuse of children, and rapes) have tripled in Carbon and Stillwater Counties over the past three years. You read that correctly: tripled. This startling phenomenon, combined with the reality that sexually based offenses are notoriously underreported, suggests that there are many survivors in our communities who need services and are not being reached.

These numbers are impactful. Our staff has watched statistics on a page translate to heartbreaking stories in our office. After 15 years of focusing heavily on domestic violence, DSVS will begin creating an outreach campaign to increase awareness and let people know we are here to help.

We are revisiting conversations with the hospital about how to better serve sexual assault survivors, and we are working with our partners in the criminal justice system on how we can all continue to hold perpetrators accountable.

How can you help? As you will see from our display on sexual assault awareness in the McCampbell building window this month (shameless plug), there is plenty you can do. If you see someone who has had a little too much to drink, make sure they get home safe. If someone confides in you; listen, believe, withhold blame or judgment, and encourage them to seek help. Most of all, be aware that these acts are happening right here in our communities. Keep your eyes and ears open, talk about it, and let others know that violence is unacceptable. If you want to do more, call us to learn about volunteer opportunities. Whatever it is, do something. These crimes thrive in silence and inaction. Please continue to Stand With Us against violence and end the silence.

Kelly Heaton
DSVS Executive Director

BOXHOLDER

PRSRT-STD
U.S. Postage
PAID
Red Lodge, MT
Permit No. 75

We ran a lot of silly covers and controversial editorials, made things up for "Red Lodge Believe It or Not," and even got in pissing matches with other publications from time to time. But one of the most controversial things we ran, surprisingly, was this cover. People complained that we shouldn't put an article like this on the front page of a "family newspaper." I disagree. That's exactly where an article like this belongs.

Montana 1830's Encampment

Living History Rendezvous at Howell's Camp

Historically authentic wares, food, clothing, arms and accouterments of the Rocky Mountain Fur Trade, at an **original historic fur-trapper location** that was used in **1836, 1837** and **1838**. Located at the confluence of the Clark's Fork River and Rock Creek, with lots of shade trees, lush grass and running water, while still within quick and easy reach of US Highway 212 and "civilization." **Howell's Camp** is a living history event, a little piece of **1830's Montana!**

What's a "Rendezvous"?

It's an historical re-enactment carried out by dedicated folks from all over the world. These lovers of America's history get together and create an old-time Mountain Man camp that re-creates the authentic costumes, sights, sounds, smells, flavors, events and feelings of the 1830's. Our "traders" have goods of the era for sale, and daily seminars of historic interest are presented. Speakers include:

- Ron Garritson: *Plains Indian Sign Language*
- Bob Garritson: *Primitive Technology*
- Gary Johnson: *Metis Culture*
- Louella Johnson: *Crow Legends*
- Randy Tracy: *Scottish Clothing*
- Jay Kirkpatrick and Rick Rivard: *Wild Horses*
- Bill Newton: *Guns of the Fur Trade*
- Kate Williamson: *Indian Dolls*
- Jerry Fahrenthold: *the History of Howell's Camp*
- Terence Luff: *Red River Carts*

32 Miles North of Red Lodge, turn East from Rockvale onto "Grapevine Road." Just follow the signs!

Public Welcome!

June 24 ⇔ July 2, 2005, 10am – 6pm

- Daily Seminars and Demonstrations
- Authentic goods of the Era for sale
- Daily muzzle - loading competition
- Music of the Era
- Good, Clean Family Fun!

Admission: Adults, $3.00;
Kids under 12, $1.00;
Kids under 6 **FREE**
Family Passes available
R.V. parking available

For more information: hrt.tripod.com

June 2003

Carbon County place names
By: Mike Majerus

Here is a look at towns and settlements in Carbon County. Some of these are well known, others are long gone and remembered by only a few.

Fox – Named for J.M. Fox of the Rocky Fork and Cooke City Railroad. It had two grain elevators, several stores and a school. Mr. Fox is also the namesake for Mount Maurice.

Cherry Springs – Between Roberts and Bridger, it had a one room school house.

Warren – A stop on the Burlington Route Railroad is known for shipping limestone.

Tony – Had a post office from 1902-1906 to serve West Red Lodge Creek, it was later known as Fairbanks.

Bridger – Early settlers came to mine coal and called it Stringtown, although some claim it was called Georgetown for a man named George Town who made the first coal discoveries.

Red Lodge – Originally called Rocky Fork after the creek that flowed through town, it almost was renamed Villard for Henry Villard the president of the Northern Pacific Railroad. The NPRR bought the bankrupt Rocky Fork and Cooke City Railroad and completed the line which provided a link to ship coal to distant markets. Local residents were grateful and some wanted to name the town after Mr. Villard but he was a bit modest and thought Red Lodge was a better name.

Washoe – A corporate name used by the Anaconda Company was named for the Washoe Indians of Nevada.

Wade – A projected town sight between Bridger and Warren had a general store.

Luther – Named for the Luther family who ran the general store. During the early part of the 20th century, it boasted a saloon, lumber yard and blacksmith shop.

Joliet – The post office was established in 1893. It is said that the town was named by a Northern Pacific official who came from Joliet, Illinois.

Silesia – Silesia Springs provided the name for this settlement as well as the water for the brewery that was built there in 1905 by Julius Lehrkind.

Roberts – This town was named for W. Milner Roberts, a chief engineer for the NPRR from 1870-1873. Broadcaster Chet Huntley caught his first fish in Rock Creek here when his father was the station master.

Montaqua – While drilling for oil in the 1920's hot water was found and the plunge and dance & dining halls were built. The Yellowstone earthquake of 1959 shut the water off and the resort closed.

Linley – The namesake here is Walter Linley who operated the general store. Linley and nearby Luther were often called the twin cities.

Roscoe – Robert Morris was an early settler on the East Rosebud River and the town was named for him. Post office officials often confused Morris with the town of Norris in Madison County and asked that the name be changed. Mr. Morris chose Roscoe which was the name of her favorite horse.

Shriver – Nettie Shriver was the postmistress here from 1915-1938.

New Caledonia – Near Washoe was a settlement of clannish Scots who worked at the Anaconda Company mine nearby.

Scotch Coulee – Another Scottish settlement of coal miners between Bearcreek and Washoe.

Gebo – A coal mining town near Fromberg believed named for Mose Gebo. The post office was established in 1897 and discontinued in 1907. Gebo was also known for a time as Coalville. The only remnants today are the cemetery and what is left of the bank vault.

Alpine – Located on the shores of East Rosebud Lake it had a hotel, general store and a post office from 1914-1953.

Chance – Chance was a stop on the old Meeteetsee Trail. It was named for Nathan Chance who built a toll bridge across the Clark Fork there.

Riverview – Named for its location along the Clark Fork River, it had a post office from 1901 to 1906.

Carbonado – A coal mine provided the name and employment for this town near Joliet. All that remains today is a slack pile.

Castagne – Had a post office from 1919 - 1935 on Red Lodge Creek. It was named for Frank Castagne who is thought to be the first soldier killed in World War I.

Rockvale – It had a post office from 1894 – 1914.

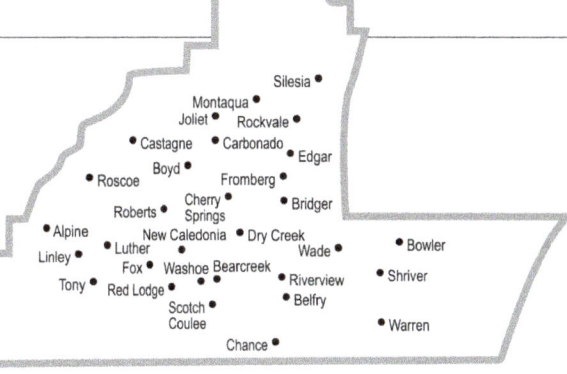

Map of Carbon County – (including historical town names)

Fromberg – Was known for a time as Poverty Flats before irrigation made it profitable to farm the area. Fromberg became known for its good apples and was sometimes called the fruit basket of Carbon County.

Belfry – Platted in 1905 and named for Dr. William Belfry, it was the headquarters for the Montana, Wyoming and Southern Railroad. The M, W & S provided passenger and freight service from Bridger to Bearcreek.

Edgar – Henry Edgar was a member of the Fairweather party who discovered gold at Alder Gulch in 1863.

Bearcreek – Named after the creek which flows through town off Mount Maurice. In 1943, it was the site of the worst coal mining disaster in the state's history.

Boyd – Named for a homesteader John Boyd, its post office began operation in 1901.

Bowler – John Bowler opened a trading post here in 1894.

Dry Creek – The Ohio Oil Company established this settlement to house workers for its oil and gas operations.

January. The first month of 2010. It is named for Janus (that's Ianuarius for you Latin-speakers), the Roman god of the doorway, because January is the doorway to the new year; the gateway to lengthening days.

January's birthstone is garnet, the flower is the carnation or snowdrop, and January is National Soup Month. Time to hit your favorite Carbon County restaurant and check out their soup du jour, or perhaps prepare your own special soup or a batch of chili.

January History in Montana

Jan 1, 1919 — Montana goes dry (prohibition takes effect)

Jan 10, 1864 — Sheriff Henry Plummer captured and hung by vigilantes in Bannack

Jan 13, 1901 — Mary MacLane scandalizes Montana by writing *The Story of Mary MacLane*

Jan 17, 2001 — William Clark finally promoted to Captain, only 198 years late

Jan 18, 1803 — President Jefferson proposes creating a "Corps of Discovery" and funding it for $2,500

Jan 20, 1931 — Nye Post Office reopens after two-year closure

Jan 23, 1870 — Colonel Eugene Baker massacres 173 Piegan Indians, not realizing they were allies

Jan 24, 1916 – Largest 24-hour temperature drop ever recorded: from 44°F to -56°F in Browning, MT (that's 100 degrees in 24 hours!)

Jan 31, 1964 – The Milwaukee Road railway ceases passenger service to Montana

The Smith Mine Disaster 60th Anniversary

February 2003

By: Mike Majerus

February 27, 2003 marks the 60th anniversary of one of the most tragic events in local and Montana history. The event has become known as the Smith Mine Disaster. To understand the event, it is important to understand the time. In February of 1943, the United States was only 14 months into the Second World War. Coal production was very important for heating and factory production had increased to aid the war effort. Montanans answered the call by increasing coal production and working extra hours in the mines. Montana Coal and Iron Company, which owned the Smith Mine, was the largest coal producer in the state and was working extra shifts to meet the demand. The 27th of February, 1943, was a Saturday, which meant time and a half for those who worked that day. This translated into much needed extra money at home for the families of the miners, not something many of them could afford to pass up.

This Saturday in winter started like so many do in the country, as a pleasant, mild day. The weather and the lives of nearly everyone in the area would change as 77 miners entered the shafts. After only about an hour and a half into the shift, three miners working together near the entrance felt increasing pressure in their ears, but no sound. At that moment, the lights in the mine went out and Alex Hawthorne, Willard Reid and Eli Houtonen headed for the mouth of the mine. Mr. Hawthorne reached the phone and called out that something was very wrong – the power was out and they were heading to the surface. Almost immediately, Hawthorne was overcome by gas and dropped near the phone. A gale force wind then knocked Reid and Houtonen off their feet, and smoke and debris hit them full force. It is important to understand here that in a mine like the Smith, an explosion underground travels down the shafts and portals much like the barrel of a gun contained within the shaft. It was about this time that a hoist operator on the surface noticed smoke coming from the mine entrance and sounded the alarm. Those whistles blowing sent fear up and down the small Bearcreek and Washoe valleys. Rescue workers went to work quickly and found Hawthorne, Reid and Houtonen where they had fallen. All three were still alive and would be the only survivors.

Typically dressed early miners. The oil lamps on their helmets were used until about 1912, when carbide lamps came into existence.

As the temperature dropped to frigid levels, all attempts to communicate with lower levels of the mine became futile. All power had been lost and the large vent fans that kept the gases from building up in the mine were not functioning. Rescue workers from mining operations around the region and state were called. It was obvious as the hours and then days dragged on that the chance of finding more survivors was fading. In-

Stories of lost gold

April 2003

By: Mike Majerus

Ever since the West was discovered, gold has been a big part of settlement and migration. Our area has been a part of this. Although there have been no large gold discoveries in Carbon County, many prospects were made. Along with that prospecting came tales and legends of gold strikes lost. Who knows? Maybe they are just legend or maybe they are yet to be found.

Stormett Butte GOLD!

In the scrub pine hills near Joliet around the turn of the century lived a man with many horses. He raised and sold them without any additional help. To keep watch over the herd, he camped on a butte overlooking the horses, a butte that now bears his name. It was from this vantage point that he watched the herd and could also keep an eye on anyone trespassing in the area. As Stormett aged, he became less able to tend the herd. He decided to sell the herd and retire.

Two train car loads of his finest stock were sent to Boston to be sold. Upon returning, Stormett is said to have had $25,000 in gold coin. About ten days after his return, he was found dead. No cause for the death was ever determined. The cabin in which he lived was in order and the only thing missing was the gold.

He was buried on the butte where he had spent so many years. It is said that for years, many locals searched the countryside for the gold with no results. To add an eerie twist, some claim that on dark nights, a small bright light appears on the butte. Perhaps the ghost of Stormett Butte is watching over his gold…

Grove Creek GOLD!

Just after Red Lodge was settled in 1884, it was common for locals to picnic and spend time in the mountains. It is important to remember that this was only 8 years after the Battle of Little Big Horn.

Well, to get back to the story, a group of settlers encountered a band of Crow Indians at Grove Creek near Mount Maurice. A fierce battle was waged between Indian and white man and a 17-year-old girl was wounded.

As soon as the attackers were driven off, the group headed to Red Lodge – a very difficult trip to make in haste. Along the route, the young lady died. The group, fearing more attacks, found a spot in a canyon between solid rock walls to bury her. While digging the grave, a good number of large gold nuggets were unearthed. Not wanting to wait around any longer, the party returned to town to tell the tale.

Later, when it was considered safe to return to the area, searches were made for the gravesite and the gold but neither was ever located.

Coal Creek GOLD!

In the summer of 1880, a man and his son were prospecting for gold on Coal Creek, west of Red Lodge. After much searching, the tale tells of a fairly rich strike. The decision was made to go to Coulson for fresh supplies and provisions. Not wanting to take all the gold with them, the legend states that a root cellar was constructed and the gold was placed in jugs inside. A tree was placed across the constructed cellar to help mark the spot.

While on the return trip with provisions, the man and his son were killed. No trace of the strike they made has ever been found. There is a tale of some lo-

cal residents finding the dugout cellar with a jug inside but no trace of that precious yellow metal.

Silesia GOLD!

At the turn of the century, one of Montana's most famous brewers established a brewery at Silesia. Julius Lehrkind called the enterprise The Carbon County Brewing Company.

The stone two-story building was known to many and was an established stop between Red Lodge and Billings.

In those days, Indians still roamed the area, so it was not uncommon to see teepees. Mr. Lehrkind noticed a lone teepee not far from the brewery and walked over to greet the occupant. He found a lone Indian, violently ill. Julius did what he could to aid his new friend. Lehrkind spent a good deal of time with the Indian attempting to aid him, but to no avail.

Before he died, the Indian handed his benefactor two large gold nuggets and said "eight days west from here." Julius Lehrkind and some friends spent many days after this trying to find the gold deposit the Indian had told of. They traveled by foot, slow horse, fast horse, travois and wagon for eight days, but never found even a hint of gold.

These stories were recorded in book form by the Senior High Class of 1951 for Carbon County High School under the guidance of Grace Bosworth. It may be the first oral history project ever done. These and many more great stories and tales would have been lost if not for this wonderful project.

> It would be hard to imagine anyone living in the area at that time who was not affected.

side the mine, many were killed by the outright blast but several managed to escape into a workshop deep within the mine. These men were seasoned miners and they knew that without ventilation, the gas would seep in and make survival impossible. After eight days of non-stop rescue operations, the bodies of all 74 miners were recovered. In the underground workshop, heart wrenching messages to wives and children were found. These brave men knew the fate that awaited them and understood that time was running out so they left chalk messages on pieces of old dynamite boxes.

One of the most asked questions when people first hear about the Smith Mine Disaster is how it happened. State and federal mine investigators, as well as miners and company officials, were called to testify at the coroner's inquest held April 12-14, 1943. The jury found that the miners had lost their lives due to concussion and gas poisoning caused by a gas and dust explosion in the mine. It was also found that in November of 1942, state mine inspectors had discovered safety violations. Mine operators claimed that because of the war production and manpower shortages, these problems could not be corrected. There was also contention that a very methane-laden part of the mine was sealed off by order of the mine inspectors, after protests of the company that this would allow methane to build up behind a concrete wall. The true cause will never be fully known. The debate continues to this day.

It would be hard to imagine anyone living in the area at that time who was not affected. Many families lost uncles, nephews, brothers and fathers. One family was planning to move to a farm and a new life with that Saturday being that miner's last day of work at the mine. Another family lost both father and son – the two men had never worked together prior to February of 1943 and they enjoyed being able to travel to work together. In a small community such as ours, everyone knew nearly everyone else, which added to the devastation.

The Smith Mine site still stands on Highway 308 near Washoe, serving as a ghostly reminder of a bygone era of mining in our community and the sad day 60 years ago that changed the lives of so many.

Photos provided by the Carbon County Historical Society and LuDon of the Washoe Quilt Shoppe - thank you!

60th Anniversary of the Smith Mine Disaster

As part of the Carbon County Historical Society's Lecture Series, a panel of local citizens will discuss this local tragedy. This discussion will be held on February 20 at 7 pm at the Peaks to Plains Museum. Free to the public, call 446-3667 for more information.

The 74 who died...
Because WWII had just begun, many of the younger men in the area were overseas leaving the older men to work in the mines.

Sam Alexander (57)	Wayne Jones (31)		
James Allison (51)	Andrew Jordan (21)		
Emil Anderson (40)	Mike Korinko (33)		
William Appleton, Sr. (50)	John Krop, Sr. (59)		
William Barry (26)	Louis Kuhar (56)		
Sam Barovich (56)	Edward Kumpula (35)		
Jules Besinque (51)	Edward Laird (55)		
William Beeney (53)	Edward J. Laird (49)		
John Bone (59)	Clem Lodge (51)		
Leland Cline (26)	John Madden (53)		
David Davis (42)	Richard Mallon (68)		
William DeBourg (55)	Ignace Marinchek (57)	William Nelson (51)	William Slaby (38)
August Deruelle (62)	Abe McDonald (59)	William Noble (68)	David Sommerville (60)
Pat Doran (38)	Josheph McDonald (42)	Frank Pajnich (53)	John Sommerville (34)
Marcel Fages (40)	Robert McDonald (42)	William Pelo (55)	Frank Starkovich (64)
Joe Ferro (51)	James McNeish (60)	Elmer Price (53)	John Sudar (28)
John Germanetti (60)	John Meikeljohn (53)	William Pryde (32)	Frank Sumicek (65)
Pete Giovetti (39)	Herman Mejean (19)	Zino Rahkola (27)	George Thompson, Sr. (?)
Matt Hallila (57)	Joe Meyer (39)	Fred Rasborschek (61)	Adam Wakenshaw (72)
Art Halpin (42)	Frank Mourich (42)	Martin Ratkovich (46)	Robert Wakenshaw (47)
Dewey Hardy (46)	Jack Mourich (36)	David Reid (33)	Robert Whitehead (47)
James Hawthorne (31)	Wilber Muller (22)	Lawrence Reid (41)	Clarence Williams (42)
John Hodnik (31)	David Murray, Sr. (56)	George Saarela (33)	Lloyd Williams (45)
Walter Joki (30)	Earl Mus (51)	William Shepard (69)	Vid Zaputil (50)

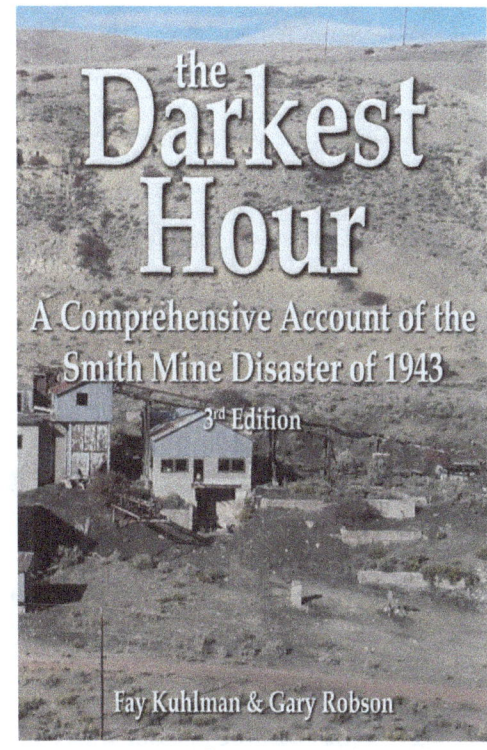

For more information about the Smith Mine disaster, I might modestly suggest this little book.

The Very Best of the Red Lodge Local Rag

history

February 2003

The towns of Bearcreek, Washoe and Scotch Coulee were once bustling communities filled with the rich culture of the many nationalities of the miners and their families who lived and worked there until the Smith Mine Disaster.

Bearcreek

In the late 1860's, "Yankee Jim" George first discovered the extensive coal deposits lying in the Bearcreek area.

Several small mines began operation in the 1890's. Miners hauled their coal in wagons over the hill to Red Lodge. The Northern Pacific Railroad head had been established in 1889 in Red Lodge.

The Montana, Wyoming & Southern Railroad was established in 1906 and the direct transportation and the rising demand for coal turned Bearcreek into a boom town. From 1906 to 1921, the town actually suffered from a perpetual housing shortage.

People from all over the world were attracted by the mines and the community was settled with immigrants from Serbia, Montenegro, Italy, Scotland, Germany, France, Scandinavia and Austria. The melting pot of nationalities became incorporated in 1906 and received a post office. According to the Bearcreek school newspaper in 1934 said "The efficient founders, in avoiding the extra shift for Capital C on the typewriter, dubbed the town 'Bearcreek'."

By 1907, four coal companies were operationg extensive underground workings. Two years later, 290 men were employed by the mines, making the town the dominant community in the district. The commercial sector had 23 businesses, including 10 saloons and three general stores. By 1910, Carbon County was the leading coal producer in Montana.

The coal market continued to expand. Employment in the mines increased to a high of 428 men in 1914 with the population of the town reaching about 1200. The war created even more of a boom but the Bearcreek mines were often shut down because of the poor construction of the railroad grade and a chronic shortage of coal cars.

The post-war depression struck Bearcreek in 1919. The dwindling demand for coal, competition from the Red Lodge mines, and the deteriorating rail line caused an economic downturn in the 1920's, and by 1923 commercial coal mining had virtually disappeared.

Interior of the Clark-Wright Bank, Bearcreek. J. Harry Wright, cashier; man on right - Jesse George "Doc" Forney, dentist in Bearcreek from 1915-1931.

World War II again stimulated production but in February of 1943, 74 miners were killed by an explosion and poisonous gas at the Smith Mine. Miners, families and even buildings were relocated to Bridger, Belfry, Fromberg and Red Lodge. The last mine, owned by Frank and Leopold Janskovitch closed in 1970.

Washoe

The town of Washoe, named for a Nevada Indian tribe, was established in November of 1906 when the Washoe Coal Company, a subsidiary of the Anaconda Copper Mining Company, opened its #1 mine. The Montana, Wyoming and Southern Railroad was extended into Washoe in 1909. Coal from the Washoe mine went mainly to Butte and Anaconda while coal from the Smith Mine went mainly to the Northern Pacific Railway and markets in Washington state.

The Washoe Post Office opened December 2, 1907 with Earl E. Lombard as postmaster. It closed July 31, 1959. The building also served as the mine office and now is the newly renovated Washoe Quilt Shoppe.

In 1911, an 8-room brick school opened with about 26 students attending. Many students would walk across the hill from Scotch Coulee to attend classes, (probably uphill both ways.) When the schoolhouse burned down, make-shift classrooms were set up in the Company Store. The school closed in 1955 when the lack of work drove most families to find work in other towns.

At its peak, Washoe had a population of about 900, all dependent on the mine for their livelihood. There was a large general store, the Washoe Trading Company, pool hall, boarding houses and many residences, along with the mine buildings. The Mine Superintendent had a house built for $2400 - $400 for the foundation and $2000 for the house. The home is still there and has been beautifully renovated. The only building in Washoe that cost more to be built was the Tipple, with a cost of a whopping $3000.

When Anaconda Copper converted most of its operations to electrical power, the need for coal dwindled, eventually resulting in the mine closing on December 9, 1943.

Main Street of Bearcreek, circa 1912

After the mines were closed, many of the buildings were moved on skids to Red Lodge. The Company Store was one of the buildings moved and it was a popular dance hall in Red Lodge until it burned down.

To look at the Washoe skyline today, it's hard to believe it was once a bustling town full of activity. The only form of commerce is the Washoe Quilt Shoppe and LuDon, the owner is happy to share her knowledge of the area with visitors.

Scotch Coulee

The land in the Coulee was owned by The Anaconda mining company. The residents owned their houses and had to pay $8.00 a year ground rent to the mining company.

There was no TV or radio. The families made ice up at Lamport's Pond. There was ice in the winter and the kids would come up and skate on the frozen pond.

Liquor flowed through the Coulee like a river. There was always lots of wine. Everyone had 2 to 3 large five-gallon vats of wine at their house. The women did not drink and liquor was never offered to the kids.

There were stills in the Coulee, on the mountain and on the Clarks Fork. Frank Planichek remembers his Dad talking about "all" the stills in the Coulee. There must have been a bunch. He tells the story about a cow eating too much of the 'mash' and falling down the stairs that go to the basement in Mary Mourich's house. He said the chickens would walk around 'drunk' too."

The Slovenian Hall had a dance floor and a stage with curtains and in one corner there was a piano. There would be plays on the stage. Behind the stage there was a room where wine and whiskey was served. Frank Planichek's dad used to tell him that the day after a dance, the sage brush would be lying flat from the guys fighting and all the Coulee kids would hunt around for any money that might have fallen out of the guys pockets.

Another victim of the mine closures, the lively town of Scotch Coulee was quickly deserted, houses and families were moved to Belfry or Red Lodge and all that's left is the stories.

Thank you to the Carbon County Historical Society for information and photogs. Information about Scotch Coulee supplied by Terry Cestnik. Find more information at www.cestnik.com/henry.htm

February History in Montana

Feb 3, 1864 — Vigilantes hang Bill Hunter as a member of the Plummer gang

Feb 5, 1865 — Official Montana territorial seal approved by Governor Edgerton

Feb 7, 1865 — Virginia City becomes capital of MT Territory

Feb 11, 1805 — Birth of Jean Baptiste "Pomp" Charbonneau, son of Sacagawea and Toussaint Charbonneau

Feb 14, 1848 — Birth of Plenty Coups (Aleek-chea-ahoosh), later to become Chief of the Crow (Apsáalooke) Nation

Feb 19, 1877 — Fort Missoula established by the U.S. Army

Feb 21, 1862 — "Tin Cup Joe" files Montana's first lawsuit

Feb 22, 1897 — President Cleveland sets aside four million acres as the Bitterroot Reserve.

Feb 25, 1865 — Montana Historical Society founded

mountain news

On Ullr
By Ullr (a.k.a. David Kallenbach)

Blame it on a couple of (stiff) Martinis! Now every time I run into Brad Logan, he groans the low, guttural "OOH-LUHR" in my direction. I'm not sure that Brad even remembers my proper name at this point, but I like the ring of the nickname, even though a few years ago I had never heard of Ullr. I'm now a true believer.

Blame Blake Chartier, who deftly conned me into his sizely duties as Ullr a few winters back with the promise of a few of his exquisite Martinis. "*All you have to do is…*" Sure, all I have to do is dress up like Raquel Welch in *One Million Years B.C.*, holler out a Shakespearian prologue like a Viking, lead a parade of revelers across the parking lot to set torch to a bonfire, and make dubious sacrifices. Sound fun? It is! I took the role of the Norse snow god seriously and employed my finest method acting to become Ullr, "god of brightness and glory."

So who is Ullr, and why should you care, ye fine, sophisticated readers? At the heart of the legend, Ullr represents no less than the bringer of snows, the god on skis, whisking around the North country hunting. In places where livelihoods depend on the white stuff falling in great quantities—farmers, ski area personnel, beer vendors, shop owners, road maintenance workers—little-known Ullr fills an important role at Asgaard. No less important to Scandinavians than rain gods to Native Americans, or the witching wand and the Farmer's Almanac, Ullr represents something to believe in, the eternal optimism that is necessary to will water onto a dry landscape. Each year we toast Ullr, that his benevolence and bounty will grace us again this winter. And against the backdrop of greenhouse gases and global warming, is there a better time to celebrate Ullr?

Ullr was the son of Sif, a Norse fertility goddess, and a father of unknown origin. When Sif became wife to Thor, the great Thunder God, Ullr became Thor's stepson. Some sources have that Ullr's actual father was Egill Orvandil, the god of archery, and this makes some sense, when you consider that Ullr is most identified as a hunting god with a long-bow made of yew in hand, as much as he is known as the god of skis.

In fact, it is likely that the concept of skis originated from the shield that Ullr always carried, as it is said that he had almost magical powers of transport, being able to toss his shield on the waters and travel across the seas as if on a modern-day water ski. Early skis were reminiscent of shields or boats. In the history of the ski, it is known that early skis had fur covering them, so that the hunter when he traveled on them would make no noise and would not lose traction or ice up. Furthermore, the long-bow, in order to be kept at its ready in warfare and hunting was fitted with a basket at one end, so that it could double as a pole, giving rise to the lurk so commonly used by skiers of a bygone era.

The first recorded evidence of skis is from 4500-year-old rock drawings found in Norway. Skis have also been dug up from bogs in Sweden, also dating back 4500 years. So for millennia, peoples of northern climes have made use of skis to get themselves about, hunt, and wage war on each other. This usefulness to the military sped their development—in the late 1600s the Norwegian military is known to have held skiing competitions! But skiing for recreation has relatively modern origins.

Sondre Norheim, from the Telemark region of Norway, is often credited as the pioneer of modern skiing, popularizing the sport in the early 20th century.

This illustration of Ullr is from an Icelandic manuscript from the 18th century. Few visual records exist of this enigmatic god.

Ski races and ski clubs had already come into their own in Norway by the mid-1800s, and in the 1850s in the U.S., skis were used to move the mail from the goldfields of the Sierra Nevadas. In 1888 Norwegian Fridtjof Nansen made the first crossing of Greenland on skis, becoming an instant celebrity by doing so, and fannning interest in skiing across Europe and the U.S.

Scandinavians who had settled in places like Michigan and Minnesota were responsible for bringing the sport to this country. Ski jumping and cross-country events were added to the 1932 Winter Olympics in Lake Placid, New York, while downhill and combined slalom racing were added in 1936 at the Garmisch, Bavarian Olympics. Rope tows and chair lifts were developed in the 1930s as well, bringing skiing to a widening audience. The development of ski-troops for the 10th Mountain Division deployed in World War II, bred a generation of skiing disciples who began to develop their own ski areas in numerous places across the country (including Red Lodge, Montana). Today many of these ski resorts, large and small, still operate, modern temples to Glorious Ullr.

So help us carry on the legacy of Ullr, Saturday, January 7th. Beginning at 5 pm in the Bierstube, your participation can truly make or break the winter we will have. March with us to the bonfire (David Rivers and company???), bring something to burn as a sacrifice, and have some chili and refreshments. It's all part of the warm feeling you will gain when Ullr sends oodles and boodles of snow to our little corner of the North Country this winter!

Hail Ullr!

Barefoot and Pregnant
By Erin Oley

January 2006

Prior to sleepless nights, diaper duty, before our duo becomes a trio, and before we are able to call ourselves "parents," we decided to take a pre-baby vacation. Apparently "babymoon" is the new term to describe a pre-baby vacation. According to my pregnancy magazines and books, these are becoming increasingly popular as a last hoorah for couples embarking on a new life with parental roles.

So, off we went to Florida where I could enjoy being barefoot and pregnant. This was a great time in my pregnancy to travel since I was 26-27 weeks along – over my exhausting first trimester and just before I enter the third trimester, when clinicians typically suggest travels should be limited to local places in case of going into labor early. It is reassuring though to have Billy by my side as he knows what to do in the event of that happening. Anyway, as we traveled through the airports, I could not help but take mental notes – observing all the brave parents traveling with their kids and the gear that goes with them. Amazing! Oh, something to look forward to. Some parents have the whole routine down and their gear organized for the most efficient way to travel, while others appear totally discombobulated with stuff falling all around them as they walk down the jetway. I think to myself: gosh I hope I can be one of the organized ones – all cool, confident, and collected – where the baby is just as cool, calm, and collected. Good luck, right?

Speaking of gear, that was the topic of most of my reading on the plane rides. One of my dear friends gave me a great book entitled, "Baby Bargains." This book reviews all the "necessary gear" involved in child rearing. It is amazing how many choices of baby items there are on the market and all the safety issues and concerns that are associated with them as well. It is all so overwhelming. That is when I reminded myself of the babymoon concept to just enjoy my time with Billy for the week. Apparently we picked the right week to travel since the reports in Red Lodge showed -20 degree weather while we were gone. Ahhhhh. Thus, much time was spent outside enjoying the warm air and sun.

It will definitely be a trip that I will never forget as our time to just be – on one last get-away as the couple we have been for over 11 years now. Like I mentioned in last month's article, we cannot wait to be parents, but it was so nice to take the time for us. I will never forget watching the sunsets on the water, taking long walks along the ocean canals, catching the only snook (a fish) during the week (sorry - I had to rub it in), exploring the historic islands of the area, and sending Billy off hunting for 2 days so he could get his wildlife fix in. Since I was able to relax and make myself sit still during the vacation, I was able to focus and feel the baby move quite a bit. It is still totally enchanting and miraculous to feel this sensation. Overall, it was a great week of enjoying the whole experience of being barefoot and pregnant.

making a difference

July 2003

Playground dreams come true

Imagine, if you can, Bill Karas—all 6'2", 210 pounds of him, Bill Karas, who's never been known to speak above a whisper "howling down the slides, climbing up the ladders, screaming...from tower to tower," with his wife and daughter on play equipment in Livingston last month. Truly, it's not something you see every day. But, if his lovely wife Margaret is to be believed (and when is she not?), that's the sort of thing we can expect from the new playground equipment planned for Lions Park next spring.

"It's just so much fun for bigger kids," Margaret says. "Bill and I were playing on that, and I think we had more fun than Gracie had." The Livingston equipment was designed by Leathers & Associates, the firm contracted by Red Lodge's People for Playgrounds group.

"A group of us moms started approaching the Parks Board about a year ago, about our need for a new playground," project coordinator Erin McNamara says. Dari Quirk then discovered Leathers & Associates on a vacation in Florida, "and it was this amazing thing. It had pirates, and a whale, a sandbox, trains, it was just an incredibly creative playground," she says. So they contacted Leathers, got approval from the Parks Board, City Council, and the Lions Club, and are now on track to build the 8000-square-foot playground in a 5-day, all-out, community barn-raising event next May 17-21.

One of the most exciting things about Leathers' designs, says the committee, is that they're inspired by the kids and built by the community. "Every one of them is unique," Erin says. Dari adds that "they're all custom-built to the site. Lisa has incorporated the whole design around the trees, the slope of the terrain, around the paths that were there."

Lisa DeShano, the Leathers & Associates designer, spent a day in Red Lodge this May, talking with kids and getting a feel for the area before she sat down and drew up the plans—plans which, if you're like Bill Karas, will make you want to be a kid again.

Behind the 3-foot picket fence perimeter, there'll be an old-west facade, a tipi, a train depot to climb around on, coal chutes to tunnel through, a climbing wall, performance stage, musical "instruments," towers, slides, swings, rope bridges, and to top it all off: a Lazy M slide. And it's all designed with the attitude and personality of Red Lodge in mind. "This is not Disneyland," Erin says. "This is not plastic and metal and bright colors. Lisa has taken all the wonderful things about Red Lodge and incorporated them into a playground design."

It's also leagues beyond the metal swingsets we grew up with. "One thing I've picked up, having

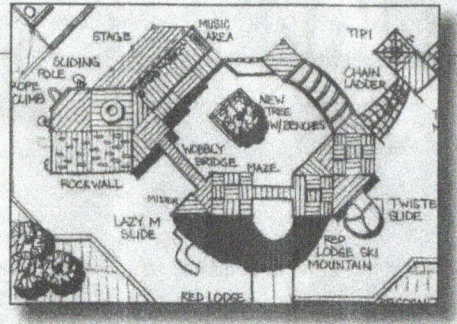

Detail of the plans for the new playground equipment. For a full view, go to www.CityofRedLodge.com/playground

a child, is the importance of creative play that teaches and improves the children," Margaret says. "There are components for developing gross motor and fine motor skills as well as social and imaginary play. So it's not just sitting on the swing; it's not just going down a slide. This is something that Red Lodge lacks in existing playgrounds."

The structure itself is built of pressure-treated lumber and recycled plastic—the stuff the boardwalk at Old Faithful is made of—and can be cut, nailed, and painted the way wood can, but has fewer maintenance issues, and a greater lifespan.

The project is going to require thousands of volunteer hours in the upcoming year, and since the entire thing will be pulled off with donations, grants and volunteer work, there are countless ways to help out. The group invites everyone, those with kids and without, to take part. For more information, contact Erin, at 446-4243 or red_lodge_playground@yahoo.com.

---

bizness

December 2004

This ex-Ranger's still working in the Pines

It's like something out of an Old West movie, "just bury me in a pine box up on the hill," the old cowpoke says. But to retired Forest Service Ranger Rand Herzberg, it's getting to be serious business. Cowboy Coffin and Pine Box business, in fact. "I got this idea a little over a year ago," he says. "A really good friend of mine went to the cemetery in a pine box on a wagon led by mules. And I thought, you know? That's really classy."

Rand was so impressed with the simplicity and the dignity of that ceremony that he began looking into it. He'd been doing finishing work on his own homes since he was a kid, so this summer with retirement stretching out in front of him and a lot of basic carpentry training behind him, he started researching the coffin business.

"There's a lot of people who are doing it," he says. "About ten years ago, the laws regulating this changed, making it legal for people to buy a coffin from anyone. I just liked the simplicity of it, and I wanted to provide people with an alternative."

Rand uses ¾" tongue-in-groove pine with simple rope handles and brass hinges. And though he expects most of his work to be custom, his standard box is six feet long, with dovetail joinery, a one-inch foam padding on the bottom and lined in white muslin. "I like using dovetail joints because they're very strong and require less framing. I don't let any of the nails or screws show on the outside. They're very pretty, very nice looking handcrafted boxes." And rather than staining them, he uses a paste furniture wax.

"This isn't for everybody; it's for the person who wants the simple burial. It's an alternative. You can be buried the way you want and it can still be dignified," he says. He adds that the coffins aren't just for cowboys. "I can bury clowns, too."

The response he's been getting has been great. "People are really interested; they think it's funny in a way. They'll see the sign on my truck and just can't believe it. Someone's always asking me—'Do you really build coffins?'"

He was delivering a coffin in the back of his pickup truck earlier this year, and "the truckers flipped out. They could read my sign and were high enough to see into the bed of the pickup—they'd go by honking their horns, half wondering if there's somebody in there, I'm sure."

And while Rand's generally got a sizable sense of humor, coffins really aren't a joking matter for him. "I try to explain to people that it doesn't have to be funny. When someone starts asking me about a box, you can tell they've got someone in mind."

But, he says, "a lot of people don't think about it ahead of time, and then they're at the mercy of their emotions, really." He can build a coffin in two to three days, but with shipping and/or delivery, it can take a week or more. Or you can order it early and store it in the garage until you need it.

Above: *Rand at Mule Days in Drummond this June.* **Far Left**: *The framing on a 6-sided box.* **Left**: *The 6-sided box finished.*

Rand has made several coffins so far via Internet order, as well as a couple of pet coffins and cremation urns. He expects that he'll do half of his business over Internet, and half locally. "I don't want this to take up a lot of my time, half of it is that I wanted to have an alternative. And it's something I can do in the winter." Asked if he wants to be buried in one of his coffins, he explains that he plans to be cremated, "but I could probably make my own urn."

You can find out more about Rand's pine boxes at www.cowboycoffin.com or give him a call at 446-2121.

art connection

A passion for simplicity

This profile of Nick Kosorok was in the October 2003 issue.

You walk into Nick Kosorok's studio: full of light from windows on all sides, Clapton and BB King on the late-70s cabinet speakers hanging from the ceiling, a thin film of shavings and sawdust covering every surface and an obviously well-used basketball hoop perched just over one workstation, and you know this is a man who loves his work. "It's heaven, as far as I'm concerned," Nick says.

2004 will be Nick's 20th year with the furniture studio. "I started woodworking in '78, when I was still with the Highway Department part time. Then I bought a home, remodeled it and took a real interest in power tools." He planned to slowly transition from part-time power tool magnate to full-time custom furniture and cabinet maker but things didn't quite turn out that way. "I was going to do my business, and still work part-time for other people. I've only worked for someone else two times in twenty years, though. It seems like when I start to worry, the phone always rings. Somebody's watching out for me."

The art education article featuring Nick's brother, Mike on the facing page ran in May of 2008.

He started out making custom furniture for interior design companies in the area, and now has pieces in 14 states, including Alaska and Hawaii. These days the business of working for other companies has trailed off, and he gets most his jobs by word of mouth. "There's always a big 'What If' floating around, but it always works out."

While it's furniture – beds, entertainment centers, armoirs – that he started out making and loves to do, "the big surge right now is in custom cabinetry. We've done high end to low end kitchens, big ones to small, you name it." He also feels fortunate to have been working these past four years with John Metcalf, who is "very good. John has made kitchens really fun."

Not at all a wood snob, Nick does a lot of work out of alder and maple. He also enjoys working in cherry and walnut, but "I won't work with rainforest mahogany. I just refuse to. There is some farmed mahogany, but it's not as pretty. You have to stain it up nice. And that's basically the thing: you take a nice piece of alder or maple, stain and varnish it up well, and you'll have a piece the customer will be proud of. You'll also save them some money."

He does really like playing with exotic veneers, though. "The thing about these elm leaf burl veneers is that you don't see the design until you've varnished it. I did one bed we called 'Two Tigers,' because when the design came up, there were two striped tigers facing each other on the headboard. It was incredible; I had no idea they'd be there like that." He also has a story of a very disturbing burl veneer that showed him a head with horns and a tail when it was stained. Luckily, the customer saw a frog in the design instead. "I was afraid that bed was hexed."

When he gets an order for a job, he gets the basic information and then sits down to draw up a design for the customer to approve. "I've got close to 200 drawings; 75% of them have ended up as furniture." And in one of the really odd Red Lodge coincidences, Nick studied drawing in high school from his brother Mike, who is 12 years older than he is. Nick didn't comment on whether Mike was a tough teacher or not, but he did say he was darn good!

The jobs he loves, of course, are the ones when the customer says "Do whatever." And while his portfolio is filled with lots of complicated designs – soaring curves, intricate carvings, delicate wood inlays – his favorite piece is a singularly elegant hutch, almost Shaker-style in its design. "I love simplicity," he says.

"At first I was really wanting to be the best I could be, make every single piece as elegant as I could, and it wasn't me. It got to be too much." So now he claims to have relaxed a bit. "Number 1: I don't want to copy people. I want to learn from those people but not become them. You've got to find your own niche. And not at the expense of other artists," he muses, "and sometimes you never find it. But in the meantime, I've built a lot of kitchens."

"And I'm still having fun. There's a lot of tools out there still to buy. I'm doing what it takes to stay in Red Lodge and have a quality life. And listen to the Blues. I'm the luckiest man alive."

We thought this January 2008 ad for Richard Gessling's dental practice had the perfect slogan!

You won't feel a thing!

Richard Gessling, DDS
Appointments taken Monday-Friday
446-1010

The Very Best of the Red Lodge Local Rag

FISH STORIES AND HORSE TALES

Don Coutts has been giving free horse and wagon rides up and down Broadway for 20 years now, and working horse teams for nearly four times that long. This past fall, he was inducted into the Montana Draft Teamster Hall of Fame, joining his longtime buddy and competitor George Miller from Absarokee. Don chatted with us about horses, fish stories, and how he got to the Hall of Fame.

Tell me about winning the Hall of Fame.

Well, my family all came to this thing in Deer Lodge. I couldn't believe it. I was amazed that whole gang showed up.

But I want you to know that you can't win a Hall of Fame by yourself. It has to be competition with your buddies and all the friends that you've worked with. They don't like you some times, but you need them.

And one of the driving forces of this system is my wife, Gloria. She encouraged me to go & do things, & get things done. I'm a guy that gets things done, but sometimes a guy needs a little help. She needs to get the credit for that.

Tell me about your trophy.

The Montana Draft Mule Association had a collar. If you win the championship in the competition, you get one of those plaques. If anybody ever wins it five times in a row, they get the collar. And I did. Five years in a row, I won that collar. Nobody else has ever done that.

It looks here like you stole it from George Miller, who'd won it the three times before you.

Yep.

What's your favorite event in the competition?

I do the best at cultivating. You take a two-wheeled cultivator and a team, and there's a hundred bottles. You steer it so you drive the team right over the row, so the horses don't knock over the bottles. Every bottle you knock over is a point off.

One time, I and my buddy George Miller did a competition at Metra. They set up 100 bottles at each end of the arena, and we had to do both sets 10 times. George beat me by 1 bottle. 2000 bottles, he knocked one bottle over, & I knocked two. The crowd was going wild.

How long have you been competing?

Since '82. I've won almost 250 ribbons.

Sounds like you've been winning these things for a long time.

Oh yeah. One guy—he's about 60, and he's a real avid teamster, and he works real hard. He comes to these shows, and he has never beaten me. Last time when I won, he comes up to me and says, "When the [censored] are you gonna die?" Then he just walked away. He never said another word.

So can you still compete, now that you're a Hall of Famer?

Oh yeah. Unless I go and die.

How did you learn to drive teams?

I was born & raised on a sheep ranch. We did all our work in those days with horses: plowing, cultivating corn, harrowing.... We didn't even have a tractor. My dad was an old Scotsman, and he was the only one who didn't go broke. All our neighbors went & borrowed money & it was depression time. My pa said, "You know boys, I can't figure out for the life of me, how we're gonna get $800 to pay for that John Deere tractor. We've got all these horses, we've got all this grass, all this machinery. We just oughtta wait until we get going better." Us boys wanted a tractor, of course.

Who are your team horses these days?

Lady & Belle. I raised them from babies, and they're 22 & 23. And they've been doing it all their lives.

How did you get started doing the free rides on Broadway?

Well, I got an idea: how would it work if I ran free rides down Main Street, & got a few bucks out of the city? This is 20 years ago. So the first year, I went around town to get money, and I got $2,500. Then I gave free rides for two hours every night. For 100 days, from Memorial Day to Labor Day. People can just get on, and have a free ride. And I [tell stories]. I lie to them, do every damn thing.

Once a guy asked me, "is the fishing very good here in [Rock Creek]?" I said, "Oh boy, there's some big ones in there." I told him I was fishing off my saddle horse one day, and I caught one of them big ones, and that damned fish jerked my horse out from under me & drowned my horse. The lady said, "boy, that's a fish story."

biz ness

Betty Waters - bridging the generations

A few years ago, a question was posed: "Can you buy underwear in Red Lodge?"

The answer is apparent if you shop at Waters Department Store. In fact, about 10 years ago, (after being in business for nearly 50 years), the store was actually picketed by some newcomers who wanted to "clean up" the town. The newly located couple chose Betty's store because she had some boxer shorts on display in the window and they also targeted a neighboring T-shirt shop. Betty was surrounded by friends who were willing to help with the protesters, and then she called the police. Tony Krumheuer came by and asked if Betty wanted to press charges. She declined, but informed the couple that they were not welcome in her store. Apparently, other residents had the same reaction, and the couple moved away after about six weeks in town.

Betty has a lot of friends in the area because she has lived here her whole life. She grew up in Bear Creek and was a senior in high school when she and some friends were at the Bear Creek post office, (at that time the town had a population of about 7000). They heard the mine whistle, drove to the mine, slid down the hill and were able to see the three survivors come out of the mine. One friend was overcome by the gas coming from the entrance and became ill. Betty then saw the bodies of the victims being hauled out. Even all these years later, it is understandably difficult for her to talk about that day.

Her graduating class began at 25 and after the Mine Disaster, the class had 7 graduates. Most classmates had lost fathers in the disaster and although Betty's father had died earlier in a mining accident, her mother was to marry a man in June. While helping with the mine victims, he was exposed to the toxic gas and died as a result.

In 1945, Wesley Waters was discharged from the Navy and although Betty hadn't met him, he knew her parents. One day he went to visit them and saw a photo of Betty on the piano. Later, he went to Natali's Bar and saw her there and asked her to dance. Betty always knew she wouldn't marry a miner, so she was happy to learn that Wes owned a clothing store. The rest is local history.

Waters' Department Store originally served as a men's store with John Peters, a rotund Scotsman, the original owner and local tailor. John Peters and Wes' dad ran the store while Wes was stationed overseas. The original building was skidded across town from Old Town and was about 25' x 25'. When you visit the shop, the poles mark the dimensions of the original building.

In 1969 the Waters' bought The Red Lodge State Bank building next to the store, tore a wall out and expanded their business from only men's wear to include squaw dresses. "I don't know why we chose squaw dresses, but that was the first women's item we carried," says Betty.

> Her secret for keeping a business alive in Red Lodge for 59 years? "Give people individual attention."

Betty didn't much like working the store so she worked for a lawyer for 10 years. Wes, however, loved retail and bought another store in Worland, Wyoming in 1974. He ran that one, and Betty ran the one here in town. In 1988, he had a heart attack, so they sold the Worland store.

In 1978, the oldest Waters son was instrumental in adding the ski shop. That went well until the son left and since Betty isn't a skier, she kept the clothing items but got rid of the skis etc. She just wasn't comfortable selling the hardware. "If people asked about snowmobiling, I could help them with that, though," she says.

Betty continues to operate the store and still meets once a year with her Bear Creek classmates. They always have an all-school reunion. The first reunion had about 450 people attend - not bad for a school that had all its records destroyed. Last year they had 149 participants. The school closed in 1950, was torn down and the bricks were sold. How does a boom town become a ghost town? Just ask Betty.

Her secret for keeping a business alive in Red Lodge for 59 years? "Give people individual attention. Don't ignore people. Wes established the store on visiting."

Stop in and say hi to Betty and if you have a little extra time, she'd be happy to show you her books about Bear Creek back when it had 7000 people living there. And the store is almost as nice as Betty.

January 2003

---

books, movies, music, etc.

Park your car here: A short intro to the world of garage bands

By Viv Vinyl

Why did some of our contributors, like "Viv Vinyl" from this 2003 column and "Stylus T. Table" write under pseudonyms? Some worked for other publications and couldn't write for us under their real names. Others, like Wil Stifya, didn't want to be treated differently in a restaurant when he went in to review it. And some, like the Round Man (Jim Kujala), just liked the name and weren't trying to stay anonymous at all.

For the ultimate trip in rock 'n' roll you couldn't do much worse than visit garage land, fondly remembered in song by the Clash. Essentially an American phenomenon, after all this country can afford the space to banish guitar-screeching teens to play amid the spilt oil cans, car top carriers and tool boxes, garage bands rose to the surface in such proliferation that it would put Hitler's U-Boats to shame.

The rise of the cheap electric guitar, Mop Top hair and British languor helped to nourish a disenchanted garden of suburban kids who wanted more than civil service careers or bag packing at their local grocery store until they were 40 years old. Thrashing away on those tinny guitars and lopping around in their best Jagger persona could be found ace group like the Seeds, the Electric Prunes, the Sonic, Count Five, the Amboy Dukes (fronted by a young Ted Nugent) and Love, initially called Hate.

Raucous, menacing vibes oscillated forth from these groups to disturb the neat crescent-shaped rhododendron shrubs out front but really, who cared if a few of the petals fell here or there, this was the first wave of punk. Every generation should bend an ear to the urban pleas of lost love and life tossed into a food processor and turned to destroy.

It makes the knees tremble to listen to these groups a decade before the Damned or the Sex Pistols spat at our screens, 25 years before grunge, and 30 years before Nu-rock screamed the same stories out at us. And it wasn't even 1966 yet. And because garage bands deserve respect, a breakdown will follow next month of the best of them, plus what to buy and where.

History

In Red Lodge: 97 Years and Counting
by Anne Rood

Many stories about how someone found Red Lodge includes the mention of a brother or sister; the story of Joe Papez' arrival here 97 years ago is no exception.

Joe's parents Frank and Mary were newly emigrated from Slovenia, living in Franklin, Kansas where Frank toiled in the coal mines of southeastern Kansas, just a few miles from the Missouri border. Mary worked at a miner's café while raising two young sons, Frank Jr. and Joe who was born there in December 1907. In the spring of 1909 the Papez's were once again lured away from home. This time by letters from Mary's brother Wally Savsek who told them of Red Lodge, the mountains, plenty of coal mine work but summers in the fresh air to farm and harvest timber, not to mention a chance for a family homestead.

So Frank and Mary loaded up their steamer trunks again, their newly-purchased used furniture, two young sons and with friends Mark and Mary Faygal took the train to Red Lodge. Met at the depot by the livery stable owner John Weaver who, with his drayman, loaded their belongings on wagons and took the Papez's to their new home on South Adams Street.

In those days Red Lodge's main business district went along an east-west route on 16th Street where the present-day Café Regis is located. (Regis Grocery was not built until 1941.) Joe remembers about five stores being there including Gibbons store and a farmer's market. But the Papez's relied on their garden as Joe recalls, "we were mostly vegetarian in those days." An occasional snowshoe rabbit, blue grouse and even porcupine ("rich in fat") rounded out their meals.

After a couple years in town, Frank chose a 320-acre homestead site west of town on Cole Creek beneath the Palisades. Frank labored in what little spare time he had to build a one-room cabin for his growing family. Joe shakes his head remembering his father struggling with the rented team from Weaver's Livery Stable when he took the family up the rutted logging road to their new home, "he wasn't good with horses."

But good at work he was, first clearing the quaking aspens, then with the help of Wally plowed the land with horses "digging up a good garden" then handseeding their first crop of oats for the horses and cows. They bought wheat for the black laying hens and slowly built it up "a good place little by little." Joe and little Frank contributed by setting traps for rabbits, weasels and muskrats; money from fur helped with clothes and school.

Joe and his older brother, Frank

When Joe was 14 his first day of school was also the inauguration of the Draper School that still stands – as a house – on Highway 78. As he got older he and his brothers helped their father with the summer timber harvest. Joe loved and respected horses so his father was happy to let him hitch the team to haul logs to the mine "prop yard" at the foot of the West Bench near the present day hospital.

Joe's reputation for handling horses garnered him good jobs but they weren't always easy to get to. Beginning in the 1920s, Joe, Frank Jr and now brother John would walk from home to three miles north of Bridger to work at the Great Western Company Ranch. There the brothers would work 10 hours a day for a dollar an hour driving teams planting the beet crop. After a two-week stay, living in the company bunkhouse, the brothers would walk back home taking the same route back to Bridger, up Dry Creek and back to Red Lodge and home.

Joe loved breaking wild horses on ranches as well riding on new trails he and his crew built as a new Forest Service employee in the summer of 1928. Corral Creek up to Line Creek was his very first. The crews spent a summer living in camps hauled in on horseback, toiling with only shovels and picks building other trails such as Richel Lodge to Camp Senia and East Rosebud to Mystic Lake in later summers. In winter Joe conducted wildlife surveys along these very routes on snowshoes and skis.

Joe says simply that Red Lodge is a "complete change" from those days. He stood outside his house near downtown Red Lodge and looked up at the mountains and said he missed the mountains and then smiled remembering "a fast ride on a wild horse."

The Local Rag

hangin' out

July 2003

Joe Papez: a man of honor and humility

By Chuck Salladé

Ten years before America joined in to aid Western Europe in defeating Germany during the Great War, and five years before the unsinkable Titanic went to the icy bottom of the North Atlantic, Joe Papez was born. Joe was born in Franklin, Kansas on December 19, 1907. As a toddler, his parents packed up their family and moved to Montana as homesteaders. The homestead is just west of Red Lodge, and the log cabin, though in severe disrepair, is still standing today. Aside from his first two years of life, and five more during the second world war, Joe has spent his entire life in Red Lodge; 88 years!!

As a young man, Joe made his living in several ways: timber hauling for the mines, trail man for the USFS, wildland firefighter, and USFS game surveyor. As seen in the photo, Joe was a strong, healthy outdoorsman. Joe showed me a picture of himself toward the end of a bet he and his work buddies had going. The bet was over ice cream, and was that the last one to shave was treated to ice cream. In the photo Joe's beard is slightly shy of his mid-chest. He won. At the age of 35 Joe was drafted.

Joe rose to the rank of Technical Sargent Platoon Leader during the war. He served under General Patton in North Africa, General Mark W. Clark in Sicily, and General O'Daniel in Italy. He was part of the 30th Infantry Division, 15th Infantry regiment. During his time in battle he bravely earned three Purple Hearts. At the battle of Anzio, Joe was given the order to take his men to find and destroy an enemy artillery piece that was harassing their position. It had hit the field headquarters and killed everyone. Joe led his men around the backside of the enemy and struck the artillery piece, thus eliminating that immediate danger. Joe's men were all killed in doing so; all but Joe! When told he would be receiving the Silver Star he asked if his men would be receiving them posthumously as well. He was told they would not be, and so he refused it. During Anzio Joe was hit by a shell, and both the shrapnel and the concussion ended the war for him. After that hit, the next thing Joe remembered was waking up in Virginia. From there he went to Denver, to Oregon, and to Santa Barbara, all to VA hospitals for recovery. Joe's brother was also in the war. He was at D-Day at Normandy, and was in the Battle of the Bulge.

When the war was over Joe paid for all of his medical treatment and medication out of his own pocket because the government lost his records! Trying to make a go of things, Joe applied for a homestead in Powell, WY, and in Oregon, but was denied because of his disabilities, and yet the government was not paying him for disability because he could not prove it with his records which the government lost in the first place!! Eventually his records were found in an old desk in Salt Lake City, UT. After years of fighting with the VA, Joe was finally given full disability, but was never compensated for backpay. Moral of the story: If you are, or were a soldier, make sure the VA has detailed records, and that you do too!!

In 1976, Joe met a nurse named Doreen at a hospital he was in for post traumatic stress syndrome. They are married to this day. Nowadays, Joe and Doreen live a quiet life in town. Joe is in all of the parades, and wears the uniform he was issued as a draftee. He has raised the flag on Memorial Day for 50 years without missing a single year.

Joe seems to have disdain for our current situation as a nation, and feels that $72 billion could be spent much more wisely than for a war on terror. However, if asked, he would gladly serve his country again. I am humbled to have been able to interview the oldest living veteran of WWII, and a man of such courage and honor that I have never felt, yet I did not only interview Joe. I interviewed Doreen as well. I could not have written this without her presence because of Joe's humility towards what he has done. By circumstance this is the first double interview I've done, and I wouldn't do it differently if I could. Thank you Doreen and Joe.

Clockwise: Joe and his brother, Frank in 1909; Currently; and in 1936 on game patrol near present-day Line Creek Road.

Who am I?

Guess who this local is! The first person to come into our office with the correct answer between July 5th & 16th will win the ever so cool Local Rag T-shirt!!!

I'm on the left. I've always loved a parade, and while freshman year at Carbon County High School seems like just yesterday, I'm having a milestone birthday this month.

The big clue for this 2004 "Who am I" is that she's always loved a parade. Indeed, she's been running our Home of Champions Rodeo parade for many years now! That is Glory Mahan on the left, posing with Shirley Roat.

Why two articles about Joe Papez? There were actually a lot more than that! We just ran out of space.

This Theatorium Halloween party was in 2004.

Haunted House Of Horrors
two nights of terror
Oct. 30, 6-9 & Oct. 31, 6-8
at the Red Lodge Theatorium
$3 per person
RLHS Fund Raiser
The thrills will chill you right down to your snow boots!

The Local Rag chatroom

May 2002

Charles Ringer, Artist

I recently had the pleasure of spending the morning with Charles Ringer, transformer of trash to treasure.

Q: What sort of art training do you have?

I'm self-taught artist. When I was 6 or 7 I'd walk two miles to the dump with my little red wagon. I'd come home with it heaped full of junk that I'd use for projects. My mom, Mary, would just scratch her head in amazement. Now I have a pick-up that I fill with junk and my mother still scratches her head in amazement. She's an artist too, so that helps her understand me a bit better.

I grew up in the Minnesota woods, and my education came from the natural environment surrounding me. At an early age I began noticing things like perfect light and I still take long walks to get ideas from nature. It's hard to make a living as an artist. It's been a long, unusual trip. Most artists require documents and trust education. I encourage people to trust their individuality and pay attention to their senses. Do what you like, not what peer pressure dictates to be good. Artwork doesn't have to match your sofa. Art means anything to anyone – it can't be taken literally, there are no words involved.

My view of life is, you're born, you experiment, you die. We're all a part of infinity. I'm a player so I'm gonna play good. We're all just standing on a planet flying through the universe.

Q: How did you end up in Joliet?

After leaving Minnesota, I spent two years at the University of Colorado. I left Colorado to pursue my career. My wife, Emily, and I traveled the country for three years, living on the road and working out of a mobile studio that I built.

We liked this area and in 1971 we bought a condemned wrecking yard in Joliet. We converted the existing buildings into studio, gallery and living space.

It took us six years to clear all the cars out of there. We had to cut each one up individually. We set up housekeeping in an upstairs apartment that was featured on Home & Garden Network's show "Extreme Homes".

A few years later, the building next door came up for sale so we bought it too. That's now the gallery. And we moved to a bigger house behind the gallery.

Q: When can people visit your gallery?

The gallery is open by appointment only, at least until summer, so call ahead. The gallery is a fun place; the important thing is that something grabs you.

Q: About how many sculptures do you create in a year?

A couple hundred pieces a year. I'm glad to know they are out there influencing people. There are hundreds of hours in each piece, but it actually took 53 years for each one to be built.

Q: So, the big Creature sculpture is pretty famous...

The Creature sculpture is now known locally as the Snowboard God. People leave offerings of food and beer, and sometimes toss change out their car windows at it. Or they'll leave snowboards and old skis.

Q: Aside from the sculptures outside your gallery, people are probably most familiar with your kinetic sculptures. They are in a lot of restaurants and galleries around Red Lodge..

I've sold about 90 pieces thanks to the Pollard. I appreciate their support. I bought one of my own kinetic sculptures for $1 at the Salvation Army. That was definitely a humbling experience.

The cool thing about kinetics is that there are no batteries to wear out. They're interactive artwork. Most people tell me they don't have room for one of my big kinetic sculptures. I tell them to move their TV out of the way, then they'll have room. And they'll enjoy watching it a lot more too.

I haven't increased prices for 10-15 years. I think everyone should be able to afford one of my sculptures. I'll take payments or barter. Once I traded a sculpture as a down payment on a piece of land. People buy my art because they like it, not because I'm some famous artist. At least they should.

Q: What is involved in creating one of your kinetic sculptures?

Each large sculpture has about 2700 welds; each weld has to be ground and polished. The hard part is the base. You have to allow for welding warpage, you gotta be sure you take your time and remember the mistakes of former sculptures. It doesn't do any good to get mad if you screw up, you just have to take it as a learning experience.

All my designs come from dreams – I don't make sketches or anything, I just dream the plans from start to finish, then I go to work on it. I always have to finish a sculpture once I start it or I can't sleep at night. I have to complete it to get it out of my head.

My definition of creativity is, "Hey, where did this come from?"

Q: Where do you get the materials you use?

I go to scrap sales, I never know what I want until I see it. You look at things out of context material-wise at a scrap yard; you're not confined by anything. I don't see stuff for what it really is, I'm a customizer. I took everything apart as a kid and put it back together as well or better than it started. I made lots of rockets, I had my own lab at 10 years old, I like to see sparks fly.

Sometimes I just have stuff donated to me. I have Joliet's old bridge; it's the oldest bridge in Carbon County and was built in 1901. They were gonna cut it up, I asked the county guys if I could have it, and a group in Billings want to use it as a pedestrian walkway on Montana Avenue. I'm trading them the bridge for a new Harley Davidson.

Q: What plans do you have for the future?

I'd like to do a sculpture garden that would be open in the summer. I want to build a catapult so when people get frustrated with their TVs or computers, they can bring them in and for a fee, I will smash the item of their aggravation to bits.

Q: Anything else?

I just feel very lucky to live in such a beautiful place and to have the title "artist" after my name and to never have had to have any other job.

June is named for the Roman goddess Juno (or Hera in the Greek pantheon). Juno was the wife of Jupiter and daughter of Saturn, and she is considered the protector of marriage and the households of married couples, which may have led to the tradition of June weddings.

June's birthstone is pearl, and the flower is the rose or honeysuckle.

In both leap years and non-leap years, no other month begins on the same day of the week as June.

June History in Montana

Jun 5, 1872—Congress creates the Flathead reservation for the Salish, Pend d'Oreille & Kootenai tribes

Jun 10, 1893—Joliet Post Office established: Maud Smith, Postmaster

Jun 13, 1805—Lewis & Clark reach the Great Falls of the Missouri

Jun 15, 1907—Gebo, MT (west of Fromberg) changes its name to Coalville

Jun 15, 1921—Chance Post Office (south of Belfry) closed

Jun 17, 1876—Battle of the Rosebud

Jun 22, 1898—Golden Post Office established between Belfry & Bridger: Joseph H. Graham, Postmaster

Jun 25, 1876—Battle of the Little Bighorn

Jun 29, 1935—Castagne Post Office (west of Roberts) closed

Jun 30, 1912—Golden Post Office (between Belfry & Bridger) closed

June 2003

Under the Sea – C-Map Systems, Inc

Next time you need to take high resolution underwater photographs, give Doug Smith at C-Map Systems a call. Located across from the Red Lodge Post Office, Doug moved here from Park City, Utah before the 2002 Olympics and chose Red Lodge because he always liked the area and because, "There is a good combination of things I like here. The airline service is good from Billings and it's a cheap place to live as second tier ski towns go. It doesn't matter where I'm at thanks to the internet. My hours tend to be long, but they are also flexible." His job requires a fair amount of traveling to California, Florida, New England and several times a year he takes trips to Europe, Australia and Saudi Arabia.

Doug and Braindead his dog, (who is second in command), provide video, imaging, navigation and instrumentation analysis by using robotic hi-res underwater digital cameras. The machines he supplies are used mainly by the petroleum industry for inspecting pipelines, the military for mine hunting and surveillance, the nuclear industry and by people doing research work – "the kind of stuff you see on the Discovery Channel." Not surprisingly, 100% of Doug's business comes from out of the area. "My closest customer is 800 miles away," he says. "My overseas customers love coming here so they can go to Yellowstone." He has an employee in Salt Lake City, various manufacturer reps who sell for him in the US and overseas, and machinists who do the actual building of the machines.

Doug Smith of C-Map Systems with second in command, "Braindead."

How does someone break into the world of Ocean Robotics? "When I was in college, I ran out of money as most students do, and I got a job in the North Sea doing sea floor survey work," he explains. "I did that for awhile and was also in the research branch of the Navy." He gets a lot of emails from kids asking how to get into the business and his advice for them is "If you don't want to starve, don't get a degree in Marine Biology – get an engineering degree. Most Marine Biologists end up working at McDonald's. It's one of the most unemployable careers a person can choose."

In his limited spare time, Doug enjoys skiing, playing golf, hunting and riding motorcycles. Experience some amazing underwater photographs at www.cmapsystems.com.

From theater to clowning,...and back

Red Lodge seems to attract artists and visionaries of all sorts, of whom Jeanne Thomas, a.k.a. *Pippi the Clown*, is an extraordinary example. "I've been a professional clown for, oh...20-some years I guess," she says. Her entertainment business, grown out of a life in theater, has taken her all over the United States as well as Japan, Egypt and Mexico. And this summer, she's moved to Red Lodge for good.

"I kept coming by here, traveling through the Park to do fairs in Montana, Wyoming and Idaho," she explains. After meeting "many wonderful, friendly people," she decided Red Lodge was perfect for her and began looking for a house—over 6 years ago. She finally bought one after looking for five years. "When I saw this, I just knew it was it. I bought it right away." And now she's finally able to move in and begin calling Red Lodge home.

She wants to continue her theatrical pursuits here, and last month offered an acting class at the Depot Gallery she feels very encouraged by. "I had such a great class, each of the students, by the end of the class was able to touch every one of us with their performance. They were great; I'd love to work with all of them."

Jeanne has taught theater in Florida, New York and San Francisco, and wants to get a professional theater troupe going here. "I've always had a dream to have a theater. And I just thought Red Lodge would be a perfect location for it. The arts industry fits so well with Montana's vision of itself."

"I've traveled all over the world; I've got the opportunity to work at the really big fairs—LA, but I found that I didn't want to be there. I wanted to be in small towns. I have wanted a town to love, and this is a size I can grasp."

PIPPI THE CLOWN

Jeanne began her professional life in theater. "My mom says I was always doing theater. I would organize the neighborhood kids and we'd do plays. When I hit twelve or thirteen, I started doing talent shows."

August 2004

The Local Rag art connection

June 2003

Carving out the Red Lodge life

By: Kari Mitchell

With an eye that sees luminous beauty in an old, discarded fencepost, woodworker David Ritter has carved out the ideal Red Lodge existence, making decorative bird decoys from old hardwood.

His distinct style of satiny smooth wings and a rough, textured body combines for a surprisingly elegant look. "I always hated sanding in wood shop classes in high school. So when I started, I tried making the whole thing smooth, but that was way too much sanding. Then, I tried doing it all textured and that hid the beauty of the wood. So my look has really evolved."

Dave makes only about 13 species of ducks and geese. "Since decorative decoys are not painted, you have to be able to identify them by profile." The lack of paint also allows him to highlight the character of the wood. "I like to work with knots—where you work a knot in, you get lots of color and swirls."

Like a kid showing off his favorite toy, Dave gets excited describing the history of his decoys. "A lot of the wood I use is from old barns in Ohio—the pioneers cut this stuff by hand. You can still see where two beams were joined together 100 years ago."

He points out axe marks in the unfinished wood and draws attention to names written on the ends of 10-inch square beams. "When a gallery gathers this wood, they write on it the name of the farm it came from." He includes all that history with the information that goes with his work, and takes pains to highlight imperfections in the wood, like knots and burls, axe chips and the occasional bullet. "I like

"I like to leave something natural in every decoy I make."

to leave something natural in every decoy I make."

Walking over to one of his many wood piles, we pick out an old juniper fencepost with a deep gnarl. Dave explains how he will use that "imperfection" as a selling point, and then shows off a beautifully finished piece in which the contrast looks stunning.

His tiny, dimly lit basement studio, no bigger than a park bench, is chaotic with the tools and smells of his trade. "To anyone else, this place is a mess, but I've been down here long enough, I can grab any tool I want any time I want it." Piles of wood set aside for head and neck pieces, body patterns by the dozen, power saws and grinders, files, drills, and—oh yes—decoys in various stages of creation are crammed into the tiny space.

"People always ask me how long it takes to make one, and I never know how to answer, because I'm always working on six or eight at a time. So it's two minutes here, six hours there." He does admit, however, that he puts about eight hours into one decoy, 80% of which is spent on the head.

He was running a photography studio in Crestline, Ohio when he first got the idea of carving decoys. "I would walk across the street to the antique shop and talk with the owner, and one day I saw a few antique decoys for sale for fifteen dollars each. I said 'Wow! That's a lot of money! I should do that.'" That was 27 years ago, and what began as a hobby has now become a way of life.

Dave moved to Red Lodge with his family in 1975 after spending the summer traveling and looking for a town to live in. "I'd always wanted to move out west, and we had narrowed our choices of towns down to three (of which Red Lodge was not one). I'd never been to Montana, but I had a friend in Roscoe, so while I was out here, I stopped in to see him. He told me 'You have to see Red Lodge before you make up your mind.' We took one look, and that was it." Dave has been here ever since.

He started in Red Lodge with a combination photography/wood carving studio on Main Street and eventually sold the photography half when both had grown to where he couldn't keep up. "When I sold the photography business to Merv [Coleman], I had about three years worth of back order on the decoys."

Now down from creating three decoys a week to just one, he considers himself semi-retired. "I work in the mornings until about noon, and then take the afternoon off. Take the dogs out, go fishing, bird hunting." His work can be seen these days at the Depot Gallery, Common Ground, the Coleman Gallery, and the Pollard.

LINDA ROGERS
OFF BROADWAY WORKSHOP
• COSTUMES • PROPS •
• SPECIAL EFFECTS MAKEUP •
406-446-9141
Oh yeah, I also do Alterations and just about anything sewn

September 1997

How sweet... a shotgun wedding! CONGRATS, KATE & MAREK! YOU REALLY DID IT! We wish you an eternity love and happiness together!

chat room

Sitting down and chatting it up

With the Friends of the Library banquet coming up, we stopped by to chat with Librarian Jodie Moore. (See calendar for banquet details.)

AR Since no one is interested in the fact that we are both Floridians....

JM Nobody.

AR We will talk about the library. One thing my hometown has in common with Red Lodge is that both towns have Carnegie Libraries. Is Andrew Carnegie still revered in library science circles? Is there a sense of what would have happened in small towns without him?

JM It is amazing what Andrew Carnegie did. He did something great for these small towns. You wonder if they would have come up with the money on their own. In Red Lodge there was a woman's club that was doing library services but they would have never been able to fund the building. Today though there are frustrations involved with it because the Carnegie Libraries were supposed to be very showy but they are not necessarily user friendly, definitely not handicapped accessible and very difficult to retro-fit. We have this entrance, which is very steep and very sudden and impossible to put a ramp up into it. It's a beautiful idea that he had -- that going into a library should be an experience of opening your mind, it should be grand, but it's horrible. It's not just the handicapped who struggle but mothers with strollers or people with a bum knee with a bag of books.

Librarian Jodie Moore has a few words for Andrew Carnegie.

AR So you've got a building you can't retrofit, there are more and more books, not a ton of room -- who decides what book stays and what book goes?

JM There are whole philosophies, sciences and textbooks dedicated to collections development and management. The layman's term is "weeding." The basics are how does the book look and has it been read? Maybe 30 years ago it was a best seller but if only one person has checked it out in two years, that's a problem. And then if a book is locally important you might keep that book too. The Red Lodge Library Board sets the policy for collection management and I carry out their policies. How-

May 2007

chat room
......still chatting

ever, it's a very difficult thing for many librarians to weed books.

AR Is it like going through your clothes closet and saying, "I might wear this again?"

JM Exactly. And it does happen, you have to face reality in a library this size, that in a community this well read, and this interested in life, we will never have every book that every person wants. That used to be a much bigger issue but with inter-library loans and the online accessibiltiy it's much easier to get books quickly. And for that reason it makes it a little easier to let go of these books you might have held on to before.

The other issue that has caused a lot of controversy in the last couple years is you have a lot of large library systems that are getting rid of Classics for the first time ever. They are saying, "You know what, no one has read this Hemingway in three years, we don't need it." But if you put an article in the paper saying we just got rid of this book you're going to get phone calls saying it's unacceptable. Although the librarian does the weeding, what stays and what go is entirely in the hands of the patrons -- if they are taking a book out it will stay.

AR Any thoughts on why we own so many books?

JM I think there's an emotional thing, a physical thing. We are attached to them. A book can hold a memory in way e-mail never will. For me, a book, I hold it and think back to where I was when I read it, who I was then, and what I was thinking at the time. It's more than words on a page, it becomes the experience, it becomes a very deep connection. I think they are just unique. Think about it, you fall asleep with it in bed.

AR Would you have a thought on a *One Town, One Book* for Red Lodge?

JM Someone like Stanley Gordon West has been very popular, he wrote *Blind Your Ponies* which has to do with small town high school basketball which, for a lot of Montanans, rings true for them. I think a book like that would have a fairly big impact. At the same time a lot of people have already read it. There's this Mark Twain book about classic books, it's like "A classic is something everyone wants to have read and nobody wants to read." And I think the book club books and *One Town, One Book* choices have the same sort of feeling for people. They want to say they have read it and they want to be involved in the discussion but at the end of the day very few people want to actually read the book. Also, it seems like in the selection of those books, while the committee says they want to pick something local, they usually pick something further away and further back in time and I think that's because they don't want to pick a local, current author because that puts them on the spot in some ways.

So for all those reasons, I think of Stanley Gordon West because he's close but not too close.

Ed. note: Coincidentally, Stanley Gordon West will be at Red Lodge Books on Saturday, May 5

The Local Rag
hangin' out

January 2003

The world accordian to JK
By: Chuck Sallade

This month I thought I'd write the living history article about somebody who's always lived here. Following the Hilderman's suggestion, I came up with a person known not only to most Red Lodge residents, but also to people all over the country who have passed through this area.

When I walked into JK's Variety Store, owned by Joe Kosorok, I was welcomed like an old friend with the "Love Me Waltz" played by JK on his Gabbarnelli accordion. When he finished, he played me a bonus song that was a traditional Yugoslavian polka. His fingers are molded to this instrument as if it were an extension of his arms.

JK was born in 1916, and will soon celebrate his 87th birthday. His son and his attorney told him he needs to slow down, so even though he's taken their advice, he still is quite active.

Joe was in the U.S. Army 77th Division in Camp Roberts, California, when the war ended in 1945. He was scheduled to go over to Japan as part of the American Occupation Army, but was discharged to work in the Smith Mine instead. He was awarded medals for good conduct, honorable discharge and marksmanship and proudly wears the medals on his hat. As a matter of fact, his marksmanship was so excellent that by aiming a few degrees high of his target on the firing range, he was single-handedly responsible for scaring the Japanese into surrendering due to his bullets landing in their front yards! His honorable discharge was sped up because the Captain at Camp Roberts was his neighbor from Red Lodge. It's a small world.

JK married his beautiful wife, Mary Anne, in 1941. They had three children, Mike, Nick, and Judy. After many years of marriage, Mary Anne passed away 20 years ago. JK has nine grandchildren and two great-grandchildren.

JK's advice… eat right, live healthy and not take for granted what you have.

JK was a 1934 graduate of Red Lodge High School, (which was located where the city pool is now), and has a photo of his graduating class. He said the class had 74 students, and most of them are gone now. Surviving are Eddy Weydt, Erma Doty (maiden name), Mrs. Walter Bloom, and Della Cobetto to name a few.

Joe feels very thankful for what he has. His store, which he opened 26 years ago, has provided for him and his family. He was an employee for Pepsi Co for 18 years prior to opening his store. Upon reflection of the years past, he says he's a very wealthy man. Not in a monetary sense, but because he has his health, his family, and his music. His advice to me was to eat right, live healthy and not take for granted what you have. That is what he calls wealth. Pretty sound advice, if you ask me. By the way, he also boasts that he has beautiful legs. Smooth as butter cream. I've seen them, and it's true.

When the interview was over, I asked him if he had anything he'd like to add. He did. He wanted to thank Red Lodge and its people for supporting his business all these years.

Also, his birthday is January 8th, so stop in to wish him a happy 87th. Happy Birthday, Joe!

The Local Rag
chat room

July 2003

One big reason we all love a parade

Jon Metcalf has been our Home of Champions Parade announcer for the last several years, and he talked with us a little about what it's like to put on the biggest show in town.

What got you into announcing the parades?
When I offered to do it, Glory said, you know Jon, it's a commitment. And I said that I was willing to commit my 2nd, 3rd & 4th of July. It's one of those things I'm willing to do to help out our community. People do different things, this is what I do. It's just that sense of community involvement, being able to give back.

What do you like most about the parades?
You know, you see your 4-H, you see the Cub Scouts, but the fun part is, you see people who actually will come to Red Lodge to have a family reunion, and participate in our parade. And that's really awesome. It's like, "…and here comes the Springer family reunion…." What a thing to do on the 4th of July! And of course, Red Lodge—the town of all parades.

Joe Papez is our Grand Marshal this year. What is that position all about?
It's an honorary position, to honor that person for what they've done for the community, the area, and in Joe's sense, in his dedication to our armed services.

The Grand Marshals that Glory Mahan arranges to have in our parade are outstanding. Joe Papez, he's a WWII vet. And he of course doesn't like to be made out to be a hero, but he is. I have a lot of respect for the man. 97 year old, and if you were up at our Memorial Day service and watched him hoist the flag…I mean, talk about a tear jerker!

How do you know the order of the floats?
As they sign up for the parade, I have a chunk of laminate, and we tape all the entries to it. So then we've got this big board with all the numbers on them, and as they're coming, D.G. [Harsha, the spotter] points to them and I read whatever blurb there is for them. It takes a little doing, if you have people who want to dance or perform, and they stop, all of a sudden, there's holes in the parade, and you have to start creating fillers. So thinking on your feet is one of the fun things.

What do you talk about during those holes?
About all the different events coming up in Red Lodge. And you've almost got 52 plugs to make, because you know darn well there's something going on almost every weekend in Red Lodge. And then you invite people to go visit the Nature Center, stop in at the Arts Guild, go to the Peaks to Plains Museum. There's countless things to continue to talk about. In a town like Red Lodge, it's easy!

It's a chance to recognize this town and what it puts out. And we're celebrating this great country's birthday, so let's make it good time!

Has the weather gotten dicey on you?
Last year it was pretty outrageous because I had the duster on, and the water was pouring off my cowboy hat like a downspout. And then it lifted right before parade time. I mean, we're talking 5 minutes before it was going to start. It was torrential. But the parade will go on, no matter what!

Where would you say is the best place to watch the parade from?
Anywhere you can find a piece of curb. Absolutely.

Any last thoughts?
I encourage anyone and everyone to jump in and lend a hand putting the parades on. It's a great group of people; They always have a little pre-function get together to celebrate that they're doing it again. To them, it's 'Hey, this is show time!'

The Local Rag
hangin' out

March 2003

...with Millicent Scanlin
By: Chuck Saliadé

Sometime around 1880 Millicent Scanlin's father immigrated to NYC from a town in Germany callled Amburg in Bavaria. He was around twenty years old. He was a machinist by trade, and went right to work in NYC. After 1 1/2 years he moved to New Britain, CT.

Millicent's mother came to the states in 1890. She was a maid/cook working in a castle where she served barons. She came from Aalan in Wurtenburg, Germany. Her older brother sent her money from the states to pay her way over. She arrived in NYC, and moved to Newark, NJ to live with her brother. Shortly thereafter, she also moved to New Britain, CT, and worked as a nanny in the home of some local factory owners. One of the children had the name Millicent, which Millie thinks is where her name came from.

In 1894 or 1895, Millicent's father's first wife died. He quickly remarried to Millicent's mother, making her instant housewife to his three children. The first child they had together was Mattilda, born in 1896, and the youngest was born in 1914, and is still living. Millicent was born in 1911, one of nine siblings.

Millicent went to normal school for two years to become a teacher, then to the University of Maine for summer credits in Bangor. This is where she met her husband Don, who had one year to go in seminary, and U of M. Upon completion he had received two degrees: one from each school. He became a minister of the Congregational Church in Ellsworth, Maine.

Shortly after the attack on Pearl Harbor they went to Kennebunk, Maine, then to Minnesota, where their daughter Elizabeth (Betsy to us) was born. They also lived in Circle, MT, Goshen, IN, Billings, MT and Red Lodge, MT. Millie taught first grade in Billings for 15 years, as well as preschool at her home. Her four children graduated from Billings West.

They came to Red Lodge for a second time in 1976, to retire. It was then that Millie became so involved in the Senior Citizen Center. In 1976, it was new, and she was the first director of operations there. After that she became the cashier, which she did for the next twenty years.

Don and Millie's children are as follows: Steve, who after leaving the naval reserves, went to law school in Boise, ID; Tom, who is a teacher of music, and math; Carolyn who is a business owner in Bozeman; and Betsy who is an attorney in Red Lodge.

Millicent - 5 years old in 1916

Millicent dressed in her German costume holding baked goodies during a recent Festival of Nations.

She also has 7 grandchildren, and two great grandchildren.

Millicent takes up her time nowadays at the Senior Citizen Center, knitting, crocheting, and tatting. She also has quite a green thumb, and is adept at raising houseplants. Coincidentally, when she needs more room in her home to raise more, she gives some to Lori and me so we can kill them in our window sills. Keep the plants coming Millie.

Anne Laird Photography
Weddings
Portraits
Fine Art Prints
Nature & Wildlife

Artwork will be on display at Bridge Creek during the month of March

406-446-2168 annelairdphoto@twoalpha.net

The Local Rag
chat room

June 2004

Augie nears 10 years of skiing year-round

He may not care for being compared to the likes of Madonna, Cher and Prince, but it's tough ignoring the similarity. Does Augie have a last name? Having a made a reputation for himself as a dedicated year-round skier, he really doesn't need more than one. We caught up to him on his regular stool at the Bearcreek Saloon, drinking the usual Kokanee beer and making plans to not ski Memorial Day weekend.

You say you're not going up skiing this weekend?
There's too many people up there for me.

Have you been up high yet?
I went up Rock Creek and scouted.

How's it look?
It looks bad. I went up to the bottom of Reefer Ridge, and it might be skiable, but it'll be a pain to hump out. It would have to be done by this week, unless they get snow that'll hold.
Compared to last year, there's just no snow. Last year I skied Reefer with friends two weeks after Memorial Day.

You've skied every month for, what, 116 months running?
115. June will be 116. October will be ten years.

What's the toughest month to ski?
None: I know where to find snow. October is the toughest — if you don't get it early, you have to hope the mountain gets snow and hike that, since they close the pass.

When did you first ski this country?
I skied Big Mountain in sixth grade. Big Sky the first year it opened. But I'm getting too old to keep track.

How many sick days have you taken to ski?
Zero. Basically everyone at work knows that I have the 18-inch rule. I'm not sick, it's just a vacation day that wasn't quite scheduled. But I did miss the big Good Friday dump of '98 or '99 — I had a salesperson who took off Easter weekend so I had to work. And in '91, the year they didn't open because they had too much snow, on the last weekend of the year, I'd driven up here all the way from Billings.

Do you ski other places?
All the time. Every March I take a week to disappear around my birthday. Which is March 14, by the way, and I haven't been in your listing ever since Lou sold the paper. I blame Tim: his brother's birthday is the same day, but somehow he never gets me in the listing.
I ski nine days straight, wherever there's snow. Salt Lake, Big Mountain, Grand Targhee. I start and end in Red Lodge, make a loop.

What's the best place to ski on top of the pass?
It depends on what you want. Rock Creek headwall, Gardner headwall. I ski Hidden because it's easy, convenient. But Reefer Ridge is probably the best: a good full day. Wherever there's snow is always the best skiing. I'm not fussy.

You hang out at Bearcreek a lot. Why?
Good people, good food, good place to hide.

How long since someone has called you by the name that's listed in the phone book?
Usually it's my mom. Nobody out here calls me by that name. If they don't call and ask for Augie, no one's home.

You're generally kinda quiet; are you ready for the fame of being featured in the Rag?
I was on CNN, playing soccer in Billings. Had my do-rag on, was interviewed at the Big Sky State Games. I got a call from an old disk jockey I used to work with, in Colorado Springs now, said, "You're on Headline News! You're on every hour!" And six months later, Thailand Joe moved back to Billings from New York City and said, "I saw you on CNN!" I'm world-famous now. I've already had my ten seconds of fame.

The Local Rag chatroom

July 2002

Sam Hoffmann, Brewer

All of us here at The Local Rag like beer. And of all the beer in town, we like Sam's beer the best. And since it's March and Sam is sponsoring Winter Carnival, it made us think about beer, which made us think about Sam, and we needed to interview someone, so we chose Sam. And not just because we like his beer. But we do like his beer. So we sat down to find out what else we like about Sam. Here's what we found out:

Q: Where can we get Red Lodge Ales?
A: It's sold in Red Lodge, Cody, Billings, Bozeman, Yellowstone, Cooke City and all points in between.

Q: How long have you been brewing beer in Red Lodge?
A: We'll celebrate our 4th year in April. Everyone should be sure to come in and join the Sam's Taproom Brewers Club so you can get invited to the Anniversary party in April. We'll have live music, lots of food and beer. I'll be releasing a brand new beer for the party. I have a full-time Brewmaster working for me now. His name is Tim Mohr and he has a degree from UC-Davis.

Q: Oh, I remember that party last year. That was WAY too much fun! Last month when I asked Tom Kohley from Beartooth Mapping, (one of the 40 Under 40), what organizations he was involved with, he named Sam's Taproom Brewer's Club. What does it take to become a member?
A: Well, you pay $20 a year and you get $2 pints of beer and $5 growler refills.

Q: Why weren't you one of the 40 Under 40?
A: I just didn't think about it. Maybe next year. Why weren't you in it?

Q: Because I'm not under 40.
A: Maybe they could have 45 Under 45.

Q: I'd fit into that category. You're pretty busy in Red Lodge. What all are you involved with?
A: I'm on the Board for the Boys & Girls Club, I'm sponsoring Winter Carnival, I'm in the Chamber and Jaycees, I sponsored a team for the Town Series. I like to support and encourage area artists by displaying their work...

Q: And you're one of Red Lodge's most eligible bachelors. What a dream guy....you make your own beer! And really good beer! And Sam's Taproom has the coolest bathroom in town.
A: I'd like to encourage anyone with retro posters or memorabilia from '80's TV shows to bring stuff in to add to the collection in the bathroom. If I get some things I don't have, I'd give the person a beer.

Q: My daughter loves your bathroom. I shouldn't probably say that, since she's under age. Sam's Taproom seems like a pretty kid-friendly place, as drinking establishments go, though.
A: It's not illegal to have kids in bars in Montana, just so they don't drink. We have root beer and other pop. And the fact that we limit everyone to 3 beers means we don't get a real rowdy crowd in here. The Taproom customers aren't people just coming in to get drunk, they're folks who just want a good beer and some conversation with their friends.

Q: So are you willing to give brewery tours?
A: Yes, although I think most of the people in Red Lodge have already seen it. But if I'm around, I'm always happy to show people around.

Q: What sort of plans do you have for the future?
A: I've been working with the manufacturing councils and engineers to look into the possibility of bottling my ales, and I'm thinking about building a grain

silo for bulk malt. The wheels are always turning for new business expansion ideas.

Q: It would be great to be able to buy Red Lodge Ales by the 6-pack. The growlers are nice, but then you're committed to finishing it once you start. Not a HUGE problem, but , well, I'm babbling. Is it 4:00 yet? Can I get a Glacier Ale?
A: You still have a few hours to wait.

Q: OK, I'll be patient. Anything else?
A: I'd like to thank everyone for their support over the years. Red Lodge is a great town with a lot of really fun, really nice people living here.

Q: And some really good beer.

The Local Rag bizness

July 2002

The Village Shoppe - family business, family clothing

In the 1920's Mr. & Mrs. Levine owned the building that was then known as Hoffman's Department Store. When Mr. Levine died, his wife and son, Bobby, ran the shop. Mrs. Levine suffered from Parkinson's Disease and her son would push her around town in a shopping cart.

McCarty's took the business over in 1975. They purchased the building and all of the inventory, including sport coats with toothpicks in the pockets which were left there by Bobby when he'd wear the jackets off the rack. Although the inventory wasn't quite up to the standard McCarty's expected, they weren't happy to learn that Bobby would sneak in and take bits and pieces of it out, then push it down the street in the same shopping cart.

They sold the store in 1996 and recently acquired it again. The newly renovated facade is a historic recreation of how it might have originally looked.

Marge McCarty and her daughter, Beth, are familiar faces in Red Lodge. Marge grew up in Roberts and attended all 12 years of school there. She and Beth are excited to be operating the business again and the response from the community has been very positive.

The Village Shoppe offers quality clothing at reasonable prices. A large range of sizes is available and the clothing selections are made with families and locals in mind. Special orders are gladly accepted and Marge and Beth encourage locals to offer inventory suggestions. Along with socks and underwear, The Village Shoppe carries clothing by Wrangler, Levi, Carhartt, Filson and Basics to name a few well-known brands. Anyone purchasing Wrangler jeans prior to the July 4th rodeo will be eligible to win free rodeo tickets.

After you find the perfect outfit, Kathy Sandine is available by appointment to color coordinate your make-up.

The Grand Re-opening will be held in July with goodies and prizes. During the summer months, The Village Shoppe will be open Monday through Friday from 9 am to 8 pm, Saturday from 9 am to 5:30 pm, and from 11am - 5 pm on Sundays.

The Local Rag chatroom

July 2002

This month we're visiting with Leo and Joan Wilson, the minds behind the Beartooth Rally and the Iron Horse Rodeo.

Q: How long have you been in Red Lodge?
Joan: I came here when I was 9 months old. I'm almost a local!
Leo: I've only been here 27 years.

Q: How many members are in the rodeo association?
Just the two of us. But we have about 40 volunteers that we dearly appreciate. 99% of our volunteers are non-bikers. It's hard to find bikers to volunteer because they want to be participating in the events.

Q: How can people sign up to volunteer?
Stop by the Harley store at 213 North Broadway or call 446-9856. We'll be sure to find a fun job for everyone.

Q: How early do you start working on the rodeo?
Just like that other rodeo, it's a year 'round deal. Every day we're making lists and crossing things off that we need to have done.

Q: How did the rally begin?
Leo: I used to enter and participate in biker rodeos and realized that Red Lodge was a great place for an event like this. I've lived here for 27 years and have ridden many roads but none are as cool as the Beartooth Highway. It's the best ride in the world.
Joan: We also wanted to create an event that would give back to the community. We thought this would be a great way to promote Red Lodge.

Q: Will any big name riders be here this year?
Well, we invited John Cougar Mellancamp, maybe someday he'll surprise us by showing up. Max Baucus is also invited to participate in the parade. Both John and Max are avid Harley riders. Willie G. Davidson was here last year.

Q: Is he related to Harley Davidson?
He IS Harley Davidson.

Q: What's the average attendance during the week?
We guess about 5000 from Wednesday prior to Wednesday following, but it's like counting ants. Our first year here we had 90 riders for the Poker Run and last year we had 849. It just gets mo' bigger every year. What we do know is that according to a survey done several years ago, this group spends in excess of $1 million dollars during the week. Plus last year 3 people stopped in and told us that while they were here they bought property in the area.

Q: So it doesn't sound like these visitors are here to just to make noise and wreck the town?
These people are gathering to have fun and ride in our area.

Q: It sounds like some people would be happier if you would keep all the events at the rodeo grounds. Have you ever considered doing that?
It would make things 10 times easier if we could do that, but the local business people want us to keep it in town. If we had all the events at the rodeo grounds, all the money would go right into my pocket. As it is now, the money is spread around.

Q: What do you do with the money you make off the rodeo?
Most of it goes back into next year's rodeo, but we give a lot of it to various causes. We've raised money for cancer and accident victims, the Red Lodge Rodeo Association, the Chamber of Commerce, the Police Department for overtime, the Junior Rodeo Association, we're raising money now through our Harley V-Rod Raffle to build bathrooms at the rodeo grounds, we've given money to the Christian Brothers Motorcycle Club, the Lion's Club, the Red Lodge Cheerleaders and so many more we can't remember all of them.

Q: How do you think most of Red Lodge feels about the Beartooth Rally?
I'd say 99% of the businesses support it and 75% of the locals support it. It helps everyone either directly or indirectly. We've talked to people in Sturgis, and their suggestion is to plan your vacation or just go away for the weekend if the rumbling disturbs you. We get a lot of support from the Red Lodge Chamber. This year they're sponsoring a breakfast for the bikers.

Q: What about non-bikers? What fun will they have at an event like this?
The street dance is way fun and the Iron Horse Rodeo is fun for the whole family.

Q: What future plans do you have?
Eventually I'd like our Saturday street dance to turn into a big name concert out at the rodeo grounds. I'd like to see Tom Petty or somebody perform.

Q: Who's playing for the street dance this year?
The Jared Stewart Band.

Q: Good band.
I know.

Q: Have there been any problems with the law enforcement in the area?
This is the 8th year of the rally and we've never had any official complaints to the sheriff or the police. The cops have been very cool; the bikers have appreciated them.

Q: What else?
We'd just like people to know that we've added extra security this year. Some people get the idea that biker rallys are a bunch of guys wanting to fight. They hear about things like what happened in Laughlin and think it will happen here but this rally is unique. The people gather for the great riding experience, and because Red Lodge is such a fun town to visit.

And we'd like to thank the local businesses and motels for their support. At this point, all rooms in a 50 mile radius are booked for that weekend. Montana Connections booked all of their units and so did Red Lodge Reservations. We have a list here at the store of people who are willing to rent space that weekend. Call us if you have room for somebody.

Also we could not have kept this going without the corporate sponsorships like Budweiser and Jim Beam and all the local sponsors including Beartooth Custom Builders, Peder & Maren Nees, Crazy Creek, Snow Creek, Greg Zeiler at the Snag and many more local sponsors.

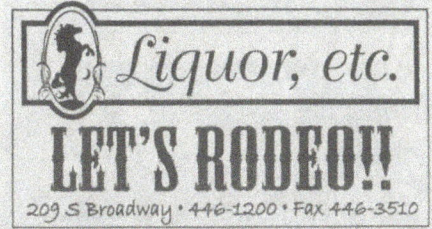

July was renamed around 400BC, for Julius Caesar, who was born July 13. It was originally known as Quintilis in Latin, because it was the fifth month of the year in the ancient Roman calendar.

The birthstone of July is the ruby. Its flower is the larkspur.

On leap years, July always starts on the same day of the week as January. On non-leap years, it starts on the same day of the week as April.

July History in Montana

July 2, 1965—Nye Post Office closes (transfered to Absarokee)
July 3, 1993—Ismay, MT becomes Joe, Montana
July 6, 1901—Morris Post Office (now Roscoe) established
July 22, 1983—Luther Post Office closes (transfered to Red Lodge)
July 24, 1897—Grebo Post Office established (West of Fromberg)
July 25, 1806—Captain William Clark pauses in his trip down the Yellowstone River to carve his name in what is now known as Pompey's Pillar.
July 27, 1901—Riverview Post Office established (South of Belfry)
July 29, 1865—A man in Helena shoots a camel believing it was a moose. The camel was part of a pack train used for entertaining, and the camel's owner demands payment for it.
July 31, 1959—Washoe Post Office closes

April 2007

Ray Kuntz learns to love the wind

By Anne Rood

Ray Kuntz admits he's been a "lifelong tinkerer". Well, he said, at least since the age of three when a shock from an electric socket "sent me flying across the room". His wife, Lea Page, thinks he's great to have on road trips because he can fix any car problem with zip ties and "things he finds in his pocket."

As a subscriber to *MAKE Magazine: Technology on Your Time* (basically DIY for garage, basement and backyard projecteers), Ray was thumbing through its fifth edition in 2006 and came across an article on building a wind-powered generator. The authors encouraged looking for parts in "your local hardware store and junk yard" and that was all the encouragement Ray needed.

The major parts were the 5 amp treadmill motor, acquired through eBay, a 21-foot steel pipe, 8" x 2' PVC pipe for the blades and then various mounting screws, locks, washers, turnbuckles, elbows, nipples and a floor flange to attach the motor to the steel pipe. Wire – copper, red and black – runs through the pole to a battery bank on the ground. A diode – it keeps power going in one direction – ensures the power goes to the charge the battery and doesn't draw it away from the battery. The pole is secured about a foot and a half into the ground and at the base a "hinge" created by a small pipe inside a slightly larger one allows for raising and lowering for any needed repairs. As a "tail" Ray used left over barn siding, about one square foot, attached to the motor by a about a foot long piece of square steel.

Ray cut the three blades from the PVC in cylindrical sections that gently curve thereby "scooping up" the wind and increasing efficiency. He cut the blades with a jigsaw (that he broke, but it was borrowed from brother Tom) and then painted the blades red to reduce the ultraviolet degradation.

Presently Ray is generating 20-100 watts, depending on the wind speed, but enough to charge his batteries for fencing and tractors. While on eBay he bought four more treadmill motors and hopes to have at least that many wind generators working in the near future. Ray figures with very little supplement he can power his 2500 square foot home. He heats his home in winter primarily with wood. Not bad for what Ray

figures is a $150 weekend, or two, project plus this resident of the East Bench says watching his wind generator "makes me appreciate the wind."

MERRY CHRISTMAS FROM PAT'S PLUMBING & HEATING • 446-3977

The Local Rag • December 2004 • Page 34

CHAPTER 5
Bathroom humor

Are you easily offended?

Then dude, put this book down and read something else! That's right: step away from the book.

For being a bunch of supposed grownups, the various editors of the Local Rag certainly managed to drag our minds down into the gutter (or the toilet) a lot.

In this case, we were helped by Maryvette Labrie, who designed a whole series of toilet-centric ads for Pat's Plumbing, most of them featuring Tom Teini, who was — for some reason — willing to put up with this.

People absolutely loved the Pat's Plumbing ads. For many readers, it was the first thing they looked for when they opened up a new issue of the Rag.

August 2004

April 2000

WARNING: NOT FOR THE WEAK OF STOMACH.
It's been four years since we last ran this list, and each April Fool's issue, it's requested. So, by popular demand:

The Poopie List

Ghost Poopie -- That's the kind where you feel it come out, have poop on the toilet paper, but there is no poopie in the toilet.

Clean Poopie -- The kind where you Poop it out, see it in the toilet, but there is nothing on the toilet paper.

Wet Poopie -- The kind where you wipe your butt 50 times and it still feels unwiped so you have to put toilet paper between your butt and your underwear so you don't ruin them with chocolate stains.

Second Wave Poopie -- It happens when you're done, you've pulled your pants up to your knees, and you realize that you have to go some more.

Brain-Hemorrhage Through-Your-Nose-Poopie or the Pop-A-Vein-In-Your-Forehead Poopie -- The kind where you strain so much to get it out that you practically have a stroke.

Richard Simmons Poopie -- The kind where you poop so much that you lose 10 pounds.

Corn Poopie -- Self-explanatory.

Lincoln Log Poopie -- The kind of poopie that is so huge that you're afraid to flush the toilet without breaking it into a few pieces with your toilet brush.

Drinker's Poopie -- That is the kind of poop you have the morning after a long night of drinking. It's most noticeable trait is the skidmarks left on the bottom of the toilet.

"Gee, I Wish I Could Poopie" Poopie -- You want to poop, but all you do is sit on the toilet cramped and fart a few times.

Spinal Tap Poopie -- Where it hurts so much coming out that you swear it's leaving you sideways.

Wet Cheeks Poopie or the Power Dump -- That's the kind that comes out of your ass so fast that your butt cheeks get splashed with the toilet water.

Mexican Food Poopie -- A class all its own!!

April 2007

The average library book has been read in the bathroom by *seven* different people.

Red Lodge BOOKS

Get your own copy!

January 2008

Mignon's *Gifts & Flowers*

Keeping the Holidays Fresh!

11 N. Broadway • 446-1100 • 1-877-4MIGNON
We send worldwide • 1-800-FLOWERS

December 2007

The Local Rag
books, movies, music, etc.

Local author does WHAT?

When this article ran in February of 2004, nobody imagined that I would end up as editor/publisher of the Local Rag a few years later.

Many authors try their hand at changing genres. A novelist may write a nonfiction book, or a historian put out a cookbook. In Red Lodge, however, you never know what's going to happen.

Local author and bookstore owner Gary Robson has been writing technical nonfiction for years. He's produced books about assistive technology for deaf people, a career book for court reporters, a specialized Internet book, a handful of computer manuals, and the 2nd edition of a booklet about the Smith Mine disaster. He has also written hundreds of articles for magazines, newspapers, Web sites, and even the World Book Encyclopedia.

Now, however, Robson has decided to break into children's books with a story called *Who Pooped in the Park?*, a kids' guide to scats and tracks. The book is published by Farcountry Press and illustrated by Elijah Brady Clark from Bozeman.

"Yes, there are lots of other books about scats and tracks," Robson said, "but I wanted to write one that was *fun*. I want kids to get excited about learning." The book tells the story of an 8-year-old boy named Michael who is terrified of bears. He goes to Yellowstone Park (Glacier and Grand Teton editions are also available) with his parents and his older sister, Emily.

As they hike through the park, their parents teach them about the animals without ever getting close enough to be scared. Michael and Emily learn what the animals have been eating by poking through their scat (poop), and how they move from their tracks (footprints). They guess how big a bear is by the scratch marks on a tree, and find an elk shed (discarded antler). There's even trivia called "the straight poop" scattered throughout the book.

All three editions of the book come out on February 21, and Robson will be at Red Lodge Books all day long serving up special treats and signing books. During the following weeks, he'll be signing at other area stores, reading at schools, and doing radio interviews.

Lodgie Award Winners
- **Poetry** – Chuck Murphy, for *Christ and the Cowboy*
- **History** – Fay Kuhlman, now deceased, for *The Darkest Hour*
- **Other Local & History** – Sam Travers, for *Christmas in the Old West*
- **Children's** – Kenneth Thomasma, for his *Amazing Indian Children* series
- **Fantasy & Science Fiction** – Christopher Paolini, for *Eragon*
- **General Fiction** – Diane Smith, for *Pictures from an Expedition* and *Letters from Yellowstone*
- **Mystery** – Jamie Harrison, for her Montana mysteries
- **Western Fiction** – Terry Johnston, now deceased, for his *Plainsmen* and mountain man series
- **General Nonfiction** – Tom Flaherty, for *Jocks & Socks*
- **Nature & Guidebooks** – Gary Ferguson, for *Hawks Rest* and other books

A "house ad" for the Local Rag itself that ran in February of 2002.

February 2005

May 2005

This photo appeared in June of 2008. Slow news month? No, just an editor who can't pass up a poop joke.

Look carefully at the bush to the left of this Yellowstone outhouse. Yep. That's a mailbox. Is that where you'd want YOUR mail to go?

ROUND MAN REVIEW

Random Restroom Review

This month's review might seem like a load of crap to you, but think about this: according to an article that I recently read, people actually make decisions on what event, restaurant, or nightclub they are going to patronize based on the restroom. Just to prove my point, ask your wife, husband, or friend how many times they have thought about "functions" they have attended or places such as restaurants, nightclubs, etc. they may frequent based on the restrooms. I think you will be very surprised to find out it is often!

I personally know many establishments that spend huge dollars to get people through their doors with specials, promotions, and various other gimmicks and then lose them to a lackluster lavatory. I thow there are many issues to worry about, like elections, world peace, starvation, etc. But damn it, man, let's put some thought to the porcelain.

I know of some local restrooms with stainless steel walls and a center drain for hosing down the place (that's what I'm talkin' about), let's get those stall doors fixed and put a lock on the door — remember the old saying about getting caught with your pants down? Just once, don't you wish you had a soft cushy roll all to yourself instead of the oval-shaped dispenser that, after searching for 10 minutes for the end of the roll you finally manage to pull out one tiny 1-ply square before it automatically tears?

I ask that all business owners take a break, run to their bathrooms, sit a spell, and ask themselves: "Is my restroom a contender for the 3P award?" That's right, the famous 3P award (perfectly polished porcelain). So let's "wipe" out one more problemfor you, the overworked business owner, and give yourselft a chance to get "flush," break out the solid oak and the Italian marble tile, and you may find that royalty will frequent your establishment to sample your wares and sneak an opportunity to sit upon the throne. Remember: I could tell you my personal pick for the famous 3P award, but only certain people are "privy" to that information.

~Jim Kujala

The September 2004 "Round Man Review" used up Jim's entire year's allocation of puns in one article.

Bogart's has new menus, redecorated interior, renovated bar, and new kitchen equipment. What's everyone talking about? The new bathrooms.

When the Local Rag reviewed Bogart's in June of 2008 after the remodel, we made sure to review everything important, not just the food.

Where do you read *your* Local Rag?

Your intrepid *Local Rag* editor will go to the ends of the world (or in this case, Hendy Woods State Park in California) to find you a safe place to go.

Yes, we are aware that there's a whole chapter in this book dedicated to where people read their Local Rags, but this one seemed to belong here.

They claim that the "smiling poo" emoji, which can be found on most smart phones these days, is a Japanese good luck symbol. Can you believe this crap?

Indoor Plumbing

You don't have to give up everything for Lent.

Pat's Plumbing & Heating
446-3977

March 2005

April 2005

COSMO PLUMBER
Premiere Issue — KEEPING THE BROWN DOWN

- 10 NEW WAYS TO WORK THE UPPER ARMS USING THE TOOLS YOU LOVE
- MAKEUP TIPS FROM A PRO: ENHANCE THE CRACK!
- Old Parts? Design These Great Gifts
- QUIZ: What Does Your Truck Say About You?
- TOUCH UP YOUR ROOTS CLEAN THAT SEWER LINE

APRIL 2005

Pat's Plumbing & Heating
446-3977

CHAPTER 6
Food & Drink

In 2015, the Red Lodge Convention & Visitors Bureau surveyed 1,100 people, asking what they loved about Red Lodge. Of course there were plenty of people talking about skiing, the Beartooth Pass, and the stunning natural beauty into which Red Lodge is nestled.

But visitors and locals alike had something else high on their list: food and drink. The Local Rag's editors and writers also share a love of eating and drinking, so there's been plenty of coverage of our area's bars and restaurants, as well as a parade of great recipes for the do-it-yourself crowd (more of those can be found in the next chapter: Columns & Regular Features).

Here's your Red Lodge trivia for the day: the town of Red Lodge has more bars per capita than any other city in Montana. Why is that? Because back when the allocation of liquor licenses was determined, Red Lodge's population was well over double what it is today, and that's what each town's allocation is based on.

March 2002

Eat Food, Drink Wine...It's just that simple at Bridge Creek

Bridge Creek flows into Boulder River near Big Timber. Anne and Peter Christ met there and it was on a footbridge on that small creek where Peter proposed to Anne. When they decided to open a restaurant, they chose to name it after that special spot.

In February of 1995, Peter and Anne moved to Red Lodge so Peter could manage the dining room at The Pollard. They saw it as a good opportunity and a steppingstone to further Peter's career, and planned to stay in Red Lodge for maybe a year. They were both surprised to fall in love with the town and community. Never feeling so connected to a town before, they decided to dig in and set up roots here.

Peter was ready to open his own restaurant and bought The Ranch House Restaurant on April 1st, 1997. After gutting and remodeling the building, the original Bridge Creek was open for business the following June. The small location behind Red Lodge Drug wasn't big enough to meet the demand for receptions and larger gatherings so Peter and Anne began searching for a larger facility. Other available spaces were inadequate, so they decided to start from scratch. The current restaurant sits on two lots, one was vacant and one had a tiny building on it so Peter bought both lots, and proceeded to make his dream a reality. Peter admits that he never thought this restaurant would be as big as it is, but it continues to thrive and grow.

Along with an incredible array of "Mountain Cuisine" featuring fresh trout, locally grown produce, corn-fed beef and fresh seafood, Bridge Creek features a full bar and serves Montana micro-brews on tap. The 10,000 square foot facility also features a temperature-controlled wine cellar that houses over 150 selections and 1,000 bottles of wine. The impressive wine list has earned Bridge Creek four awards of excellence from *The Wine Spectator* magazine.

After enjoying your meal, be sure to browse through The Market at Bridge Creek, a retail shop offering food and beverage related items.

Bridge Creek also offers cooking classes, wine tasting parties, theme dinners, comedy nights, dinner theater and many other community events.

If you are looking for a romantic dinner for two or are planning a party for 120 of your closest friends, the crew at Bridge Creek will make sure you have a pleasant dining experience.

Bridge Creek Backcountry Kitchen and Wine Bar is located at 116 South Broadway and is open for lunch from 11am to 3 pm with a light bar menu available after 3 pm. Seating for dinner begins at 5 pm. Reservations for dinner or for larger groups are recommended. The extremely popular Blueberry Brunch will begin again the last Sunday in September. Please call 446-9900 or check out the website at www.eatfooddrinkwine.com for more information.

August 2002

Steak Out: The Ale House
9 & 11 N Broadway • 446-1426

July 2002

Remember the great food that used to be available at The Ale House? You know, right after the Food Farm closed in 1999 and The Ale House opened and we all liked it and then it closed and then the bar reopened and we could get some food but not much? Well, now, the restaurant is open again.

Jody McCampbell gathered up two of her pals, Jane Chatlain and Cindy Hansen, and the three of them have created a wonderful new menu with foods that taste good with beer. Jane was manager of the Bear Creek Saloon for about 8 years, Cindy has been a cook for about 8 years and Jody is the newcomer with 3 years of restaurant experience. Along with their full line of appetizers, they offer a dinner menu featuring brats, burgers, sandwiches, steaks, ribs and seafood. A children's menu is also available, so bring the whole family. Dine in the restaurant or the bar, and enjoy your choice of Red Lodge Ales, wine, domestic beers or your favorite non-alcoholic beverage.

The Ale House, located at 11 North Broadway, is open Wednesday through Sunday from 3 pm - 9 pm, with extended hours over the 4th of July weekend.

July 2003

bizness
The Local Rag

A Taste of Carbon County: Welcome to where Pigs do Fly!
By Jon Densmore

Where can you find a comfortable atmosphere to enjoy a pleasant meal, a full-service bar, country hospitality, and racing pigs? The Bear Creek Saloon & Steakhouse, of course.

If you manage to be able to walk after dinner, then the entertainment is still to come.

Set up as a fund raiser supporting Carbon County high school graduates, pig races are not only entertaining, they provide a service to the community.

Over the past eleven years, proceeds from the races have contributed between four and six thousand dollars annually, totaling fifty-seven thousand dollars in college scholarship donations.

Lynn and Pits DeArmond moved to Bear Creek in 1982 from southern Wyoming and for the past 21 years have owned and operated the Bear Creek Saloon. After coming up with the idea of pig racing, the DeArmonds waited out the legal process of determining whether or not the races were in fact legal. Four months later, the State legislature passed a bill legalizing pig races as a fund raiser and the success speaks for itself.

With the restaurant open weekend nights, Lynn and Pits spend the remainder of their time enjoying the Montana lifestyle. When they're not traveling the country participating in dog shows with their enormous English mastiffs, they pass the time camping, fly fishing, or whitewater rafting.

On your visit to the Bear Creek Saloon, you can expect to find a casual smoke-free environment in the dining room. The menu offers an excellent selection of sandwiches and steaks including award-winning choice filet and prime rib. With a buffalo rib-eye and Cajun shrimp, you'll find something for every appetite.

The full bar proudly serves Red Lodge Ales on tap and offers house wines by the glass or wines by the bottle suitable to anyone's tastes.

Just a seven-mile drive east of Red Lodge on Hwy 308, the Saloon occupies the same building it has since 1904. Originally sharing its foundations with a butcher shop and market, the Saloon was expanded over time to make room for the dining room and kitchen.

Perhaps the best part of the establishment is the back deck where you can enjoy a view of the races, just don't forget to place your bet on the way out to the track. As a special bonus, you can bring the kids out to the playground where they can see the pigs preparing for their big race.

Bear Creek Saloon & Steakhouse opens its doors to the public Thursday through Sunday nights from 5-10 pm. Races begin at 7 and run every fifteen minutes with the final high stakes race at 9:45. For a slice of Montana you won't forget, drop in and visit Lynn & Pits for a delicious meal or have a drink and enjoy the racing. The races take place every night the restaurant is open through September 6th, and provide fun and entertainment for the entire family. For more information or to make a reservation, call 446-3481.

You won't find pork on the menu 'cuz the pigs are busy entertaining, but you can find your smile at the Bear Creek Saloon & Steakhouse.

Bone Daddy's now open

There's a new orange and black building in town, kids, and they call it Bone Daddy's. Along with his son Jerry, Leo Wilson, long-time local motorcycle sales and service guru has opened his new bike shop on the north end of town, just in time for summer's throng of motorcycle tourists. With a full-service shop as well as a clothing and biker-gear retail store, Leo's shop promises everything you need to get you up & running and back on the road.

The shop also offers ATV rentals by the day or week and buys and sells used bikes. Bone Daddy's also serves as the official headquarters of the Beartooth Rally. So stop in at Bone Daddy's, and see how cool orange and black can be.

Kibler & Kirch expands

Kibler & Kirch, after more than three months of rethinking, renovating, and remodeling, opens its doors this month on their new retail store. The old grocery store-turned-hardware store has in less than six months been converted into a fashionable, cozy display center for the oldest unique home furnishings business in Red Lodge.

Kibler & Kirch originally moved into their space at 22 North Broadway in 1990, offering both retail and design consulting. The design business remains at the original location, while the entire retail department has moved across the street.

Beartooth Custom Builders, the contracting company managing the remodel, has gone to great lengths to highlight the unique features of the building like the original pressed-tin ceiling plates, while making the space adaptable with stationery and moveable walls and dozens of electrical outlets.

Glögg

by Melissa Cross

Glögg is a traditional Swedish spiked, hot wine, which is steeped with nuts, raisins, and fabulous wintertime spices. As children, we always gathered in the kitchen to watch the grown-ups make a large pot during our holiday get-togethers. This is the recipe from my great grandparents, who were both born and married in Sweden.

Serve warm, with a spoon in the glass.

Be sure to include some of the goodies from the bottom of the pan in each cup. And watch the youngsters! I hear they like to sneak into the kitchen to taste the nuts and raisins.

Melissa has been a bartender for 11 years and loves holidays almost as much as she loves holiday drinks.

Swedish Glögg

Ingredients
- 1 bottle Aquavit (or other high quality potato vodka)
- 1 bottle of Burgundy or Pinot Noir
- 1 bottle of port
- 1/2 of cup raisins
- slivered almonds
- cinnamon sticks, broken into large chunks
- whole cloves
- cardamom seeds
- sugar
- 1 orange rind, thinly peeled and cut into slices
- 1 (2 inch) chunk of fresh ginger, grated

Process
1. Toast the almonds, cinnamon sticks, cloves, and crushed cardamom in a cast iron pan on the stovetop.
2. Soak the raisins and spices in 2 cups of Aquavit for half an hour.
3. While the goodies are soaking, make a simple syrup by dissolving 1/2 cup of sugar into 1 cup of water in a large stockpot, stirring until sugar is completely dissolved. Lower heat.
4. Add the Aquavit mixture, wine, and port. Add the orange rind and the grated ginger, simmer gently. **Do not allow to boil!**

These two recipes appeared in the December 2013 Local Rag

Holiday Spiced Elk Tenderloin

by Steven Roat

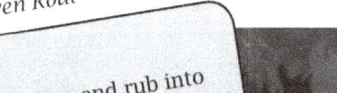

Pro tip: while raw meat will stick to the hot pan, it will release on its own as soon as it is seared properly. Try giving your skillet a wiggle. If the meat slides around, it's seared!

Ingredients

Holiday Rub:
- ½ cup of juniper berries, crushed or chopped
- 1 Tbsp nutmeg
- 1 Tbsp cloves
- 1 Tbsp cinnamon
- 1 tsp coriander

Fig Reduction:
- 1 cup figs, chopped
- 1 tsp garlic
- 1 tsp shallot, finely chopped
- butter
- white wine

Process
1. Mix all rub ingredients together, and rub into the tenderloin. Be sure rub is evenly distributed over the meat.
2. In a medium skillet, combine chopped figs and butter, and sautee for 5 to 6 minutes over medium-high heat. Add garlic and shallot, and just a splash of the wine. Stir carefully, being sure to dissolve all browned cooking material from the bottom of the pan. Add cold butter slowly, while stirring, to thicken the sauce.
3. In another pan, preheated to medium-high heat, sear the tenderloin.
4. Finish the tenderloin in the oven, preheated to 350°F. Cook to desired temperature.
5. Serve toped with fig reduction.

Steve is the sous chef at Old Piney Dell. Don't get him wet or feed him after midnight.

Slightly Out of Focus
by Gene Rodman

Christmas Family Photographs

> "However handy the phones are, they cannot compete with the features and quality of a camera whose purpose is to take photographs."

Sometimes the photographs taken on Christmas morning of the children opening presents become more valuable than the presents we give the children. As with many photographs, we sometimes only see their value when time has passed and we look back on those fleeting moments, looking to relive them again. Christmas photographs should be left to a camera which has the sole purpose of photography, rather than the camera on a phone. The reason so many photographs are even taken is because we always carry phones with us. However handy the phones are, they cannot compete with the features and quality of a camera whose purpose is to take photographs. It is well worth a little time to make sure the camera is out and ready with a charged battery and an empty memory card. Do this before the kids wake up at too-early-thirty on Christmas morning. You may even want to do some presetting of your camera to help with getting a good exposure in the morning. This includes setting a shutter speed, aperture, white balance, and ISO sensitivity. Try these to start with: shutter speed 1/60 second; aperture F4; white balance incandescent light (or whatever the type of lighting you have in the tree room); and ISO 800.

When the kids do wake before dawn, help yourself out by turning on all the lights near where the tree is located, as well as the tree lights. I'm not a fan of flash photos, so I have all the lights on in a room so I can just use a high ISO, slow shutter speed, and wide aperture to get my photos. If you do end up using a flash, having all the lights on helps with the red eye effect of the flash. Just remember that the strength of the flash may make the tree lights look like they aren't even on because the flash overpowers the brightness of the tree lights. Before there is a need to get the perfect shot, take a few practice shots to see if any adjustments are needed to improve your image capture. Keep adjusting until you get an acceptable exposure. Always remember that you may not be able to override the camera's settings when it is set to automatic. You may want to see if there is any improvement to your ability to get the camera adjusted correctly if the camera is set to manual. This may be part of your day-before preparation if you are not up on exactly how your camera works.

As the kids start opening their presents, get down on the floor to the kids' level and start framing your image so when the right moment happens all you need to do is click the shutter. Don't stop with just one photo but make a series just in case one is better than the rest. If you preview the images and see a problem, act quickly to correct it. Usually it's that the kids are moving so fast in their excitement that the preset shutter speed is not fast enough to stop the action of their movement. If you have several kids opening presents, don't try and capture everything. Remember you want to enjoy the kids excitement too. There will be more opportunities to capture them playing with their toys and the boxes and wrapping paper. As the day progresses be ready to notice cute opportunities for images and don't be afraid to get close and fill the frame on your viewfinder with cuteness. If the excitement moves outside, reset your camera's settings to that environment or just turn it back to automatic. If you have a habit of previewing your images regularly you will quickly notice when you forget to reset the settings for a different environment.

Always remember that Christmas is supposed to be fun and not stressful, so give the kids the camera and see what they come up with rather than fretting over having everything perfect. You may want to experiment with doing something totally weird – like I did when my wife started taking down the Christmas tree and I found the pile of Christmas lights on the floor. I plugged them in and experimented with a slow shutter speed and wriggling my camera during the exposure. Hope everyone has a great holiday season.

Gene Rodman and his wife, Tracy Shaw, operate a studio called Montana Photographic Arts. This article is from December of 2014.

Food & Drink

Oven-Roasted Grouse
by Melissa Davis, Pollard Head Chef

Ingredients
- 4 fresh grouse breasts
- Brine: 3 tablespoons salt and 2 cups water
- 3 apples, cored and sliced
- 1 large yellow onion, peeled and sliced
- 6 slices of smoked bacon
- 2 Tablespoons brown sugar
- 2 teaspoons salt
- 1 teaspoon pepper
- ¼ cup apple cider vinegar

Process
1. Soak the breasts in the brine for at least 6 hours.
2. Preheat oven to 360°
3. Layer the bottom of a 9x13 casserole roasting pan with apple slices and onions, reserving a bit for the top. Sprinkle about half of the brown sugar over the first layer. Lay the grouse breasts over the first layer and sprinkle with salt and pepper. Place the bacon slices over the grouse, followed by the remaining apples and onions and sprinkle with the remaining brown sugar.
4. Place the pan in the preheated oven for 15 minutes.
5. Remove from the oven, and pour the apple cider vinegar over it.
6. Return to oven for another 15 minutes, occasionally basting. Remove from oven and carefully scoop out the liquid at the bottom of the pan and pour over the top a few times before serving.

Serve with cous cous and roasted beets. Watch out for BBs!

Chocolate Lava Cake
by Melissa Davis, Pollard Head Chef

Ingredients
- ½ pound of chocolate, chopped small (I use callebaut chocolate but any kind will do.)
- ½ cup butter
- 4 eggs
- ½ cup sugar
- ¼ cup flour
- ½ teaspoon vanilla extract

You will also need
- Two 2 inch round pastry rings (or two 2 inch round ramekins good for baking)
- A sheet pan

Macerated raspberries
- Mix together one container of raspberries and three tablespoons of honey, but do not over mix. The sugar from the raspberries will bleed out and make them juicier and delicious!

Process
1. Preheat oven to 350 degrees.
2. Heat the butter in a sauce pan to boiling. Pour over the chopped chocolate, and stir until the chocolate is completely melted. Add the eggs one at a time, whisking slowly. Add the sugar, whisking slowly again, and then add the flour and vanilla (still whisking slowly!) until all is incorporated.
3. Prepare your pastry rings or ramekins with pan spray on a sheet pan. Carefully scoop chocolate mixture evenly into prepared rings or ramekins. Place in hot oven and check at 8 minutes. The sides and top should be cooked, but center of cake still gooey.
4. Remove from oven when done. Using a spatula and hot pad, place cake on a plate. If using a ring, give a gentle tug to pull the ring off (Careful, the ring will be very hot!).
5. Top with whipped cream and macerated raspberries.

Aphrodite's Delight
by Melissa Warrington, long time bartender & cocktail enthusiast

Muddled strawberries
Use either fresh sliced strawberries, or thawed out frozen ones. Smoosh with a bit of simple syrup or sugar to get the juices flowing.

Process
1. Fill a champagne flute with ice. Fill glass 1/3 of the way with Bombay sapphire gin and an equal amount of St. Germaine elderberry liquor.
2. Add a scoop of muddled strawberries and a small squeeze of lime.
3. Top with a splash of champagne.

This recipe also works well with the macerated raspberries used in the Lava Cake recipe. I've also added blueberries and blackberries.

Warning: these are strong drinks! Stay safe!

When Heather took over as editor, she started to move away from using a regular food columnist, instead bringing in a variety of different food and drink recipes from local chefs and bartenders. She focused on seasonal recipes like this Valentine selection from the February 2014 issue.

October 2002

bizness

Steak Out: Becker's Kitchen & Steak House

Gary and Angie Becker moved to Red Lodge from Hardin about 12 years ago. About four years ago, they delighted residents of Red Lodge by opening Becker's Kitchen. Originally located at Old Towne Square as a popular breakfast and lunch spot, the Becker's moved up the street a bit three years ago and expanded their hours to include dinner. Now located at 600 South Broadway, right next to the Silver Strike Bowling Alley, Becker's Kitchen & Steak House provides good, hearty meals in a family setting.

The Becker's employ about 15 people, many of them high school students. Angie and Gary like to provide jobs for the students and are happy to work around the kids' sports and school schedules.

The cozy restaurant is open for breakfast, lunch and dinner. Popular breakfasts include a sausage patty & cheese sandwich or steak and eggs. Daily lunch specials have included entrees like lasagne, BBQ spare ribs and cabbage rolls along with regular menu items ranging from sandwiches, salads, burgers and delicious homemade soups. For great steaks or prime rib at reasonable prices, this is the place to be. Complete your meal with a slice of Angie's homemade pie and your favorite beer or mixed drink from the full bar.

Becker's Kitchen & Steak House is open Monday through Saturday, 7 am - 8 pm and Sundays from 7 am - 2 pm. Call 446-2568 for more information.

The Lucky Dog

Well, it's official. The Lucky Dog has opened their doors! They will be open Wednesday through Friday for lunch and on Saturday and Sunday for lunch and dinner. Enjoy wraps, nachos, chili and your favorite Red Lodge Ale or non-alcoholic beverage. Dine inside or on the patio, (assuming the weather continues to be warm and sunny.) The Lucky Dog is located on the corner of 13th Street and Broadway.

December 2006

Mary Ringer's Ginger Cookies

Mary's favorite cookie recipe. These are soft cookies, not hard and crispy like ginger snaps. Makes about 5 ½ dozen cookies.

- 1 ½ cups sugar
- 2 cups unbleached white flour
- 1 ½ teaspoons cinnamon
- 1 ½ teaspoons cloves
- 1 ½ teaspoons ginger
- Extra sugar for rolling out dough
- 1 teaspoon soda
- ½ teaspoon salt
- 1 egg
- 6 tablespoons molasses
- 1 cup melted butter

In a large bowl thoroughly mix together dry ingredients. In a smaller bowl, mix together egg and molasses. Then add melted butter, mixing to blend well. Add the molasses mixture to the dry ingredients. Chill the batter until firm, about 1 hour.

Meanwhile, heat oven to 350 degrees. Using a tablespoon of dough, roll it with your hands into a round ball. Roll the balls in sugar and place them on either unbuttered cookie sheets or cookie sheets covered with parchment paper.* You can place no more than 10 balls on each cookie sheet. Be sure not to flatten the cookies; just leave them in balls. BAKE 9 MINUTES ONLY. The cookies will not look done! But they will look crackly on top.

Remove from oven and cool for a few minutes. Then place on a cookie rack or a cool counter. Whatever cookies aren't eaten immediately are best stored in a covered tin. They also freeze beautifully.

*Note: I like to use the French Silpat baking sheets for making cookies. They are absolutely the best! They cost about $20 and you can purchase them at any cooking store or on the Internet. They make wonderful presents for yourself!

August 2004

hangin' out

Easter dinner Red Lodge-style

By Kris Thomas

Only one day in advance, I planned a little Easter dinner at my cabin for those of us who either didn't go home for Easter or hadn't been invited to somebody else's family gathering. I started to think about what I would serve as I was laying in bed Sunday morning. Once the menu took shape in my head (Ham, Lois Potatoes, Green Bean Casserole and Mom's Cinnamon Bread) I was motivated to get started and jumped up to go to the grocery store. Things were eerily empty at the IGA parking lot. The pretty pink sign on the door said CLOSED FOR EASTER. What sort of cruel joke was this? The bigger question was, however, what were my eight friends and I going to eat tonight? I contemplated letting everyone fend for him or her self, then decided I would not let a simple roadblock such as having no food stand in the way of my dinner. I marched straight next door to Michelle's.

"Do you have any of the following items?" I barked at her. "A ham. Frozen hash browns. Cream of mushroom soup. Buttermilk." After I finished the list, Michelle led me into her kitchen and plunked a fist-sized bag of frozen green beans (which was mostly ice) down on the counter for me. "Did you try the Texaco?" she asked.

In the meantime, my friend Dusty was en route from Whistler to Boston and was going to be in Red Lodge in time for dinner. He called from somewhere near Butte, and was no help when I asked him if snap peas would be a good substitute for green beans. "Do you want me to try and hit a rabbit with my Jeep or something?" he said, in a voice that was a bit too serious for Dusty.

By the time I returned from Texaco, I had cleaned them out of mushroom soup, their one can of green beans, and a carton of milk. I stopped at Millie's house on my way home. Although she wasn't there, I knew she wouldn't mind me foraging a bit, as long as I pet the cats who were guarding the house. I walked out with one measly red onion. It was organic though, she told me at dinner.

When I got back to Fountain Park, Michelle was dancing in front of her cabin to greet me. "Eric has a HAM!" she said, beaming. Dinner had just taken a turn for the better. And then Deborah called to ask if she could bring another friend to dinner. "Um, sure," I said and explained that she might not want to have really high expectations. Ever supportive, she countered with, "I have asparagus and mushrooms. I could make a casserole if you have some brown rice." Bingo! A minute later, a phone call to Michael produced pounds of brown rice.

On my way over to Dave's I ran into John and Kari and explained my predicament. "I think I have some buttermilk powder," said John. The stuff smelled godawful but, really, what choice did I have? After I explained to Dave that I'd already ransacked his house earlier and found absolutely nothing I could use, he produced a ham steak and then led me to Erin's to rummage through her house while she was visiting her family in Powell. Erin has kids – she'd *have* to have green beans. Despondent, Dave came back to the car empty-handed. I learned later that Erin had a *case* of canned green beans sitting on the counter that he had somehow missed.

The beans were beginning to be a problem. Green Bean Casserole was an Easter tradition in my family and you might as well serve pizza for Easter if you weren't going to serve the "green bean magic" (anything tastes great with enough cream of mushroom soup). Even Judy didn't have green beans. "Judy, you're a *vegetarian*. You have a chest freezer and lots of cabinets. How can you *not* have a stockpile of beans?" I demanded.

My other next-door neighbor, whom I barely know because she just moved in, also came to the rescue. She showed up at my door wondering, could I use some leftovers from her Easter dinner – half a pound cake, a buttermilk pie and some rolls? Woman, you have no idea! I think I will like my new neighbor a lot.

I had harvested all the food I was going to get, unless I changed the menu and started all over. In the end, I did substitute some pea pods for beans. The ham was delicious, but my potatoes and beans were pretty lame. Everybody claimed everything was delicious, though. What would I ever do without my friends?

> "Judy, you're a *vegetarian*. You have a chest freezer and lots of cabinets. How can you *not* have a stockpile of beans?" I demanded.

May 2004

March 2002

Steak Out at the Bierstube

By: Bud Weimer

One of the most popular attractions of Red Lodge Mountain and the reason I go skiing is the Bierstube. Knowing that the place must have a history we started asking around but most of the patrons could not remember much. Seem's people don't go to places like the Bierstube to remember. Marcella gave me the info

In the early 60's Kenny Hancock donated the building that now houses the Stube (pronounced Schtube after 5). The building was originally a ski shop with the rental and shop area on the first level and the upstairs was a very high end ski shop that would rival the shops of Vail. Raise your hand if you're glad that went away.

There is a bit of an information void through most of the 70's attributed to most peoples need to forget things like Disco, Mirror Balls and Polyester Leisure Suits. But, sometime in the 70's the ski shop moved to it's present location and the upper floor became the Willow Creek Saloon although everyone has always called it The Bierstube, German for Ale House. The Deck was enlarged in the 80's and again in the 90's to make room for all the Neon clothing made popular in our area by Midwesterners.

Today the Bierstube is the favorite gathering place at Red Lodge Mountain. Friar's lunch and apres ski menu includes burgers, brats, sandwiches, salads, soup and Mexican food. There are daily sandwich, beer and apres ski snack specials. The full bar features locally brewed Red Lodge Ales on tap. There is live music every Saturday from 3-7 featuring local musicians.

If you're at the Mountain on weekends you will most likely see me riding my favorite chair. Chair 8 at table 6 on the Bierstube Deck.

STEAKOUT

by Wil Stifya

September 2002

We're introducing a new segment this month called, (you guessed it), STEAKOUT. Each month, unless Wil is unmasked and lynched), we're going to feature a Carbon County eatery or watering hole.

We couldn't think of a better place for our inaugural visit than in Roberts at The Lost Village Saloon and Eatery. First opened as a bar in 1946 by a local named Ernie, it was located on the east side of the street a little north of its current location. In 1948 it was put on skids and moved to its new home where it stands today. Local story goes that during the move on skids, and its subsequent reattachment to terra firma, it never closed for business. It was then called "Rudy's" by its new owner Rudy the magician. Sometime after that the building to the north was hitched on, giving it its approximate size today.

During the years that followed, it had numerous owners up to February of 2000 when its current handlers took over. Today it is owned by Jimmy and Wayne, with the help of their great crew. Extensive remodeling has been done in the last eighteen months to make the place not only a great saloon, but a place where you can get an excellent meal.

One of the things that was hands off during the remodel was the back bar. It is a classic 1906 "Brunswick" that was hauled up the river systems from St. Louis. Extensive changes have been made recently to upgrade and expand the kitchen equipment, and to enlarge and lighten up the bar and eating areas. The lunch and dinner menu is well rounded, and the service is friendly and quick.

Folks come from as far away as Bear Creek and Billings for their famous halibut and pizza. The new pizza oven features hand made soap stone shelves. There is an open back patio area that has its own bar, and has live entertainment and speciality food nights during warm weather.

Many local and out of area bands and groups light up the night at The Lost Village. Some of them are Harry Harpoon, Swingin' Richards, Canyon Magic Band and Mountain Country Band. Jimmy, Wayne and their people make local folks as well as travelers feel right at home, and The Lost Village is the kind of place where everybody knows your name. We had a great time, although we should have **hung around** for The Swingin' Richards, we hear they go to **great lengths!**

STEAK OUT
By Wil Stifya

November 2001

If a Town Crier needed material, Coffee Factory Roasters would be the place to find it. A hubbub of activitiy beginning every morning at 7 AM, Coffee Factory Roasters is a Red Lodge gathering place. Fueled by morning newspapers and community events, energized conversations waft back and forth along with the aromas from a multitude of coffee beans and flavors.

The present building was erected in 1929, and over the years, in different configurations, it has held many endeavours, with the word "saloon" not being an exception. In the 1980's a local couple coined the name "Coffee Factory Roasters". Holly and Randy, the current owners, purchased the business in July of 1999.

Holly and Randy have established Coffee Factory Roasters as a popular destination through quality products and consistent service. They roast their own beans and have fifteen varieties from both hemispheres. Every morning as the espresso machine runs constantly, fresh baked pastries can be picked from the counter display case. Lunch features homemade soups and sandwiches with bread made from scratch. Two of the most popular offerings are Chicken Dumpling soup and Brown Wheat bread. Closing time is 6-ish, and afternoon patrons are given a choice of fresh pies, cookies and gingerbread. There is also coffee and tea paraphernalia available, and customers can utilize the free internet station. Additionally, retail and wholesale bean sales perk up part of the business. They provide coffee shops in Montana, North Dakota and the Yellowstone Park Service with fresh coffee beans, and those who would like to order can reach them by going to www.coffeefactoryroasters.com.

As I peck away on my 1925 Smith/Corona trying to make my deadline for this review, Coffee Factory Roasters is quietly changing proprietors. Holly and Randy are turning the reins over to Doug, Rhonda, Ron and Kara. From every indication it looks like the new roasters will continue the traditon that the brew will be good 'till the last drop.

Editor's note: You MUST try their breakfast bagel, (jalapeno is the best).

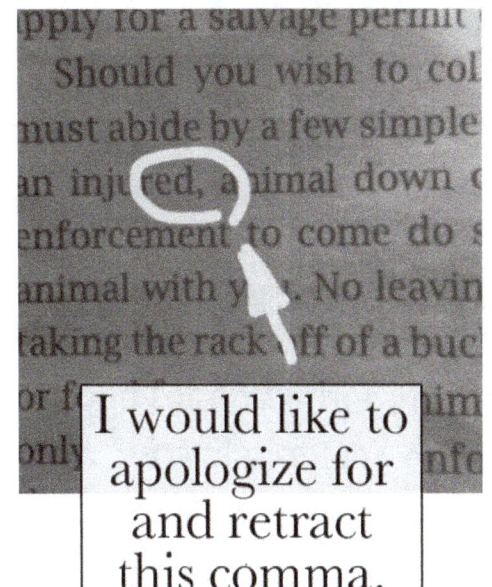

Let it never be said that Heather doesn't take her punctuation seriously! This is from the February 2014 issue.

Steak Out: Bogarts
11 S. Broadway • 446-1784

February 2002

Judy and Jodie Christensen bought Bogart's Pizza in 1984, they kept the name but added Mexican food to the menu since they both love it so much. Jodie even proposed to Judy while they were cooking a huge pot of chili verde. Prior to the Bogart name, (founded in 1974 by a Humphrey Bogart fan), it was called Beartooth Bar with the building dating back to 1906. The original bar is still in the restaurant, but it was cut down to fit more tables in the restaurant. And even with the additional tables, sometimes patrons are willing to wait awhile for a table. But the wait is worth it, and you can always enjoy a killer margarita or smoothie while you wait. The menu offers something for everyone; choices include burgers, Mexican food, pizza, sandwiches, and they offer a special menu for kids. Along with their famous margaritas, they also offer beer, wine, and yummy fruit smoothies. Many entrees have been named for loyal customers or employees. Their cheese-broccoli soup is such a favorite of Barb Thormalen that Judy makes it every Wednesday. Be sure to check out some of the unusual pizza choices, including a jerk chicken pizza (inspired by a trip to Jamaica) and a pizza with a black bean sauce. Although it seems that every customer has their favorite Bogart dish, Judy suggests that in 2002 everyone expand their horizon a bit and try something new.

Judy and Jodie serve their homemade "Ruggies" salsa, so named because Jodie used to call the neighborhood kids "rugrats" and they in turn called him "the big rug." About once a month, they head to the kitchen at the Billings Food Bank where they can crank out about 45 cases of salsa in a day. Then they seal it and slap the labels on and it's ready to sell. They consider making salsa a hobby and have hired sales reps to market it for them. Future plans include bottling their delicious marinade and even their margarita mix.

Judy credits her 35+ employees for the success of Bogart's. She says every single one of them adds something special to the restaurant.

Steak Out: Red Lodge Pizza Co., Front Bar, Carbon County Steakhouse
115 S. Broadway • (406) 446-3333
By: Wil Stifya

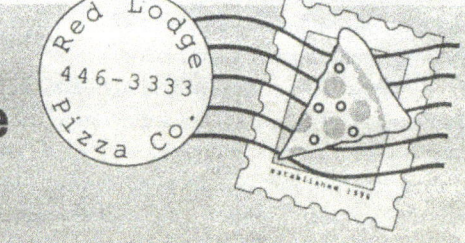

August 2006

If anyone were looking for the traditional "food court" in Red Lodge, they would find it at the Red Lodge Pizza Company and its surrounding eateries, The Front Bar and Carbon County Steakhouse. Purchased in 1996 by Tom and Eliza, these three food and beverage outlets all have their individual personalities.

Way before any of this, the building(s) had a colorful history in keeping with many of Red Lodge's main street structures. The building was first constructed circa 1900. From 1900 until 1932 it was home to a dry goods business and a Dodge dealership. The first restaurant was started in the building in 1933, and The Front Bar, as we know it, was first a saloon beginning in 1936. Prior to 1996 for several decades, Pius owned and operated the building(s) in several restaurant configurations. In addition to being a great host, Pius was also known for his famous bottle collection housed in what is now the back banquet room. During Pius' ownership the building was also known for its recognizable Natalis sign. Surprisingly, that sign dated back to the 1960s and not earlier as many of us thought. Currently, The Pizza Company has a building face sign, as well as a perpendicular sign out over the sidewalk.

Today, all three operations are busy with their individual offerings. The Pizza Company has excellent sit down, take out, or delivery pizza. The pizza pie variations are named around a post office theme. In addition to burgers, BLTs, and specialty sandwiches, they are also known for their Montana Rolls. The Front Bar offers a great appetizer and entrÈe menu, and is a popular gathering spot at happy hour. The Carbon County Steakhouse, the youngest of the three businesses, has accelerated to near the top as one of the area's premier dinner houses. Pius has returned to help Tom and Eliza in the steak house. Working along side of Pius is Heather, and the two of them together make an exceptional management and service team.

One additional area that serves the community is the back banquet room. With all of the groups that reside in the area, this room is kept busy twelve months a year. These four food and beverage outlets are serviced by two complete kitchens housed between the various dining rooms. On the horizon for the businesses is a banquet room service bar, a new pizza delivery vehicle, and hi-tech "hot bags" to keep the pies sizzling en route.

If people are hungry but can't decide what they want, then The Pizza Company, Front Bar, and Steak House can surely satisfy a variety of appetites.

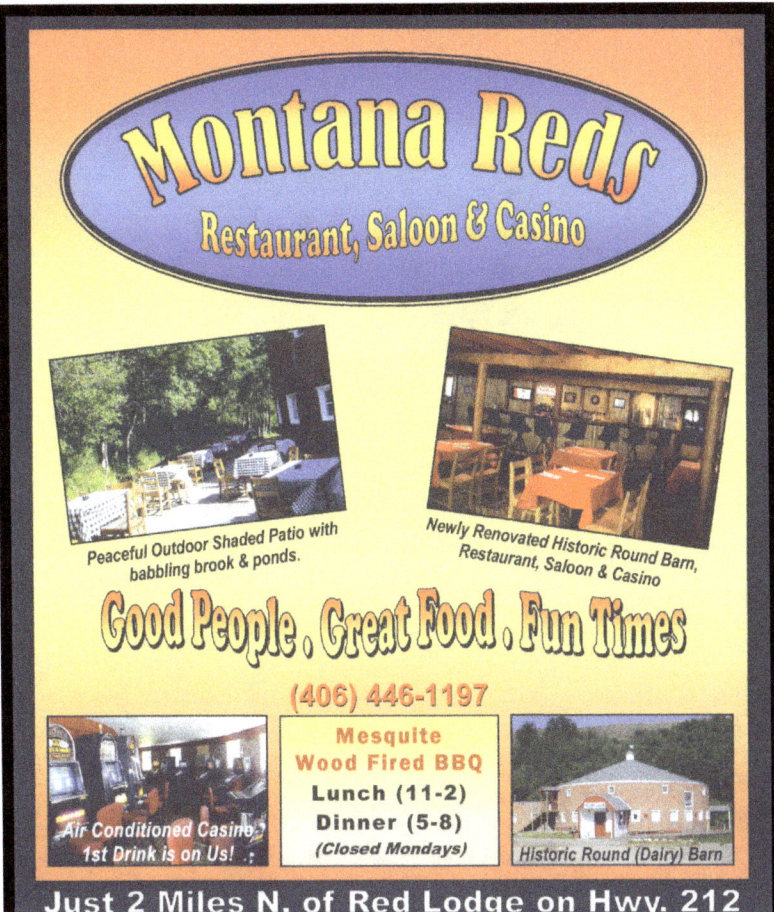

August 2006

December 2006

The Very Best of the Red Lodge Local Rag

STEAK OUT

by Wil Stifya

If ever there was a cornerstone of Red Lodge eating it's The Red Lodge Cafe. A colorful and storied institution on main street, it has served locals and visitors for well over a half of a century. To walk in on a busy winter morning during breakfast, you would think you were in the middle of a Norman Rockwell painting. As best as records can account, the building was erected in 1900. Although we don't have a calendar chronology of its ownership, we do know who has held court as owners for some time. Since 1976 Ted and Doris have owned and operated the cafe, and their son Mark has joined in as manager since 1990.

Ted and Doris sold the place briefly during this time, but ended up back a proprietors due to a set of business circumstances. Prior to Ted and Doris, a woman named Polly was in charge, and prior to Polly a gent named Charlie S. took care of business. Prior to the Feds putting the kibosh on non-inspected wild game, Charlie was known for the preparation of some incredible game menus. Charlie even had a string of small billboards all over the United States advertising his cafe, some of which unbelievably still stand today. Prior to Charlie, it was called Burton's Cafe, owned by a family named Oiler. Highlighting the exterior is the famous Red Lodge Cafe neon sign. This sign is the oldest "running" sign in the state of Montana, and is registered as such in Helena. The lounge next door was originally two long thin businesses. One was a company called Mile High Development, and the other was a haberdashery. After the lounge was in operation for some time, the back portion of the bar was added in the late 1970's. Now a pool table and big screen sports area, it was a dining room until 1993 serving lunch and dinner. In addition, the back area has served as a gathering place for local service clubs and morning coffee groups. If you take a close look at the current pool table, it is only one of two in the state that is an "8 pocket right angle billiard table". Back in the cafe, some of the decorations have a lengthy history. The current pictures on the south wall go back to 1967, the totem poles were carved by a local mechanic, and the mounted skis are pre-1950s.

But lest we get on to the important part... the food. The Cafe is open from 6am to 9 pm. The menu is arguably one of the most varied in town.

Having been in the business, I can tell you it takes a organized and steady mind to cook a large menu. Known for their "Montana" portions, some of their most requested items are prime rib, home made chili, and their hearty breakfasts. Their blueberry pancakes were even featured in an in-flight magazine. Although equally hospitable to visitors, Doris admits that her heart belongs to the local residents. Even to the point that she plans the daily specials in a sequence that enables her steady retired customers to get a specific balanced diet. All of this being served by a courteous staff of which Gloria and Marie have been a part of for 23 and 15 years respectively. The lounge is open for beverage service from 10 am to 2 am and patrons can eat in the lounge anytime the cafe is open, except for Friday and Saturday evenings when the joint is jumping. As far as eating legacies go, this is a bench mark in the state of Montana. If ever anyone wanted to see a piece of Americana, they should just step into The Red Lodge Cafe.

October 2001

Page 129

food forum

January 2004

Champagne & sparkling wine: Indulge yourself

By Bobbie Sacks

In the early 1600s, the monk Dom Perignon, tasting Champagne for the first time exclaimed, "Come quickly brothers, I'm drinking stars."

Bubbles in his abbey's wine were caused by the cold climate in the Champagne area of France as well as its short growing season. Time was too short for yeast on the grape skins to convert the juice's sugar into alcohol before the cold winter temperatures stopped fermentation. When spring came, fermentation started again, this time in the bottle. Re-fermentation created carbon dioxide, which got trapped in the bottle—thus the sparkle.

Good Champagne seems to be the epitome of elegance and sophistication, yet is no longer considered a luxury by many. You can buy it for as little as $5.99, spend $17 for Domaine Chandon or Piper Sonoma, $75 for Charles Heidsieck Blanc des Millenaires (1990), or spend over $170 for a bottle of Louis Roederer Cristal (1996).

I am a huge proponent of keeping bubbly in the refrigerator at all times and drinking it for no reason at all. And then there's the true optimist who always keeps two bottles chilled just in case....

Is sparkling wine Champagne? Well,...yes, and...no. In the European tradition, the name "Champagne" is reserved only for sparkling wines produced specifically in the region of Champagne, France. However, fine "sparkling wines" made in the US can be every bit as crisp and good as Champagne, and wonderfully unique in their own right. Napa Valley sparkling wines are easy to enjoy and don't give you the "sticker shock" of French Champagne.

Though an international agreement not to use the term "Champagne" on non-French sparkling wines was signed by all wine producing countries in the 1930s, the US was then under prohibition, and so did not attend the summit. Due to this loophole, some domestic sparkling wine producers have labeled their wine as Champagne. Call it what you will, you can't go wrong. In our country the two have become interchangeable.

"Those who have experienced good champagne are passionate about it," says Peter Christ, Bridge Creek owner. "Champagne's effervescence adds a quality that enhances dishes. It's versatile and food-friendly. If you're eating textured food such as salmon with a heavy cream sauce, the bubbles cut through the richness of the sauce and cleanse your palette and bring balance to your mouth." Peter suggests that for cocktail purposes Brut is the best. With a meal, Extra Dry is good because it's sweeter and complements the food better.

As far as words on the label go, they all indicate a wine's relative "dryness" (the smaller amount of sugar remaining after fermentation, the dryer the wine). Brut is the driest, Demi-Sec the sweetest.

He also uses Champagne in sauces because "it's a great way to liven up a dish. The frothy effervescence doesn't lose its sparkle when it's heated. Making vinaigrette with champagne along with white wine vinegar is a good combination, too."

In terms of glassware, flute-shaped glasses bring the delicate flavors and aromas to the top, hold the bubbles the longest, and show off the bubbly. Besides, they look and feel classy. But if you don't have any, by all means drink out of a wine glass. I was once playing tennis with my son and filled the tennis ball containers with sparkling wine. Now that was fun!

According to Mumm Cuvee Napa, the smaller the bubbles, the better the wine. The better the wine, the longer the bubbles will last. The best temperature to serve Champagne is 43-50 degrees F. Store it in a cool, dark place, and chill just before serving (90 minutes in the refrigerator or 15-20 minutes in an ice bath.) Of course, an ice bucket helps set the stage for a dramatic celebration.

To set the record straight, Champagne really does get absorbed faster in your body than wine. Scientists still aren't sure why. They theorize that it might be because the bubbles help the alcohol get digested more quickly, thus helping it get into the blood stream. So drink slowly while savoring that Champagne.

Here's a neat way to use the bubbly: a romantic picnic in the great outdoors with a blanket, two plastic flute glasses and a picnic basket filled with antipasto, charcuterie and fresh strawberries. And a kiss or two.

Indulge yourself even if you want only one glass. Bubbles last two to three days when refrigerated and sealed with a stopper. This means you can enjoy yourself three days in a row!

A health and food nut, Bobbie Sacks teaches Yoga at the Pollard three days a week. Call her at 446-0114 for recipes, tips, or Yoga information.

Steak Out – Arthur's Grill

May 2003

2 North Broadway, 446-0001

It's not often that the restaurant we feature actually offers to buy dinner for a guest and me. So when Sharon at The Pollard suggested I come to the restaurant for dinner, I jumped at the chance. And when Sharon insisted I bring a guest, my friend, Kim, was more than happy to help me do my job. I also brought my daughter along to test the kid's menu.

I don't go out for dinner very often, and when I do, it's usually for pizza or fast food. But after the meal I had at Arthur's Grill, I plan to do this more often.

Jackie, our waitress, was very friendly, and she offered great suggestions. We passed on appetizers so we'd have room for dessert, but Jackie did bring us really good, fresh bread while we waited. Anyone wanting appetizers can choose from smoked duck hash, blackened trout cornets, beef wontons, steamed artichoke or several choices of sushi.

For dinner, I ordered the New York Strip au Poivre, Kim ordered the Walleye, (both at Jackie's suggestion), and Katie had a burger from the kid's menu, (it was under $5!)

The soup of the day was broccoli cheese and the best I've ever had. That and the bread would have been enough of a meal, but next came the salad. Kim's actually had the cucumbers and red pepper arranged to form a smiley face and the bleu cheese dressing had big hunks of bleu cheese in it, the real stuff.

Then came the entrees. My steak in brandy cream sauce was so good, the thought of a doggie bag never entered my mind. Kim and I swapped a bit of our food so we could better critique the entire meal and I don't even like fish but the walleye was delicious. Katie's burger was big enough to satisfy even an adult's appetite and she really enjoyed the endless supply of Shirley Temples.

Although Arthur's Grill offers an extensive wine list at reasonable prices, Kim and I had mixed drinks. My gin & tonic was very refreshing.

After dinner, we were all stuffed, but took Jackie's advice when she said "if Americans knew what full felt like, we wouldn't all be so fat." So Kim and I split the espresso fudge torte and Katie had a créme-caramel. It was worth the price of the meal just for the dessert. I wanted to lick the plate, but was worried that I would offend the diners sitting at the next table. Katie couldn't finish her créme-caramel so I helped her.

As we waddled out of the restaurant, we all had big smiles on our faces, the smiles of three women who've had an extraordinary meal. There are not enough adjectives to describe the flavor of the food so I suggest you go experience it yourself. It was such a pleasant experience to sit at a table with a table cloth, (real, not plastic), and have a delicious meal in a comfortable, (not stuffy) atmosphere.

Don't wait for a special occasion to pamper yourself with a wonderful meal. Any day is a good day for dining at The Pollard.

Although the prices are higher than I'm used to spending at Burger King, they were not unreasonable. Especially when you consider the WOW factor. When questioning the price of a meal, ask yourself these questions: Can you make something just like this at home? IF you could make something like this at home, would it be worth the time and energy it would take to prepare it AND clean up afterwards? Not for me, pal. I don't go out for nice dinners often, so when I do, it better be worth the money. Both the quality and quantity of food met my "is it worth the price" criteria.

In addition to awesome dinners, Arthur's Grill is open for breakfast and although the lunch staff will be on vacation until May 20, stop in after that for a delicious lunch. The Pollard Hotel will be celebrating its 110th birthday this year, you're all invited to join the celebration.

Don't wait for a special occasion to pamper yourself with a wonderful meal. Any day is a good day for dining at The Pollard.

CHAPTER 7
Columns & Regular Features

The Local Rag

Eat, Drink & Be Merry

Jay West's food columns always had a story to go with the recipes. The name of the column was later changed to "Heirloom Recipes."

Aunt Katherine's Cranberry Banana Nut Cornbread Story

by Jay West

I come from people who cooked for others. Some, like my paternal grandmother, got paid to do it. Others, like my great-aunt Katherine, cooked on ranches and for the love of it. Katherine was my mother's father's oldest sister. She was born near here back before Carbon was even a county. Her birth year of 1880 was a "long time ago" even when I was young, which is now a long time ago, too. Let's just say my first memories of her are from around 1950. The first memory is a lesson about cooking and family history.

I was small and underfoot in her kitchen. It was a wartime holiday. My dad was overseas in Korea – a grinding war more terrible for us than the one we now have in Iraq but little remembered today.

Katherine's kitchen was brightly lit, sunshine yellow and warm on a cold, stormy day. A good day to be inside. Aunt Katherine drafted me to "help" make the cornbread dessert. With the work came Katherine's story of the "hard year."

For her, the hard year was 1896. It was the winter before she went off to teacher's college. The family had seen other hard years. A decade earlier, in 1886, the snows had started in November and didn't let up until March. All of the cattle died. But Katherine was only six that year. Being snowbound for Christmas was fun. She didn't know the cattle were dying or that the bank would take our Wyoming ranch in the spring.

The year she turned sixteen, she knew a lot more. Times were hard all across the country and especially hard for the family. The house at the new ranch had flooded out in heavy rains. The family moved in with neighbors. The neighbor's wife died. My great-grandmother — a fierce woman in her pictures — was laid up with two broken arms, inflicted when the wagon brakes failed and the wagon overturned on a steep grade. The oldest of the boys, Freddy, had been thrown and died of his injuries a few weeks later, a lingering and depressing death.

The tradition of having Turkey with Thanksgiving dinner goes back a long way!

So there it was with Katherine working like hired help in a neighbor's kitchen before dawn on Christmas. Making breakfast for 40 some-odd hands, sad children and depressed elders. She was feeling a bit sorry for herself.

Around daylight, one of the hands came in with a tree. Then neighbors came by for a Christmas visit. Like the Magi, they came bearing gifts, including jars of preserves.

Aunt Katherine said that this recipe just came to her when she saw the preserves. Fresh fruit is better but in winter you make do with what you have. What you have changes with the years and where you live. This recipe changed accordingly.

Bananas came into the mix when Katherine got her first teaching job, which was in a large city out on the coast. Cranberry sauce replaced the fruit preserves sometime in the 1920s. The powdered milk was an innovation of the 1940s.

And the peppers? Aunt Katherine said that this bread is supposed to cheer people up. Just to be sure, she started slipping jalapeño peppers into it for anybody who insisted on staying grumpy. Back then, a jalapeño was a gag like an exploding cigar. These days, it is thought to be gourmet food. Try the bread with cream cheese.

INGREDIENTS & DIRECTIONS

(makes one 5" x 9" x 4" loaf; double the ingredients to make two loaves).

Cranberry Sauce

Use one 14 oz. can or make your own:
- 2 cups fresh cranberries
- 1 cup sugar
- 1 cup water
- juice of a fresh orange and a bit of the peel (zest)

Other Wet Ingredients

- 2 bananas (older is better)
- ½ cup powdered milk
- ½ cup water
- ¼ cup oil or melted butter
- ½ teaspoon salt (reduce to ¼ tsp if you use regular salted butter instead of oil)
- 1 tablespoon vanilla extract
- 1 egg

Dry Ingredients

- 1 cup cornmeal
- 1 cup all purpose flour
- 1 cup sugar
- 2 teaspoons baking powder (skip this if you use a self-rising cornmeal or flour)
- 2 teaspoons ground cinnamon (more if you like cinnamon.)
- 1 teaspoon powdered ginger
- ¼ teaspoon nutmeg
- 1 cup broken walnut pieces (optional)
- ¾ cup raisins.

Spicy

- 1 jalapeño pepper (or more, if you like), stemmed, seeded and minced
- 1 strip of bacon, chopped
- pinch of sugar (or less).

PROCESS

1. Preheat your oven to 350°.
2. Cranberry Sauce: Boil 1 cup sugar with one cup water, stirring until all the sugar dissolves. (This will take 5 to ten minutes). Add the cranberries, orange juice, the zest and a pinch of salt. Boil gently for about 10 minutes, stirring occasionally. (You can do this with a pressure cooker — when you add the cranberries, put the lid on and let the pot come to pressure. Then turn off heat and wait for the pot to de-pressurize.) You'll only use half of the cranberry sauce in the batter; the rest can be spooned over the cooked bread or saved to serve with a holiday turkey.

Mix the Batter

3. Butter (or grease) and flour a standard loaf pan. (A standard loaf pan is 5" x 9"x 3").
4. Dice the bacon and saute over medium heat. Chop the jalapeño(s) very fine. Add to the bacon. Toss a pinch of sugar to help browning. Saute, stirring occasionally, until both the bacon bits and the peppers are browning a bit on the edges (probably about 5 minutes.)
5. Puree the bananas with the ½ cup water, the oil, the vanilla, the spices and the eggs. You can do this with a fork but it will be easier with blender or food processor or a mixer.
6. Put the dry ingredients in a large bowl and combine with the wet ingredients. The batter will be thick. If it is hard to stir, or won't pour easily, mix in a bit more water. (Don't worry if you get it too wet, though. You can just bake it a bit longer.)
7. Pour the batter into the greased loaf pan. It will be around ¾ full or maybe a bit more.

Baking

Baking will take somewhere between 45 minutes and an hour, depending on your oven. Start testing after 40 minutes with a toothpick or thin sharp knife or a piece of broom straw. When the tester comes out clean, put the pan on a cooling rack. After half an hour of cooling, turn the bread out of the pan.

You can serve the loaf warm or cool. For breakfast, it's good with cream cheese.

January 21 actually is Squirrel Appreciation Day, but this was our fake ad in January 2010.

May of 2007 was the last of many food columns from Bobbie Sacks.

food forum

A Foodie's Fond Farewell

by Bobbie Sacks

So long, farewell, auf wiedersehen, goodbye. This edition of The Local Rag will carry my last food column. Just know that I have loved writing every column all these years and hearing all of your great comments!

I am heading in a new direction as a full-time quilt designer. I need to focus my activities so that I can spend more time making quilts for shows and commissions. In 2009 I will have a show at the Carbon County Arts Guild with two other quilters where many of my handmade quilts will be on display.

However, I can't leave you without sharing one of my all-time favorites, a comforting delicious soup I call New England Soup. This hot soup is easy and always makes a big hit at any time of year.

NEW ENGLAND SOUP

You can cook this soup either on the stovetop or in the oven. Whenever I make soup or stew with potatoes, I always use a 325 degree oven. There's something about the consistent heat inside the oven which breaks down the starch in the potatoes to enhance the flavor.

- 2 tablespoons olive oil
- 1 large onion, thinly sliced
- 3 garlic cloves, minced
- 1 pound ground chuck
- 3 carrots, peeled and cut in 1/4-inch slices
- Salt and pepper
- 2 large potatoes cut in 1-inch chunks
- 1 28-ounce can tomatoes
- 1 14-ounce can sweet corn
- 1 handful of fresh green beans, cut in half
- 3 cups cabbage, sliced thinly

In a large heavy soup pot add the oil and sliced onion and cook over medium-high heat until onions are translucent and a golden color. Add minced garlic and cook just until you can smell the garlic. Add ground chuck and stir while cooking until the meat loses its red color. Add carrots, potatoes, canned tomatoes, corn, and green beans. Cover, bring to a boil, then turn down the heat so that the soup simmers for about an hour or until the potatoes and carrots are soft. Add the sliced cabbage and simmer 5 minutes longer. Season with salt and pepper to taste. Serve in bowls and pass the pepper grinder....

*Note: To cook soup in the oven follow the directions up to adding all of the vegetables, Bring the soup to a boil, remove immediately from the stovetop and place in a 325-degree oven and Bake for 45 minutes. Add cabbage and seasonings to taste and bake for another 5 minutes.

After spending close to twenty years in the food business, I still love to cook. If you ever have any questions about cooking, I would love hearing from you.

And here's how I've been spending my time lately -- designing these

quilts. And I'll still be teaching yoga regularly every week because it keeps me so balanced.

The Very Best of the Red Lodge Local Rag — Page 133

ABOUT TOWN

by Corey Thompson

Howdy!

Howdy! Howdy! Howdy!

"About Town" consists of Corey's random musings, polls, surveys, interviews, and anything else related to life in and around Red Lodge.

Awww, shucks! Montana is just a doggone friendly place! We know that because, unlike the rush of urban life, where people dash from one place to another, avoiding eye contact, we rural and small-town Montanans go out of our way to greet one another. We say good morning, we comment on the weather, and we wave at each other as we drive in cars. It's just downright good etiquette.

But let's think about The Wave for a minute. When do you wave, and how do you wave? Most folks do it instinctively, but after years of careful observation and numerous conversations with people, it appears that there are actually three different kinds of driving waves: the Acknowledgment, the Recognition, and the Regional/Special Occasion waves.

Acknowledgement Waves

These are done when the waver and the wavee don't really know one another, but just in case they do and don't want to appear rude, or are simply Montana polite, they wave to simply acknowledge one another. There are several different types of Acknowledgement Waves:

1. The Windshield. Hands are on the wheel, and one hand, either the left or the right, is raised up flat, palm out, and a windshield wiper motion is executed back and forth, just once in each direction.

2. The Howdy One. Hands are on the wheel, and one hand raises the pointer finger upright and gives it one, inside to outside, windshield wiper motion.

3. The Howdy Two. Like the Howdy One, hands are on the wheel, and one hand raises the pointer finger and the middle finger in one windshield wiper.

4. The Farmer. This is a variation on the Howdy One, but instead of a windshield wiper, the pointer finger raises up away from the wheel and then quickly back to the wheel.

5. The Ma'am. Again both hands are on the wheel, and one hand, with either the pointer finger alone, or the pointer finger and the middle finger together, is raised to the either the middle or the side of the forehead, and one salute is given towards the oncoming car.

Recognition Waves

Recognition waves are given when the waver truly knows the other driver and wants to say hello.

1. The Enthusiastic. This is a variation on the Windshield Acknowledgement Wave, but with a number of quick windshields added.

2. The Hey I See You. A more laid-back, casual form of the Recognition Wave, this one can be either a modified form of the Recognition Enthusiastic with just a couple of quick windshields, or, with hands still on or near the wheel, extend all four fingers and then quickly stadium wave them several times.

3. The Thumbs Up Wave. With four fingers on the wheel, simply raise one thumb in a universal gesture of good will.

Regional and Special Occasion Waves

These are always fun to interpret. This is an incomplete list of waves seen in Carbon County in various seasons:

1. Everyone knows the Queen's Parade Wave. The royalty will look to the left at about ten o'clock, and then with the right arm extended across the upper body and to the left, with a cupped palm, three gentle figure eights are drawn in the air. The hand is gracefully returned to join the other hand in the lap, the gaze is shifted to the right, and the process is reversed on the other side. It's a classic.

2. The Rodeo is a variation of the Queen's Parade Wave, but only because the wavers are rodeo royalty. Its hand signals are similar to the Acknowledgment Ma'am Wave, but it's a lot quicker because it's executed on a galloping horse. This wave has the rider circling the arena

several times, one hand on the reins, while the other arm is raised to the side of the forehead facing the spectators. The forearm and hand goes back and forth, from the forehead, extending out to the spectators at ten o'clock, elevated well above the horse's ear.

3. The Little Rascals. Extend one hand out about 12-18 inches in front of your face, fingers spread with palm out, and do a circular motion. This is usually done counter-clockwise, but the size of the circles drawn is a matter of personal expression.

4. Italian Ciao is actually a backwards "come-hither" wave – palm down, with all four fingers moving and the thumb sticking straight out.

5. The Hawaiian Wave, also called the Surfer Dude Wave, has the pointer, middle, and ring fingers cupped into the palm, the thumb and pinkie are up right, and the wrist is wiggled vigorously back and forth.

6. Like the Hawaiian, the Texan Wave, or Hook 'em Horns Wave, has two fingers extended upright but this time it's the index and pinkie. The other fingers and the thumb are curled together next to the palm. (Also known colloquially as the Shout at the Devil Wave.)

7. The Papal Wave. This has been known to occur among hikers and snowshoers with poles as well as, of course, the pope. The staff, or pole, is raised in an up and down gesture of acknowledgement, usually accompanied by a head nod.

8. The A-hole Wave doesn't happen very often in Montana since we are so friendly, but be aware of its existence. The thumb and pointer finger are curled together in a circle, and the remaining three fingers are wiggled towards the offender.

9. Don't forget the "You-just-cut-me-off" Salute! The pointer, ring, and pinky fingers are curled into the palm, with the middle finger extended prominently. Often accompanied by honking.

The above waves are primarily driver-to-driver waves, but all have slight modifications for driver/pedestrian encounters. For example, most polite pedestrians will wave a "thank you" to drivers who stop to allow them to cross the street. Usually this is just a quick Acknowledgement Windshield or just an arm raised up and down towards the driver; the driver will, in turn, probably execute one of the forms of Acknowledgement Waves, or even a Recognition Wave if the situation calls for it. Drivers also appreciate dog walkers who control their pets as they pass, and will show it with their own personal form of Acknowledgement Wave.

Yep, we sure are friendly folks! Next time you give or receive a wave, pay attention to which one you're doing or seeing. And the next time you see this writer, please – stick to Acknowledgement or Recognition Waves.

> "Don't forget the 'You-just-cut-me-off' Salute! The pointer, ring, and pinky fingers are curled into the palm, with the middle finger extended prominently. Often accompanied by honking."

hAPPY BEARDIVERSARY!

December 2013

The *Local Rag* would like to wish Doug Bailey's beard a happy second birthday. Doug started growing it on December 1, 2011. In a recent interview, the beard stated that it was cheerfully accepting belated birthday gifts. It quite enjoys beer, and Doug always makes a point of spilling some of his just so the beard can enjoy a taste.

The Local Rag
TechnoBabble

According to My Watch
by Gary Robson

As I write this article, it is nine seconds past 10:30 a.m. and the temperature near my computer keyboard is a balmy 72 degrees Fahrenheit. Yep, I can tell that just from looking at the new watch my wife, Kathy, bought me. Yep, a watch that measures barometric pressure, altitude, and temperature.

Kathy obviously understands men (a lot better than I understand women—that's for sure). How else would she realize how important it is for me to know that, right at this moment, I am at 5,536 feet altitude, with a barometric pressure of 827 hPa? After extensive research (which consisted of looking up hPa on the Internet because reading the manual on my watch wouldn't have been a technological enough thing to do), I discovered that an hPa is a hectopascal, which is the same as a millibar, and there are 0.02953 of them in an inch of mercury.

Yep, I'm pretty sure that means there's some weather outside. In fact, I just may go out there and look at lunchtime. But that's beside the point.

We've come a long way since the first LCD watches were introduced. Remember those? They cost hundreds of dollars, and all they could do was tell the time. Nowadays, even the watches you get free with your Happy Meal have lap timers, stopwatches, calendars, and the ability to solve simple differential equations.

The most important advance in timekeeping technology is the ability to know exactly what time it is. I'm not talking about within a minute or two. I'm talking about *precision* here.

Let's take my house, for example. We have approximately 673 clocks in our house. There are clocks on the oven, the microwave, the stereo, the VCR, the toaster oven, all three iPods, the coffee maker, and the bread maker. We have a grandfather clock, four wall clocks, at least 300 alarm clocks, clocks in our computers, clocks in our cars, and a clock in the four-wheeler (the tractor doesn't have one—it's from 1967, when you told time by looking at the sun). And none of these 673 clocks can agree on the time.

"You're fifteen minutes late," I tell my son, pointing at the grandfather clock. "No, I'm ten minutes early," he says, pointing at the microwave.

The woefully inaccurate NIST-7, good for a paltry tenth of a second per million years.

The awesome NIST-F1, over twice as accurate as the NIST-7.

The Timex 41711. non-atomic, no barometer, no altimeter.

Well, modern technology has solved this problem.

Back in the dark ages of the mid 1990s, this great country depended upon a time standard called the NIST-7, an atomic clock at the National Institute of Standards and Technology in Boulder, Colorado. Problem was, this clock had some reliability trouble. You see, every million years or so, it could gain or lose almost a tenth of a second. Disturbed by this horrible inaccuracy, Steve Jefferts and Dawn Meekhof of NIST designed and built the Cesium Fountain Atomic Clock (cleverly dubbed the NIST-F1), which can run for 20,000,000 years without gaining or losing a second. Now we're talking.

Any good watch and clock store will be pleased to sell you a watch that sets itself using radio broadcasts from the NIST (radio station WWV, for those who want an exciting listening experience). No longer do you have to worry about being a tenth of a second late for an appointment. Your watch will be right.

CONTRIBUTORS' CORNER

We love our contributors, and think you should, too! Thanks, folks.

Once upon a time, a long, long time ago, Chad Hansen thought he wanted to be anonymous. Well, anyone who's lived in this town for six months can tell you how impossible that can be! After three & a half years of contributing to the Local Rag as columnist "Spicy McHaggis," however, he is ready to be unmasked. Chad flies cargo planes for a living, which sort of explains his exotic encounters and random experiences. But only in part. Partly, Chad just experiences things randomly. Like this month's article, for instance. Take a gander, & see if it sounds like anything you've ever run across yourself.

Farewell Spicy, & Welcome to the madhouse, Chad! ~Kari

u tawkin to me?

Neologisms
(alternate meanings for common words)

1. Coffee (n.) the person upon whom one coughs.
2. Flabbergasted (adj.) appalled over how much weight you have gained.
3. Abdicate (v.) to give up all hope of ever having a flat stomach.
4. Esplanade (v.) to attempt an explanation while drunk.
5. Willy-nilly (adj.) impotent
6. Negligent (adj.) describes a condition in which you absentmindedly answer the door in your nightgown.
7. Lymph (v.) to walk with a lisp.
8. Gargoyle (n.) olive-flavored mouthwash.
9. Flatulence (n.) emergency vehicle that picks you up after you are run over by a steamroller.
10. Balderdash (n.) a rapidly receding hairline.
11. Testicle (n.) a humorous question on an exam.
12. Rectitude (n.) the formal, dignified bearing adopted by proctologists.
13. Pokemon (n.) a Rastafarian proctologist.
14. Oyster (n.) a person who sprinkles his conversation with Yiddishisms.
15. Circumvent (n.) an opening in the front of boxer shorts worn by Jewish men.

The Rag had a lot of writers with attitude, but none had quite so much fun with it as Jason Magida.
Above: February 2006 — Below: November 2003

Of course, that's not good enough for NIST. They're now working on an optical clock that uses "an energy transition in a single trapped mercury ion." They believe it will be 1,000 times more accurate than the clock Steve and Dawn slaved over for four years.

But think about this a moment. How will they *know*? Can't you just picture a group of guys standing around at the NIST a billion years from now saying, "Hey—this atomic clock over here is a fifteenth of a second slower than that one over there. Which one do you suppose is right?"

I may be a few seconds slow now and then, but I am content and secure in the knowledge that the barometric pressure has dropped by a full hectopascal while I was writing this, which probably means that a hurricane will be hitting downtown Red Lodge pretty much any minute now. Maybe I'll go read that users manual for my watch after all!

The Very Best of the Red Lodge Local Rag

Page 137

The way we were...

Just another day of interviews. Ten hours a day, every day. How will we ever staff a new restaurant that has two dining rooms, three bars, and banquet facilities for three hundred? Ten hours a day, every day.

The Library Lounge overlooks the lake. Perfect place for interviews. Who's next? Let's see, this next one has more qualifications than I do. Vivian? That's my mother's name.

She walks in wearing a blue business suit. Startling blue eyes, blond hair. The sun shining in through the bay windows over the lake sparkles back from those eyes. The dark wood of the Library Lounge makes a perfect backdrop. She owns the place.

I can no longer speak in complete sentences...

That was twenty years ago. I just heard my wife's voice again for the first time in seven weeks.

Viv and I would like to thank the community of Red Lodge for your support. We can't imagine going through this without you all.

Love, Viv & Craig

December 2006

The priveleged life of a fisherperson

By Craig Beam, Montana Trout Scout

"Privilege -- noun – advantage or favor that only a few obtain."

I got out the Funk and Wagnalls for that little bit of knowledge. Like a lot of words I use, I couldn't come up with a good definition for "privilege" off the top of my head.

It fits.

I've been trying to write about my experience last summer for quite a while. The problem I've had is, the experience is still going on. My emotions are still changing daily. My outlook changes much more often than that. Where should I start? Fear. Anger. Grief. Those were the first stages, but I'm still too close to it to write about those feelings. I'm trying to come to grips with the initial phases of this. Not quite there.

So, I'll write about how it feels now. Today. Not so scary. Not so painful. Joy has supplanted grief. Plenty of time to exorcise those demons later.

As you all know, I spend my time teaching folks to fly fish or ski, depending on the season. This can be looked at in two ways: I baby sit tourists for money, or I share my passions (obsessions) with folks who want a new experience. Sometimes these folks are easy to be with, sometimes not. The single item they share is that they want to have fun. Some don't know how to have fun. I try to show them. What could be more of a privilege than facilitating fun? Skiing and fly fishing are both difficult to learn. Very frustrating and physically demanding. Some of the folks I teach never spend time outside at all, much less dealing with the elements while trying to learn a difficult discipline. They get tired and cranky. That's when I can be the most help. If I'm not tired and cranky myself.

I have the unique opportunity to practice this philosophy with someone I love. Someone I've loved since the first moment I saw her. I wrote about that moment in the very heat of the hospital experience. It was very cathartic. I hope you all read it.

I need to say that "love at first sight" is a hard row to hoe. Sometimes, you don't want it. Sometimes, you deny it. Sometimes, you try to get out. But you cannot. Love at first sight happens, but it's not easy. You have to live with it forever. Dr. Gaddy asked me today if I remembered "for better or worse." It took me a second to realize that was a vow I took 18 years ago.

Folks I see all over town, at the IGA, at the post office, at the Red Lodge Café, etc, etc, keep saying how much they admire me. How brave I am. How hard it must be for me. They say other people would just leave. I tell them I have no choice. I'm privileged. I get to show my love. I get to help someone I love in ways that most folks never have the opportunity to do. I now know my wife more intimately than most men will ever know theirs. I now know another human being in ways that most folks would never consider, unless forced to. Like I have been.

Oh, did I mention joy? I have found more joy through this ordeal than I ever knew possible for me. Every day, Viv gets better. And I'm there. I get to be part of that. The love of my life is learning how to walk. How to stand. How to be independent. Viv was the most independent person I'd ever met. That's part of the horror of her affliction. Now she has to depend on me. Again, no choice. She accepts the help graciously. No complaints. I know she wasn't that way before.

It's a privilege.
Craig Beam
Forced to be human.

Putting my heart into it

By Vivian Beam, Garden Party

"Now abide these three: faith, hope and love. And the greatest of these, is love." ~1 Corinthians 13

"All you need is love; love…love is all you need." ~Lennon/McCartney

Faith, hope and love have delivered me to the thirtieth week in my recovery from Guillain-Barre Syndrome. Certainly all three have been tested, but love will be telling the tale from here.

Something about my attitude has changed in the last month or so. I no longer think of myself as a patient – I think of myself as a well person with a few physical limitations. Okay, so at present those few limitations are fairly key functions. But this is a completely different mindset, nonetheless. Let me explain…

One of the more dramatic incidents in my illness was a tracheotomy performed after my first week in the hospital. Among other resulting inconveniences was the fact that I couldn't talk for the next seven weeks. ("It's all fun until someone gets a tracheotomy!")

During those seven weeks, I depended largely on my eyes to do the talking. (My face wasn't totally in the game at that point, either.) I tried to convey my fears, my needs, my feelings – what's going on, can you help me, I love you. I discovered love as empathy and gratitude. I also discovered how much I love my husband and my family. Love became my reason for hanging on.

Lots of you came to visit me during that time. I studied your faces to assess my condition – there were no mirrors. I shared tears with you and held your hands and silently tried to reassure you that everything was still okay. I didn't completely believe that everything was still okay, but I had faith and hope that it would be. And love was my reason for hanging on.

One of my assignments in rehabilitation was to "re-enter" the community at large. My first attempt at this was a trip to the medical center connected to the rehab floor. We went to Subway there and I sat with my mom and Craig while they ate lunch. At that time, I was still sporting several medical accessories: tubes in my throat, arm, stomach and a catheter on my leg.

I watched people as they reacted to the sight of me. They were curious, empathetic, patronizing, repulsed and reassuring – all in a glance. Some pretended not to stare, but children openly checked out every detail – especially the bag on my leg. Parents were embarrassed and pulled them away, but there was no need to apologize. I fell in love with the human condition that day and it was impossible to be offended. Love was still my reason for hanging on.

When I began talking again, my personal contact with the hospital staff lost some of its intensity. At times, I found myself sometimes no longer looking directly at them because I could now verbalize what I wanted. An insignificant bit of my independence was returning. I didn't realize it at the time, but I was denying my caregivers the opportunity to comfort me. I became more uncomfortable with their attention, and in some small way love started to fade.

Now I'm home and beginning to "re-enter" this community. I'm in familiar surroundings, but I'm not the same. You have accepted me unconditionally and affirmed my place here. (And the hugs – thank you for the hugs!) One life does indeed connect with so many others. Love is benevolence and I can't allow that to fade.

As I said, my attitude has changed in the past month or so. I'm (necessarily) preoccupied with my physical condition, which is improving dramatically. I'm happy. I'm extremely fortunate. But… somewhere in the effort of getting better, I'm compromising love. My returning self-sufficiency is competing with my willingness to be vulnerable. I wonder – is this instinctual behavior to some extent? (Oh, really – it's just me??)

One of the few circumstances I welcomed in the last seven months was my state of vulnerability. Actually, I had no choice – for a time I was entirely dependent on everyone around me. I accepted every act of kindness given, without question or hesitation. I accepted love as never before and now I'm trying not to forget how exciting that was. It's the challenge of a lifetime.

Husband and wife team Vivan and Craig Beam wrote for the Local Rag for years. Most of the columns written by Craig Beam (the "Montana Trout Scout") were light-hearted and humorous. Vivian's were about gardening. These columns (Viv's above, Craig's on the facing page, and their thank you to the town) about dealing with her Guillain-Barré Syndrome were an exception.

get out and play

by Marci Dye   October 2006

Noah's First Summer

Our youngest just turned 6 months old! Time goes by so fast, when there are kids involved. You never realize the full extent of that statement until you are a parent. Holy buckets, did this summer go by fast!

Someone made the comment in the store the other day that with a new little one we probably didn't make it into the hills at all, but I think that taking things into consideration (newborn baby, busy summer in downtown Red Lodge, busy social calendar of the other two kids, etc...) we did pretty well. Noah got initiated to life in the mountains with some good times.

The beginning of the summer, Noah was in the front pack on a number of "flower walks." We didn't really get all that far, especially following the five-year-old tour guide who definitely has to examine every single last flower. Just think about how very little space there is between all flowers in the June fields. Moms and Dads definitely have to get out of the mode of making a particular destination while on kid-ventures, remember?

We learned that mosquitoes can pick out the "young and tender," and thus we avoided any long adventures during the heavy bug season in the backcountry this year. I didn't mind that one bit – I all-out hate mosquitoes. I'll confess, I think I used Noah as an excuse for not hitting the hills during the buggy months of late June/early July.

Mid July brought Noah's first overnighter trip. At four months old, I was still a bit nervous about getting too far into the backcountry with a baby, so we opted for the car camping adventure. We hadn't been actual car camping since well before kids, we figured out, so we did well by bringing along many comforts of home (3 packages of marshmallows, an entire cooler for beer, lots of great food, great friends to cook while I sat and drank a beer, etc...) We had a little bit of rain, a few nasty bugs, but overall, it was a perfect couple of days. While the big kids dug in the sand by the river for hours on end, Noah napped peacefully nearby with a Crazy Creek chair propped up as a little sunshade. The older kids fell asleep around the campfire, totally un-amused by the rounds of bad jokes told by the so-called adults. Noah snuggled into his fleece blankets in the tent and woke up with a smile the next morning. Very cool! With this tent camping hurdle a big success, we were now looking forward to an adventure a little further from the car!

We managed to squeeze in some day hikes/fishing adventures throughout the rest of the summer, but of course, never enough. I'll have to admit, I was very jealous at first of the fishermen in the group, as I didn't even get my Montana license this summer. At first, watching everyone from afar was very hard for me, having caught the fly fishing bug as a kid, and thus never "not fished." A mom transformation must have come over me one day, as I never enjoyed anything more than an afternoon of sitting by the lake holding one sleeping kid, while watching the other two (or three, if you count Mike) kids fish the lake shore, catch a few fish, and taking in their "mountain time" on their own. It must be a mom thing, I realized, as I remember my Mom doing the very same thing.

In the last weeks before school started, we had scheduled a few days with another busy family to hit the mountains. In deciding that we wanted more of a camping adventure vs. a long day death march for the kids, we chose a spot not more than an hour from the car. We didn't take the llamas, figuring the adults could tough it out for an hour and heft some heavy packs on our own. The Harley guys who were pulled off at the trailhead parking spot thought we were completely nuts, packing up kids and dogs, and then shouldering our own heavy packs and taking off down the trail. (Personally, I think they are nuts for spending their "fun time" at 60mph, sunburned, bug plastered, with a loud exhaust pipe by their ear, but to each his own, right?) We found a perfect campsite, the kids gravitated to the mud to play, the adults lazed around camp napping or reading, and Noah napped under his Crazy Creek baby sun shelter. I think we all got what we needed. As the day grew chillier, the warm clothes came out, and we all came to the realization that kids grow and clothes don't. There were more than one, I'd say more like three, pairs of fleece pants that were a fashionable Capri length on kids. Noah's super-warm fleece snowsuit, which I had planned on him sleeping in, wouldn't zip either – too short. Guess we learned that next time make sure clothes fit as you pack them. Noah ended up snuggling the night with me in my bag to stay warm, which wasn't all that bad either.

Noah had a great first summer! He's been initiated well, and took on his mountain time wonderfully. We even came to understand him enough to know he would rather be outside, and to take him there when he was fussy. So, if you see someone toting Noah around downtown Red Lodge, you'll know he was just exerting his wishes to just be outside.

Montana Roadkill 2013

by Emory Robinson

A website — which went live on Tuesday — allows Montana residents to apply for free permits to salvage carcasses of certain game animals after they've wandered into the roadway and met with a vehicle. Yes, you read that correctly. You are now able to collect roadkill for human consumption.

This law, along with an array of other new laws that went into effect on October 1, grants permit holders the right to legally harvest dead animals from the side of the road. If you do not have a permit and wish to scoop up some tasty morsels, you have 24 hours from the time of your salvage to apply for a permit. Nearly a dozen roadkill connoisseurs have applied so far.

"Why?" you may ask. Well it seems that some supporters of this law believe that carcasses just go to waste when left on the roadway to rot, while others believe that the animal's body could pose potential hazards to motorists when left on the side, or in the middle, of the road. Opponents of the law feel that roadkill may not be the best thing for humans to eat. While I do not oppose the law, I do somewhat agree with that point.

It is true that an animal hit by a motorist isn't an uncommon sight; actually it's downright expected on highways in Montana. This seems like a veritable wonderland for hunters who didn't get their bear tag this year; however, there are limitations. The line is drawn at moose, elk, deer and antelope. Other non-game animals, like coyotes and skunks, are always legal to scoop up, even without a permit. Permit holders are to withhold from collecting bobcat, bear, sheep and other furbearing animal carcasses due to their high value. Birds of prey are also excluded. Collection of animal carcasses is also prohibited on reservations, with or without a permit.

Some believe that allowing motorists to collect those remains will actually promote the intentional running down of these species, and that is a no-no in the roadkill game. If you do, however, hit one of the approved animals and Montana Highway Patrol or a County Sheriff must respond, you will be able to apply for a salvage permit on-site.

Should you wish to collect animals from the roadway, you must abide by a few simple guidelines. These include not putting an injured, animal down on your own. You must wait for law enforcement to come do so for you. You must take the entire animal with you. No leaving the entrails on the shoulder or just taking the rack off of a buck. You may not use the carcass for bait or food for any other animal; roadkill is for human consumption only. Sorry, Fido! Law enforcement may also inspect any part of the animal any time they wish, which doesn't make entirely too much sense, but roll with it.

Emory Robinson loves reading & writing, long walks in the mountains, and pontificating in many of Red Lodge's finer drinking establishments.

Apply online today with Montana Fish & Wildlife for your very own roadkill permit and get out there and harvest away. I must say though, as a hunter who has ruined shoulders of game with one small projectile, I can't imagine the viability of the meat on an animal that met its maker at the business end of a semi. Happy Hunting! Or should I say, "collecting"?

Visit LocalRag.com for a link to the application page.

Fishing Report &

by Craig Beam, Montana Trout Scout

OK. Everyone knows me as the Trout Scout, fly fishing purist. Wouldn't touch a spin casting rod to save my life. Every time a client refers to my hand-tied flies as "bait" I have a seizure.

It wasn't always so.

I grew up in rural Oklahoma. My dad taught me to fish with everything from Captain Bob's Blood Bait to minnows. Chicken parts were a favorite. Our shed always stank to high heaven of "stink" bait because, no matter how tightly you screwed the lid back on, you could never get that genie back in the Ball jar. I would try to describe the smell for the uninitiated, but that's impossible. Have to smell it to believe it.

Now, cat fishing in Oklahoma comes with some other odd baggage. The tools used are not always as sophisticated as a spinning rod. Sometimes all you need is some heavy nylon cord with a huge grappling hook tied to the end. Attach chicken parts to the hook and tie the cord to a tree sticking out of the (man-made) lake you're fishing. Go away for the night, come back and harvest. Take the catch home in a gunnysack and throw the catfish in a rain barrel. Cats are notoriously hard to kill, so they live for several weeks in a barrel. Voila! Fresh fish.

Okies are proud of their catches, just like all fishermen. For most of us, paying a taxidermist to mount a fish was out of the question. Why hide that huge flathead inside the house, anyway? Don't you want every passerby to admire your fishing prowess? The accepted method of displaying your fish was to leave the heads hanging from a tree in the yard. What could be more efficient? You have to hang the really big ones, like a deer. Gut 'em, skin 'em with a pair of pliers, and cut steaks off the carcass. Leave the head hanging there for all to see! Many's the time my dad and I drove all over creation, looking for the tree with the biggest heads. Then we'd stop, knock on the door and ask to fish their farm ponds. After the hour or so of obligatory bullshitting with the owner, down to the pond we'd go. Those were the days!

I remember one day we were heading out to set "limb lines" on a local lake. We'd been given directions to the best spot by a farmer whose tree was decorated with many very large heads. A couple were too big for me to get my 12 year old arms around! Very impressive. The old timer had told us to look for the coyotes. In those days, fish weren't the only trophies folks liked to show off. It wasn't uncommon to see coyote carcasses lashed to fence posts by the hind legs. Sure enough, we came to a fencerow festooned with coyotes. Some had been there so long only the hind feet remained. There must have been two miles of fence posts, each one with a trophy. The reasoning was that the carcasses served as a warning to other coyotes to stay away. Similar to the dark ages practice of impaling your foes for all to see. Very effective.

Now, at the end of the fencerow, a right turn took us down to the lake. It was a great looking spot with many half-submerged trees sticking out. Perfect limb-line territory. We took the old, beat-up aluminum boat out of the pick-up and tossed it in the water. No motor, just a couple of paddles. We weren't trying to cross the lake, just get to the trees in 8 to 10 feet of water. An easy task for two eager anglers. We set about twenty lines, each huge treble hook adorned with a lovely chicken leg, thigh, wing, or (always best) glob of rancid guts. Tasty.

The hard work done, we drove back to town. Now that's fishin'!

Next morning, back we went. Hello, fish heads! Hello, coyote feet! In no time, we were pulling up fish after fish. Easy as pie. About halfway through the harvest, one of our lines was thrashing around furiously. My dad put on his work gloves for this one! "Looks like a real monster!" he exclaimed with glee. Dad grabbed hold of the line and pulled with all his strength. The thrashing reached a crescendo; the line came up a foot or so, then stopped. I lent my weight to the tug of war. Nothing happened. We couldn't budge that line.

Both of us were white faced and panting as we paddled back to the truck. What to do? We couldn't leave a huge fish like that! My dad decided to drive back to the farmer's house and ask for help. Even though we would have to share the glory of the catch.

We pulled into the farmhouse just as the farmer was driving off on his tractor. I jumped out the door without waiting for the truck to stop, waving my arms and shouting! The farmer's tractor wheezed to a stop. I ran up, panting. "What's the matter, boy? Look like you seen a ghost!" he shouted over the backfiring engine.

"FFFFFFFish!" was all I could choke out.

About that time, Dad strolled up and casually asked the farmer if he would bring his tractor down to the lake. Even though my dad was trying to act like nothing out of the ordinary was going on, the farmer immediately started asking questions. Soon the whole story was out, and the farmer was tearing down the road (at about 3 miles an hour) to get a look at this monster catfish.

Associated Exaggerations
April 2006

When we pulled up to the site of the battle, my dad and the farmer had a little strategy conference. It was decided that we couldn't risk attaching the relatively light fishing cord to the tractor. Might break the big fish off. Now, the farmer had a heavy rope and hook in the box behind the tractor seat. He tied one end to the tractor and my dad and I took the hook end out in the little boat. We slid the hook down the fishing cord, hoping to get it into the fish's mouth. Sure enough, we hooked something solid as a rock!

"Let her rip!" shouted Dad!

The tractor backfired twice, belched black smoke from the stack, and started forward. Dirt and grass flew from the back tires! And, low and behold, it started to gain ground. A foot at a time, slowly, the beast was being dragged to the shore! I could barely contain myself! The wait was excruciating! "Floor it!" I shouted.

Then, slowly, slowly, a rusted metal shape began to emerge from the depths. An old car! We had hooked onto an old Studebaker. The farmer dragged the car out onto the bank. Then, we noticed that SOMETHING was alive in the car's trunk! There was a furious banging and slapping coming from the car's trunk! I ran up to the rear of the car and peered in through the jagged rust hole in the trunk, out of which was sticking the fishing line.

Low and behold, the biggest flathead catfish you'd ever seen was trapped in the trunk! Our chicken guts had dropped right in the rust hole and the cat had eaten it! No wonder we could only get the line to come up a foot! The fish's head was three or four times as big as the hole. Amazing.

My dad and the farmer pried the trunk lid open. I stood ready with a 12-pound sledge to finish the monster off. I looked in that fish's eyes and he gazed steadily into mine. Then he grinned and said "Thanks, fellas! It was getting a bit cramped in there!"

April (no foolin') Fly Box
April means bugs! Yahoo!

Baetis (BWO) imitations: olive parachutes, olive comparaduns, size 16.

Pheasant tail nymphs, size 18

Green sparkle pupa, size 18

Brachycentrus (Mother's Day Caddis): greenish-brown elk hair caddis, size 16

Dark cased caddis nymphs, size 16

Dark reddish brown hare's ear nymphs, size 14.

Rhithrogena (March Brown) imitations: brown parachutes, brown comparaduns, size 12.

Captain Bob's Blood Bait, treble hooks and sponges. Clothes pin for your nose. Transport this in the bed of your truck or duct tape to roof of car.
DO NOT CARRY IT INSIDE YOUR AUTOMOBILE. No foolin'.

Slightly Out of Focus
by Gene Rodman

He's so fast! I wish I could stop him

The world is always moving, and much too fast for me, thank you. I became interested in photography because it captured a moment, a special one, any one I decided. Just one moment that can easily be missed. I don't need to be entertained anymore. I enjoy silence, simplicity and these individual precious moments.

Making a still image consists of two components: shutter speed, and f-stop or aperture. Stopping time involves the shutter speed part of the exposure and is measured in seconds, or usually, fractions of a second. It is the length of time the shutter is open and light will be hitting the film or the sensor in your camera. The aperture is like the iris of your eye that opens and closes the pupil to vary the intensity of light entering your eye or the camera.

Since shutter speed is measured in fractions of a second and may be noted on your camera as 15, 30, 60, 125, etc. remember that that number really means 1/15, 1/30, 1/60, and 1/125 of a second. If you think about it, trying to hold your camera still at anything slower than 1/60 of a second is going to create a blurred image simply because you just can't hold the camera still when the shutter will be open at slower speeds. At that point you need a camera stabilization device (tripod) or you need to support the camera against a solid object like a wall, tree, or fence post depending on the shutter speed you'll be using.

> "You can follow a moving object with the camera while taking the photo and the background will blur in a panning effect."

When you think about the image you wish to capture, ask yourself if anything in your photo will be moving, and if you want to stop the action of the object or maybe have it blurry. Moving water will blur even though the rocks surrounding it will remain sharp if a slow shutter speed is used and the camera is on a tripod. You can follow a moving object with the camera while taking the photo and the background will blur in a panning effect. If you want to stop the action of someone in a sporting event you have to make sure that you have a shutter speed fast enough to stop the action. The faster the object is going the faster the shutter speed you'll need to use. In the 1930's and later Harold Edgerton created images with a special flash that could stop the action of bullets going through apples, a crown created by a falling milk drop, and a balloon popping.

If you'd like to experiment with the slow end of shutter speeds you can go for a second or two exposure in the evening to capture the lights of the city with the blurred lights of the cars on the road. I've even set up my camera to record the stars in the sky as the earth moved creating arcs of different colors. That exposure was several hours long.

The great advantage of using a tripod is that image blur due to camera shake is non-existent.

Gene Rodman and his wife, Tracy Shaw, operate a studio called Montana Photographic Arts. This article is from March of 2014.

The photos with this article are of some water in Beartooth Lake taken with the camera on a tripod and a motorcycle photo Tracy took during the Beartooth Rally that shows the panning effect.

The Very Best of the Red Lodge Local Rag — Page 145

The Local Rag
Zymurgy Corner

by Gary Robson   November 2007

Red Lodge "Bent Nail" IPA Wins Bronze Medal at the Great American Beer Festival

Last month, Red Lodge Ales claimed a bronze medal at the 2007 Great American Beer Festival Competition, the largest national beer competition that recognizes the most outstanding beers produced in the US today. The top three winners in the competition's 75 beer-style categories were announced October 13th at the 26th Great American Beer Festival Awards Ceremony held at the Colorado Convention Center in Denver, Colorado.

Red Lodge Ales was recognized in the American Strong Pale Ale category for its Bent Nail IPA, an American style IPA brewed with copious amounts of hops. The beer, named for the hard working contractors ("nail benders") who make their living in Red Lodge, is available on draft and in bottles around Montana and northern Wyoming. Red Lodge Ales is a 1750 barrel microbrewery located right here in Red Lodge that specializes in "good times and good beer."

If you want to congratulate the winners, stop by Sam's Tap Room in Red Lodge (417 N. Broadway) between 4:00 and 8:00 p.m. You can have a pint of Bent Nail IPA, and then try a couple of their other award-winning beers while you're at it.

The 2007 GABF competition winners were selected by an international panel of brewing experts from an impressive field of 2,832 entries received from 474 U.S. breweries. More than 1,500 breweries were invited to compete. "The Great American Beer Festival is the premier judging event for the American craft beer industry," says Nancy Johnson, Festival Director.

India Pale Ale

There's a fascinating story behind the IPA style. In the early 1700s, when India was a British colony, beer spoiled on the three-to-six month boat trip across the ocean from home. English brewers worked to create a beer that could survive the trip to India without refrigeration. Louis Pasteur was still 150 years away from inventing pasteurization, so the only defenses the brewers had against spoilage were alcohol and hops.

The India Pale Ale, or IPA, style came from a brewer named George Hodgson at the Bow Brewery in East London. He started with a basic pale ale recipe, added a considerable extra dosage of hops, and upped the alcohol content. The result was a durable and drinkable beer, which is popular to this day.

Traditional IPA is hard to find in the U.K. these days, but it's produced by quite a few breweries in the U.S. Typical alcohol content runs over 7%. Don't slam down a sixpack of this stuff and get in the car!

Other Local Winners

Red Lodge Ales wasn't the only winner from our area. Montana Brewing Company in Billings and their brewer Travis Zeilstra picked up a variety of awards, including Small Brewpub and Small Brewpub Brewer of the Year.

They also won a gold medal for their Whitetail Wheat (American-Style Hefeweizen) and silver medals for Sandbagger Gold (English-Style Summer Ale) and Custer's Last Stout (Export-Style Stout).

The name of this column was soon changed from "Zymurgy Corner" to "Beer Snob" because it appears that only brewers know what "zymurgy" means.

Meet Ninkasi
the Goddess of Beer

The Local Rag salutes the ancient Sumerians. The Greeks and Romans may have had their gods of wine (Dionysus and Bacchus), but our favorite diety has to be Ninkasi, the Sumerian goddess of beer, whose name means "the lady who fills the mouth." Much of what we know about her comes from a poem entitled "Hymn to Ninkasi." A portion of the poem reads:

You are the one who handles the dough [and] with a big shovel,
Mixing in a pit, the bappir with sweet aromatics,
Ninkasi, you are the one who handles the dough [and] with a big shovel,
Mixing in a pit, the bappir with [date] - honey,

You are the one who bakes the bappir in the big oven,
Puts in order the piles of hulled grains,
Ninkasi, you are the one who bakes the bappir in the big oven,
Puts in order the piles of hulled grains,

You are the one who waters the malt set on the ground,
The noble dogs keep away even the potentates,
Ninkasi, you are the one who waters the malt set on the ground,
The noble dogs keep away even the potentates,

You are the one who soaks the malt in a jar,
The waves rise, the waves fall.
Ninkasi, you are the one who soaks the malt in a jar,
The waves rise, the waves fall.

You are the one who spreads the cooked mash on large reed mats,
Coolness overcomes,
Ninkasi, you are the one who spreads the cooked mash on large reed mats,
Coolness overcomes,

You are the one who holds with both hands the great sweet wort,
Brewing [it] with honey [and] wine
(You the sweet wort to the vessel)
Ninkasi, (...)(You the sweet wort to the vessel)

The filtering vat, which makes a pleasant sound,
You place appropriately on a large collector vat.
Ninkasi, the filtering vat, which makes a pleasant sound,
You place appropriately on a large collector vat.

When you pour out the filtered beer of the collector vat,
It is [like] the onrush of Tigris and Euphrates.
Ninkasi, you are the one who pours out the filtered beer of the collector vat,
It is [like] the onrush of Tigris and Euphrates.

It was through this poem that modern brewers like Fritz Maytag at Anchor Brewing have been able to recreate the original Sumerian recipe for beer, dating back 3,800 years. So next time you tip a pint, think of the noble history of the brew you drink.
All hail Ninkasi!

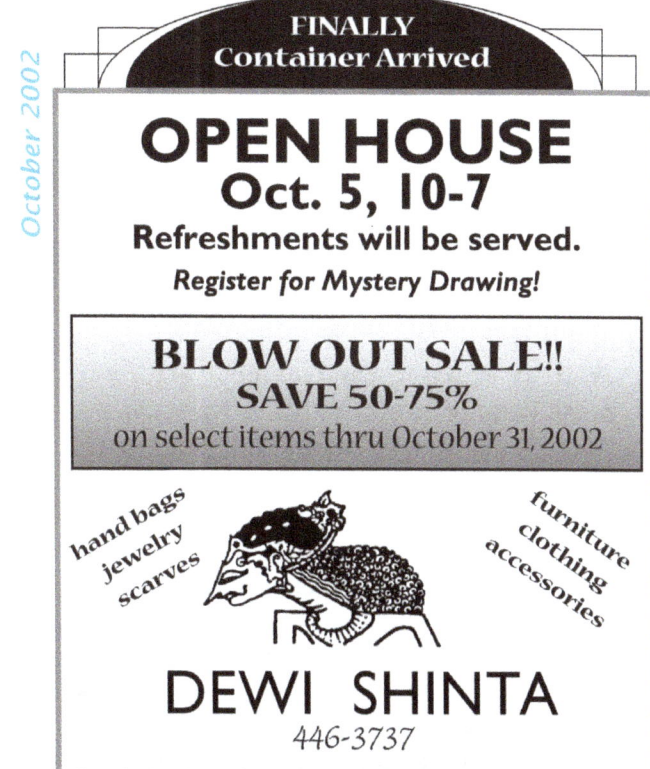

I wonder if this is why dogs aren't allowed at Sam's Tap Room any more. Were they keeping away the potentates?

Sass & Class
An Honest Column about Fashion for Real Women
by Amber Enos

Due to the impending summer season, I really think that it is the perfect time to address some warm-weather fashion no-no's. Let me preface this article with the fact that I don't condone nor support fashion bullying, but there are just certain things NO ONE should wear! And if you are a fan of tube tops, daisy dukes, wife beaters, or Crocs with socks; READ THIS ARTICLE.

We have all had our eyes burned by that one gal or guy that must have gotten a little mixed up on dress codes for the summer. You know the one: she's rocking the daisy dukes that are covering... well, um... I'm not so sure what they are covering, but I have a pretty good idea of what they should have been covering. Don't get me wrong, I am a Dukes of Hazard fan, but other than Daisy there is really no girl that should try to sport her shorts. Have you seen that guy strolling down the street with the white tube socks with his red, white, and blue Crocs, and his super sexy wife beater matched with that oh-so-hot Hawaiian shirt? This is NEVER sexy!! Never. Often one must wonder if they were going to look like this on purpose for laughs, but alas, I'm pretty sure it was not intentional.

So rather than cause utter distain, dirty looks, and gawking passers-by, avoid these ensembles and you will get whistles and compliments, instead of job offers to be a carnie or a... well, you know.

Ladies, please understand that a tube top – though it may be presentable in Vegas by a pool – when worn out and about, will most likely earn you a weird glance or two. If you are a diehard fan of tube tops, layer it with a flowy tank top and great pair of capris! This is going to look fun and flirty, and give you great confidence in knowing that the stares are for your epic sense of style rather than your extreme showing of the skin.

Now let's address the men in our lives. Here's the deal-i-oso, wives, girlfriends, and sisters: I plead with you to stop supporting terrible summer men's fashion trends! I can't even count how many times I have seen a guy sporting his Crocs with tube socks, shorts, and a Hawaiian shirt (Have I mentioned that I hate this outfit?!). Now I'm not sure if this is just due the fact that you are so exhausted after dressing yourself and your little minions that your hubby ends up sneaking out of the house in this epic get up and you are just willing to let it slide, just this once. But please for the love of all that is attractive, stop this! It's kinda cute for a little guy around age three to sport this look, but by 45 the nostalgia has more than worn off.

I get it, we are often too busy to address our men's wardrobes, but that is why you have a trash can in your laundry room. When you spot those nasty, little fashion "what the ficus" ensembles, toss them in the bin and blame the missing items on the Sock Monster! Next time you're out shopping, grab him some no-hassle wardrobe pieces that always match. Find him great shirts, shorts, and a steadfast pair of foot wear that will not allow socks. That way he'll always look great, and you, my dear, get to actually claim him in public rather than walking behind and praying no one notices that you're together.

There are many trends that are being offered this summer, and you should totally experiment and find one that fits your style!! From flowy skirts, tops, and hi-low tank tops, to colors that you are sure to fall in love with, be adventurous, and find your new fave! And when in doubt about what is a great look for your guy, go with the steadfast polo shirt, denim shorts, and a great pair of sandals. Remember the easiest thing about the guys in your life is that if you make sure they have a closet full of coordinating items, they will always look good!

Amber Enos owns a Red Lodge clothing shop. She has an insatiable passion for fashion.

June 2010

Robin Hood (2010)
Could have used more tights
by Doug Robson

Robin Hood: A classic tale told through the generations of a rebel who stole from the rich to give to the needy; a man who, with his pack of merry men, took resources from the people who didn't need it, and helped out the poor. Truly a hero of legend, Sir Robin of Loxley. His story has been told throughout the ages, and has been told many different ways. In this, the year of 2010, director Ridley Scott took it upon himself to remind people of this legend in the form of a film. It's a revitalization of the epic tale told through the eyes of one of the greatest directors in all of Nerdom. Here's a plot summary.

We all know Robin Hood and what he did, but this is doing what has not really been done within my very limited knowledge of the subject: Scott told us how Robin Hood gained his fame, where he came from. An appropriate title could have been "Robin Hood: Origins," but Wolverine stole that one. This is a tale of how Robin Longstride, a lowly archer in King Richard the Lionheart's legion, stole a dead man's identity, and used it to do great things.

It stars Russell Crowe as Robin Longstride, Cate Blanchett as Marion Loxley, Oscar Issac as Prince John, and Mark Strong as Godfrey.

This was an interesting experience for me. I, as of this writing, have seen this movie twice. The first time, I walked out thoroughly unimpressed. The movie overall seemed confusing, boring, and not overly great. Perhaps it was because I was tired, or maybe my mind was simply wandering. After seeing it a second time, not of my own accord, I walked out of it happy I was dragged in again, for I enjoyed it. "What?" you ask. "How can this be?" Well, my confused compatriot, I'm not sure. Perhaps I was studying it more thoroughly the second time, or maybe my mind was just in focus for once, but I enjoyed it.

I don't know if this means you should watch it twice or not, because I don't know what state my mind was in the first round. All I know is what I am saying now. The movie was fun. It had its flaws, but it was fun. The acting was great for the most part. Crowe did a great job as Robin, but he was still too old to play the role. Issac played a great John: twitty, jerkish, and outlandishly arrogant, just as John should be. Strong, as usual, was fantastic (I'm a fan of him). Blanchett, as usual, was bad (I'm not a fan of her). Kevin Durand played a great Little John; it was a very fitting role.

The effects, where applicable, were fairly good. The one place I will point out the effects is the beginning of the credits. They did this animated painting style of art that just turned out astonishing. It made me want to sit there and actually read all the credits presented there, which means it worked. Another scene, which I chalk up to cinematography rather than effects, (even though it was mostly due to effects) was towards the end. I won't spoil anything by giving context, but it involves a mass of archers shooting arrows into the sky at once at an army, creating a rain of arrows. The angles given to this scene (in particular, the "coming right at you" angle and the "side view" angle) were just stupendous. They made me marvel in the glory of Scott.

The issues I had with this movie? Well, not much beyond Crowe being too old and Blanchett being in it at all. There was one thing, however, that peeved me. There are quite a few coincidences that I am not buying. Just in case you're sensitive to spoilers, even though they are within the near-beginning, I'll throw a spoiler alert in.

Effects	A-
Story/Plot	B+
Casting	C+
Captivity	A-
Overall	**B+**

SPOILER ALERT!
They just expected me to accept that Robin and his gang, as they were wandering out in the woods, just so happened to come upon Sir Robert of Loxley's cavalcade shortly after being ransacked. Then I'm to believe that Longstrider and Loxley just happened to have the same name, thus making stealing his identity easier. And to add onto that, when he gets to Nottingham, the father just so happens to think of Longstrider's plan before it's ever mentioned to him and suggest it, then Walter just so happened to know Longstrider's father before he died. And also, as he's wandering through town, Marion is the only one who could see that the new Robert of Loxley was not as he looked before? No one remembered what he looked like enough to know he couldn't have changed that much? Not even his father's servants who have been there for oh-so-long? Right.

Setting aside my inner pedant, this movie was enjoyable. I had fun watching it, and liked it overall. The acting was good, it had at least one beautiful cinematic shot, and it had Russell Crowe. Even if he was too old for the role, he's great. I didn't expect Mark Strong to be in it, so that was quite a pleasant surprise. I'd suggest you watch it if you like the Robin Hood kind of scene. You know the kind of genre I mean. Again, I'm not sure if it must be seen twice, or if I was just loopy the first time, but I enjoyed it my second time. I'm not sure what you should take from this, but if you take anything, I'd say take away that it is a good, fun time, and that you should probably see it once.

Doug Robson is an avid movie and videogame fanatic who runs a review website called www.ecoticity.com

We like Malagasy Giant Rats. We didn't hurt any in April 2009, and we won't hurt any next month, either.

ABOUT THE LOCAL RAG

The Local Rag
P.O. Box 1630 ◊ Red Lodge, MT 59068
Editorial: 406-446-3999 ◊ Gary@LocalRag.com
Advertising: 406-860-3245 ◊ Ads@LocalRag.com

Staff
Gary Robson, *Editor/Publisher*
Kathy Robson, *Comptroller*
Heather Robson, *Ad Sales Manager*
Paul Johnson, *Graphic Designer*
Douglas Robson, *Web Tech*
John Overton, *Ombudsman*

The Local Rag is published monthly, and is distributed to every P.O. Box and mailbox in Bearcreek, Joliet, Fox, Luther, Red Lodge, Roberts, Roscoe, and Washoe. It is also distributed free at many restaurants, bars, and hotels in those towns plus Belfry and Bridger.

Warning: The Local Rag may contain citrates, cyclamates, glutemates, chlorates, phosphates, and acetates, but (alas) no playmates. No Malagasy giant rats were harmed in the making of this paper.

Circulation varies by season, from 4,200 to 5,500 copies per month.

Subscriptions are available for $20 per year to U.S. addresses or $15 to locals in the armed forces (via APO) or local students away at college.

Notice: The opinions expressed in this issue are not necessarily the opinions of the advertisers, writers, editors, proofreaders, harp seals, good housekeeping seals, or navy SEALs. I'm pretty sure my dog agrees with everything in here, though.

THE GREEN SCENE

by Clare Witcomb

The History of Red Lodge's Pride Park and the All Nations Garden Club

July 2009

The idea of writing a history of the All Nations Garden Club in Red Lodge has been percolating in the back of my mind for several months, and just when I'm the busiest at the Beartooth Nature Center, I decided to take the bull by the horns and just do it. I've asked several long-time members to give me as much information as they are able to remember, to give me a thumbnail sketch of how the All Nations Garden Club came into being.

In reading through the various scrapbooks kept over the years, I assumed that Grace Larkin was the one who came up with the idea of forming a local garden club, but that was not the case. Tom Flaherty recently emailed me say that it was actually his mother, Dorothea, who first came up with the idea. She mentioned this idea to Grace; the rest is history.

Dorothea's original idea was to help with the Festival of Nations. Back when the Festival ran for 10 days (I remember this schedule when I first moved to Red Lodge 20 years ago), the All Nations Garden Club helped with the arranging of flowers in the different Nationality rooms, which were held in the Mountain View school. This was the way things were done from the beginning of the Festival of Nations. The All Nations Garden Club was formed in 1952 when the Festival of Nations began. The Club has grown and its activities increased the effort to "Spruce Up Red Lodge" as the club motto states.

Long-time member Estelle Tafoya gave a history of Pride Park at the May All Nations Garden Club (ANGC) meeting this year. We all learned at that meeting just how very important the ANGC has been to the community of Red Lodge. Because of work the ANGC has done at Pride Park, these groups and boards have come into being: Community Forestry, the Tree Board, the beginning of work on a trail system for Red Lodge, becoming a member of National Arbor Day, becoming a member of Tree City USA, and the Red Lodge Parks Board.

Estelle was also able to get grants through the Community Transportation Enhancement Program (CTEP) for the development and beautification of Pride Park. I traveled to Billings several weeks ago to learn of the beginning of Pride Park from Ruth Pitcher Von Fossen. Her memory is still quite sharp for someone who just turned 80!

The land where Pride Park is now located used to be the Swinging Door Saloon, which burned down in 1975. It then became a vacant lot and a parking lot for Flash's. With hard work by Ruth, Exia Clark, and other dedicated ANGC members, a fund drive was started to raise money to purchase the lot. $8,000 from the sale of a lot on South Platt started things rolling. The ANGC also purchased 100 spruce trees from Pat Melaney north of town for $16 each and sold them for $20. The ANGC then sold memorials for $5, $10, and $25.

Eventually $20,000 was raised, the lot was purchased, and Pride Park was born. Then the ANGC turned Pride Park over to the City of Red Lodge. The City now pays for power and water and clears the snow in the winter. The sprinkler system was installed in 1988. Ruth remembers the tall spruce tree by the raised flowerbeds in the front of Pride Park was dug up from her home south of Red Lodge as a sapling. Other trees in the Park were dug up from the grounds of Cedar Wood Nursing Home. An interesting story Ruth told was that before the old Drug Store was built across 12th street from Pride Park, the ANGC planted trees, grass, bushes and flowers on that lot, too. An idea was floated to close 12th street from Broadway to the alley and have a park from the empty lot to the north end of Pride Park, but it was voted down.

In reading the minutes of ANGC meetings over the years, it's very interesting to see the changes that have occurred since the club was first authorized on March 27, 1953. The ANGC was certified by the Montana Federation of Garden Clubs. The first years of minutes were painstakingly handwritten in pen or pencil, and all of the members were written down as Mrs. [last name]. Very seldom were their first names mentioned. The dues in the beginning years were 15 cents a meeting. Since I joined back in the 1990's, the dues have remained at $10 a year.

These are a few more things that the ALGC has done for Red Lodge: We take care of the Christmas lights at the Library and at Pride Park. On Festival of Nations weekend, we set up a lemonade and cookie stand at Pride Park, which is free to the public. We adopted the Pocket Park next to Junction 7. We donated trash cans to the community, which are placed up and down Broadway. We are working with the Main Street Project and Red Lodge Proud and Beautiful in trying to obtain funding for bear-proof trash cans on Broadway.

Our big fundraiser of the year is the Plant and Bake sale, which is held every June. Through the tremendous hard work of member Jeannie Hull, who raises most of the flowers for sale from seed in her greenhouse, we are able to raise money to continue the work of the ANGC. Also, many thanks to Vivian and Craig Beam for donating so many annuals over the years. The colors from their flowers certainly help brighten up the corner of 12th & Broadway.

Every Monday morning through the growing season, you can see various members of the ANGC gather at Pride Park to plant, weed, prune, and keep things looking beautiful. Over the years many groups and individuals from the city of Red Lodge have helped in so many ways to help the club members keep up Pride Park. There are now comfortable benches and picnic tables for the public to enjoy. In July, we plan to have another concrete pad and picnic table installed on the West end of the Park. We also have a new trash can, thanks to Greg Zeiler (former owner of the Snag) and Tim Buckstead of Bone Daddy's. There are plans being discussed to redo the map on Flash's wall.

I know I have only hit the main events over the years about the ANGC and Pride Park. I hope everyone has a chance to enjoy the beauty and convenience of Pride Park. All members of the All Nations Garden Club thank the public for enjoying Pride Park and keeping it clean. What a great place to sit and watch the world go by!

Clare Witcomb is the Chair of the Carbon County Resource Council. She's green in more ways than one—she is also responsible for a lot of the gardening at the Beartooth Nature Center.

Cheapskate WINE SNOB
by Randy Tracy

Tasting Notes: Fact & Fiction

July 2009

Randy Tracy is the Concertmaster for the Billings Symphony Orchestra. His Scottish heritage qualifies him as a cheapskate. We have no idea what qualifies him as a wine snob.

The "tasting notes" on a manufacturer's wine label can be fascinating fiction. I've often hoped for a "truth in advertising" label to show up some day, something that reads, "This haphazardly- manufactured wine is produced by the tanker-full by indifferent, underpaid and unskilled labor. A nose of burning hair and overheated vacuum cleaner invites one to discard this immediately. It exhibits flavors of rancid coffee grounds, cough syrup, dishwater, bath water, cat pee, and tennis shoe. A particularly unwelcome finish of moldy oatmeal lingers far longer than one would like."

But no. I end up tasting a cheap, thin, bitter Chardonnay that leaves me annoyed, and the label reads, "Redolent with subtle nuances of Georgia peach and Valencia orange, and a luxurious finish of Citron and Quince." Yeah, right.

But still, tasting notes can be useful, if they are written by someone who isn't trying to sell you the wine, someone with a balanced view, someone who's tastes you can trust. The perfect person to write those notes is, of course, yourself. I know it seems "fussy" to take notes on wines you taste, but if you do, then you'll remember the wines you liked, and why, and your palette will become sharper quickly. If you don't take notes, then you end up wandering into a wine shop and saying things like, "I think I've had this before, but I can't remember if I liked it." And then there's the favorite of everyone who works in a wine shop: "My friend had a bottle of wine, I think it was red, and it was really good... I think it had the letter 'R' in the label... can you find that for me? I really liked it."

If you are like me, and somehow the habit of taking notes slips away for an entire month, you end up with a shelf of mysterious empty wine bottles. I saved all of them because I liked them, and planned on writing about them, and there they sit, staring back at me reproachfully, because I can't remember how they tasted. I do remember a few things:

- **2006 Razon, Spain**, $14. It was good. I liked it.
- **2007 "Writer's Block" Grenache**, $16. It was good. I liked it.
- **2001 Taurino Salice Salentino Riserva**, $12. It was good. I liked it.
- **2006 Cuvée Terroir Chinon**, $23. It had some nice herbal flavors and some French class. I liked it.
- **2002 Salar de Randez Rioja**, $18. It was from the Basque region. It had some fiery spiciness. I liked it.
- **2003 Tedeschi Ripasso**, $14. It had some of the extra "Oomph" that you'd expect from a Ripasso, and some tannins. I liked it.

Finally there were these three, which stuck in my head somewhat better:

- **2001 Tedeschi Amarone**, $25. Really nice. Classy, dark flavors, lots of chocolate overtones, deep and intense, very long finish.
- **2005 Moulin-a-Vent**, $12. A screaming deal; real class and tons of fruit, some nice complexity and very likable for everyone at the table.
- **2006 Le Pigeoulet en Provence** (80% Grenache, 10% Syrah, 5% Cinsault, 5% Carignan), $13. I bought this strictly based on the label; not the front, but the back, which described the varietals that go into this blended Rhone-style. It had a "Châteauneuf-du-Pape" weight and flavor, and I was very excited to find something in this price rage with this kind of sophistication. Unfortunately, the 2007 vintage came in at $18, but if it's anything like the '06, it's still a great bargain.

But how exactly did they taste? Beats me. I really gotta go back to taking notes.

MONTANA Fashion

by Ryan Sankey

The sexiest garment ever invented is not the teddy. It is not the lace bikini. It has never been a "hottest item of the season" at Vic's. The sexiest garment ever invented is... the starched white shirt.

Roll your eyes if you must, but I have evidence to back me up. Think George Clooney in Ocean's Eleven; Robert Redford on safari in Out of Africa and, the defining hotty in a white shirt, Mr. 007 himself. Rest assured men do not have the corner on this market. Take for example Elizabeth Banks in Seabiscuit or Kristin Scott Thomas in The Horse Whisperer. When the time came to seal the deal with their man both were wearing the iconic, and incredibly seductive, white button down. This is more than mere coincidence. The appeal of the white shirt is its effortless effect. I mean, how calculated can a simple shirt be? Well, just like "natural beauty" there is more than meets the eye when it comes to your sassy selection.

The very basic of basics is the suit shirt. Minimal tailoring and virtually no details make it beg for a jacket. But, from such humble beginnings comes fabulous variations. Leaning on the feminine side is the tailored blouse, featuring darts and fitted seams. Caution: Fit is essential with the fitted blouse. Nothing takes a look from amazing to ghastly quite as fast as button-gap across the bust—except maybe muffin top and panty lines, but that is another article. So, wear the appropriate undergarments and try it on first! My super trendy sister-in-law showed off the white shirt perfectly last Christmas when she wore is out over black trousers and layered long necklaces as accessories; sharp and classic. Equally as stylish, you can wear it untucked under a semi-fitted sweater with a bright scarf for a look that is easy and pulled together.

On the other end of the spectrum is the "boyfriend" shirt. Simply an oversized variation of a classic style, the boyfriend shirt has multiple possibilities. The usual design is untucked, with the sleeves rolled one turn and nearly uptight jewelry. This is where an element of balance is essential. Keep the shirt starched, or better yet buy one that is iron-free (gee, where could you get one of those?), the jewelry minimal and you must stand up straight! Anything less will make you look like the frumpy result of a poorly planned one night stand. Alternately, and every bit as sexy, even if it is a little more put together, is the tucked-in version. Turn up the collar and add an amazing multi strand necklace and stud earrings. White hot takes on a whole new meaning.

Take a hint and embrace the starched white shirt. So many high budget dramas can't be wrong.

Ryan Sankey owns Sagebrush Sirens with her partner in crime, Kim Jacobs. When she isn't in Red Lodge she is on the road mixing music at rodeos across the country.

Jeff the Nature Guy

I've never been blessed with a large stature. Like any man, I often flex in the mirror and dream of having biceps as thick as my legs. However, all that stares back at me is a lanky, boney frame. But you know, I'm okay with that now. Sure, I received the occasional swirly in school and often used my little size to outrun bigger thugs, but now that I'm an adult—at least I think I am—size really doesn't matter to me anymore.

After all, I'm a dad. I was man enough to spread my seed, so who needs muscles, right? Sigh, maybe I wish I had at least one. Anyway, I'm still going to call myself Big Daddy, in honor of Fathers Day. And to all you big daddies out there, thanks for your hard work. In the big daddy spirit, I'd like to tell you about my three favorite dads in the animal world; the worst, the best, and the largest.

Let me begin with the easiest, the worst dad. In the animal world, finding an incompetent dad is not difficult to do. For Pete's sake, we can find that within our own species. With all the bad ones out there the worst has to go to the grizzly bear. Now a deadbeat dad is one thing, but grizzlies will actually kill their own cubs, and yes, occasionally eat them. To be fair, these big boys will often kill any cubs they come across, not just their own. Despite this, I'm not too sure many mama grizzlies will be showering their man with new ties this Father's Day.

Next we move onto the best dad. I know many of us would like to nominate our old man, I know I certainly would, however, I have to give this honor to the seahorse. This delicate, odd little creature really goes to bat for his youngsters. So much in fact, that he delivers them. No, he's not there to witness or help with the birthing process, he *is* the birthing process. Yes, you heard me right, male seahorses carry and give birth to their young. The female simply deposits her eggs into a brood pouch near the male's stomach; he then fertilizes the eggs internally and carries them until they emerge as fully developed, mini seahorses. What a pop pop!

Last—but certainly not least—is the award for the largest dad. When it comes to sheer size, nothing beats the male blue whale. Considering this behemoth can weigh over 180 tons and an entire football team can stand on its tongue, nothing in today's world comes close to this hulking dad. More importantly, this big boy means business when it comes to producing his offspring. With a 10-foot appendage to do the job, I'm sure there are several mama whales who agree the male blue whale is the biggest daddy of them all. Now that I've crushed every dad's confidence, stand proud, value the love you give and have a great Father's Day!

You can tell Jeff Ewelt is a "nature guy" by the way he walks around with a vulture on his head. The Beartooth Nature Center hired him anyway.

CHAPTER 8

Red Lodge Believe it or NOT!

Red Lodge Believe It or Not!

Red Lodge Man Markets Bear Arms

A local inventor known only as "Griz" has come up with an answer to what he calls "My right to bear arms." He will soon be marketing a new line of Bear Arms designed to be surgically implanted on humans. According to Griz, three models will be available for adults, Grizzly Bear, Black Bear and Polar Bear. "Women will love the Polar Bear arms because they can dye them to match their outfits!" exclaimed an excited Griz. Children's models will also be available in various sizes and colors and will be marketed as "Teddy Bear" arms. "Of course I will require any underage customers to have a signed permission slip." Griz is quick to add.

Griz claims the idea came to him while watching TV. "The NRA was talking about our right to bear arms and I thought, hell yeah, I'd like to have bear arms. The claws would have lots of uses like opening beer cans and my arms would never get cold." When it was suggested to Griz that the NRA might have been talking about our right to own firearms, Griz commented "Oh."

AMAZING BEAR-MAN CLAIMS...

"Hell yeah... I'd like bear arms. Who wouldn't??!"

May 2002

SIZE MATTERS!

Sean Robichaud recently unveiled the redneck dream vehicle - a stretch flat bed pick-up. When asked why, Sean replied "Basically, I just got tired of everyone bragging about how damn big their pick-ups were. I had some free time, a 12 pack and a new welder, next thing you know I had the biggest damn truck in the whole county."

July 2002

Red Lodge Believe It or Not!

ARMS TO RIGHT BEARS

An alarming trend among bears in The Custer National Forest near Red Lodge has prompted officers of the Beartooth Ranger District to develop a method to set slumbering bears upright in an attempt to wake them up. Apparently, due to the mild winter last year, many bears started hibernating later than usual, and are now having trouble waking up. Armed only with a long pole, leather gloves and safety glasses, Rangers nudge the sleeping bears into an upright position. "Once we get them on their feet they usually just sort of wander off." Says Ranger Josh Charles "It's pretty damn scary when you run across a grumpy one though."

"We considered just letting them wake up when they felt like it, but then we knew their internal clocks would get all hinky," announced Rand Herzberg. "We've got to get them back on the right schedule, it's our job."

June 2002

Red Lodge—
Believe It or Not!

TRUCKERS BARE RIGHT ARMS

A group of area truckers are up in arms about the difficulty of getting a tan on their right arms. There is no problem getting a tan on their left arms as they usually hang them out the window of their trucks while driving across country. "At first we just tried to get Peterbilt to move the steering wheel to the other side of the damn truck cab, seemed easy enough enough to me, but they didn't think it would be cost effective," said spokesman, Jimmy Kujala. Searching for another solution, the band of teamsters have contacted truck drivers in Europe, whose *right arms* are tan, and are organizing an exchange program. Jimmy learned about the plight of the European truckers while selling ATV's to British hunters via the Internet. "They're just average joes like you and me," he reported. "You know, they have their steering wheels on the opposite side of the truck so this just seemed like the logical solution." The group of 17 truckers will stay in Europe until the tan on their right arms matches that of the left. "I hear it's kinda rainy over there, so this might take awhile," quipped Kujala.

"Red Lodge Believe It or Not" ranged from serious political parody to complete goofiness. Most of the time, it ran on the back page of the Rag, which made it very visible when you first unfolded the paper.
For the most part, people read it and laughed (or read it and said "huh?"), but every now and then someone would fail to realize that if an article starts with "Believe It or Not," it's always safest to go with "not."

Some of the gags generated angry letters or emails; sometimes people actually called. We ran one about changing the name of Fox, Montana to Hannah, Montana (see next page), and one fellow called to chew my ear off about the real history of the name. He not only believed that the name had been changed, but he thought the Local Rag was somehow responsible for changing it and could change it back.

Red Lodge — Believe It or Not!

January 2008

Town of Fox changes its name to *Hannah*, Montana

Fox is a nice enough town, but the name just lacks a certain sizzle. Following the example of Ismay, Montana, which changed its name to "Joe" in 1993 after the famous quarterback Joe Montana, the residents of Fox have renamed their town for the Disney pop star, Hannah Montana.

Miley Cyrus, the actress who plays Hannah on the Disney TV series, said, "Wow! I'm, like, really flattered to have a town named after me. I mean like after my character, y'know?"

When asked about the name change, a Fox resident who wishes to remain anonymous said, "Look. Fox gets no respect around here. Everyone playfully calls Roberts 'Bob.' People have 'Where the hell is Roscoe' bumper stickers. Ismay became world-famous when it was renamed Joe. We figured if it worked for them, then by golly, it'll work for us."

The town of Hannah is currently accepting bids from local painters to paint the pop star's picture on the famous Fox grain elevator. ✻

November 2007

Red Lodge — Believe It or Not!

Real Estate Market "Too Damned Good"

The upturn in the market has finally arrived, and real estate is selling in Red Lodge.

"It caught me by surprise," says Myrna Wright of Montana Realty. "It all sold. All of it. The prices were so good I just couldn't say no. My house. My office. My little cabin in the woods. I even got an offer I couldn't refuse on my car."

Myrna, like several other Red Lodge realtors, is now living in doorways and alleys, pushing her dog Captain around in a shopping cart and begging for help until prices drop enough to buy another house.

"I guess it's true what they say," Myrna mused. "You really do have to be careful what you wish for."

May 2004

Red Lodge
Believe It or Not!

MATTEL INTRODUCES RED LODGE BARBIE

"Our very own Barbie!" announces Mayor Richard Gessling. "I sent a 26 page proposal to Mattel about Red Lodge and they loved the idea of a small town theme." She comes dressed in her Snow Creek cap, Bone Daddy's hoodie and Sylvan Peak rafting shorts. With her own Jagermeister bottle in her hand and battery operated arm movement you can actually make her drink by pressing a button on her back. Careful though, too much drinking action will give Barbie a hang-over, her skin turns a slight shade of green and that chipper smile disappears. Buy one for yourself or as a gift. "I'm expecting to have her in stock by mid June but get your name on the preorder list, they'll go fast." says Jewel Karina at Radio Shack. Red Lodge Barbie accessories include skis, hiking boots, a pink bar stool and her own 501(c)3 application, all sold separately. But Red Lodge Barbie has left surrounding towns saying, "What about Bob's Barbie!" and "Where the hell is Roscoe's?". Over the hill they ask "Have road closures delayed the launch of Bearcreek Barbie?"

Real Drinking Action!

give Barbie a hang-over!

OZZY TO SPEAK AT GRADUATION

Sources report that rock star/TV phenomenon Ozzy Osbourne will be the guest speaker for this year's graduation ceremony at Red Lodge High School. "We wanted someone with a strong anti-drug message," reported Principal Rex Ternan. "I think just seeing the results of years of drug abuse first hand is a good way to steer kids away from drugs."

Osbourne will be in town to perform with the Classic Rock All-Stars on May 25. "I'll probably do a few songs at The Pollard Pub after the concert," says Ozzy. "We'll be staying there with our dogs anyway, so I plan to sing for my supper."

The family will also go on a fishing trip with long-time pal, Mel Gibson. "I always like to fish with Mel at least once a year," said Ozzy via speaker phone. "Sharon and the kids love to camp out under the stars. We eat lots of s'mores and sing campfire songs. It's very bleeping wholesome."

"Jack wants to attend college at MSU-Billings so we're also checking that out," said Sharon. "He plans to major in veterinary science. He really likes Montana because people drive around with rifles in their pick-ups. And of course, Ozzy is eager to see some of those Belfry Bats."

When asked what his speech will be about, Ozzy mumbled a few incoherent sentences followed by a string of expletives.

June 2003

Red Lodge
Believe It or Not!

NEW FESTIVAL EVENT! BARBARIAN DAY

The Festival of Nations has added a new day to this year's annual festivities and has dubbed August 4th Barbarian Day. Although the idea started out as a simple typo, misspelling the word Bavarian, the Festival board is very excited about the possibilities of this new day. "Barbarian Day should greatly raise interest in the hunters and gatherers contingent. And besides, the outfits are great, we will stay much cooler dancing with our shirts off," commented a Festival board member, who now wishes to be known only as "Holman the Barbarian." Barbarian Day events were still being planned but will include "Grog Chugging" and "Village Plundering." The day will end with a Roast Beast Slaughtering Competition and BBQ. Locals and visitors alike are encouraged to grab their wenches and join in this exciting new addition to the Festival.

July 2003

October 2004

BLACK BEAR ADVOCATES ATKINS

After returning home late from a potluck dinner, Charlotte Rice left her remaining salad in her car overnight. The next morning she found her car covered in mud and surrounded by bear prints. On inspecting the interior she realized the salad was gone, bowl and all. She made a call to her friend Rosalie McQuillan who was working at H bar S, saying "The bear must have crawled in a window and eaten my salad!" With even further inspection and a second phone call, she told Rosalie that not only is the bowl nowhere to be found but the bear left a full bag of potato chips that had been in the car and had taken her breath mints. So beware, Red Lodge, of the carbohydrate-avoiding omnivore with minty fresh breath.

November 2004

TUNNEL TO YELLOWSTONE

Construction is nearing completion on the tunnel through the Beartooth Mountains into Yellowstone National Park. "Wahoo dawgie, will it ever!" says an enthusiastic John Toler when asked if he thought it would increase tourism.

"It'll keep us busy all year" says Carl Jr., Snowcreek Saloon owner, "and maybe those folks from Cooke City won't be quite so strange, if they can get to town more often during the winter."

Soon Red Lodgers and surrounding communities will all be able to take the tunnel. This will surely bring overwhelming opportunity to the community and business owners.

May 2007

Red Lodge Believe It or Not!

Amazing Dog Does Massage

Some massage therapists might be slowed down by a broken arm. But not Threse Fuchs of Bearcreek, who has passed on her gift to her Jack Russell Terrier Sadie.

"Sadie's a very smart dog, so she's picking this up quite quickly," says Threse. "And the clients get an extra benefit because she likes to lick up the massage oil when she's done."

To train Sadie, Threse placed treats at strategic points on her clients' backs. "One thing I didn't have to train her on, though, was the lower back area. Like most dogs, she's always ready to sniff somebody's bum."

On her very first engagement, one problem came when Sadie started barking toward the end of the massage. "But it turns out she was just doing her job," Threse says, "letting us know that the next client was here."

That first client, XXX, says she would gladly repeat the experience. "Sadie's massages are different from Threse's, of course, but no less effective. Between the delicate touch of the paws, the occasional digging action, the gentle breeze of the wagging tail, and the more insistent, colder, wetter nudge of her nose, Sadie really got at those deep tissues. I felt incredibly relaxed -- I think I could curl up in my favorite chair and sleep all day."

The experiment has gone so well that Threse even debated giving up massage entirely, to focus instead on her vast entrepreneurial talents, opening a chain of franchised dog-massage parlors known as JackBacks. "We were going to start in California, and I was thrilled by the opportunity to travel to strip malls all over Los Angeles inspecting my JackBack franchisees. But as I was sitting with my financial advisor, I started getting jealous of Sadie, who got to have a close, touching relationship with people.

"So as soon as this arm heals," Threse concludes, "I'll be back at the massage table, and Sadie will have to find some other furniture to jump up on."

August 2008

Obama Picks Running Mate!

Presidential candidate Barack Obama has selected prominent Carbon County Democrat Betsy Scanlin to fill the Veep slot on his ticket. "I'm proud to have Mayor Scanlin on board," Obama said. "She's an asset to the party and to my campaign."

Pundit James Carville commented, "It's a stroke of genius on Obama's part. He's got an experienced party loyalist from the West—and she's a woman!"

When the news hit, former Red Lodge Mayor Brian Roat was quick to congratulate Scanlin. "I wish her all the best, and I'm ready to fill in when she vacates her current office!"

Obama announces to an enthusiastic crowd that he's picked Red Lodge Mayor Betsy Scanlin as his running mate.

September 2002

SHUTTLE TO LAND IN RED LODGE

NASA officials are working with a group of Red Lodge citizens to build a new runway large enough to allow the space shuttle to land. An unidentified spokesperson was quoted as saying "It's the same as the airport, I don't care where the landing site is, just as long as the shuttle doesn't fly over my house."

Reportedly, NASA will pay to pave the strip once the land is provided by the city. "Right now, we're trying to decide between downtown Red Lodge or Hwy 212 near Rock Creek Resort," said the source. "Those are the only two pieces of land flat enough for a strip of the necessary size. We figure by leveling the downtown area, we could encourage merchants to set up temporary booths that could be moved easily when it was time for the shuttle to land. The tourist revenue would be incredible!"

Along with the runway, the facility will require the city to build an $8 million radio tower. "We could pay for it by increasing the Resort Tax, just think of the jobs this project will generate," added the source. NASA officials had not returned phone calls as of press time.

SHROOM ATTACK!

During the Festival of Nations, a giant alien mushroom attacked a local woman walking alone south of town. Luckily for her, but not so lucky for the alien, she was accompanied by Red Lodge's own intrepid Scottish terrier, Tess (registered name Tess the Terrierable). Tess grabbed the toadstool where it really hurt and the alien fell to the ground. In it's dying breath it confessed that it's "cap was fried" because the Alien Nations of Shroom were not included in the Festival activities (except as appetizers). It did not express remorse at its horrendous act. The mushroom was taken to Professor Randy Tracy – a noted fungologist (mushroom nut). When pressed by our interviewer he responded sadly "the giant mushroom was really and sincerely dead." With a gleam in his eye he stated that it was either a rare alien giant Suillus (or possibly Bolete?) mushroom. The Shroom weighed in at 22 lbs. with a cap diameter of 9 in. and height of 8 in.

Professor Tracy also noted that "Indeed, this was an heroic act by our wee bonnie lass, Miss Tess," and that "We have all come to expect great things from her!"

As for the victim of the attack, she has no visible scars from her encounter. Unfortunately she is experiencing an exaggerated startle response (read: screams and hides) when anything bounces within 100 yards.

– By Gwen Williams

Red Lodge — Believe It or Not!

Some of the staff get acquainted with the newly-rebuilt lodge.

One of the new rides at Red Lodge Santa's Village.

December 2007

Red Lodge Mountain becomes "Santa's Village" Theme Park

The new owners of Red Lodge Mountain have decided to convert the ski area into a Christmas-based theme park, taking their cue from the "Santa's Villages" that used to dot the country in the 1960s.

A spokesman for JMA Ventures, the company that purchased the Mountain last month, said that "Ski areas are a dime a dozen, but Christmas-based theme parks? They rock, man!"

The rumor mill says that George W. Bush will be playing the role of Santa after the upcoming presidential election. "I just want some love," he reputedly said. "Everybody loves Santa, don't they?"

March 2005

Red Lodge — Believe It or Not!

The Fowl — A MONTANA MAKEOVER

Sometimes, The Fowl believes, the essence of the Ultimate Makeover is minimalism. Subtraction. Advice from the More-is-Less school of thought. Our team of plastic surgeons, reconstructive dentists, and implant specialists can remake anyone – and make them more beautiful, stronger, sexier than their own imperfect DNA would ever allow – but is all that is really needed? Especially in a place like Red Lodge, where so many people want to simplify their lives. Simplify, simplify, simplify. Such was The Fowl's message to Red Lodgian Paul Beck. Take, for example, his musical career. Though we loved his 2000 album Of the Forest, why, we asked, did he record it under the name "Paul Eugene Beck"? Why not simplify? And so, with our help and some color-blindness inducing contact lenses, he has become simply Beck, and the rest, well...the rest is obvious.

"I suppose I always had it in me," Beck (Paul now wishes to be known exclusively by his simpler moniker) says. "I guess I just needed a little fowl attention."

BEFORE / AFTER

TAKE-A-PENNY THIEF APPREHENDED!

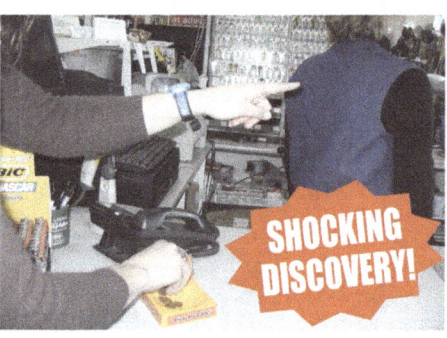

SHOCKING DISCOVERY!

In the latest development of the scandal we reported on last month, Lincoln "Take A Penny" Blake has been apprehended by Michigan police following his terrifying Red Lodge crime spree. "He cleaned us out twice" said Vanessa Gilbertson at Buckin' Bronc Coffee counter. "It didn't seem like any store was safe," said Trevor Culp.

Thirteen cents here, four cents there, it all added up to sizable loot for Blake, who fooled cashiers by posing as a polite, unassuming retiree. "He'd buy a pack of gum or something, and then poof! the penny tray would be empty," said one clerk, who asked to remain anonymous. "It's really shaken my faith in the essential decency of mankind."

Red Lodge
Believe It or Not!

"THANKS, RED LODGE DATING SERVICE!"

Are you a Red Lodge single looking for love? Red Lodge now has a dating service available to anyone at no cost. Just send your personal information, the type of person you're looking for, hobbies, activities, annual income etc. to RedLodgeSinglesLookingForLove@yahoo.com and they will match you with that perfect someone.

It worked for Tom Rickbeil and Melissa Kaufmann who after dating for 2 years got engaged at the Bogarts 20th anniversary party May 11th. "I did it on a whim one night, I sent RedLodgeSinglesLookingForLove@yahoo.com my info, and they matched me with Melissa" says Tom.

"I really had no idea what was going on when Tom called the first time," explains Melissa. "I guess my mother heard about the service and gave my profile and picture to RedLodgeSinglesLookingForLove@yahoo.com but now I'm glad she did."

"And the rest is history" they said in unison.

Take it from these two love birds, Melissa and Tom a true RedLodgeSinglesLookingForLove@yahoo.com success story. It's fun, it's free and who knows you may be lucky in love. TRY IT TODAY!

CURVY CROSSWALKS

Just in time for summer, the crosswalks have been updated in the Social District of downtown Red Lodge. Now more user friendly to locals and tourists alike, a calculated curve has been added to help with late night pedestrian safety. "A study of walking patterns in this area between June and August 2003 indicated the conventional crosswalk was not meeting people's needs" says city planner David Stauffer. "People can easily stay between the lines now and we'll have fewer problems with jaywalking" adds Chief Pringle. Thanks Red Lodge for putting safety first.

Where were these crosswalks during the Great ADA Street Corner Controversy of 2015? We had the problem solved in June 2004 and completely forgot about it!

January 2011

Red Lodge
Believe It or Not!

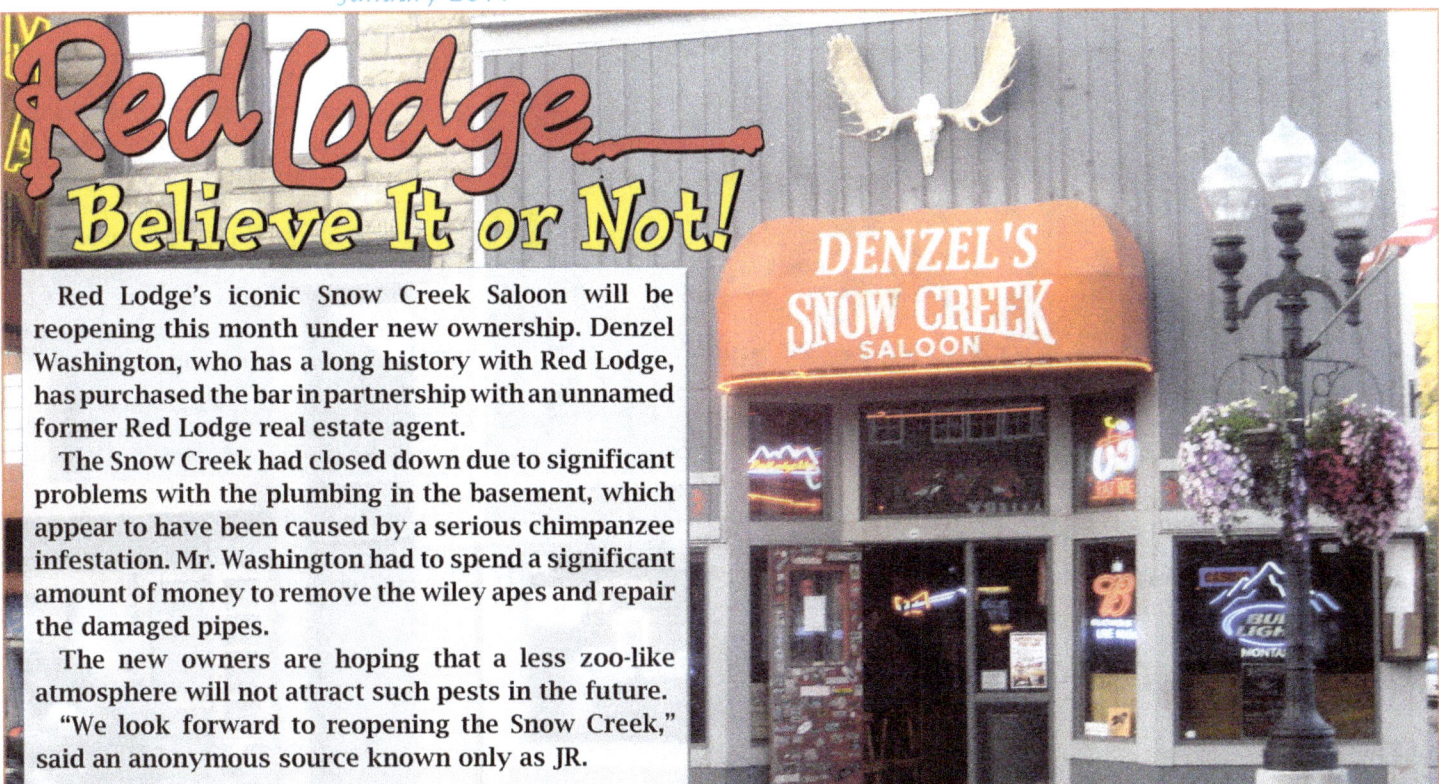

Red Lodge's iconic Snow Creek Saloon will be reopening this month under new ownership. Denzel Washington, who has a long history with Red Lodge, has purchased the bar in partnership with an unnamed former Red Lodge real estate agent.

The Snow Creek had closed down due to significant problems with the plumbing in the basement, which appear to have been caused by a serious chimpanzee infestation. Mr. Washington had to spend a significant amount of money to remove the wiley apes and repair the damaged pipes.

The new owners are hoping that a less zoo-like atmosphere will not attract such pests in the future.

"We look forward to reopening the Snow Creek," said an anonymous source known only as JR.

Red Lodge—Believe It or Not! Box Store Opens in Red Lodge!

Corporate executives from Thinkoutsidethe Corporation pose outside their first store in Red Lodge.

Young and Ferguson's company cars: matching limited-edition Porsche Boxsters.

Ferguson and Young show just a small sampling of the wares for sale at Thinkoutsidethe Box Company.

February 2008

In response to the growing interest in chain box stores in Carbon County, Thinkoutsidethe Corporation is pleased to announce the opening of a new Thinkoutsidethe® Box Store in Red Lodge.

"We hope to provide the community with close to 200 minimum-wage jobs without benefits," said CEO Gary Ferguson, "and two jobs that pay *really* well. Everybody needs boxes, right?" CFO and Corporate Counsel Kent E. Young agrees.

"In recognition of the forthcoming boon to the economy," Young told us, "Thinkoutsidethe Corporation has approached the City Council, County Commissioners, Planning Board, EDC, Chamber of Commerce, and Main Street Committee seeking waivers of taxes, utility hookup fees, license fees, and pretty much all other fees, as is common in the industry."

Thinkoutsidethe has already negotiated a steep discount on the property for the store, right behind the Café Regis. The savings were enough to purchase a pair of shiny new Porche Boxsters for the corporate executives.

"Advertising," said Young. "They're Boxsters. Get it? BOX-sters? They're tax deductions."

Thinkoutsidethe will be stocking a wide variety of both new and used boxes in a wide variety of sizes.

"In addition to boxes, Thinkoutsidethe will be selling accessories such as box cutters, boxing gloves, boxer shorts, box seats, shadow boxes, box office receipts and box tops," Ferguson said. "We plan to underprice all competitors to achieve our aggressive growth goals. Prices may, however, have to go up after all of the competition is gone.

Future franchise opportunities are available for interested (and qualified) investors in the burgeoning communities of Edgar and Roscoe, Montana; and Frannie, Wyoming.

For the time being, however, Thinkoutsidethe is looking forward to boxing up the market in Red Lodge. ✳

CHAPTER 9
Christmas in Red Lodge

December 2007 • Volume 18 • Issue 12

Around Town
What's Happening in December . . . 18-19
Christmas 14-17
Halloween Wrapup. 5
The Not-So-Great Mall of Red Lodge 8
High School Goings-On 9
Agriculture: Pigs? In Carbon County? . . 27
Round Man: Tribute to Stano Bustos 24
Birthdays & Anniversaries 29
Helping Hands 30

The Arts
Artist Profile: Dominique Paulus 32
Book Review: *The Animal Dialogues* . . 22
Book News: Local Authors 23
Music: Symphonic Rock 34
Photography: Taking Pictures in Snow . . 31
Architecture: Archi-texture 20
Fiction: Cody Quarterline, part XVI 25

Food & Drink
Nana Inga's Pepparkakor 10
The Cheapskate Wine Snob 12
Eggnog: Not Just for Christmas 15

Outdoors
The Willow Creek Trail 6
What to do in Winter in Red Lodge. 28
Fishing Report 7
Bird of the Month: Kingfisher 13
Garden Report (or is it?) 26

Fun & Games
Find the Fake Ad! . . . . ??
Red Lodge Crossword Puzzle 35
Red Lodge Believe It Or Not 36
Cartoon 6

PRSRT-STD
U.S. Postage
PAID
Red Lodge, MT
Permit No. 75

BOXHOLDER

Red Lodge had many Christmas-themed covers over the years (about one per year, if I recall correctly), but the 2007 cover was the start of something new. Billings artist Benny Gillet submitted a piece of artwork for the Red Lodge Christmas Stroll poster contest, not realizing that there wasn't going to be a poster that year. We purchased rights to the painting to use as a Rag cover, and thus a new tradition was born. Over the following years, a different artist was featured each December — and Benny's painting did end up becoming a Stroll poster a few years later.

The 2008 Christmas cover featured artwork by Dolly Frerichs (now Dolly Stuber), owner of the Strawberry Patch frame shop.

In 2009, we decided to go to Red Lodge High School to search for artists. Our first stop at the school, of course, was with Art Teacher Extraordinaire Mike Kosorok. The masterpiece on the front cover, as it turns out, came from a student that isn't even taking art from Mike this semester, a Junior named Mariah Greathouse. Mike approached her in Algebra class. "Mariah is tremendously talented," Mike told us. "Especially with lettering. She has a future in commercial or graphic arts if she chooses to pursue it."

Mariah's picture was inspired by the snow at sunrise. "I love the weather around here," she said. The lettering and outlines are pen & ink, and the background is watercolor.

December 2014

BOXHOLDER

FREE and worth every penny!

Please recycle your Rag

PRSRT-STD
U.S. Postage
PAID
Red Lodge, MT
Permit No. 75

The December 2014 Local Rag cover is a Christmas Stroll poster contest entry by Suzanna Bailey. The artwork is a 9x12 mixed media work, made with colored pencil and acrylic paint on a fiber paper sketchpad. Suzanna has a background in interior design, so her art was done with a heavy focus on architecture, perspective, and the technicalities of the buildings. She added the chandeliers to create sort of an ethereal, dream-world kind of feel, she says. Suzanna was inspired by the story of the Twelve Dancing Princesses by the Brothers Grimm, in which the princesses sneak off each night to dance in a secret other-worldly castle, only to return each morning with their shoes worn out from the journey.

The 2013 Christmas cover was on the first issue back after a publishing hiatus of almost three years, hence the "we're back" headline.

My favorite music of the Christmas season

by Kathy Robson

Nothing to me evokes the holidays like Christmas music. My family can tell you, I start listening to Christmas music *way* too early for their taste. I used to sing in a large choir, and we started practicing for our "Singing Christmas Tree" in early September. I still remember listening to my practice tape in the car, blasting out "*White Christmas,*" and realizing I was stopped at a stoplight, with my windows down (the temperature was in the 80s), and the person in the car next to me was looking at me like I was insane. Why is Christmas music one of the few genres that can only be listened to one month out of the year?

Music goes a lot further than just being something nice to listen to. Music has been used as therapy for seizures, to lower blood pressure, treat children with A.D.D., treat mental illness, treat depression, aid in healing, treat stress, and even insomnia. In his book *Musicophilia: Tales of Music and the Brain*, Oliver Sacks says "Listening to music is not just auditory or emotional, it is motoric as well. We keep time to music, involuntarily, even if we are not consciously attending to it." It is believed that there is no one single musical center of the brain, but rather it is the involvement of dozens of scattered networks of the brain working together (this is a great book, by the way).

On an emotional level, who doesn't feel like a kid again, when singing *Frosty the Snowman* or *Rudolph the Red-Nosed Reindeer*? And there's always the modern favorite, *Grandma Got Run Over By a Reindeer*. But now that I'm a grandma, I kind of understand why my grandmother never quite got the humor of that song.

By far my favorite Christmas song of all time is *O Holy Night*. This is largely due to memories of my father, with his beautiful tenor voice, singing this every year at our church. And when I was old enough, I got to accompany him on the piano. Not only do I have over 600 different Christmas songs on my iPod, I have 28 different versions of *O Holy Night*, including versions by the Canadian Brass, Mannheim Steamroller, Brian Setzer Orchestra, Bing Crosby, and Trans-Siberian Orchestra. I cannot listen to this song quietly, or non-physically. It just has that effect on me. Some people feel the same way about the *Hallelujah Chorus*.

I do love the classics, Bing Crosby's *White Christmas*, Elvis Presley's *Blue Christmas*, Frank Sinatra's *Silent Night*, Tony Bennett singing *The Christmas Song* ("Chestnuts Roasting on an Open Fire"). But here are a few of my newer favorites:

- **Trans-Siberian Orchestra**
  The Lost Christmas Eve
  Orchestral music set behind driving electric guitar

- **Il Divo**
  The Christmas Collection
  Great Italian male quartet

- **Celtic Woman**
  A Christmas Celebration.

- **Gaither Vocal Band**
  Christmas GVB Style or
  Still the Greatest Story Ever Told

- **Brooklyn Tabernacle Choir**
  Oh What A Love

- **Mannheim Steamroller**
  Any *Fresh Aire Christmas*

- **Woody Phillips**
  A Toolbox Christmas
  Christmas carols played on various hand and power tools

- For something really bizarre and irreverent, **Bob Rivers**
  More Twisted Christmas or
  Chipmunks Roasting on an Open Fire

Whatever your musical preference, crank it up and enjoy the music of the season – soon enough there will be people saying, "Why are you still listening to Christmas music?!"

> "On an emotional level, who doesn't feel like a kid again, when singing *Frosty the Snowman* or *Rudolph the Red-Nosed Reindeer?*"

During the Christmas Stroll, everybody loves the goodies! How did people find out what goodies were available where? Why, the Local Rag, of course. This list is from the December 2006 issue.

CHRISTMAS SPIRIT IN RED LODGE

December 2006

by Kathy Robson

I've always loved the Christmas season. I'm the one who starts listening to Christmas music way before my family is ready for it. I do sneak out a few decorations a little early, but I am a traditionalist when it comes to really decorating for Christmas—I have to wait until the day after Thanksgiving and then blast it all at once. When I lived in the city, I think I looked forward to the Season because everyone seemed to be much happier, and helpful to each other. They may have been rushed and stressed, but it was a "good" bustle. Since I've been living in Red Lodge, I've noticed that what other people call the "Christmas Spirit" is abundant all year long!

We had been here about a year when Gary was diagnosed with cancer. Within days of word getting out, he was inundated with people coming into the bookstore asking if they could help, offering to help at the store even though they didn't work for us; cancer survivors that came to offer inspiring stories or offer an ear; the local lady who took her hat off to show her bald head and said "I'll show you mine if you show me yours." And especially the employee who put Gary's chemo treatments on her calendar, so that she wouldn't book herself to do anything else for a few days following each treatment, so she could work as much as we needed. She said that was not only for Gary's benefit, but she wanted me to be able to stay home and help him, and not worry about the store; I still tear up thinking about that.

Kathy and her big brother Larry a few Christmases ago

Everyone has a story of people coming out of the woodwork when they need it: the ones who help pull people's cars out of snow banks; the ones who help push stuck cars away from the curb; the homes that were opened up to people who had to evacuate because of the Cascade fire. The list is endless.

But it's the everyday attitude of people here that shows the Christmas Spirit all year long. The fact that even teenage boys still hold the door open for you (not to mention the older gentlemen that run ahead of a lady to get the door, just like my Montana grandfather used to do), a stranger that will offer to help you lift something heavy out of your car and help you carry it into your home or business. People take the time at the post office, the grocery story to catch up on what you've been up to; and people still stop on Broadway to let pedestrians cross.

And do we love a parade! The big ones, yes. But I remember when a local girl was going to compete in the Special Olympics, and we threw a parade for her. It was just one convertible, with her riding in the back waving to the crowd. But people came out to cheer her on and wave flags.

It's this attitude that brings people here to visit. All summer, I have people coming into the bookstore talking about how nice everyone in town is, and everyone seems genuinely happy. They say that is different from even other small towns our size. It's why people who come here for Christmas save their shopping for Christmas Eve in downtown Red Lodge, because they say they know we always have unique items, and that they love the spirit downtown; they'd never save their shopping for December 24th in the mall!

Let's try to never forget what a special place we live in, and that we are all here because we choose to be. It's the people; that's what makes it special.

ROUND MAN REVIEW

Livin' and Lovin' the Holidays

Ah,…the holidays. How could you not love them: family, friends, days off, sights, sounds, smells, parties, gifts. This is the time of year where it just seems like one big holiday from Thanksgiving right into the Christmas season followed directly by New Year's Eve. I think once Thanksgiving hits, our minds go into a whole different mode until after the New Year. Personally for me it's the time of year when business doesn't seem quite as important as the rest of the year, even though I subconsciously know it is. I go into the Whistle While You Work mode, you know the mode where if we had a great year, I'm tickled and if we didn't, it's to damn late to do anything about it so why worry?

At times for me it's a bit overwhelming, the shopping standing in line waiting for a crack at the new Tickle Me Elmo that walks, talks, goes to school, grows up and has a career, you know the toy. Crowds can be a small irritant for me, but for the most part it's all about the joy of the season. Giving, sharing, celebrating that warm fuzzy feeling we get this time of year.

A huge build-up to the finale, of course, is New Year's Eve. That's right, the night when the ball drops and we are into a whole New Year of 2007. This is the night when we all have to make some serious decisions. These decisions are easier for some than others. There's the "Do I stay home by the fire with someone, pop some popcorn, play games, watch Dick Clark, wait till midnight, pass around the kisses, and head off to bed" kind of Play It Safe New Year's, or…? That's right, you guessed it: the "Party Like It's 1999" mode. Start about noon with putting Prince (or formerly know as something) on the CD player or mp3 your choice, you start pumpin' that subwoofer at warp 10 with some "Little Red Corvette" and move right into "1999" and you are off and running. It's time to choose your proper attire for a night on the town, something classy yet practical and something that you won't mind throwing away when in the morning you discover it has cigarette burns, booze stains, possible foot prints and various other foreign material all over it.

Then you discover you might as well have a little holiday cheer to kinda get primed. You, my friend, are on your way to Amateur Night as we musicians like to affectionately call it. This is the night when some people who never indulge are going to. You will find that about 9:30 you start to speak drunkineese and even though the bartender can't understand what you just said, you're sure it was "Bartender, may I please have another glass of that delicious tequila?" You're starting to think you can dance way better then the eight people up on the bar on you know it would look way better with some naked choreography. By now you have danced, consumed mass amounts of swill, discussed and solved every economic and political problem we had in the past ten years with anyone who will listen. Now all that's left is to make it to the magic hour.

At one minute to twelve the only thing clear to you is the one person way back in the corner heading your way puckered up. Even though they are less than desirable, they look like the latest centerfold from your favorite fashion magazine. The clock strikes twelve, you just received the best kiss you had in 2006, and within minutes the delicious beverages you had earlier aren't setting well, or maybe it was the peanuts and cigarette butt combo from the bowl on the bar, whatever. Your main goal now is to get safely home to your spinning bed and porcelain statue that you will grow to love by morning, at which time you will wake up to find yourself uttering that world famous phrase: "Where the hell am I?" Have a safe, fun and Happy New Year!

~By Jimmy Kujala

January 2007

The Very Best of the Red Lodge Local Rag

COOKING WITH JOHN
SHARING CHRISTMAS RECIPES

by John Overton

Yummy Salad

Ingredients
- 1½ cups crushed pretzels
- 2 tbsp sugar
- ½ cup melted butter
- 1 8-oz pkg cream cheese
- 1 cup sugar
- 9 oz Cool Whip
- 1 6-oz. pkg raspberry Jell-o
- 2 cups boiling water
- 2 20-oz pkg frozen raspberries

Process
Mix crumbs, sugar and butter. Spread in 9x13 ungreased pan. Bake at 350°F for 10 minutes. Cool. Combine cream cheese, sugar and Cool Whip. Mix well. Spread on crumb crust. Refrigerate for two hours.

Dissolve Jell-o in water, stir in raspberries. Allow to thicken slightly. Pour over cheese mixture. Refrigerate overnight.

Serves 12-16

Christmas is a great time to dig out your old family recipes and share them with your friends. So guess what? I've found some that have been in my family for years, and I'm sharing them with our loyal readers.

BON APPETITE

Merry Christmas to you and yours.

Chicken Cordon Bleu

Ingredients
- 8-10 boneless, skinless whole chicken breasts
- 20 slices Canadian bacon or ham
- 32 oz (two pounds) sliced Swiss cheese
- 2 10-oz cans cream of chicken soup
- 1 regular bottle white wine

Process
Place chicken breasts in greased 9x13 pan. Bake at 375°F for about 35 min, until done. Place 2 slices Canadian bacon and one slice cheese on each breast. Reheat until cheese melts (about 5-10 min.)

Sauce: In a medium-size saucepan, mix the soup with the remaining cheese (torn into small pieces) and 2 cups of wine. Heat until cheese melts, stirring frequently. Spoon sauce over the chicken.

Reheat until sauce is bubbly, but not brown (approx. 10-15 min).

Serves 8-10

Frozen Peppermint Dessert

Ingredients
- 1 box vanilla wafers
- 1 stick butter
- 1 cup chopped pecans
- 2 qts. peppermint ice cream
- 1½ cups whipping cream
- ¼ cup cocoa
- ¾ cup sugar

Process
Combine crushed wafers, melted butter, and chopped pecans. Reserve ¼ of mixture for topping. Press mixture into bottom of 9x13 pan. Bake for 8-10 min. at 350°F. Cool completely.

Filling: Soften ice cream and spread over crust. Place in freezer.

Topping: Whip together cocoa, sugar and whipping cream until soft peaks. Spread over ice cream, sprinkle remaining crumb mixture. COVER and freeze until ready to serve.

Serves 15-18

December 2008

John Overton is the Local Rag's ombudsman and staff chef. He believes that food is to share.

CHAPTER 10
That strange *Local Rag* sense of humor

FAKE ADS

For the most part, we thought our fake ads were pretty obvious, but we got calls about some of them. As expected, there were more calls about the kitten than the husband.

We were told by several people that the cuddle marmot picture was the creepiest thing we've ever printed.

PICK ONE!
Free to good home

6-month-old tabby kitten. Beautiful, affectionate, playful, and litterbox trained. Comes with all supplies, including food, toys, bed, and litterbox.

23-year-old husband. Good-looking, playful, doesn't like cats. Says it's him or the kitten. Comes with a car and a 12-pack of cheap beer.

Check out both and see which one you like best. Call Annie at 555-3253 today

interesting inc
MAKING PEOPLE INTERESTING SINCE 1970

WE PROVIDE YOU WITH...
- A NEW WARDROBE
- A MINIMUM OF 26 TWITTERS A DAY
- GUARANTEED 1000 OF FACEBOOK FRIENDS
- A BRIEFING EVERY MORNING WITH DOZENS OF INTERESTING THINGS TO SAY TO PEOPLE.

$300.00 Special

DOWNTOWN RED LODGE   555-FUNGI

Let us fill in what's missing

Beartooth Escorts
Prices start at just $4,300

New to Red Lodge
POLKA TOWN

* Polka Records (33's & 45's)
* Best Accordian prices since JK
* Live Polka Music every night
* Free Polka lessons
* Special Polka Video Games

**at #34 Old Town Square
1-8pm daily**

THE JOY OF WET SHEEP

by Gary Robson

Once upon a time—and yes, this is true even though it begins with the words, "once upon a time,"—we lived in a warmer place. A place warm enough, in fact, to have a swimming pool. It was a nice swimming pool. An honest-to-goodness in-ground swimming pool with a deep end, a shallow end, and steps. Generally, it only froze over a couple of times a year.

It was a warmer place, but it was still a windy place sometimes, much like here. So, to keep the leaves, pine cones, dust, insects, frogs, and other windborne detritus out of the pool, we decided we needed a pool cover. Just to be clear, we didn't have windborne frogs. They were more self-propelled, wandering up from the creek to explore this new and different body of water.

And despite being a warmer clime, it wasn't exactly the Sonoran Desert, so we decided we needed a thermal pool cover that would keep the pool not only clean and frog-free, but warm as well.

So we found a pool cover that looked remarkably like blue bubblewrap, cut it to fit, installed the roller holder system, and had a well-protected, warm, and clean pool. Until the next big windstorm.

I know what you're thinking, and you're wrong. The wind didn't blow the cover from the pool. All it did was knock a whole bunch of apples off of our apple trees. "What does that have to do with pool covers?", I hear you cry. Hold tight. We're almost there.

I asked my kids to pick up the apples. Being clever little tykes, they let their 4-H sheep out to do the work for them. One of these sheep was a big ol' wether from the prior year (for those not up on their sheep terminology, wether is to ram as steer is to bull—he was a castrated male). I know some of you see this coming, but don't ruin it for everyone else, okay?

So, this big ol' wether, who went by the moniker of "Spaz," filled up on apples with the rest of the flock, and then wandered casually off toward the pool (yes, it's easy to be casual when you have the IQ of a cow pie). The kids, foreseeing trouble, attempted to head him off at the pass, and Spaz broke into a trot.

At this point, I heard two sounds that you just don't want to hear superimposed: loud splashing and screaming kids. I ran toward the ruckus to find that Spaz had not only attempted to trot across the pool on the flimsy floating cover, but had torn up said cover with his wildly-flailing sharp little hoofies.

The children were panicking, but not nearly as much as the sheep, who was bleating madly in sheer terror (sheep terror?) as his flockmates crunched apples and looked the other way. Spaz was working his way toward the deep end of the pool, shredding the cover and inhaling a quart or two of water every time he bleated.

Being a man of action, I ran to the edge of the pool, reached out and grabbed the sheep, and tried to pull him out. I'm not a small fellow, as many of you know. In fact, I even outweighed this 220-pound shrieking wether, and (believe it or not) was once in pretty good shape. But have you ever put a wool sweater in a tub of water and then lifted it out?

Spaz's wool had absorbed somewhere in the neighborhood of 16 tons of water (everybody sing! "You absorb 16 tons, and whaddya get?"), and there was simply no way I was going to drag him out. So I handed my wallet to the kids, kicked off my boots, and leaped in. The water was about five feet deep there, and I'm 6'5" tall, so that put the flailing hooves right at chin level.

Let me elaborate on that last point. That put the sharp, sheep-manure-encrusted, flailing hooves uncomfortably close to my face. I managed to maneuver around beside Spaz while he did his best to climb on my back for a piggy-back ride, got my arms around his middle, and dragged him over to the stairs at the shallow end.

I think I already mentioned that he was panicking, bleating in terror, sucking in water, and had the IQ of a cow patty, right? It took a swift kick in his wooly little butt to encourage him to climb out. I swear he had soaked up so much water the pool level dropped a half-inch when he got out. I could have wrung him out like a sponge and watered my whole lawn.

I followed him out of the pool (dripping a not-inconsiderable amount of water myself), waved my arms, and yelled to encourage him to head back for his pen. He took several steps backward, shook like a dog, lost his balance, and fell in the pool again.

To this day, I don't think my daughter knows how close we came to having leg-o-lamb for dinner that night.

> "It's easy to be casual when you have the IQ of a cow patty."

Caught Red (Lodge) Handed

I moved to Red Lodge just last year
And bought a great big hat,
A pair of boots, and Wrangler jeans
To cover where I sat.

I stole a couple flannel shirts
And threw away my ties
And raised my glass of Red Lodge Ale
And looked 'em in the eyes.

I thought that they'd all take me for
A good ol' Red Lodge boy,
But, there was one thing missing from
My good ol' Red Lodge ploy.

A local copper saw at once
The whole thing was a front;
He watched my blinkers, turning left,
And stopped me with a grunt.

"I'll have to shoot you, pop," he said.
"Your driving's crossed the fence;
Turn signals used in Red Lodge are
A capital offense!"

Doug "Rabbit" Sutherland
February 2003

CRACK SHOT...

Sometimes the personals in the Rag tended to get rather ... personal ... as they did in this congratulatory message in October of 1998.

Congratulations, Bucky, on shooting your first 25 clay pigeons in a row at the Cody Shooting Complex... bummer about your prize Subaru hat! (The prize for shooting 25 in a row is that everyone else gets to shoot your hat, not while your head's in it, of course!)
Love, Kimberly

Editor's Note: Happy birthday, Bucky, on October 4th. And now we know how you look in your birthday suit, don't we? (Only in Montana....man, I love this state!)

HOOTERS or bust!

by David Kallenbach

My former wife dragged me to a Hooters restaurant one time. Being the equal-minded sensitive new-aged guy that I am, I would never have suggested this, but if someone of the more-enlightened female persuasion drags you to a Hooters, you don't exactly say, "No!" Besides, she was driving.

What I learned that day (amongst other things!) over a big bucket of greasy hot-wings, Coronas, and (s)hooters of tequila, was a powerful lesson in economics—sex, liquor, smokes, and junk-food ARE good business! Stick with me here. My articles always come back around to the greater good of the community at some point.

I was born and raised in Louisville, Kentucky so I know a few things about vices. I've been to Colonel Sanders' mansion near Shelbyville, just outside Louisville, and knew about fried chicken long before I ever heard of McDonalds. No "KFC" here; I *proudly* pronounce it "Kentucky Fried Chicken"!

I was certainly too young to wager on the thoroughbreds at Churchill Downs. But you can sure bet I understood what gambling was from an early age, though growing up in the house of a Protestant minister I never got to practice it much.

And, after North Carolina, Kentucky grows more tobacco than anywhere else. My house was right next to a bona-fide tobacco warehouse where they hung the long bales of brown wavy weed from the rafters. It was bigger than a football field inside—we used to break in just to explore around in there. The whole neighborhood smelled of sweet tobacco at times.

Then, of course there's one of Kentucky's most famous vices—the brown volatile liquid endemic to Bourbon County, Kentucky that utterly dominated the economics in my area. Whisky distilleries were everywhere. Now, "small-batch" bourbons are all the rage from those little rural distillers. I remember my first sip of mint-julep—way too sweet for me, just like the iced tea in the South. Now, older and more sophisticated, there's nothing better than a nice bourbon on the rocks!

The really intriguing thing about this picture is that it comes from the April 2007 issue of the Local Rag. There was, of course, no roundabout in front of the fire station then, although the plans to put one there had been approved. Good Photoshop work!

So it warmed my heart with nostalgia, the way bourbon whisky warms the insides, when recently word was released that not one, but TWO of my three favorite industries revealed plans to open up plants in the greater Red Lodge area. This, after a study by MSU—Billings' Scott Rickard concluded that conditions around Red Lodge were right for a micro-distillery, a cigarette factory, and a chicken parts outlet. Where I come from, down south, that's like the Triple Crown!

Called "the biggest coups in Red Lodge business history" by a gleaming Mayor Brian Roat, the City of Red Lodge came to agreements with Morningstar Farms, Inc. of Pine Bluff, Arkansas in late February, and with Millenial Distillates of Vancouver, British Columbia this past week to open up operations at undisclosed sites north of town. "We're certainly disappointed Brown and Williamson (cigarette manufacturing titan) pulled out of negotiations," Mayor Roat added, "but heck, winning the Kentucky Derby and the Preakness Stakes, isn't too shabby…Barbaro didn't quite win the Belmont, either, you'll recall, and he wasn't a bad horse…may he rest in peace."

It's anticipated that these two industries combined could bring a nearly $20 million windfall to a region hit hard by loss of ski customers due to climate change. Estimates in this study predict that nearly 800 new jobs would be created. "All the real estate agents should be kept pretty busy for the next few years", said the mayor. Asked if this region's workforce would readily take to the chicken processing and liquor production industries, Mayor Roat responded, "Heck, if we can can peas by the bucket loads, we can sure make some good hooch!"

Red Lodge beat out such larger economic markets as Coeur d'Alene Idaho, and Grand Island, Nebraska. "We were really enticed by the willing work force and low wages abundantly found in the Red Lodge area," said Morningstar vice-president for Marketing and Development, Chester Friedkin. Friedkin added, "This facility will be primarily producing edible chicken products left over from the choicer breast meat cuts taken initially in the slaughtering process…we use the byproducts to make dinosaur-shaped chicken nuggets for kids, as well as the ever-popular wings for the older bar crowd."

A spokesperson for Millenial Distillates, Martina Tyson, who was reached by phone in Seattle and declined a full interview at this time, did say that one product being produced at the new Red Lodge facility will be a vodka drink with an energy-boosting Chinese herbal infusion. "We see it as the 'beer alternative for active adults'—it's really quite distinctive! We make it in small batches the way Master Distiller Todd Bateman's cousin used to make it." Millenial Distillates is best known for its Dekuyper line of liqueurs and cordials, but the company has expressed an interest in developing its micro-distilled line of hand-crafted vodkas produced with local Montana grains. "We think the growing biker crowd will readily take to our local products," said an ebullient Tyson.

These two industries join King's Cupboard Chocolate and Red Lodge Ales to make Red Lodge 'the Vice Capital of the United States!'

So all this got me to thinking about my own economic development, and I started to reflect back on Hooters. Hmm!…Now there's a highly recognizable restaurant chain….Well supported by the NASCAR crowd (don't they have their own car?)…. And, since one of the things Mr. Rickard found in his study was that Red Lodge and its surroundings are about 5-6 fast-food restaurants below the average this area is capable of supporting, why not put a Hooters here? They serve chicken products….People smoke there….I would advertise that I use only locally made products at my restaurant and hire only local girls…And what about THIS? Boyd Motor Speedway! Let's really bring 'em in here! My Outward Bound career is winding down and I need a challenge to keep me going through my prime professional years. Why not?

Oh, the sun shines bright on my old Kentucky Home!

Happy April Fools Day!

hangin' out
Rejected sign submissions

When the historic light poles went in downtown, the Chamber was considering options for banners to hang on the poles.

In the April 2007 issue, the Local Rag obliged.

In the August 2008 issue, Kathy and I published a collection of signs from our last trip to the U.K. (that's Kathy hanging out in the "Broad Sanctuary")

Most of these could be applicable to Red Lodge — we even figured out where to put them. The only one still puzzling us is the frog one. There just aren't that many frogs in Red Lodge!

April 2008

The Very Best of the Red Lodge Local Rag Page 181

The Local Rag Chat Room

April 2006

Local Fiddle Band Goes Punk

"Sometimes life just gets, you know, boring," said Red Lodge's Randy Tracy. "I've done the symphony thing, I've done the Celtic fiddle, I've done the Scottish folk music, I've taught violin lessons. It's time for something new!"

The something new, revealed in this exclusive interview for the *Red Lodge Local Rag*, is punk rock. Still a bit uncomfortable with his new "do" and a red, swollen tongue piercing, Tracy met our intrepid *Local Rag* reporter, Gary Robson, at the new mosh pit he just completed upstairs in the Bull & Bear.

So tell us about Glynfiddle's new sound, Randy.

Well, it's not Glynfiddle anymore. Now we're "Sgian Dubh to the Groin." A Sgian Dubh is this knife in my sock, you know.

Very nice. Put that away. What about the sound?

You know my symphonic background, right? I wanted a cool, melodic sound with a driving beat, screeching bagpipes, and a bunch of yelling. I opted for kind of a cross between The Pogues, Jethro Tull, and Yanni.

We checked out your demo CD, and that first cut, *Eat My Haggis You Wanker*, has quite a unique sound to it. Who did the pipes?

Brad Logan is our new piper. The unique sound came from stabbing his bagpipe with my dirk during the last chorus. Between Brad's scream and that nasty farting sound from the bag, it really added some depth to the piece, don't you think?

How about the vocals on *Death to Englishmen?* They're truly inspired.

Yeah. Sue Logan wrote most of it. The part about the ghost of William Wallace strangling Prince Charlie in Balmoral Castle with a spikey dog collar was mine, though. The vocals are provided by the Nordstrom brothers [Tim & Mike], and they play the guitars, too. You get a whole different sound out of those guys when they go electric. Tim only knows three chords, of course, but this is punk rock, so who cares. And wait 'til you see Mike's new piercing! It'll be the highlight of the show.

Do you feel ready for your first concert here April 1st?

Oh, yeah. I don't want to give away too much, but when I set my violin on fire during *The Devil Went Down to Glasgow*, Brad's going to leap out into the audience and start beating people with his bagpipe. It'll be awesome! I just hope I have time to get my new tat done by then.

A new tattoo?

Over my whole chest. It'll be the Loch Ness monster eating a whole boat full of tourists. Computer programmers from Seattle. Nessie will be crunching down, baby! Blood everywhere. I'll be wearing a kilt for the concert, but no shirt. And under the kilt --

Well, thank you very much for talking to us today, Randy. We'll be looking out for the new CD from Glynfiddle soon.

That's Sgian Dubh to the Groin now, not Glynfiddle. The CD is called "Grizzly in a Kilt," and it'll be out by the concert. See you all there!

localrag@redlodge.com

It's hard to put out a newspaper funded only by ad revenue, but the Local Rag managed to remain free from 1991 to 2014. Not bad...

CHAPTER 11
The Cody Quarterline Saga

Cody Quarterline

The Cody Quarterline story began in April of 2005 as a spoof article. Since then, it's been passed around, from one volunteer tale-spinner to another. We gave each author the freedom to do whatever they liked with Cody, and frankly, we're still not quite sure what's going on. We do know, however, that we've got some creative people in town with time on their hands and maybe a few too many Mickey Spillane movies under their belts.

Part I

Cody misses the funeral

By Dan Upton

"Things aren't good," Cody thought to himself. He had just left I-40 at the exit to Brevard, and he had been chuckling to himself after reading a bridge sign marking the French Broad River. Yep, instead of Aimee or Adrienne, the third oldest river in the world was so anonymously titled, probably by a hungover Scotsman on an excruciating and confusing Saturday morning.

Cody now stood waist-deep in the same French Broad wondering what the hell had just happened. For ten years, there had been no threat to his life prior to the witness protection program. But either the driver of the black Continental who just pushed him through the guardrail really meant business, or Carolina drivers are very discourteous. But deciding on the former option only brought on a rush of questions. Was his fiancée safe? How (and when) did they find him? Why did he wear his Italian suit and why the hell hadn't he taken those swimming lessons in third grade?

Noticing that traffic on the bridge was still moving, he assumed he was safe to go on. The driver of the black Continental must have continued on his way, timing impeccable, because surely if someone had witnessed his "accident," they would have stopped to help. The South was renowned for its hospitality and generosity, was it not? Or was he confusing Southerners with nuns?

No Southerner or nun was in sight to be of assistance however. In fact, the only thing Cody could see was a curious raccoon peering at him from the shore. Cody took a mental inventory of all his bones and important organs, and except for painful bruising from the jerk of his seat belt and a gash on his leg, he seemed to be in good condition. His pounding headache was a result more from the tense phone conversation earlier that morning than from his current situation.

Luckily, he had long ago learned to travel light and never to become overly attached to any place or object, so nothing he loved had been damaged in the wreck. He removed from the half submerged rental car just one item, a linen-wrapped package, and laid it over his shoulder. Then came the daunting task of footing his way to shore, hoping that the Broad was no deeper than the spot where he now stood.

The area had suffered extensive flooding six or seven months ago, and although the water had returned to an almost normal level, there was still debris accumulated along the edges of the river, making his journey more arduous than his Italian loafers rated. Several times he misjudged the strength of a branch or the stability of a rock and was plunged into the icy cold water. The long process gave Cody time to think about his situation, too much time, some might say.

Cody Quarterline was certainly not his real name, nor had he so much as spoken his real name in years. Maxwell Prine had suggested it two days before going into official protection. Cody was his favorite pet. Quarterline was the street where he grew up riding wheelies on his BMX. Cody thought the name would be great if the whole adult film acting thing ever worked out. It seemed terribly obvious for a WPP name change, but it worked. It worked, that is, until tonight.

Max was renowned for reciting quotes (and misquotes)… "The dubious intentions of the few should not be seen as a benchmark for the masses." Cody groaned as that struck on the irony of this situation. Was he really in town just for the funeral of a friend, or was he being baited?

As always, so much time to think offered nothing but confusion over the reality of his situation. Perhaps he had misjudged the situation. People got in car accidents all the time that had nothing to do with their long and tangled pasts. Yes, it was strange that the driver had not stopped, but as Max was always quick to point out, people suck.

Cody steadfastly realized three things as he walked through the rhododendron on the east bank of the murky water. He had to get these leeches off of his legs. He had to solicit one hell of a tailor. And he was, under no circumstances, going to miss this funeral.

Part II

The gunfight in Boone

By Chuck Sallade

Cody couldn't help but to think that the driver of the black Lincoln who put him ass deep in the French Broad was no other than the reputed mob boss Giuseppe Di'Lampedusa, a.k.a., "The Leopard." Since he spilled his guts at the Congressional hearings, and told the world things that he knew he would wind up dead for, Cody had moved to a small town in Montana under the guise of a chiropractor, in hopes that he and The Leopard would never meet again. In actuality, chiropractic was only a front for his heroin trafficking. Old ways die hard.

Four days ago he received an e-mail from Maxwell's wife Shirley telling him that Max had died suddenly from food poisoning, but now he wasn't sure that Shirley was the sender after all. At the foot of the Appalachians in the Carolinas, hiding in the woods, he tried to figure out how to get to Boone with his linen package, but without anyone finding out about his accident. That would inevitably involve police, and the press; something that would not only be inconvenient, but also potentially life-threatening.

Cody headed east, skirting the road just out of sight in the trees. Eventually he came upon a small house with several cars parked outside. He bolted out of the trees, and jumped into the Chevy Cavalier. Hot wiring it would've been easier than any of the others, but the keys were in it so it didn't matter anyway. Off he went in a blaze of rubber and Carolina red clay dust; off to Boone. Now heading north and west on Rt. 321.

Having never been accused of being a thinker or one to reflect on his actions, Cody felt the rush of his previous life. The feeling like a moth to a flame. After switching out three cars, i.e., hot wiring them so as not to be too noticeable, Cody made his way into Boone, NC. He went straight to Shirley and Maxwell's house only to find the house eerily abandoned. Little did he know, but they hadn't lived there for two years. In fact, Maxwell and Shirley had also been relocated via the witness protection program, but apparently they hadn't been hidden well enough. The Leopard and his men found out their locale, kidnapped them, and forced them to get in touch with Cody just before they executed them and buried them deep in the woods of Virginia. The plan worked, and Cody took the bait hook, line, and sinker. However, as soon as he peaked in the window he knew he'd been set up, and oddly he didn't much mind. He was boring of his life as a quack back cracker/small-time heroine trafficker.

Knowing his predators were somewhere close, and probably watching, he ran around the back of the house and kicked the door in. He ran up the stairs and hid the linen package, but only after removing the pistol out of it, and carefully re-wrapping the remaining contents. Sure enough, just like clock work, up pulled the black Lincoln, dents and dings and all. So predictable! Cody hid behind the door to the kitchen which had a vantage point to both ends of the house; he waited. As the thugs surrounded the house and began creeping in, Cody felt a grin spreading across his face. Oh how he missed the excitement. The first man in was a large man who he vaguely recognized, but never knew his name. That didn't matter now, because he would be the first to die today. When he came around the corner Cody pistol-whipped him in the forehead, and again in the back of the head as he was crumbling to the floor. Cody calmly picked the gun out of his hand; two was always better than one.

Just as Cody stood back up and hid behind the wall, the front door came crashing open with the two remaining thugs coming through in force. "Morons," came out of Cody's mouth, and bullets came out of his guns. The first one through the door fell like a sack of rice motionless on the floor. The other fell back out of view, but left his weapon in the middle of the floor, with the trigger finger still in it. While the thug screamed in agony, and tried to figure out how to get his gun back, Cody snuck through the dining room and behind him.

"Stand up," Cody demanded. Thug number three stood up with his arms automatically going up above his head. "Just get it over with," he said. Now in any good mob movie the hero would have something clever to say, or do. Maybe he'd make the thug wish he were dead as he tortured information out of him. Not Cody. "OK." Thug number three first hit the floor with his knees, then his face. The slug embedded itself the wall opposite Cody. Amazing how such a small little piece of lead could cause so much damage.

Since nobody had reported the Lincoln missing, and nobody even knew it was missing yet Cody helped himself to it. "Fill 'er up, Chief," he told the gas station attendant. He popped the trunk to see what kind of goodies it might contain. The cache of weapons didn't interest him nearly as much as the brief case. He popped it open and his jaw hit the ground. He estimated it to amount to $1.5 million all in twenties. He tipped the gas guy handsomely, and headed for the Ashville Airport where he bought a ticket to Caracao.

Knowing the connecting flight would be in Miami, and he'd need a passport, Cody made a few calls from the payphone to make the proper hasty arrangements. It would cost him, but he did have a lot of cash, and of course the linen package. Fencing the package in Miami would be quite lucrative since he couldn't take it through customs. As per the arrangements, locker #1324 had Swiss bonds amounting to $22 million. He placed the linen package in locker #1325, dropped the key off to its recipient's desired location, and made his way to his gate.

Part III

Cody & Cheyenne meet up in Tampico

By Maryvette Labrie

Cody woke up to the flight attendant's voice saying, "The weather is clear and 81? in Port of Spain." "Hope that guy on the last flight makes it to his destination," Cody thought to himself, "rather nice of him to leave that boarding pass sticking out of the book."

How the Leopard found him, Cody couldn't stop wondering about. If Casper was still in the area, Cody had to find him and get the bag back before things got even more difficult. Trinidad had changed very little, Cody couldn't help noticing; maybe that was a sign that finding Casper at the Blue Moon would be a possibility. If they'd found him stateside they could find him here, and Cody couldn't afford that chance. He walked the last two blocks enjoying the sun and light breeze coming in, picking up the pace when he heard that old familiar steel drum from the bar.

Cheyenne got off the plane and looked around the tarmac. Not impressed, she thought, he'd better have things organized this time. Not like when they took that trip to Tampico. She found a cab and was soon zipping along the congested thoroughfare past the colorful shanties. Mulling over how much her life had changed since Cody had been placed in the program, Cheyenne didn't notice the blue mini trailing close behind the cab. The hotel lobby was empty and she was quick to get into the room. Her next instructions were encoded around the room. Finding the charter was the easy part. The docks were full of all types and each suspicious, whether they were the local Trinis or the visiting yachties. Even with the new hair color and style and quick self-tan, Cheyenne felt exposed.

Cody and Casper headed down to San Fernando after they picked up Jackson. If everything went according to plan, which normally didn't for Cody, he would see his beautiful fianceé, Cheyenne, in a couple of hours. Jackson had an odd look about him, like a lonely carpenter just waiting to pound his nail. They continued on down the road past the sugarcane fields to LaBrea. It was almost unbearable walking the trail through the tar pits. Casper had become strangely quiet and Cody didn't like to think what that meant. He had his little friend just in case.

It was the sudden sidestep of Jackson's that saved Cody; his bullet hit the stranger in the left eye and he spun around in time to grab Casper's arm with the large machete and heave him over his shoulder into the nearest tar pit. Jackson was almost to the exit when the bullet shredded his cervical spine and cored his Adam's apple. Cody quickly searched the stranger and rolled his body into the bubbling ground nearby. As he was heading to the car he could only hope that Cheyenne was faring better.

Cheyenne was almost to Turtle Beach; the sun getting low made landing the boat difficult. She could see Cody's headlights weaving down the hillside. They embraced briefly, long enough for her to get a quick adjustment, that short stint as a crack doc in Montana comes in handy. "We can't go back to the hotel, we'll have to head to the colony until we hear from the buyer," Cody explained as they took off, keeping low in the boat. The motor quit about two miles from the shore, and a high drone of a speedboat approaching could be heard. Cody hid under the canvas and the first two to step on the boat didn't know what hit 'em. A bullet grazed his ear and Cody rolled to the left. The first punch took him by surprise, but it was the only one. He managed to slam his would-be assassin's head against the large hook hanging down—blood spurted across the deck. Cody gently rubbed his jaw as he took stock of the situation.

Cheyenne already had the other boat ready to go, and once he was on board he heaved the unfortunate seaman over the edge and let go. With a satisfying splash Cody collapsed and closed his eyes. Cheyenne turned the boat around and headed out to the north side of the island, beaching it just yards from the Maricaibo beach.

Cody knew the leather bag would be too noticeable, and casually picked up a swimming tourists' stuff sack. The bus ride was long and cramped, winding through the jungle and finally into an older part of the aging city. The Savannah, as the large local gathering place is called, was filled with people, a good place to blend in for a while and enjoy the bacchanal air. The last time Cody was here he'd just been starting in the business; the Leopard had thought he was the cat's meow.

Cheyenne's scream brought Cody out of his reverie. She was being dragged toward a blue mini by a very large woman. Cody jumped over the short fence and launched himself toward her. It gave Cheyenne enough time to deliver a sharp deadly blow to the kidneys. As a crowd slowly started to gather, the two of them jumped in the mini and started careening through the narrow streets. Finding another boat wasn't difficult, Cheyenne had already checked out the option earlier. The Leopard would yowl at the thought of Cody disappearing again, and what better place to go than the old leper colony off the coast. He patted the beach bag and made the call.

Part IV

Cody meets the Leopard

By Jon Phillipsborn

As Cody and Cheyenne reached the harbor and readied to hop on a boat to the leper colony, a one-armed, noseless man walked past them with a faded blue t-shirt that read "I'm With Leper: Spring Break 2004." Cody paused a moment to rethink his plan to hide there. "On second thought babe, why don't we go to Belize," Cody spoke to Cheyenne, as he gave the passing leper a wink. "My uncle Roscoe has a deep sea fishing charter and we can stay with him on the beach. Besides, nothing says sexy quite like Belize in July." Cheyenne smiled back at Cody and tickled him under his ear.

Cody loves a good ear tickle.

Thanks to all this running from The Leopard, Cody had earned enough air miles to get the both of them first class seats into Belize City. The flight was half full, and a Ben Affleck movie would soon begin. As the plane took off Cheyenne reclined in her seat, thankful to be heading towards humidity (complexion), and back to the mainland. She took the wet cloth that the stewardess handed her and started dabbing her neck. The air condition kicked on at the same time, and as Cheyenne had worn her extremely tight, white halter-top, Cody noticed that the erotic index had just reached new highs. Remembering why he killed her first husband, Cody was interrupted by the stewardess, "Care fo a wet towow, Meesta Quarterwine?"

Shocked to hear such a Japanese accent on a United flight to Belize, he took his eyes off of Cheyenne to discover that the stewardess was indeed Japanese, and as beautiful as Lucy Liu, circa 1993. He was helpless beneath her seducing eyes and was dumbfounded by how tight her black leather union suit was. "Meesta Quarterwine, you are spiwwing yor beverwage," were the words he watched purse off of her silky lips, as he felt the cold whiskey fill his lap. Cheyenne, realizing Cody was in a bind, grabbed the wet towel from the stewardess' hand, and elbowed the Japanese nymph in the side to mosey her along. "Cody," she said, "don't you think it's odd that the stewardess knew your name?"

Cody, cooled off from the dose of alcohol to his loins, grabbed the towel and unfolded it: "Meet me in Dangriga if you know what is good for you. P.S. I have your wallet." Written in red crayon, signed, The Leopard.

Panic-stricken, Cody grabbed at his pockets. Empty. Bastard! He does have my wallet! Cody pulled his hand to his mouth and started to chew on his knuckle – as he tends to do when panicked, turning to the window, just in time to see the Japanese girl parachuting away.

Uncle Roscoe, clad in cut-off jean shorts and a Hawaiian shirt with none of the buttons done, revealing four scars and a giant fishhook pierced through his left nipple, was waiting outside next to a pickup. His dog, Jasper, was yipping away in the back. The two men shook hands and exchanged a pat on the shoulder. Roscoe turned to Cheyenne, said hello, and then started making out with her. Cody watched, a bit confused, but shrugged it off as just one of those things that Cheyenne does.

"Roscoe, looks like we've got to head to Dangriga, The Leopard has my wallet, and who knows what else in mind. But all I know is that I am sick and tired of running. This ends here. In Belize." Cheyenne sighed, long past being humored by Cody's ultimatums, but fully enjoying the 100% humidity and what it was already doing for her skin. "Great," said Roscoe, "That's where I live. I've been exploiting cheap labor successfully in Dangriga for going on 4 years." But as Roscoe took his seat, a beautiful and tiny frog skirted out of his shorts. Roscoe began to say "Hey, I've got a tattoo of one of those on my ..." but fell over dead before he could finish.

"Poison arrow frog," said Cody as he pushed Roscoe's dead body out of the car and grabbed the wheel. "The work of The Leopard. I'd bet my woman on it. Buckle up sugar, we're heading south."

They made Dangriga just in time to close down happy hour at the "Shark's Dive."

Cody tried to order a bottle of rum and two straws, but the bartender had another suggestion. "Senor Cody, there is a man sitting at a table waiting for you both. You are to sit with him. But he has recommended tequila shots first." The bartender put two shots in front of the pair and pointed to a poorly lit corner in the back where a whale-sized man was visibly panting from the heat. Cody began walking over while Cheyenne downed both shots, winking at the guy behind the bar as she slammed the empty glasses on the counter.

"So we finally meet, Leopard," Cody said as he sat down at the table, his eyes fixed on the swollen face. "I'm sick of you chasing me. I want answers! Why are you trying to kill me? And where is my wallet!"

Cheyenne stood behind Cody, holding on to his shoulders to keep from swaying. The large man's mouth opened. "Calm down Mr. Quarterline," he panted as he took a gulp of ice water. "I am not 'The Leopard.' My name is Colby, though my friend's call me Meatball, and I am 'The Leopard's' personal assistant, and his money manager." He snickered, as if telling a joke. "Perhaps, Mr. Quarterline, you are asking the wrong questions. Is 'The Leopard' really chasing you, or are you chasing him? Or, perhaps you are simply running, Mr. Quarterline."

Cody, very happy to have not taken the tequila shot, was not expecting such a turn of events. And the fact that Meatball over here kept putting quotes around The Leopard's name only increased the confusion. His stare at his counterpart thickened as Cheyenne's hands began to massage his shoulders. It had been years since Cody remembered being forced to be so introspective. And frankly, it frightened him. Could it be that all this time, despite the attempted murders and Roscoe's death, no one has been chasing him? And if he dared to humor that thought, who, or what, is "The Leopard," that he keeps running from? Or to? And what was in that linen package he had left in the locker at the Miami airport, so very long ago?

The setting sun spilled like yoke into the Caribbean, and Cheyenne was now nibbling on his ear. Meatball smiled slyly from across the table at Cody, who all of a sudden, was not even sure if he liked what Cheyenne was doing.

Part V

Cody tries to think

By Spicy McHaggis

The first thing that Cody thought was "Ouch." He thought this because he found himself rather unable to actually say it. But it was not immediately clear to him why, exactly, this was the case. Currently, much was unclear to Cody.

They say there are benefits to one's life falling apart. Like finding the humor in Carl Heisenberg's Uncertainty Principle. Cody himself had never been the intellectual sort. Except, of course, for the back cracking deal. Ordeal, as it were. But he reckoned that as more of a distinguished guise than an intellectual endeavor. But at the present time, this time of certain uncertainty, Cody was forced to see things differently. Like trying to find a set of lost car keys, he was reduced to back tracking his steps to as early as he could remember. Only it was not his car keys he was looking for. Not by a long shot. Cody was looking for himself. He was looking for his past, be it years or minutes. Because that what you do when you lose something. Go back to the last time you remember having it, then take a look around. On his way back he passed by his senior year of high school and Mr. Shebly's science class. It was there where he learned about a peculiar little thing called the uncertainly principle conjured up by some whack job named Carl Heisenberg. In a nutshell is goes like this: the more certain you are about one thing, the less certain you are about something else. Indeed. Cody suddenly found himself intimately familiar with this notion. Take away everything, strip yourself of all that you once held true and familiar, remove all doubt of having any doubt. Be absolutely certain about being uncertain. Do this and things you never before dreamed will become glaringly obvious. Nothing from nothing is nothing.

All these things went through Cody's head before he lifted it from the sand. "Ouch," he thought again. Perhaps this time his lips moved. There's probably a name for that peculiar state between dream and reality. This place where Cody found himself this moment contemplating these fantastic notions. That place of time where dreams seem more like reality and reality more like dreams. The place were Nobel prize ideas are from. The place were the Mona Lisa called home. But as soon as your head is set upright, all these things that rest beyond our normal senses fall to our heels, to our tenia infected feet, our fungus ridden toenails, our vericosed veins, where all the other garbage goes.

When Cody lifted his swollen head from the sand, Heisenberg was gone. He stood to find himself badly sunburned, crusted over with salt, a sizable gash on his side, and still without his wallet.

They say there are benefits to one's life falling apart. Like starting over. When, like the old saying goes, you can't go home again. When the proverbial junkies heart explodes and the room, life, suddenly goes flatline. BEEEEEEEEEEEEEEEEEEEEEP. Checked out. Like the eight ball on some dank, central American billiards table - whack, over and out. When all that's left is nothing, you can start over with everything.

Cody found himself realizing this as he walked himself sober on the white sand beach of anywhere. Which is where he might be, anywhere. Slowly he pieced back together what he could remember of last night, or was it days, was it months?

His memory started with the last thing he saw - Meatball's smirking face, the last thing he heard - the chime of the front door of the Shark's Dive Saloon as somebody walked in behind him, and the last thing he smelled - the hard tequila breath of Cheyenne as she whispered in his ear, "We got 'em now." After that, his memory was a stew pot of broken images. Shackles and chains, hot and cold, boats and airplanes, water and sky, laughing and screaming (or was it the same?). He remembered Cheyenne, his fiancee. Was she in on it or merely a hapless victim. Was she trying to out fox the foxes or save herself? Her exact role wasn't clear in Cody's muddied memory but perhaps it'll come to him. Either way, she's as gone as a bug in a hurricane, as gone as an opportunity lost, as gone as, well, Cody Quarterline himself.

They say there are benefits to one's life falling apart. Like disappearing. Cody had often wondered what it would be like to be dead. He entertained the idea to it's furthest mortal extent, enrolling in the federal WPP, but apparently that wasn't dead enough. They'd dug him up. Like Night of the Living Dead. Like Friday the 13th. But now he was on the other side of the fence. Meatball and his goons had killed him, or so they thought. He remembered his attempted escape from the jungles of the Cayo district of interior Belize and the pursuit to the coast. They caught up with him in Placencia, the end of the line. He remembered being drug out behind a boat and through the coral reefs of the Bugle Cays. They had beat him, drowned him, and left him for dead. "Perhaps I am dead, at least to them," he said, his lips moving now.

They say there are benefits to one's life falling apart. Like choices. You either have them in unlimited quantity or very few. Feast or famine. Sink or swim. Cody had exactly two. Be dead for the rest of his life, or just until his killers see the whites of his eyes, then he'd trade 'em, their life for his.

Cody didn't know exactly where he had washed up, where he was wandering in circles trying to get his wits. But it didn't much matter. Not far down the caye there was buoyed a Twin Otter on floats. A respectable plane with a high capacity for cargo and survivablitly, qualities he learned from his previous life as a "tree top flyer", or smuggler, if you must.

The Belizeans are a bartering people. Food for tires, rooms for labor, airplanes for good information. Money is a questionable asset in Belize, which was fortunate, because Cody was still without his wallet. But dead men don't need wallets. He did, however, have something better. He knew where there was a very valuable linen wrapped package in Miami. He knew where there was a fat bastard named Meatball who was sitting snidely on a fat stack of bills, surely a substantial amount of drugs, and an unfortunate score to settle with a dead man. He knew that somewhere out there was a woman with a lot of answers, or no tongue. He knew that his new best friend, Rojie, the Twin Otter pilot, would be into all these things.

The blue waters gave way to bluer skies, the plane banked low over the palm trees, and the dead man and his pilot turned north, quite certain of their intent, uncertain of their plan. There are benefits to one's life falling apart.

Part VI

What a long, strange trip

By Stylus T. Table

The Twin Otter coughed its merry way through a cloudbank and was suddenly awash with the bright hues of a mighty bright sun.

"Christ," murmured the "dead" Cody covering his eyes, "The Pearly Gates beckon." Cody's newfound friend, Rojie Joint, turned back from the controls to look at the crumpled heap on the cabin floor.

"U al rite?" he shouted, in appalling Belizean English with a hint of Byzantine revelry.

Cody stared at the noise with knitted eyebrows and listened to the face before answering, "You what?"

"U al rite?" returned Joint, somewhat muffed.

Cody shook his head, his eyes rolled in their sockets. On any other day he felt he could have scored a double six with them and taken away the shake-a-day prize. But here he was, eight miles high and climbing, according to his stomach, trying to communicate with a pilot who looked like an extra from a '60s sitcom about shipwrecked folks. This was worse than the seventeen beatings he'd taken in the last six months. The plane skipped and floated peacefully enough over the sugarplum landscape of frothy-looking German beer and turned right away from the gleaming sun. The cabin was suddenly colder than a gremlin's nipple and Cody bundled up tighter than a pair of socks after being laundered.

And it was while Cody lay folded up on that very same floor that Rojie let out the universal word for "Crikey." "Huh oh," he said.

"What's huh oh?" Cody moaned back.

"Huh oh," Rojie replied without looking back.

"Bugger it," thought Cody, "the least he could do is look back, at least give me a face to look at, so I can translate the 'huh oh.' Don't make me crawl up there." Cody crawled to where the co-pilot seat should have been and tapped on one of Rojie's frantic mambo-dancing shoulder blades.

"What the hell's happening?" screamed Cody.

"It nah gaud, stom mulch baaad," blurted out Rojie as he jiggled with the wheel. Cody looked out towards the future facing them. From out of nowhere there loomed, on its throne of ready-whipped folds, the biggest, blackest cloud Cody had ever seen, aside from the time he got a thumping from Shark Bait, an old girlfriend of his from the Bronx. The swirling mass, complete with crown and scepter, pulled the hapless Twin Otter on into its lap.

Rojie tried the radio. "Belize tower, this Space Man calling, come in."

"That's funny," thought Cody, "he can talk perfect English. Well, who cares, as long as we get out of this."

But they didn't. The Twin Otter was grabbed by the throat and flung into the maelstrom of fear.

"You know, I've been reading the map upside down," laughed Rojie.

"What?"

"I've been reading the map...," continued Rojie.

"And," interrupted Cody as the plane lurched and plummeted. "Do you know where we are?"

"I think we're over that Bermuda Triangle thingy," resumed Rojie with an air that was calm compared to Cody's furiously pumping heart.

"Just great," said Cody.

"You don't believe that mumbo jumbo?" snickered Rojie as he tried to read some sense into the flashing lights on the dash. Cody, feeling his sanity reaching for the parachute by the second, nodded an affirmative nod.

Rojie could only roll his eyes in disbelief, "and you from the New World as well."

Cody had by this point had enough. "And while we're on the subject, and before we die, how come you're speaking better English than before?"

"Storms do that to me," answered Rojie. "I don't know why."

Cody sat back on the floor and clutched at one of the seats behind him. The plane spun, spinned, cartwheeled and pirouetted on its fin. "This reminds me of a poorly rolled spliff," said an ever-greenish Cody.

"Ohh, non ritengo bene," cried Rojie in beautiful Italian at the plane, now at the mercy of the raving ringlets. "Ik denk wij het mijn vriend hebben gehad," said Rojie now in perfect Dutch.

"I think so to," abruptly answered Cody, pulling up quickly. "How come I understood you?" he queried.

"C'est le donner l' assaut à," said Rojie with a sublime French shrug of his shoulders.

"It's the storm," Cody repeated in English. "That's amazing. Say something else."

"Wie was?" said Rojie, who had now given up with the controls and was leaning back in his seat.

"Like what? I don't know," grew an ever-excited Cody. "Anything."

"Quisiera ir a la isla de coney y ver a muchacho de la langosta," said Rojie.

"You what? Never. Is that you're last wish, visit Lobster Boy at Coney Island fair," said an incredulous Cody. "This is great. Umm, what shall we do next. Wanna play I-Spy?"

"Okay with me," said the flattered Rojie.

The Twin Otter glided on and on towards the earth and just as suddenly stopped. The two men looked at each other. Everything was suddenly still. Quiet. But that wonderful quiet you get after Iron Maiden has stopped singing. Cody got up and looked out. A pink hue with red fringes enveloped them and started pulsating to colors of varying purples. It occurred to Cody that the beat was similar to a top song from the past. "You hear that?" he asked Rojie.

"Nah," replied the sulky pilot, now back to his standard tongue.

"If I'm not mistaken, that's the Grateful Dead's Barbed Wire Whipping Party," said Cody. They cautiously listened and sure enough the words, like droplets of rain, spelled themselves out of the fluorescent theater of lights around the plane.

"Meat, meat, gimme my meat
Meat, meat, gimme my meat
Meat, meat, gimme my meat..."

"I wonder if that bastard Meatball was around here," thought Cody. They felt the Twin Otter land on something and gingerly they made their way to the outer cabin door. Rojie pulled on the latch and the glowing light show poured in. There was a huge roar, not that of an animal, but a crowd. Cody peered out and saw a figure run up towards him. "Did you bring the linen wrapped package?" said Jerry.

Part VII

Cody finds some answers & shoots them

By Craig Beam

The dead leader of the "Dead" skidded to a stop on the rain-soaked tarmac of the runway. The storm was worsening, and so was my disposition.

"You really think I'd bring something as valuable as the LWP (linen wrapped package) on a long, strange trip like this? You fat hippie, I oughta give you the gun right here."

Meatball's jaw dropped. He expected the carefully constructed hallucinations to confuse me to the point of inaction. Rojie had slipped peyote in my coffee. I'd learned years ago not to let drugs control my mind. That's when I gave them both the gun.

Between flashes of euphoria and snatches of visions from my past, I took stock of my situation. I was standing on the tarmac of an unused airstrip, surrounded by giant clowns with scary lips. Wait, that last part was just the dope. No clowns. I was alone.

That's when it hit me! I recognized this place. It was one of the Florida air strips Max Prine and I had used in our drug running days! I was only miles away from Miami.

I dumped the two bodies in the swamp. The boat that Meatball had used to get to the airstrip was tied to a small pier. I sped off in the general direction of the Miami airport.

After a brief but fierce battle with the alligator people, I emerged from the swamp right next to a road. I leapt from the boat to the bank as a long, black Lincoln came screaming down on me! The Leopard leaned out the back window, heater blazing. I drew my gun and fired. Blood splattered the back window like a red exclamation point. The limo slewed crazily from one white line to the other, then sped off.

I started walking. Black clouds hovered all around and flashes of lightning accented my mood. Rain poured down in torrents. I flipped up the pin-striped collar of my jacket and pulled my fedora down to my eyebrows. My revolver was a hard lump in my armpit. Cheyenne was a hard lump in my …throat. Where was she? I needed my ear tickled, and bad.

Suddenly, a bullet-riddled blue mini came screaming around the corner! It skidded to a stop within inches of my stomach. My pistol was already leveled at the driver. She climbed slowly from the car.

Cheyenne's long, black hair glistened in the pouring rain. Above her high cheekbones, piercing black eyes flashed. She wore a black rain coat over a short skirt, her long, shapely legs woven into black fishnet stockings. The hard lump got harder.

Our lips met and the lightning flashed again. Thunder clapped so suddenly that I barely felt her hand inside my jacket! In an instant, she had my gun pointed right between my eyes! Never trust a broad in fishnets.

"You drive," she hissed. For a second, her pupils appeared vertical, like a snake. The after effect of the drugs, no doubt. I drove.

Silence filled the mini like the black mood filling my skull. This woman is my fiancée! My most trusted (after Max, of course). After a second or two of self-pity, I quit whining. I'd been kicked in the teeth more than once. Now what? I felt my old confidence return.

"So, where are we going?" I asked.

A smug smile adorned Cheyenne's beautiful face. "To the Miami airport, of course. To retrieve the LWP. The buyer killed himself before we could extract the location of the key from him… but not before I had a bit of fun. This was his car, you see. Very convenient."

"You're working for The Leopard, of course".

Cheyenne's laugh was like a million soft bells at first, building in a maniacal crescendo. "That criminal?" she finally spat. "I just killed him. Who do you think put the holes in this mini?"

"Who, then?" was all my reeling mind could come up with.

"All you need to know is that we want the LWP. And we'll do anything to get it." The look in those beautiful, horrible eyes made me believe it.

"That's the one thing I can't deliver," I sighed. "Why do you think I had to go to Max's funeral, even if it cost me my life? Max had the chip that makes the LWP work! If he was killed, I had to get it off the body. Now he's worm food."

I picked that moment to slam on the brakes. The mini screeched to a halt. Cheyenne's face smacked the dash. Blood poured from her broken nose as I snatched the gun from her limp hand. Those beautiful black eyes were white as I dumped her out of the car. I floored the mini and sped off into the darkness. "Easy come, easy go," I thought.

Part VIII

Cody has a prophetic nightmare

By Vivian Beam

"Oh, Cody, Cody, Cody, Cody (etc…) Cody – you tragically deranged; yet eminently fascinating, blip on the radar of human existence. How could you hope to continue this charade indefinitely? Your self-propelled spiral into the depths of depravity has finally landed you face down in the muck with no defense. You don't even know who I am - do you?"

"I should leave you right here and never look back, but still – I'm morbidly curious. Did you not see this coming? All the signs were there and then some. You yourself felt neurotically compelled to boast of your fantastic hallucinations and perpetually delusional state of mind. There were far too many clues, my sorry friend/lover/whatever-you-think-you-are-to-me…."

"It could have been great – the whole thing. We set you up to be the hero, but you got lost in pointless mind-meanderings and attaching significance to every lackluster occurrence. In short, you marked the trail well, dog – and I've been the perfect scent hound to track you down.'

"Blah, blah, blah," thought Cody. "If there is any justice left at all in the world, then WHY is she still talking? Luckily, this imposter is not only an egotistic windbag; she's a poor shot, as well." His body lay paralyzed with the searing pain of his wounds – how many, he couldn't be sure. And, amazingly enough, it didn't seem to matter. The Cheyenne look-alike stood above him, her poor eyesight enhancing the illusion of his impending death. In his semi-conscious state, he tried to consider his next move. It was a moot point, since he didn't even have the energy to open his eyes.

"Cheyenne" continued her self-indulgent discourse. "Of course, you were chosen early in the game to be The One who would alter humanity's course toward a slow and certain death by Political Correctness. The Leopard? Meatball? Cheyenne? They're all your friends, fool. How arrogant of you to assume incompetence in their attempts to stop you from transferring the LWP. Of course, they're all alive and well – protected by the same web of hallucinogenic manipulation that you are."

Cody was beginning to sense a glitch in the program. The voice was taking on a decidedly mechanical tone. He barely opened one eye. The facial expression, though pert, seemed fixed on a point in some vague landscape. She seemed frozen on the spot – determined to ride her train of thought all the way to the next depot. Something else he noticed; no blood on her face – no sign of the broken nose from their encounter in the Mini.

Just then, "Cheyenne" fell strangely silent. After a brief moment of hesitation and appearing to establish her bearings, she quickly turned and broke into a dead run in the opposite direction. Cody opened his other eye just in time to make out the inscription on her neck, at the base of her upswept black hair: "Clones R Us" 1-800-CAT-COPY……………………

I suddenly came to, gasping for breath. What a nightmare! My searing pain was the result of apparently landing belly-down in a dry creekbed. A curious situation indeed, considering my location in southern Florida. I had long since ceased to question the details of my whereabouts.

Raising my head, I could see the old bullet-ridden blue Mini thirty yards away, resting on one side in the same dry creekbed. The engine was still running, which immediately gave me hope. A fast healer, I leapt to my feet with a sudden giddiness and sense of purpose. Find Cheyenne!

Just then, an encouraging voice came booming down at me from the road above. "Can I help you, Poindexter?"

What?? Could it be? Only one other person in the Northern Hemisphere knows my real name. "Max!" I shouted. "Max, I thought you were dead – and buried in Virginia. Is it really you?"

"Yes, my friend, it is I," Max answered, in his characteristically even-toned and somewhat dramatic slow drawl. "I saw your fall on my game board back at the office and decided it was time to bail you out."

Like some good-humored sidekick in a movie with a happy ending, Max scrambled effortlessly to the bottom of the dry creekbed. Together, we uprighted the mini by pulling on the passenger side roll bar and settled ourselves in; Max in the driver's seat. A quick detour through the creek drainage led us back to the main road.

"Where are we going?" I found myself asking, in a repeat of an earlier scene.

"To Miami, of course." Max answered, apparently also echoing the verbiage of incidents past. "You see, you have the key to unlock the LWP and I have the chip that activates it – together we can find the buyer and save the world," he continued. "Everyone in the company – The Leopard, Meatball, Cheyenne and the others – needed to learn how you would perform under extreme conditions of personal injury and emotional betrayal. You're in, kid. Let's go get em!" he shouted triumphantly.

Stunned but smiling, I looked at the road ahead. I didn't care what the "game board" was that Max referred to, nor was I curious about his "office" or "the company." I was only slightly hurt and confused by all the pain I'd endured since entering the WPP – it was seemingly all behind me now.

A slow, brilliant realization began to gel in my consciousness. The nightmare at the bottom of the creek bed was totally prophetic! Everything "Cheyenne" said in the dream was true. I had been lost and led by the nose down a countless number of dead-end paths. I began to see the meaning of the clone in the dream – Cheyenne had been playing the heavy to test my loyalty! Wait a minute….

"That's right," Max said, gently interjecting my thoughts which he somehow seemed to be following perfectly. "Cheyenne is special – Cheyenne IS the key to the LWP. And there she is now!"

Unbelieving, my eyes focused on a familiar tall, sleek, female figure at the side of the road. She had one hand resting jauntily on her left hip – the other hand in the air with the thumb extended. As we screeched to a halt, the smile on her flawless face widened. (In yet another strange turn of events in an endless chain of strange turns, the broken nose seemed to be perfectly healed.) "Poindexter!" She exclaimed. "Max found you!"

Ever the athlete, Cheyenne vaulted over the roll bar of the mini and landed squarely in the center of the back seat. Max floored the gas pedal and the tires squealed in celebration. Together again!

[How is Max not dead? Are they really all on the same team? But then what about the clones? Tune in next month when another author takes up the saga.]

Part IX

Cody returns to Montana

By John Clayton

"We are going to a tailor," Cody said.

"But Poindexter—"

"Look, honey, I've been wearing this bad Italian suit ever since I first fell into the French Broad River. I started on this quest with three goals. One of them was to get to a tailor."

"But at least you did take care of those leeches," Max said. Then, after a pause, "Didn't you?"

Cody ignored the question. "Plus it chafes. In the crotch."

"All-righty then," Max said, and swung the bullet-riddled blue Mini to the left.

"And then I'm going back to Montana," Cody continued, emboldened by his new forcefulness. "All this time I've been bouncing around: North Carolina, Trinidad, Belize, Florida… If I see one more Jimmy Buffett impersonator I'm going to scream. I'm going back to Red Rock, Montana, where everybody knows me as a lovable fishing guide and incompetent chiropractor. I'm going to crack some flies, toss some backs—or is it the other way around?—and sort everything out. Alone."

"But, Poindexter, don't you love me?"

"You," Cody snorted. Suddenly he grabbed Cheyenne's head and yanked it forward toward his lap.

"Cody, not now, not in front of Max!"

"Shut up! I'm looking for your serial number!" He pulled up her black hair, expecting to find the "Clones R Us" logo he'd first seen on her neck in his dream.

And suddenly the blue Mini was airborne again. The last thing Cody remembered was the mangrove leaves brushing the windshield.

"This one's wasted away," said Jimmy Buffett, "again."

"And here's another lost shaker of salt," said Jimmy Buffett.

"I think this one's alive, though," said a third Jimmy Buffett.

Cody blinked and looked around. Were there really three Jimmy Buffetts wandering about the wreckage of the bullet-riddled blue Mini? There were indeed, although now that he looked closer, one of them appeared to be Chinese and another, if Cody was not mistaken, was a profoundly overweight 18-year-old African-American female.

"Here, dude, nibble on this spongecake," said the most-realistic Buffett. Cody pushed it aside.

"Not enough protein, right?" Buffett responded. He yelled, "Hey, somebody get me a cheeseburger!" He studied Cody's bleeding shoulder. "Dude, you got a brand new tattoo. What happened?"

"Max was driving," Cody said. "Suddenly we were airborne."

"Looks like this guy blew out his flip-flop," said the Chinese Buffett, who was standing over Max's body. "That could have affected the steering."

"Dude, you cut your heel too," said Cody's Buffett.

"Yes," Cody said, "and I need to cruise on back to Red Falls, Montana."

"Changes in latitudes," Buffett said, "changes in—" Cody pulled out and cocked his gun. "Don't you dare finish that lyric," he said.

As Cody descended to the baggage carousel, he realized what a terrible error he had made. In his desperation to get away from the Jimmy Buffett impersonators, he had asked the ticket agent for the first flight to Montana. "Missoula, Bozeman, Great Falls?" the agent asked. "Or—"

So he'd hopped on that last flight without first visiting a tailor. But now that he was here in Receivables, there was no way he'd be able to find someone to fix his bad Italian suit.

With no baggage, he went immediately to the rental car counter. "Do you have any Minis?" he asked.

"We have a gorgeously restored 1979 Ford Pinto coupe," the girl said. "In puce."

"Close enough."

Cody stayed in Receivables just long enough to visit a pawnshop, where he loaded back up with weaponry. Since he was flying, he'd donated his guns to the female Jimmy Buffett at the airport bar. (She was thrilled. "Another round of brew!" she called. "Why don't we get drunk and—" but when Cody glanced daggers at her she asked if he wasn't a "Son of a son, son of a son, son of a son of a—")

Unfortunately the underpowered Pinto had trouble making it up even the gradual slope to Red Barn. And it troubled Cody to be in such a lousy vehicle, for he had a serious dread of what he would find waiting for him in his old hometown.

[Who is waiting for Cody? How many Cheyenne clones will end up eating cheeseburgers in paradise? And what color is puce, anyways? For the answers to these and other questions, check back in vain next month when another writer takes up the saga.]

Part X

Cody gets within 60 miles of Cody

By Kari Clayton

As the Pinto whined its way up the hill toward Cody's back-crackin' hometown of Red Yurt at a tedious 48 miles an hour, Cody had plenty of time to think—an art he'd never really perfected.

Trying to sort out the events of the past year, he couldn't help but feel like some kind of puppet on a string. Jerked here and there—Tampico and Belize, Louisiana and Miami, and whatever that was with the crazy-talking pilot. He remembered the day Max told him that Witness Protection would change his life—but somehow this seemed too much. He wondered if this was happening to everyone. Or if it was even happening to him. Clones "R" Us? The "Plan?" Some days, the only part of the last year that made any sense to him at all was that drug-laden Twin Otter ride.

All this thinking was making Cody's head hurt, but fortunately, he was coming up on the old teepee billboard that told him he was nearly home. The steady stream of farm tractors passing him was beginning to get old.

"Just let me go home, take a hot shower, and get out of these damn Italian loafers that have been killing me since I landed in that stinky French Broad River," Cody said aloud in the car. He sometimes found that talking helped him not to think.

Suddenly though, the thought of "home" became more painful to him than his feet. Hadn't he been living with his girlfriend Petunia when he left for that funeral so long ago? Sweet Petunia, and her daughter Marjoram. Cody never could get enough of Marjie's cute high-pitched squeal. S'pose 'Tunia would even let him back into the house? He had to admit he hadn't written, or even thought much about her since he left—he was like that sometimes. Come to think of it, he'd even managed to get himself engaged to Cheyenne—whatever her deal was—while he was away.

"Petunia's not gonna like that," he thought, and remembered why he didn't like thinking in the first place. If he could only get what he came for here in Red Yurt and get back out again before Cheyenne tracked him down, he might be in the clear, Petunia-wise.

Pulling into town, he decided he'd better not go straight to her place, not before a shower, anyways. He slid into a parking space at one of the motels on the edge of town. The motel looked a lot nicer than it had when he left—he was encouraged that maybe Red Yurt was on an economic upswing. Good news if he had to stay around and do some back-cracking for a while.

Cody was sad to hear from the motel clerk that his favorite department store had been turned into condos while he was away, but remembered a great second-hand clothing shop where he should be able to find something to wear. "Anything will be better than this pitiful Italian suit," Cody said to himself, walking into town (two and a half hours in that puce Pinto had been enough for a while).

He started getting some strange glances from passing drivers, making him paranoid again that Meatball and his thugs had followed him here. Maybe put the word out. A price on his head. He just realized, passing the trusty Laundromat, that he could be walking into the worst trap of his life! What had he been thinking, coming back here?!? But, then again, it was possible that he just looked like a psychotic homeless man, barefooted in a tattered suit, walking along the highway with a deranged look on his face. "Gotta take to the alleys, I think I remember a couple," he said. "And stick to talking to out loud. It's safer."

Once Cody finally found an alley to hide in, and set things straight with the resident dumpster dogs, the going got easy. He was able to cruise right in to the familiar clothing shop, and as luck would have it, today was Dollar-A-Bag day. "Who says you can never go home again?" Cody whistled to himself.

Comfortable finally, in cast-off hiking boots and maybe-they're-in-style-again plaid trousers, Cody headed for Main Street.

"Shit! I'm screwed!" Cody half-shouted to a row of gift shop windows. Coming toward him was Cheyenne, of all people, walking with a couple of guys who had to be plumbers (nobody else tells those jokes). He ducked into the corner drugstore, hoping she hadn't seen him. Flattened against the wall, watching her pass by outside the window, Cody nearly collapsed.

"No! How can my Cheyenne be tickling some other guy's ear? And a plumber's ear, at that," Cody wailed to the wall of Hallmark cards. Come to think of it, he wasn't even sure Cheyenne was the real deal. Was this the Cheyenne-clone? If only she'd had her hair pulled back, he could've looked for the tattoo again. That was fun the last time. He started to swoon, thinking about it.

Trying to get his bearings, Cody noticed the sly grin on the face of a Round Man who just might give him a square deal. "Another of Meatball's goons?" he thought. No, as it turns out, Cody was standing in the feminine products aisle, fondling a box of pregnancy tests. "Damn, there goes that rumor again," he said out loud.

Figuring it was safe for him to go outside, Cody paid for the box of tests—he'd sort of crumpled the package thinking about Cheyenne—and headed for the alley. He was just nearing his friend Jackson's old wood shop and was about to stop in, when he remembered that Jackson had bought it early on, at the tar pits of LaBrea. He never did figure out where that bullet had come from—the one that split Jackson's Adam's apple. Had it been his gun? Jasper's? The whole episode was a little foggy to Cody. But he was getting used to it.

[What did Cody come to Red Yurt to get? Will plaid trousers ever be in style again? And why do all these people seem familiar? For answers to these and other questions, check back in vain next month when another writer takes up the saga.]

Part XI

Cody takes R&R along with reflections

By mac...

Ahhhhh... the Pinto parked and settled into a much-needed rest. Cody fell into a deep sleep as his mind went over the recent events. Though it's not always good to sleep on an empty stomach. Cody had gone to his favorite sandwich shop only to find it closed and all of the contents auctioned off. Damn! They made good sandwiches.

The leopard was still out there, and Cody was not sure where he stood with Cheyenne. Max was the only one he could trust; he had given him a number to call. Sleep first and then he would look for the answers.

Having awakened to the sound of the wind and looked out, he saw at least 3 feet of fresh snow. "Looks like it will be a day of couch potatoing and calling Mr. Buffet," Cody thought. He had to be careful. Even though this was a good town to hide out in, you can never be too trusting. First things first: coffee. Must have coffee.

Looking out the window, Cody started putting together all that had come to pass. The key was in the contents of the linen-wrapped package, the LWP. "I will have to go back to Miami to get it," Cody decided.

He dialed the number given to

him by Max. A gentleman answered the phone: "Can I help you sir?" Cody was not sure how to respond, so in the usual manner he replied, "Yeah, Max sent me." There was a pause, and then a voice came onto the line. "Cody, go to the Found Saloon. You will find a package behind the Dart machine; this will have what you need." The line went dead.

Cody sat there and pondered the message "it will have what you need." Heck, he didn't know what he needed.

Cody called Max and told him of the short and direct conversation. Max said, "Follow the instructions in the package and then contact me." Cody knew he would need help now, but where was Cheyenne? He needed to get this sorted out before he went to retrieve the package. She had to be in trouble and this could help her, too. He called Max back again and asked him how to find Cheyenne. Max replied, "She will find you" and hung up the phone. Cody sat back on the couch very confused, trying to sort this all out in his head. Then came a knock at the door. No one but Max knew he was here. He went to the door and there was Cheyenne!

Cheyenne sat on the couch with Cody and told him that Max had contacted her and instructed her to help him. He'd told her that Cody would have the instructions and that it would involve the LWP, of which she was the key. Neither of them understood any of this, Cody wondered if they where just pawns being used to perform tasks for a sinister group of conspirators.

Some of it was making sense. For instance, the funeral for his friend Max had got him out and on the run again. Now people of great power were using him. Was Max really his friend or also being controlled? Now there were more questions than answers.

And the Leopard, where did he fit into all of this, or was he also being used as a pawn? Cody knew all too well the misuse of power;

a local judge had once used her power against him unjustly. She was just a small fish in this sea, so he knew he had to be very careful. Cheyenne gave Cody a hug to help comfort him. They would rest and get ready to go for the package; nighttime on Friday would be best. Dance over to the dart machine and quietly pick it up. They would then be off to Receivables and off to find the answers.

[What the heck color is puce??? Where will this next adventure take Cody & Cheyenne? The LWP holds the answer to many of these questions so check back next month for a chance in hell you will get the answers or just be taken deeper into this dark underworld.]

Part XII

Cody and the magic diary

By Gary Robson

Cody Quarterline woke up abruptly, not recalling having fallen asleep. For a moment, he couldn't recall where he was, but then it came back to him, and so did his fiancée Cheyenne. She walked into the room carrying a steaming cup of Earl Gray tea for him and a double lite mocha frappuccino deluxe with whipped cream and chocolate sprinkles for herself. He was back home in Red Chalet, Montana.

Despite the lengthy conversation he'd had with Cheyenne the night before, he still faced more questions than answers. Before he ran off looking for the Linen-Wrapped Package™, he wanted a better understanding of what, exactly, was going on. Life had been so simple just a few short weeks ago, before Max died and came back; before the peyote, Jimmy Buffett impersonators, and assorted beatings.

"Cheyenne," he said, "I have a few loose ends to tie up. Wait here. We'll need some sandwiches for

the trip. Would you mind packing us a good lunch?" He pulled on his ill-fitting hiking boots and strode purposefully out into the snow. His rented puce Pinto was buried, and it took him fifteen minutes to dig it out and get it started. Priority one would have to be his girlfriend, Petunia. He hadn't spoken to her since leaving for Max's funeral, and he owed her an explanation.

When he walked into her empty apartment, all he found was a note taped to the fridge, which said, "You haven't spoken to me since you left for Max's funeral, you thoughtless ape. Marjie and I went back home to Bob." Disappointing, he thought, but that's one less complication at the moment. I'll track her down again when this is all over and explain about Cheyenne.

He hopped back in the puce Pinto, thinking that it really had more of a terra cotta hue, but that just wasn't as alliterative. He wrestled it into gear and slipped down the icy roads to the Found Saloon, which was uncharacteristically quiet, even for this early hour.

"Hey, Cody," the bartender greeted him. "What'll it be this morning?"

"A bloody mary and the use of your phone, if you please." The bartender handed Cody the cordless phone, and he dialed the one person in the world he could still trust. The one person who had never forsaken him. The one person who loved him no matter what.

"Mom? It's Poindexter. Yes... Yes... No, don't hang up! Mom! Please!" He clicked off the phone and let out a string of profanities that stunned a passing housefly. The fly fell into his bloody mary just as the bartender added the third kind of hot sauce. It sizzled softly and sank. He redialed, and walked across the room so the bartender wouldn't hear the conversation.

"Mom, listen to me. I really need you, Mom. I know I haven't called in three years. Mom, I've been in the witness protection program.

Really. Look, if you'll help me with this, I'll pay off your mortgage. What? Yes, fine, I'll pay off the Caddy, too. The WHAT? When did you get a boat? Fine. Look, Mom, here's what I need...".

Carefully, Cody outlined the situation. Locker #1325 in the Miami airport contained a Linen-Wrapped Package™ and locker #666 held a briefcase and a duffel bag. He'd overnight her the keys, and she would FedEx back the LWP and briefcase. He didn't tell her about the $1.5 million in twenties the briefcase contained, but he did tell her that the duffel bag contained millions in Swiss bonds.

"Keep the bonds safe, Mom. Use as much as you need and save the rest for me. I promise I'll come visit soon."

Cody handed the phone back to the bartender and paid for his drink, adding a hefty tip for the long-distance call. He quietly stepped over to the dart machine for a quick solo game while he drank. After the first set of darts found their targets, he approached the machine, eyeing the bartender surreptitiously. When the bartender looked away, Cody slipped his hand behind the machine and pulled out the thick envelope that was waiting for him. He slipped it into his pocket and took another sip of the bloody mary. When the enamel on his teeth stopped smoking, he set the drink down and walked outside to the puce Pinto, already covered with a dusting of fresh snow that made it look almost salmon pink.

Secure in the privacy of the car, he opened the envelope and found a tattered black leather book with a strap and a lock. The lock was open, and the book followed suit. It was a diary. Wonderful. It was a diary that had gotten him into the Federal witness protection program in the first place. But this diary was different. It was Cheyenne's diary. He settled back to read it.

Reading the diary was like an hour-long epiphany. Everything began to clarify. Like a peyote vision two days late, the diary ripped the mist from his eyes.

It wasn't the Leopard that had set him up. It was Max's wife Shirley all along. She killed Max and hired an impersonator after the funeral. She had tried to buy off Cheyenne, and when that failed, she created the Cheyenne clone (which she had named Frannie). It was Shirley driving the black Continental that sent him hurling into the French Broad River. Shirley hired Jackson to kill Cody in Curacao, and the Meatball to kill him in Curacao. When those attempts failed, she tried to use Rojie, the peyote, the Max impersonator, and Frannie to get him on the way home.

Cheyenne was writing the final pages of the diary from a locked basement somewhere in Wyoming. That could only mean that it was Frannie the clone who was making him sandwiches at home.

As he turned the last page of the diary, a note fell out. He picked it up, and read, "Mr. Quarterline, I am sending you Cheyenne's diary to prove that we have her safe and sound. When you crossed Shirley Prine, you made a very dangerous enemy. If you can return my Linen-Wrapped Package™ safely to me, you're free to keep the money and the bonds. I'll deal with Shirley. I'll even give you Cheyenne. I just want the LWP. You know how to reach me."

The note was signed, "Giuseppe Di'Lampedusa (The Leopard)."

Part XIII

The flying lunchmeat

By Charles Mitchell

When Cody returned to his room, he found Cheyenne (or was it Frannie?) nicely aspected on the bed surrounded by lunchmeat. Taking in the view, he thought of what was missing: the pickle, the condiments, the real Cheyenne. But what was real? This was here, this was now, now was real. If you can't be with the clone you love . . . .

Cody was jerked from his lascivious reverie by a mashed up ball of smoked turkey and roast beef careening off of his forehead. The real Cheyenne did not have such good aim; she had other weapons that were more effective and more covert (those eyes, those lips, those aspects). So this clone was for real; a real clone.

"Where have you been?" she asked in such a convincingly whiney voice that Cody marveled at the wonders of technology. "Off with that Petunia and her little spice girl?"

"Will wonders never cease?" he mused. "A jealous clone! Who needs the real thing when you get the whole package in a store brand?" Cody studied the faux Cheyenne, Cheyenne his foe. Her tears seemed real, her disappointment and look of betrayal authentic. "Now sweetie," he reassured her, "they've left town. Remember, I left them behind to come find you, and here we are. We're together baby, you and me, now whaddya say you put some of that lunchmeat between some bread so we can get on our way?"

Cheyenne seemed to regain her composure, no easy feat for a cloned bombshell sitting on a bed surrounded by cold cuts: the girl with the pearl earring in her natural setting. "You sure you weren't off with parsley, sage, rosemary and thyme?" she asked, in a tone that was more alluring than accusative.

"Scout's honor," he replied. "If you want, you can come by our old place and see that it's empty."

"No, that's okay, I trust you, Cody. It's just that these last few weeks have been a bit stressful." She got up from the bed and wandered over to the kitchenette in search of bread.

For a clone, Cody thought, she had mastered the art of understatement, recalling the strikingly banal naiveté that Cody had come to adore in the real Cheyenne, the kind of girl for whom a hangnail was a cause of much grief. Which set him wondering again. How was he to know what was real and what a replication? His Cheyenne had never seemed like the diary-keeping type. She was too vain to indulge in that kind of self-reflection. Besides, she couldn't spell all that well either, and her carpal tunnel syndrome made it painful for her to hold a pen. And who thinks to keep a diary when they are locked in a basement in Wyoming?

Cheyenne returned from the kitchenette with a loaf of Wonder Bread and a jar of Miracle Whip, mercifully repriving Cody of the headache his thinking was about to cause. "So where are we going anyway? How many sandwiches should I make?"

The question struck Cody as odd. It was the type of question for which there should be a ready answer, an easy answer, a clear answer. Cody thought a little; the headache threatened to return. He remembered asking Cheyenne to pack them a good lunch, which seemed to imply that they would be going on a trip. But a trip to where? And for what purpose? His mother was on the case regarding the LWP and the briefcase, so there was no need to go to Miami, and who brings sandwiches to Miami? It was as if this trip idea had been dropped in his lap by aliens. Was it the peyote aftertaste? A voice from beyond, from Max, telling him to go on a trip, to get out of town? Was it a typo?

"Now honey," he said, trying to regain some control over the course of events, "if I told you where we were going it wouldn't be a surprise! You make us two sandwiches each, and I'll head out and pick up some other goodies to lubricate the journey." He needed to get back out in the fresh air, to give his mind a chance to work away from the distraction of Cheyenne's delectable Cheyenne-ness; most of all, he needed to figure out where he was supposed to go on this trip.

The streets of Ocher Hacienda are not the sort of place a man should go in search of direction. Eclectic did not begin to describe the mix of people and commercial venues to be found there. In fact, eclectic did not describe it at all. Walking down the streets of his adopted hometown was like wandering in the twisted canyons of his own mind, an adventure Cody would wish on no one, least of all on himself. Halter-topped Harleyites mingled with corn-fed mid-westerners and over-dressed city folks as they browsed the moose-themed gift shops, ye olde ice cream parlors, and real estate offices promising five hundred thousand dollar cabins of your dreams. Whether your tastes ran to fudge or elk tenderloin, choices abounded. And that was Cody's problem: he needed direction, not options.

Cody reasoned (a rare occurrence in itself) that if someone were trying to speak to him from beyond, to send him on a trip for his own good, then trying too hard to hear the voice would only drown it out; he'd have to let that voice find him. He started down the side street leading to his chiropractic office with its sign reading: "Come in if open." And just as he passed the combination auto-repair/aromatherapy boutique, he heard it: "Hey mon, ova here." He looked around, fully expecting to see no one, and he was not disappointed. Then again: "Hey mon, here is where U got to go." The voice came from a poster on a kiosk, a poster advertising the annual Mountain Man Rendezvous. Cody studied the poster until the picture caught his eye: Rojie in fur cap and buckskin. If the Bermuda Triangle was real, then so was this.

He hurried back to the hotel to pick up Cheyenne and the sandwiches. They had a trip to go on.

[How much lunchmeat can Cheyenne put away? Where does Rojie think they should go? And what about Naomi? For answers to these questions and more, check back in vain next month when another local author takes up the saga.]

Part XIV

Cody deals with Frannie

By Angela Schilz

Cody needed to leave fast and to do that he would need a car (a truck would be even better) and a cooler for the sandwiches. He didn't have time to make his own sandwiches and he couldn't go back to the hotel without bringing Frannie, so he would have to bring her along too. Cody's wishes were answered by some trusting tourist who had left a Ford F-150 running in the parking lot. Cody ran to the room, grabbed the sandwiches and Cheyenne (or Frannie or whoever she was), left some money for the room on the dresser and headed for the already running vehicle.

When the sun finally went down, Cody was able to breathe. His ease had nothing to do with the darkness; no, it was the fact that Frannie had fallen asleep. "Do clones really sleep?" Cody thought, but Cody couldn't trouble himself with these thoughts now. He had to concentrate and if he had any distractions...well he didn't know what would happen, he had never had to concentrate before.

Cody continued driving in silence, waiting for mile marker 54 where he knew he would have to turn onto a dirt road that was almost impossible to see. Cody grabbed a sandwich, being careful not to wake Frannie. He thought it might help him focus, or at the very least keep him awake and provide some noise.

After four hours of driving they were almost there, only three miles left. The sandwiches had served their purpose and kept him awake. They were also delectable; was there MSG in the dressing or was Frannie just that good? Cody didn't know what had compelled him to eat all 32 finger sandwiches until he hit mile marker 52. Only 2 miles left and he knew he wasn't going to make it. Frannie had drugged the sandwiches, that's why they were so good. He had thought he could stop drugs from affecting his mind, but he forgot that Rojie was a medicine man. Whatever Frannie had put into the sandwiches was hitting him and causing the road to swim in front of him.

That was when Frannie woke up—clones don't sleep, Cody had been set up again. He should have just gotten deli sandwiches, he should have left that imposter in the hotel, but it was all too late now. Cody was on this ride and there was no getting off.

Just before he hit mile 54, Frannie turned and looked directly at him. Those piercing black eyes hardly resembled Cheyenne's and Cody wondered how he had ever thought this imposter was his beautiful fiancée. Then she started to speak, but it wasn't Cheyenne's voice, no, it was Rojie. Of course! How could Cody have been so stupid, Frannie couldn't be that good, she was merely a clone and another pawn in Shirley's sick game.

Out of Frannie's mouth, in Rojie's thick accent, came Cody's only chance for survival. One piece of advice that could save him, "u got to free ur self in to't mon." That was all Cody needed. He was back just in time to slam on the brakes and take a sharp left onto the dirt road that he could hardly see.

It was as if he were part of a river. Cody had followed Rojie's instructions and he knew (perhaps for the first time in his life) exactly what was going on. He hadn't been set up, the Belizean medicine man had the answers and he was sick of being a pawn. Rojie had used Frannie to get to Cody so that he could get out of this mess.

Frannie!!! What was he going to do about Frannie? Cody saw his chance to get rid of her. A bison was charging straight for the road in front of them. If Cody could time it right he could bail out just before the bison hit the truck and Frannie sitting in the passenger seat. The animal was closing in and the collision was going to be timed perfectly. 3...2...1... Cody jerked open his door and did a perfect barrel roll out of the truck and into the grass lining the road. He turned just in time to see the bison hit the truck flipping it one, two, three times.

Cody slowly approached the truck which had rolled enough to land up-right. Frannie appeared to be unconscious. Even if she hadn't died this would give Cody plenty of time. He wasn't far from Rojie's camp but it was so late it was getting to be early, and Cody had to get there before sunrise.

Part XV

Breakfast and a makeover

By Edward Terry

"Damn!" Cody exclaimed as he stumbled on another rock. The boots he had gotten on dollar-a-bag day could not be laced properly due to the missing eyehook and so his steps were somewhat iffy.

He was mostly certain that he was traveling in the right direction—mostly. The past few weeks of his life were enough to disorient almost anyone. Shoot, come to think of it even the last hour would be enough. Most people never jump out of a truck—so that a buffalo could hit it—trying to dump a girlfriend—who was cloned. Well, there was Dwayne, but Cody didn't think his old girlfriend was a clone.

"At last!" thought Cody as he came over a rise of sagebrush. There before him was Rojie's camp, that was what Rojie liked to call it. Stuck out here in the middle of nowhere the collection of cabins and pole buildings was a welcome sight, and he had made by sunrise—in time for the fabulous pancake breakfast! The cook at camp, Skeeter, was known in these parts for the incredible pancakes she created. Everyone knew that she heated the syrup but no one knew how she could get them so light and fluffy. Cody headed toward the mess hall.

As he got in line to get a tray, Cody reflected how this place had evolved. This used to be a militia training ground belonging to The Sons of the Brothers of the Fathers of Fairness or something along those lines, whose organization folded. Probably had too long a name. Any way, Rojie's brother-in-law had loaned him the money to buy the place. Rojie had turned the place into a camp for inner city kids who had no idea how to use cosmetics. His thinking was that if they were ever to become "beautiful people" they should get early training.

While he was debating on getting a second serving of pancakes, the head of the lipstick department sat down next to him. "Hi, Co, long time no see." This natural redhead was always a tease to Cody, and it was nice to see her freckles and crooked smile again. "What you been up to? Staying out of trouble?"

Cody opened his mouth to speak, changed his mind and just said "No."

Ruby was just the one Cody had wanted to see. He needed her help. She had more skill with lipstick, mascara, and blush than any rancher in the county. "Ru," Cody explained, "My mom is slipping into senility and hasn't seen my sister in years. She keeps asking about her and wants to see her but sis is doing 7-to-12 at Sing Sing so it's not going to happen. What I want to do is dress up like my sister, surprise my mom and make her happy as I am taking her to the nursing home."

The open mouth and blankish stare from Ruby told Cody that she would need a moment for his story to sink into the recognition section of her brain. Trouble was, this is the most plausible story he could create. How could he tell her that he had to go in disguise to see his mother?

How do you explain that you have been hiding for years, called your mom to pick up a very important package (linen wrapped), and FORGOT TO TELL HER WHERE YOU ARE! He knew that by now she was probably being watched and would be spotted before he got near her. This was the only way.

Ruby shifted her position in her chair. "Well, aren't you the considerate son? I don't know anyone else who would do this for his mother. No, no one I know." She smiled that crooked smile and told Cody she would help in any way she could.

They went back to her salon station and as Cody settled into her chair, Ruby asked about his sister.

"Well, her posture isn't as good and she is more of a summer than I am."

"Oooookaaayyyy" she said.

"Can you give me more so that I know what I am going for?"

"She looks mostly like me only female." Cody lied. How could he explain he needed to look good enough to be a woman—not too good looking to draw attention, and not so ugly to draw attention either. Ruby started to work.

Cody's eyes wandered around the room, noting the animal heads spaced out on the walls. He couldn't help but smile at the moose wearing lipstick. City kids—guess they need something to practice on but any fool knows better than that. All a moose needs is a little blush and some hair product. Now an antelope on the other hand....

The creaking door should have put Cody on instant alert, but somehow he missed it. The first bullet turned Ruby's white smock into a mockery of her freckled shoulders. The second one spun Cody on to the floor. Lying there, unable to move, he saw a face he knew come into focus above him.

"Hi ya, kid."

The Leopard leveled the .45 at Cody's head. "Wait," said Cody. "Will you at least tell me what has been going on here? Who is my friend and who has plotted against me? Please tell me the truth before I die!"

"Truth! You can't handle the truth!!" The Leopard shouldn't have been this upset—he had the gun.

Why is he in a marine general's uniform?

Cody made a jerk as he woke up. "Man I hate that Few Good Men dream." Ruby had stepped back but was now coming forward with brush and pencil. "That's okay, Co, lots of people go to sleep in that padded chair. Now as I was saying, my cousin, you know, the one who is also my twin, well, he and his girlfriend—the one who drives a taxi in Miami—"

"Oh, yeah," thought Cody. "Miami."

Part XVI

You want chip(s) with that?

By Whispy McCloud

"Oh damn, not again." He was lying in the sagebrush with a freezing mist soaking his good suit, his only suit. He had wrapped himself around the large bush like he was trying to make love to it. "Doesn't quite smell like sweet Petunia." The light was dim, and it was almost dark. "I wonder if it's morning or night. What the hell did Ru put in that makeup?" It got a little lighter, and he could make out the mountains. "I must be on the Chaphands bench about forty miles from Red Dog."

He pulled himself to a sitting position leaning against the bush. Every movement brought a new pain. He felt like he had been through the spin cycle on a front loader. When he was able to stand, he could see far away headlights moving across the bench. He pitched forward onto another sage bush. A sharp stick rammed into the back of his arm. When he rubbed it for some relief, he felt a lump. "What the hell is this?" It was square and about an inch on a side, just under the skin. "A microchip. Those bastards loaded me with a chip. No wonder they're always in my face. It's got to come out now." He reached down in his sock where he kept a small knife for emergencies. It was still there. It was a little bit of a gymnastic trick to cut the right underarm with his almost worthless left hand. It took three determined slices before he could get it out. There were several leads on the chip, but he broke them off in his hurry to get the thing out.

It lay there square and shiny. The source of most of his troubles. He shoved it under the sage. He couldn't tie the bandage one-handed, so he just put on his soggy Italian suit jacket, stuffed his knife back in his sock and hoped for the best. He staggered toward what seemed to be the highway. After about a half a mile he went down and couldn't get up. As he lay there, he heard a vehicle churning through the sand and brush. He watched on his hands and knees. It stopped, and men got out and looked around. After a while they got back in and roared back to the road. I've got to get the hell out of here before they come back. It took a long time to get to the road, and longer to get a ride. Finally, an older pickup stopped for him. It took the last of his strength to crawl in. There was a woman driving, and she looked awfully good. Before he passed out, he noticed two jeeps out in the flat where he had been.

He opened his eyes. This time it wasn't bad. He was warm, dry, naked, and clean. He felt his arm, and it was bandaged. The woman sitting in the chair noticed he was awake.

"Soon as you get a little more awake, I'll feed you some supper. You've been out all day. You're about the worst case of a half-drowned pup I've seen. I hope you don't mind. I burned your clothes. They were covered with some kind of nasty stuff. I shoulda burned them outside. They stunk up the house. That was a really fancy suit though. I never saw one before that had wires everywhere in the coat."

"Wires in the coat? What the hell? How did they get there? Oh, maybe when Petunia took it in to be cleaned. It never did fit quite right after that. I wonder. I bet it was Petunia who set me up for everything." He didn't mention to her that there had been $1,500 stitched into the lining for emergencies. "How about supper? I have no idea how long it's been since I ate."

"Elk stew coming up. I like to keep one hanging, then, I don't have to go to town."

"What did you say your name was?" Cody asked as he slurped down the stew.

"I didn't. There's people on both sides of the law who don't like me. Just call me Chrysy. That's short for Chrysanthemum. You know, you did a real hack job on your arm. When I was cleaning it up, I found two little tubes like Norplant sticks. I'll bet they were drugging you."

"Then maybe everything that seems to have happened in the past few months was an hallucination." Cody flopped back in despair and fell asleep. Sometime later, he opened his eyes to see Chrysy standing at the foot of the bed. She had changed into a nightgown and was obviously ready for bed. "There's one more thing. The house has only one bed, and you have to share." She blew out the lamp and got into bed. She didn't smell as good as Sweet Petunia. Hell, she didn't smell as good as the sagebrush. He fell back asleep in spite of the snuggling Chrysy.

"You sure do sleep soundly. I'll give you one more chance to socialize with me. Here's your breakfast." Cody got out of bed and put on her robe. Outside, the world was white. He clearly wasn't going anyplace for awhile, so he might as well just stay here with Chrysy.

Later, he lay around thinking, his head being clearer than it had been in months, There is something I know that everyone wants to find out. I wonder what it is.

Part XVII

Cody and the Malodorous Mademoiselle

By Tam McDowell

Cody was warm, dry, and at ease for the first time in several episodes. For a few brief moments no one was chasing him, drugging him, or bugging him. It was kind of pleasant. I could get used to this, he thought. Maybe I should just let Mom keep everything. The bad guys can hassle her for a while. He stretched and took a deep breath, catching a good whiff of Chrysy in the chair opposite him. Then again, maybe not, he thought as he pushed his chair back from the fireplace to try and put some distance between them.

"Uhh, Chrysy? Would you mind if I freshen up? I'm still feeling a little out of it and a shower would help me clear my head." Cody thought maybe he could ease into the topic of hygiene and not offend his host.

"Showers are a summer activity in this cabin. It's outdoors and solar. But I did build me a nice sauna out back. It's wood-fueled. We could fire that baby up and sweat the rest of those drugs right outta you." Chrysy jumped up and headed for the closet. "You'll want a pair of flip-flops for getting out there; we got a lotta deer hanging out in the yard so ya don't wanna go barefoot. Kinda messes things up for rolling round naked in the snow after sauna, too. You gotta look for a good clean spot before ya lie down."

Cody considered the possibility that he was still a little foggy. Surely she didn't just say flip-flops. There were six inches of new snow on the ground. And why didn't she mention clothes? He was going to need some sooner rather than later if he was going to get back to Red Dog.

"Hey Chrysy, I hate to bother you, but do you maybe have some clothes I could borrow? If you could just give me a ride into town, I can probably shower at my place." Cody wrapped the robe he was wearing a little tighter and cinched the belt.

"Well now. You're mighty anxious to be on your way aren't ya?" Chrysy turned from the closet with a pair of turquoise-colored fuzzy flip-flops dangling from her fingers. "I considered this while you were gettin your beauty rest this morning, and I've decided I like havin' company. It can git a little lonely out here, ya know."

Cody's spider sense was starting to tingle. Something about Chrysy just wasn't quite right. He stood up and took a few steps back, putting furniture between her and him. For the first time, he realized Chrysy outweighed him by at least fifty pounds, most of it pure muscle. She had a weird gleam in her eye and the smile fixed on her face looked a little forced. Amazing how perceptive Cody could be when not under the influence of this, that and the other.

Chrysy gestured with her flip-flop-adorned hand. "Don't be a stranger. Come on over here and get these shoes. You're gonna need em. You can wait in here while I get the sauna heating up."

"Maybe I'll just take those clothes instead. You've been a great host, but I really have to be on my way." Cody backed up a couple more steps and loosened his limbs, preparing for the possibility of having to fight his way out of this.

"Oh, I don't have no clothes that'll fit you. And you'll recall I burned that nasty suit. I figure if all you've got is my robe and a pair of flip flops, I'll have company until at least June." Chrysy chuckled and came closer. "Quit lookin' so alarmed. You'll get used to the idea. Sides, it ain't like I'm keeping you indefinitely. Just til the weather warms up." She dropped the shoes in the chair and pulled on her parka. "I'll be back in a few. Go ahead and slide those babies on your feet, okay?" Chrysy walked out the door yodeling "Saaa-oooonaa" at the top of her lungs, while Cody stood frozen in amazement.

Cody's mind was working furiously, which was really quite a feat since he wasn't much on thinking. How was he going to get out of this? He could make a run for it, but he wasn't going to get far on foot in turquoise fuzzy flip flops and a pink chenille robe. Even if he did make it, the thought of someone seeing him clad so outrageously was enough to make him shudder. The truck! He could steal the truck. Cody rushed to the back window, looking for Chrysy. She was barely visible around the side of the sauna. He frantically looked for some clothes to pull on, realizing he didn't have a lot of time before Chrysy came back to tell him the sauna was ready. A stocking cap lay on the floor next to the front door. He snatched that up and tugged it down over his ears. He was just pulling Chrysy's extra pair of pants out from under the bed (from the looks of them, Chrysy was wearing the clean ones), when she opened the back door.

Their eyes met across the room and for a second neither one of them moved. Then all was pandemonium. Cody scrambled for the front door, pants in hand. Chrysy let out a roar and leaped over the kitchen table trying to reach him. She's pretty fast, for a girl, Cody thought just before she tackled him. He felt the air rush out of him and everything faded to gray, but Cody bravely fought his way back from the brink of unconsciousness. He couldn't afford to pass out now. He'd seen Misery. He didn't want to wake up tied to a bed with two broken legs. He kicked out at the woman on top of him, and gave her a good jab in the face with his elbow.

"You knocked out my front tooth!" Chrysy yelled, spitting blood all over the back of his neck. "That. Wasn't. Very. Nice!" She punctuated each word of her sentence by banging Cody's face into the floor. Cody threw every ounce of his 180-pound frame into rolling over and knocking her off of his back. He scooted backwards for the door, struggling to regain his feet. Chrysy was crawling toward him faster than a crab can scuttle across the beach. He grabbed a spittoon sitting next to her chair on his way past and threw it at her, hitting her squarely in the head. Tobacco juice splashed everywhere. Chrysy paused in her forward progress to wipe the muck out of her eyes and Cody seized his opportunity, opening the door and making a run for the truck.

He was almost there when he felt her yanking on the spare pants he still had in his hand. He let them go and kept running. In no time she was on him again, catching hold of the collar of his robe. He tore his way out of the robe and left Chrysy kneeling in the snow clutching it. Cody locked himself in the truck and went to work hotwiring it. Chrysy was pounding on the window now and begging him to stay just a little longer. Cody saw the keys were in the ignition and abandoned his efforts to hotwire the truck. He peeled his way out the driveway, Chrysy running after him in futility.

Cody spared a glance in the rearview and breathed a sigh of relief. No one would ever believe he had just escaped the clutches of an amorous mountain woman wearing nothing but a stocking cap and a pair of flip flops. Speaking of which, he was getting pretty dang cold. Various and sundry parts of him were threatening to freeze and fall off. Cody turned on the heater and headed back to town.

He needed an airline ticket and a new suit, not necessarily in that order. He was going back to Florida to visit dear old Mom. Who says you can't go home again? Cody's brain was in overdrive thinking of all he needed to accomplish. It was more thinking than he'd done in a very long time. How was he going to look driving through town stark naked? Would anyone even notice? Should he ditch Chrysy's truck and take the pinto back to Billings instead? So many questions! His brain was done. "I won't think about that right now," he said to no one in particular. "I can't think about it now. I'll think about it tomorrow." He raised his eyes to the heavens and lifted a fist in the air, banging it on the ceiling. "After all, tomorrow is another day!"

Part XVIII

Cody and the Irate Agent

By Ethan McDowell

Needless to say, Cody made it to Scarlet House in one piece. But now he was faced with two slightly larger problems: whether to take the truck or the Pinto to Billings, and how to get some clothing without attracting too much attention to himself. The former problem worked itself out when Cody turned to the news on the radio. "The forecast for the week ahead is snow, snow and more snow, shortly followed by a long warm spell sure to force the closure of several local winter activity centers. If you need to do some highway travel, vehicles with four-wheel-drive are a must as Highway 212 will be closed at Billings and Scarlet House to anything but four-wheel-drive vehicles," the radio quickly spewed at him. "Well that answers that question, but leaves the more important one," Cody muttered bitterly.

Just then an elderly man in a blue jumpsuit knocked on the window, asking in an overly loud voice, "Are you Witness number 2114583: codename Cody Quarterline?" Cody rolled down the window and replied with a shocked "Yes".

"The name's France, Nort France, I work for the Secret Service, I have very important information for you. But first, let's get you some clothing, and maybe a coffee. You wait here," The man said, matter-of-factly.

"That last part wasn't really necessary. Where the hell else am I supposed to go?" Cody said softly.

After Cody spent a few minutes waiting and contemplating what he was going to tell his mother when he showed up at her door, Nort returned with a pair of plaid golf pants and an early 70's low-neck shirt. "You'll just have to keep the shoes for now; they were out of them at the senior center," he said, quite happily. "Now, let's get that coffee and I'll tell you more about why I'm here.

They took a short stroll down the block to the local coffee shop, where the barista, Pam, took their orders with only a little bit of an amused look at Cody's clothing, and dispensed the coffee from a large urn behind the counter. "Thanks for coming in, Nort!" she said with an overlarge smile of job satisfaction on her face. Nort just shrugged her off.

Nort jumped right into his story when they left the coffee shop, "I've been working undercover here for a long time now — can't actually remember how long — rooting out subverters and crooks for the President. I chose this disguise because I can go anywhere in town with it. My main target is local writer, Haul Combusts. You've probably seen him around, he has a great bushy beard and hangs out at the coffee shop a lot. He may actually be an infamous diamond thief. That's enough about me though; I was told to tell you that the government thinks the Leopard knows who and where you are, so be on the lookout for anything suspicious."

"Well, that's good to know," Cody said with a small smirk. "It's probably good that I'm on my way out of town today then."

"Where are you headed?" Nort asked conversationally

Cody replied, "To see my mother. I'll be gone about a week."

"Well, I'd better get back to my job," Nort said with a touch of a grin. "Bye," he said before turning and walking briskly away.

"Thanks for the clothes," Cody called after him. "Now, I'd better get to Billings before the weather gets any worse."

Cody ran back towards the truck. He got in and took it to get fuel for the trip at the local station. After an uneventful fueling session he started for Billings. He made it about five miles before the snow really set in. The snow was coming down so hard he didn't see the curve and continued straight into oncoming traffic. The elderly driver of the oncoming Jeep never saw him. They collided at well over fifty miles per hour. The icy road conditions sent both vehicles sliding off the roadway, luckily, because a large eighteen-wheeler had been following the driver of the Jeep. Cody climbed out of the twisted wreck of the truck with only a few bruises on his shoulder and legs. Cody pulled some flares from under the truck seat, lit them and threw them on the roadway. He then checked to see if the other driver was all right.

"Hey, you all right?" he called above the wind. There was no reply, so Cody went over to the Jeep and pounded on the door, yelling "Hello, are you all right," to the man inside. Again there was no reply so Cody opened the door and found that the man had hit his head very hard on the steering wheel and was unconscious. Cody looked around for a phone, but couldn't find one. Luckily enough a passing vehicle saw the road flares and stopped to see if everything was okay.

"Hey, are you okay; do you need to call an ambulance?" the people in the vehicle called.

"Yea, this guy hit his head really hard," Cody called back. Then Cody heard the woman in the passenger seat talking on a phone for a bit.

"The ambulance is on its way, do you need any more help?" the woman called.

"No, we should be all right now, thanks for the help," Cody replied. The vehicle drove off. "Well, this puts getting to Mom's on hold. Why does this stuff always happen to me?"

Just then he heard a loud banging noise and the Jeep caught fire. "Why me?" Cody asked as he ran over to get the elderly driver out of his vehicle. He got the man to safety and returned to the truck to get his money from the envelope he had it in. He got the money, and turned around, facing away from the wreck, just in time for it to explode. Cody went flying into the ditch. Luckily enough for him, he found a soft patch to land on. Luckily enough for the softball sized chunk of asphalt kicked up by the wreck, it found a soft part of the back of Cody's head to land on.

The last thing to go through Cody's mildly-concussed mind before he blacked out was, "Why did the sky hit me?"

Part XIX

The Leopard and the Babe

By David Alsager

Cody woke to find himself slumped against the passenger door of a moving pickup and the next slight bump helped him to focus on the screaming pain in his head.

"Argh." Oh, yeah. The sky had hit him. He wondered why.

"Ah, you're awake. Good," said the attractive dark-haired woman driving the truck. Cody thought she was a real babe but realized that she looked strangely familiar.

He wondered who the hell she was.

"Who the hell are you? You're a real babe" Cody also wondered why he was in this truck and where they were going.

"Well, I'm..." she started to say.

"Why am I in this truck and where are we going?" He noticed it was still snowing heavily.

"Cody, I'm Kay...."

"Hey, it's still snowing."

"Will you shut up!"

"Sorry."

"I'm Kaycee, Cheyenne's little sister and we're headed to the Cody airport to..."

"My airport? I have an airport?"

"The airport in Cody," she said, a little tartly.

"In Cody? But I'm Cody."

"Cody is a town in Wyoming. It has an airport. Did that blow to your head addle your brain?"

"No, I'm always like this. Why Cody? Isn't Billings closer?"

Kaycee explained patiently that it wasn't snowing in Cody and they had a chartered jet waiting to take them to Miami. Cody noticed then that they were crossing the Wyoming state line and the weather was indeed clearing ahead of them. He wondered why they were going to Miami.

"Why are we going to Miami?"

"To meet with your mom."

Okay, Cody knew that, but how did Kaycee know? He decided to ask the obvious question, but she was ahead of him.

"Your mom sent me to get you. She seemed worried that you would have trouble getting there on your own. I guess she was right; it was a good thing I came on your accident when I did.

"Before Cheyenne died she told me about you and Max, as well as the Leopard and the LWP. She knew you were going to need help......"

Wait, wait. Cheyenne has a sister? And she's really a babe! As Kaycee talked on, explaining her connection, Cody's mind was lancing to the heart of the matter.

"...and what's with those plaid pants? You don't really think they're back in fashion--as if they were ever in fashion--do you?"

Cody was still noticing that Kaycee was a babe and he rather belatedly realized that she had stopped talking and left a question hanging.

"What?"

"The plaid pants. I thought you wore Italian suits. And my god, those shoes."

So Cody began filling her in on the last few chapters. They arrived at Cody's airport; I mean the airport in Cody, and found the chartered jet waiting for them. Soon they were airborne, heading towards Miami. Cody slept for a long while, then woke with a start. Kaycee was still sitting in the lounge across from, a pleasant aspect. He'd remembered something.

"I thought my mom was going to FedEx the LWP and the bonds to me. Why are we meeting her in Miami?

Kaycee looked a little confused, "How would she get into the locker? You have the keys."

"No, I don't. I mailed them to Mom."

"You what? When?" Kaycee appeared seriously concerned now.

"I think it was back in chapter twelve. Why?"

"So she has the keys to the locker?"

"Well, she should."

Kaycee jumped up and went forward to the cockpit, opening the door. Cody couldn't really hear the conversation with the crew but it appeared to be about a course change. He thought he heard "Cozumel." When she returned, she was holding a cell phone, "It's me. We're heading there. The mom's got the keys. The idiot mailed them to her. What?! How could she escape? You're on an island. Yes, yes, I know about boats; don't be a smartass. Well, you need to find her. What? What does Cinco de Mayo have to with the search? Oh great. And I suppose they'll be too hung over tomorrow." She listened a moment, "Well, we'll head your way unless something changes."

Cody was more confused. Who escaped? What island? And what does this have to do with his mom? And Cheyenne is dead? What does Cinco de Mayo have to do with anything. Is there any tequila on board? He began to ask these questions of Kaycee but she cut him off. Yes, she explained, Cheyenne was dead, Shirley Prine had killed her. The rest she glossed over, saying he'd find out when they got to Cozumel, but she did get up and find a bottle of tequila in the bar.

Cody felt the plane bank as the cockpit door opened and one of the pilots came aft, explaining that there were big thunderstorms over Texas and they were going to have to divert to the west. That would add distance and they would have to stop and re-fuel in San Angelo. Kaycee was clearly impatient, but there was little she could do.

A couple of hours later, the plane was on final approach to San Angelo when the cell phone rang.

"Biloxi? How did she get to Biloxi?" A long pause, then," Well, I never trusted that Rojie. Did the guys at least save the Twin Otter? Okay, good. Does she have the keys?" Another pause, "Okay, okay. When we're done refueling here, we'll head to Biloxi, then we'll take her to get the keys."

That began Cody thinking again. His mom lived in Biloxi, maybe they would see her. But wasn't she in Miami? And what are these keys Kaycee keeps talking about? Maybe they'd see Rojie there. He liked Rojie. He started to ask Kaycee but she seemed a little distracted.

"Cody, "she said, kind of exasperated, "your mom is in Biloxi, that's why we're going there. So we can get the keys to the locker. And Rojie is dead."

Oh.

"Well, then what do we do?"

She looked at him, "We go to Miami, open the lockers, get the LWP and the bonds and that's it."

"What are we going to with them?

And what about the money?"

"We aren't going to do anything with them. I am going to take them to Giuseppe. And what money?"

Oops.

"Cody? What money?"

Cody was forced to tell Kaycee about the 1.5 million in yet another locker. Man, even his mom didn't know about that. On the rest of the flight to Biloxi, he began to think that he and his mom might be in a little trouble. How come Rojie was dead? Who was Kaycee talking to? Was she really Cheyenne's sister? Boy, she really was a babe. Who's Giuseppe? Perhaps he should come up with a plan.

After a while he remembered who Giuseppe was. Giuseppe Lampedusa, aka "the Leopard." Holy crap. Was Kaycee working for the Leopard? Now, he really needed a plan. But before he could put one into place they were landing at Gulfport-Biloxi International Airport and taxiing over to the private aviation hangers. The plane came to a stop in front of one with a sign, "Panther Jet Service." There was a black BMW 7-series parked by the door. It was raining. Dark, too, because they had left Wyoming in late afternoon. Kaycee led Cody down the stairs and over to the BMW, where a heavy-set Hispanic-looking man held open the back door for them. As Cody leaned down to climb in, he saw a rather bedraggled older woman sitting by the far door.

"Mom! Are you okay? What's going on?" Kaycee pushed him the rest of the way in and climbed in herself as Cody's mom said, "I'm okay, Poindexter, but they're making me give up those keys."

The BMW drove off and headed out of the airport as Cody and Mom caught up. He was astonished at her story. He'd had no idea that she'd been kidnapped, escaped and caught right here in Biloxi. It seems the Leopard was using her as bait to get the keys and locker numbers from Cody.

"But I didn't have the keys, Mom, you did."

As his mom was explaining the nuances of this to her son, the BMW was passing through downtown Biloxi to her house in the Back Bay area. It was still raining, remnants of thunderstorms that had passed through hours before. Cody gradually became aware that she was talking about someone named Dubois.

"Mom, who's Dubois?"

"He's my boyfriend."

"How come I don't know about this boyfriend?"

"Maybe because you haven't called me for three years."

"Oh. Well what's he do? Is he retired? Did you meet him at the senior center?"

"No, I met him at the library." She was a semi-retired librarian. "He and his brother, Lander, are bounty hunters. But, what I was trying to say was that he and Lander are at the house and..."

The car turned into the driveway of a twenties bungalow surrounded by tulip and magnolia trees hung with Spanish moss. They parked behind a late-model puce-colored Cadillac DeVille. The Hispanic man, who had ridden in the front passenger seat, opened Mom's door and Cody and Mom got out. As they walked around the car and joined Kaycee on the wide front porch, Cody noticed that it was still raining.

"Hey, it's still raining."

As they approached the door, Cody's mom slipped and grabbed his arm. Caught off guard, he slipped, too, and they both fell to the porch floor. Instantly, the front door exploded outward and dozens of double-ought buckshot pellets slammed into the Hispanic man's chest, knocking him off the porch. A second blast caught Kaycee in the abdomen and put her down. At the same moment, an elderly man wearing a raincoat and a floppy hat stepped from the side of the house and fired two rounds from his Ruger Mini-14 into the BMW, killing the driver.

Stunned, Cody helped his mom up. "Are you all right?"

"Well, no thanks to you, you idiot. Anyway, this is Dubois," indicating an even older gentleman coming through the ruined door carrying a stainless steel Remington 12 guage. "And the man with the rifle is his brother, Lander."

After introductions, Cody's mom went into the house while Dubois and Lander moved the BMW onto the street and started the Cadillac. Shortly, she emerged carrying a small package and a larger bundle and they all climbed into the Caddy, she and Cody in the back.

"What's in the packages?" Cody wondered.

"These are all the keys to the lockers and this is a pair of trousers and some decent shoes. You are not traveling with us wearing those horrid plaid pants."

As Dubois powered the Cadillac down the street, Cody was curious, "Where are we going?"

"To Miami, of course. To get that #$%*ing linen-wrapped package."

It was still raining.

Part XIX appeared in May 2008. Now, over seven years later, we are proud to finally present the conclusion of the Cody Quarterline saga. And as an aside to my high school English teachers, yes, I split that infinitive in the last sentence ON PURPOSE, and I know this is a run-on sentence because that's the best way to make my POINT! Okay. I'm done now.

Part XX

Epilogue

By Douglas Gunn
A.K.A. Diarmund "The Ferret" van der Merwe
A.K.A. Mackenzie Guffin
A.K.A. Doug Robson

"Um..."

She stuttered as she stared at the papers scattered over the desk between them. The man looked expectantly at her, excited, though purposefully nonchalant.

"I don't understand."

"What do you mean?" He spat the words indignantly. "You seen *Face/Off*?"

"What?"

"*Face/Off*."

"I really don't see how that's relevant."

"Have you seen it?"

"Yeah, the John Woo flick. Nic Cage? Travolta?"

"What? No. The... The— The Brad Pitt, Ed Norton, punchy punch—"

"*Fight Club*?"

"Yeah, *Fight Club*! Obviously. You seen that?"

"Well, of course."

"You get that?"

"Get it? Yeah, I got it."

"*Twelve Monkeys*?"

"Yeah."

"*Butterfly Effect*? *Memento*?"

"Sir, get to the point."

"The best movies ever made are all mind-bending psychological thrillers. You can't dismiss this just because you 'don't get it.'" He threw as much insult into the last words as possible, flipping his scarf over his shoulder as he did.

"Mister Spampinato, you can't expect me to believe you actually think this is on par with the works of Chuck Palahniuk or Terry Gilliam."

"It's brilliant! Of course it is!"

"Just because it makes no sense doesn't mean it's great."

"You're missing the nuances of it."

"It's not nuanced, it's broken. The story falls apart at least three times."

"No, see, that's part of the nuance. The milieu."

"Every chapter's written by someone different. There's no cohesion."

"No. See, that's why it's a work of art. It's not like any existing movie 'cause every chapter in it is done by someone different. It's a collaboration, an evolving, growing, twisting art project."

"The name of the town changes every chapter. It changed twice in one chapter."

"You're missing the whole point," Spampinato huffed. "It's poking fun at the classic detective dramas and noir pieces that were so long in the tooth that they couldn't keep details right. It's parody! It's also a joke on the concept of changing authors in a single piece, so it's, like, self parody at the same time. Come on, Mrs. Derbogosijan, I thought you were in the film scene."

"What the hell is a hacienda anyway?"

"A large estate or plantation with a dwelling house. In Spanish speaking regions." She stared blankly at him. "I looked it up."

"Sir, I just don't think this Cody Quarterline of yours is the right fit for a Hollywood movie."

"I already adapted it into an internet radio drama. It's a podcast, and it has thousands of dedicated fans. I even have a store set up. My 'What the Hell is Puce' and 'Why did the Sky Hit Me' shirts are selling like hotcakes. Hotcakes, Raven."

"How much is hotcakes?"

"Like, ten." She stared at him blankly. "Okay, five. We've got a plushie Rojie on the way, and the pre-orders are through the roof. Jimmie Buffet even came on the podcast to voice one of the impersonators."

"I don't believe you."

"Alan Moore is doing a comic spin-off of Cody Versus the Alligator People."

She stared at him with vacuous eyes, begging this meeting to end.

"He says it's James Bond meets Johnny Quest."

Her eyes bored into his, asking wordlessly if he was done. Evidently, he was. She tried to divert the conversation, but couldn't help asking.

"Seriously? Alan Moore?"

"Well, no, not THAT Alan More, he's—"

"Sir, I'm going to have to ask you to leave."

"You're not seriously passing up on this? You could make millions off this. People are clamoring for fun spy-action-thriller since Bond went all dark. This is your opportunity, Mrs. Derbogo—"

"There's no opportunity, Mr. Spampinato. You have a thrown together mess of a script with no cohesive plot, characterization all over the place, no clear end, which, by the way, where's the end?"

"There is no end," he spat with a tight, serpentine glare. "Everyone talks about how refreshing a 'bad ending' is, or now 'happy endings,' 'cause we see so many bad. Happy or sad? Hopeful or dread? Confusing or clear? Obviously, the answer is don't even write one. No one will see it coming!"

"Sir, I'm done. My doorman will see you out."

Spampinato stood, grabbed his briefcase, and stormed out. Before he hit the door, he spun on his heels and stared her in the eyes. "My twitter followers won't be happy about this."

"Uh huh."

"You'll regret turning me down when Guillermo del Toro picks it up!"

"Goodbye, Mr. Spampinato."

He slammed the door, and she sighed, leaning back into her chair. She stared down at the pages littering her desk, ordered them, and opened Twitter on her laptop. Searching his name brought up an account with under a hundred followers, a link to a GeoCities site, and podcast feed with two episodes dated over a year ago. Smiling, she opened the drawer to her right, drew her cell phone from it, and glanced at the small package delicately wrapped in a fine linen resting underneath. She shut the drawer, flipped through her contacts, tapped one, and waited.

"Mr. Spiripopulous' office, please... Hey, Aldous? Idris Elba never got the Bond role, right? Tell him I've got something for him."

THIS PAGE INTENTIONALLY LEFT BLANK

no, it isn't

You know what I mean, I'm leaving this verso page blank so the chapter will start on a recto — oh, never mind

> **MICHIGAN STATE UNIVERSITY**
> **MSU Libraries | Guides**
>
> **Recto and verso**
>
> When you open a book anywhere, you'll see two pages: a left-hand page and a right-hand page, which face each other. These two pages together are called a spread.
>
> Each section of your book should start on a right-hand page. The title page is always a right-hand page, the table of contents begins on a right-hand page, chapter 1 begins on a right-hand page, and so on.
>
> Book designers call these two pages by the Latin terms "recto" for the right-hand page and "verso" for the reverse or left-hand page. This usage may help you remember that each new section always starts on the recto or right-hand page, not on the 'reverse'.

I don't want to hear about your "recto"

CHAPTER 12
Red Lodge Major Events

THE LOCAL RAG

JULY 2009 FREE
& WORTH EVERY PENNY

RED LODGE • BEARCREEK • FOX • JOLIET • LUTHER • ROBERTS • ROSCOE • WASHOE

Home of Champions Rodeo
page 10

Beartooth Rally & Iron Horse Rodeo
page 24

National Day of the American Cowboy
page 36

Red Lodge Resort Tax
page 6

BOXHOLDER

PRSRT-STD
U.S. Postage
PAID
Red Lodge, MT
Permit No. 75

July is a great month for big event lovers in Red Lodge, as the month kicks off with the Home of Champions Rodeo & Parade on the 2nd, 3rd, and 4th, and then goes into the Beartooth Rally and Iron Horse Rodeo a few weeks later. This cover attempted to show a little of both, with Doug Bailey attempting to rope his Harley in the arena at Aspen Ridge Ranch. It took two photographers (Kevin Aukema and me) and over 100 shots each to get this picture.

This cover went even farther, putting rodeo champion Deb Greenough on a motorcycle and Beartooth Rally founder Leo Wilson on a horse.

Red Lodge FESTIVAL OF NATIONS 2008

All Nations Night

This area was settled by people who came here to work in the coal mines and in agriculture—all seeking the opportunities promised by this country to its immigrants. Beginning in 1950, the Festival of Nations founders chose to honor all of these courageous and adventurous people who left their homelands for the promise of a better life by preserving their traditions and customs. We continue to honor them in the All Nations Gala on Friday night, August 1st, in the Civic Center. In keeping with the tradition of the first 52 years, this Festival of Nations event is FREE.

For the first 52 years of the Festival, each of the original nationalities and Montana presented a separate evening program filled with dances, bands, singers, skits and all types of entertainment showing off the traditions and customs of that nationality. On the 9th day of the Festival, the Festival of Nations culminated in an All Nations program. Bob Moran, the Festival coordinator, acted as Master of Ceremonies and host, introducing the 2 to 3 best dances or songs from each of those nationality's programs. The All Nations night program was considered the very best of the Festival of Nations, and the Civic Center was packed on both sides, with standing room only, with audiences from all over the United States and beyond.

This year, as the opening night of the Festival, we will once again present the All Nations Night as a gala event. Just as was done historically all those many years, you will see dances from each of those original nationalities: Scotland, England, Ireland, Italy, Germany, Finland, Scandinavia, Greece, and the former Yugoslavia. Many of the dances will be performed to live music: bagpipes, accordions, fiddles, and brass bands. You will see many new dances from those regions as well as some old favorites back by popular demand.

Celtic Fusion, led by Tonya Kosorok, will surprise you with some new dances, including a German dance in honor of her own heritage. As has always been the custom, the national dance of Scotland, "The Highland Fling", will be danced by any and all highland dancers who attend, whether from Billings, Red Lodge, Miles City, or Canada.

Returning as our special guest is the Billings Caledonian Pipes & Drums, carrying on a long tradition begun by Red Lodge's Scottish piper, Bill Flockhart. Folk dancers from Butte, Bozeman, and Missoula will join with the International Folk Dancers. The International Folk Dancers have been in existence as separate groups in Red Lodge and Billings since the early 1970s and, after dancing in the Yugoslavian program together for many years, the two groups officially joined in the late 1990's under the direction of Marilee Duncan. They will be performing dances from Greece, Hungary, Serbia, and Croatia. They are honored to have been asked to perform two Finnish traditional dances as well.

Dansairrean competition Irish step dancers will present a variety of jigs and reels, including a joint dance with Celtic Fusion. The Montana Morris Dancers will present a traditional English dance. Il Gruppo Folklorico Italiano, also known as the Natali Italian Dancers, sponsored by the local Italian Girls Victory Club, will perform three favorite dances and will also be showing their heirloom costumes. Our local Scandinavian adult dancers and children's group will also be featured, wearing their beautiful traditional costumes.

Doors open at 6:30 with a prelude from Red Lodge's community band, "Alte Kamaraden," which means "Old Comrades." The program begins at 7:00. Come early to get a seat! Join all of the participants for a social dance afterwards, with more music from Alte Kamaraden.

Red Lodge FESTIVAL OF NATIONS Montana

SPECIAL 8-PAGE PULLOUT SECTION

August kicks off in Red Lodge with the Festival of Nations. The Rag has always been supportive of the Festival, as some of the editors have served on the Festival board — and others just liked kilts. It became a tradition for the Rag to print schedules, and in later years (like this 2008 example), to produce full programs as pullout sections in the middle of the paper. In the top photo on this page, I'm celebrating my father's heritage by wearing a kilt and holding the Canadian flag as my wife, Kathy, sings the Canadian national anthem. Pius "flagmeister" Meier graces the lower photo.

Red Lodge FESTIVAL OF NATIONS 2008

The Dancers

The Festival of Nations is all about dancing. You can join in on Friday night after the opening ceremonies, attend the Contra Dance workshops Saturday and Sunday night, or just sit back and watch.

Opening night is a flurry of different ethnic dances performed by local and imported talent alike, mostly to live music. Saturday and Sunday provide some longer shows where you can spend more time with a particular type of dancing.

The picture at top left shows the Finn dancers at the 2002 Festival of Nations. This group is one of the largest traditional dance groups in the area.

Red Lodge's Celtic Fusion perform at the 2003 (above) and 2000 (below) Festivals. Celtic Fusion, led by Tonya Kosorok (granddaughter of one of the founders of the Red Lodge Festival of Nations), performs traditional Scottish and Irish dances, and Tonya manages to work in bottle dances and other ethnic treats.

Tajamuul, shown at left at the 2005 Festival, is a Red Lodge belly dance troupe.

The Very Best of the Red Lodge Local Rag

THE SCENE, BY JEANNE

I am very pleased and excited to remind you that the **Red Lodge Music Festival** will be celebrating its 46th season this year, bringing world-class chamber music and jazz to our fair city. This fabulous festival begins on **Saturday, June 6th at 7:30 PM** at the Red Lodge Civic Center. Tickets are available at the door, and I encourage all of you to set aside the evening and just go! You'll be transported and astounded at the virtuosity of the musicians and the wide variety of music on a scale most of us experience only in major cities and venues.

The Festival will continue on Sunday, June 7th, Tuesday, June 9th, Wednesday, June 10th, and the faculty portion finishes up on Saturday, June 13th. All concerts start at 7:30. The admission is nominal and the music is phenomenal! The student concerts are also delightful and totally free! They are on Thursday, June 11th at 7 pm, Friday, June 12th at 11 am and 7 pm, and Sunday, June 14th, @ 1:30 pm. More information is available at their website: www.redlodgemusicfestival.org

The Red Lodge Music Festival was started 46 years ago by four tenacious people with a dream: Nancy Critelli, Ann Rylands, James O'Brien, and Mary Critelli LaMonaca, who formed a festival quartet, hired six musicians, and brought in nine students. Now the festival has a world-class faculty of 32 members, two of whom are stars in our own community: Sue Logan on the oboe and Randy Tracy on the violin (both play for the Billings Symphony). Currently the Festival brings in over 200 students every year.

46th Anniversary
Red Lodge Music festival
Montana's Premier Music Camp
June 6-14, 2009

Leonard Garrison

This year the Festival has an exciting new artistic director, Leonard Garrison. His face will be familiar to everyone, as he has been associated with the festival, in one way or another, for most of his life; six years as a student, later a counselor, then a faculty member, and now as the artistic director of the Festival.

A consummate flutist, Leonard has been associated with the festival since 1971. His résumé is impressive, and he has an extensive performance schedule and two critically acclaimed CDs. I love both of them, and intend to purchase them at the festival. You can hear wonderful and enchanting snippets at his website: www.uidaho.edu/~leonardg. The site itself is really interesting. It contains not only his credentials and music, but advice on flutes, practicing, and links to a lot of useful sources for any admirer of the flute and its arts.

This year the Festival is continuing a tradition of focusing on celebrating musical anniversaries, both births and deaths. This year is the 200th anniversary of the birth of Felix Mendelssohn, 1809, which will be commemorated at Wednesday's concert with the overture to "Midsummer Night's Dream" Op. 21.—this will be a wonderful preamble for all of us attending the Hospital's June Fundraiser: "Midsummer Night's Dream" Beartooth Ball, which will be held on Saturday, June 13th. There will also be pieces celebrating the anniversaries of Haydn, who died in 1809; Ernst Bloch, who died in 1959; and Harold Genzmer, born in 1909.

Leonard Garrison says the Festival always strives to provide a balance between presentations by all the instrument groups; strings, winds, and piano; and a good mix of sizes and textures of music; as well as a blend of solos, duets, and quintets. Wednesday's concert ends with a presentation by the Jazz Faculty Combo, and from my own experience this is not to be missed. There is also an ongoing tradition at the end of the last program, on the last night, of presenting a sensational eight handed piano work, featuring two pianos and four musicians.

This year's pieces, chosen by the artists and arranged by the director, will include three world premieres; two of them by John Harmon, who has one foot in the classical world and one in jazz. The third premier is by Robert Leve, who has been associated with the Festival since the 1970s. His new piece was written for Loren Marsteller who will be performing it here.

In addition to the premieres, the Festival concerts will include selections from all four basic eras: Baroque, Classical, Romantic, and Modern; as well as most instrument groupings. So no matter what your taste in music, you will find pieces to delight your ears and energize or soothe your soul. It has been said that music is the great uniter, so come on out and be part of the celebration!

Jeanne Thomas is a lifetime devotee of the performing arts. In Red Lodge, we see both her serious side as a member of the Performing Arts Consortium and her fun side when she performs as Pippi the Clown.

June 2009

CHAPTER 13
Local Rag Election Coverage

Election coverage in the Local Rag isn't like other newspapers. While we've always realized the importance of the election, we've also realized that candidates for local offices are people that we interact with every day. Those other newspapers will tell you how they feel about the big issues of the day; we'll tell you how they feel about dogs vs. cats and whether they catch & release or cook the fish they catch.

The Local Rag political reporting has gotten pretty serious at times, but it mostly stayed light and positive.

The "debate" below is from October 2003, and the 4-H election news is from December 2006.

> "The best defense of democracy is an informed electorate."
> –Thomas Jefferson
>
> "If we don't have an informed electorate we don't have a democracy. So I don't care how people get the information, as long as they get it."
> –Jim Lehrer

In true ELECTION NEWS….
By Gunnar Nelson

Beartooth Bums 4-H Club elected the following in landslide WINS! (no need for recounts, recalls or concession speeches!) Reporter: Gunnar Nelson, Vice Presidents: Callie Wollenburg & Quinn Entenmann, President: Hannah Wollenburg, Secretary: Ceily Rae Highberger, Treasurer: Jamie Nelson, Historian: Becky Martin

The Local Rag chat room

Mayoral debate sizzles

With elections coming around, we at the Local Rag want to do our part in keeping the public informed of the truly important issues at stake. So we sent our crack reporter out to attack the hard-hitting issues of the Mayoral Race, because we know that YOU, Red Lodge, deserve to know. What follows are a few highlights from the debate.

If you had a superpower, what would it be?
Richard: MRI eyes (Magnetic Resonance Imaging).
Smokey: I'd like to be able to fly. I was a tailgunner in Korea and I've always loved flying.

How many pairs of shoes do you have in your closet?
Richard: Ten.
Smokey: You don't even want to know!

What's your favorite cartoon?
Richard: Road Runner—he always makes me laugh.
Smokey: The Flintstones, I just watched it last night.

If you had an entire day to do whatever you wanted, what would you do?
Richard: Swim and lay on the beach at the ocean.
Smokey: Go hunt and fish.

What brand of jeans do you wear & why?
Richard: Wranglers—they fit.
Smokey: Whatever's on sale.

What's your worst habit?
Richard: Licking my wounds.
Smokey: Not learning how to use the cell phone.

Do you put the milk or the sugar on your cereal first?
Richard: What's cereal??
Smokey: I eat Wheaties, the Breakfast of Champions! But yes, I put the sugar on first.

Do you eat your corn on the cob around in circles or typewriter-style?
Richard: Typewriter-style.
Smokey: I kinda gnaw around it.

What's the oldest article of clothing you own that you still wear?
Richard: An Oregon Duck Rally sweater.
Smokey: My Harry S. Truman hat.

What's the greatest invention of the 20th century?
Richard: The Roto-tiller.
Smokey: The doggone cell phone, cuz I can't work mine.

And now for a final question, gentlemen. Tell me about your nickname—where did it come from?
Richard: I can't tell you - my wife gave me the name.
Smokey: We used to go fishing in this marshy area when we were kids. I was 7 or 8 and I'd smoke to keep the mosquitoes away. So my doctor, Dr Ferrando, called me Smokey. I kept the name, but quit smoking.

On the November Ballot

Mayor
Richard C. Gessling
C.R. Smokey Owen

Ward 1
Tera Reynolds

Ward 2
William M. Alberta
Doug Carpenter

Ward 3
Glory Mahan

Ballot Issues
To change the expenditure limitation for the Red Lodge City Resort Tax, in the following proportions:

	Proposed	Current
Property tax relief	15%	15%
Merchants' collection fees	5%	5%
City administration	1%	1%
Capital improvements to streets, water, sewer, parks/sports facilities	76%	79%
Marketing and advertising	3%	0%

Bearcreek

Council Member (4-year)
Kathy Burgener
Patricia Cenis

Council Member (2-year)
Carl Peterson

Please vote November 4th!

Polls are open from 7 am - 8 pm at the Civic Center

Your intrepid reporters set out to ask twenty questions of each of our 2007 Red Lodge mayoral candidates. Not all of our questions are earth-shattering. Heck, some of our questions aren't even serious. But each question tells you something about each candidate and how he or she thinks.

"And what's Martha Young's dog doing in there?" we hear you ask. Well, please remember what newspaper you're reading. We're mixing the other candidate's perfectly serious answers with Roscoe's just to make the interviews a little bit more fun.

Speaking of write-in candidates, you will find Tera Reynolds and Betsy Scanlin on the ballot, but Brian Roat filed after the deadline, so you'll have to write in his name on the ballot if you wish to vote for him. Roscoe never got around to filing at all.

On to the rules: Each candidate was interviewed live and in person, with no opportunity to review the questions in advance. The responses were typed in the candidate's presence, and they were given an opportunity to check their answers before leaving. Nobody saw anyone else's answers.

And so, with no further ado, we present you with our 20 questions, and the candidates' answers:

RAG: Dogs or cats?
REYNOLDS: Dogs.
ROAT: We have a dog, but that doesn't mean I don't like cats.
SCANLIN: I've had both, but I currently have neither. My beloved dog Ralph died last January.
ROSCOE: I do have a cat, but I prefer dogs.

RAG: What kind of business does Red Lodge need the most?
REYNOLDS: An office supply store.
ROAT: There's a conflict – we need businesses, but we don't have the people to work them. We could use something like a Pamida store, a general store like we used to have.
SCANLIN: Given its character, I'd say we should serve the health industry, especially for the elderly. We're a remote community. It would provide the town with good, living-wage jobs. Internet businesses are definitely up there, too, because our remoteness doesn't lend itself well to manufacturing and shipping.
ROSCOE: An animal shelter.

RAG: Who is your favorite Presidential candidate?
REYNOLDS: Ron Paul.
ROAT: Our office is non-political, and I'd like to leave it that way.
SCANLIN: This is a non-partisan race, and I appreciate very much not having to take political sides on local business. I'd really rather not go there. I understand that we have diverse political feelings here.
ROSCOE: Mitt Romney sort of sounds like a dog's name, but I'm not sure I agree with his politics.

RAG: How far would you go to prevent Paris Hilton from moving to Red Lodge?
REYNOLDS: I don't think it would be a bad thing. It's an open-gated community.
ROAT: Not very far. We already have some Paris Hiltons in Red Lodge. This town has some interesting characters.
SCANLIN: Who's Paris Hilton?
ROSCOE: I'm opposed to all chains. I realize she's just a person, but she's connected to the hotel chain, so I'd go to any lengths to keep her out.

RAG: How do you feel about Red Lodge businesses importing employees from other countries?
REYNOLDS: I feel fine about it. They provide great service, and good quality service is what this town's all about. If that's what it takes, then bring them in.
ROAT: The businesses have to get by. They have to survive.
SCANLIN: I think it's truly an example of our history of international diversity. On the other side, I'm very sad that our own locale cannot provide workers for the service industry that we all enjoy.
ROSCOE: I'm very much for diversity. I'll accept attention and doggie treats from anyone.

RAG: Last year, Red Lodge collected $614,828.10 in resort tax revenue. This year could be even more. How do you feel this money should be spent?
REYNOLDS: It should be spent on the parks and the infrastructure, just like the law says.
ROAT: It has to be spent by the formula. The part that's designated to the City for infrastructure, should go to water & sewer.
SCANLIN: Clearly our ordinance anticipated that question; 79% goes to infrastructure, and that's a pretty broad field. We've seen a lot of benefit to water, sewer, and streets. I'd like to see more attention to parks and trails. We need to continue to pay attention to the basics, but work more on things like trails.
ROSCOE: I think Red Lodge needs to be safer. We need better streets and sidewalks so my friend Joe can get to the Post Office. My main interest, though, would be more fire hydrants.

The Very Best of the Red Lodge Local Rag

VOTE NOV. 5 — ELECTION 2007

RAG: What was the best concert you ever attended?
REYNOLDS: Stevie Ray Vaughn. Front row.
ROAT: The Oak Ridge Boys at the Metra.
SCANLIN: The Willie Nelson concert at the rodeo grounds. I can't think of a nicer place and a greater personality to listen to. The firefighting planes were just an extra thrill. You're not going to find that in Madison Square Garden.
ROSCOE: Three Dog Night.

RAG: What will it take to fix the streets in town?
REYNOLDS: Hot asphalt.
ROAT: If you think they're bad now, you should have seen them when they were gravel. Are they really that bad? Go to Billings and then come home and compare.
SCANLIN: A comprehensive plan.
ROSCOE: The will to make it happen.

RAG: How important are ranching and farming to the future of Red Lodge?
REYNOLDS: Very important. I'd like to see more farmers and ranchers enter their property into conservation easements so that they can continue their way of life without pressure from the developers.
ROAT: At one time they were probably the most important part of our economy, outside of mining. I recognize the survivors as being important, and I wish them well.
SCANLIN: They're absolutely essential. Not only do they define our setting, but they're some of the finest, hardest-working people that you could live with, and they're a key component to our economy. We need to be concerned about their viability.
ROSCOE: I come from a long line of ranchers. My dad was the best cowdog in the county. I think ranching and farming are crucial to the viability of Red Lodge and Carbon County.

RAG: What's your favorite gun?
REYNOLDS: I own a Ruger .30-06, but my favorite would be a phaser from Star Trek.
ROAT: Model 94 Winchester.
SCANLIN: Squirt.
ROSCOE: Top Gun.

RAG: What's your opinion of the USA PATRIOT act?
REYNOLDS: It's a perfect example of what happens when Congress reacts too quickly to a situation and passes a bill without enough debate. Some of the provisions in that bill invade too much of our personal liberty and should be re-examined carefully, with the unconstitutional parts removed. No matter how bad things are in the state of war, we must remember that our civil liberties make the United States of America the best country in the world.
ROAT: It's been taken advantage of by the administration to interfere with our rights as American citizens. The concept is probably good, but the implementation isn't.
SCANLIN: Most of us don't fully appreciate the individual liberties that we have, and we're unique among nations because of them. We cannot take our liberties lightly. We have a check-and-balance system and we need to make sure it remains in place and is not abused.
ROSCOE: I've learned a lot about patriotism from my neighbor Joe. I think it's the most un-patriotic thing that's happened in my lifetime.

RAG: Beef or venison?
REYNOLDS: Beef. If they issued cow permits for $600, I'd go shoot a cow.
ROAT: Beef. The deer in my front yard that look in my window with the little noses and the little whiskers and the eyelashes are very different animals from the ones I used to shoot. They're more like pets now.

Tera Reynolds is a new RE/MAX real estate agent, and is currently president of the Red Lodge City Council.

Brian has been the mayor of Red Lodge for 12 of the last 16 years, and he owns a heating and air-conditioning business in Red Lodge.

Elizabeth (Betsy) Scanlin is a three-term councilmember and grew up in Red Lodge. She has practiced law for 30 years.

Roscoe moved to Red Lodge as a puppy 17 years ago, and is campaigning on a platform of doggie treats at the Christmas Stroll.

Scanlin: Is there such a thing as a "deef"? I like them both—especially locally grown.

Roscoe: Whichever is handiest.

RAG: How do you feel about continued development around town?

Reynolds: The city has mechanisms in place through our growth policy and development code to embrace it, and in turn control it and shape it into the Red Lodge vision.

Roat: I recognize it as being inevitable, and I'm really pleased with the way the developers are working with the City.

Scanlin: Growth is our key issue. I think we could handle it better. I wouldn't be running if I didn't think we could handle it better. We need to be welcoming but we need to understand what it's doing to the basic character of the town, and we need to be aware of the economic disparity, particularly with housing.

Roscoe: I'm concerned about having places to run. I think development should take place in more confined areas.

RAG: What's more important: justice or law?

Reynolds: Justice.

Roat: Justice is more important, but law is supposed to produce justice.

Scanlin: I would hope they're compatible. If they're not, you need to change the law.

Roscoe: Justice.

RAG: What would you fix for dinner if you had twelve distinguished guests?

Reynolds: A brisket with mashed potatoes and asparagus, with a pie for dessert.

Roat: Ribeye steak. On a grill.

Scanlin: I've done this before. I'd serve Legends beef, City Bakery bread, King's Cupboard Caramel over locally-grown apples, vegetables from the Farmer's Market, and beer from Sam's.

Roscoe: Wheat bread and canned milk for an appetizer, steak tartare for the main course, and chicken strips for dessert.

RAG: Should Red Lodge be more dog-friendly?

Reynolds: Yes.

Roat: I don't think Red Lodge is dog-unfriendly.

Scanlin: I think it *is* dog-friendly, although the town could really use a dog park where dogs can run together.

Roscoe: Yes.

RAG: How about bicycle friendly?

Reynolds: Yes, although I think we're fairly bicycle-friendly now.

Roat: I don't ride a bike, but I don't think Red Lodge is bicycle-unfriendly. We don't let people ride bikes on Broadway for safety reasons, but I've never had anyone complain that we're not bike-friendly enough.

Scanlin: If elected, I will be the first Mayor who rides her bike to City Hall. Regularly. As I do now. Given the level of traffic, the town is pretty bicycle-friendly now, but we need some better links to surrounding areas.

Roscoe: Yes.

RAG: Are skunks cute indigenous wildlife to preserve, or a scourge to be eliminated?

Reynolds: Skunks in their natural environments are cute, but when they're rummaging in the alleys, they're a scourge, just like the bear, the moose, and the deer.

Roat: They have as much right to be here as we do. If we didn't put them on Earth, then why should we get rid of them?

Scanlin: If you live on the west side of town, they are a scourge. But they're a cute scourge.

Roscoe: They're a lot of fun to chase.

RAG: Describe why you'd be the best mayor—in 25 words or less.

Reynolds: I bring my experience serving six years on Council and participating actively in Red Lodge. I listen, understand, and find solutions to the city's issues.

Roat: I've been privileged to serve as mayor for twelve years, and I get a great deal of enjoyment out of serving the people.

Scanlin: Among worthy opponents, I hope to offer the best blend of hometown perspective, experience as an attorney and civic activist, and passion about Red Lodge.

Roscoe: I have a unique perspective, I'm smart, I can herd, I stay with the job until it's done, and I let sleeping dogs lie.

RAG: Where do you read your Local Rag?

Reynolds: At the office.

Roat: In my living room chair—that's where I do my evening reading.

Scanlin: Wherever I am at my first opportunity after I pick it up. I took it with me to Belgium.

Roscoe: On the kitchen floor.

The Very Best of the Red Lodge Local Rag

A word (well, 464 words) from your humble editor
VOTE!

May 2010

"Meh. Why vote in the June election? It's just a primary, and it's all local stuff. It's not like we're voting for President or something."

This attitude, all too prevalent among American voters, has things exactly backward. Of course it's important to vote in a presidential election, but it's local elections like the one coming up next month that really affect your life on a day-to-day basis. And you can have a much larger effect on the outcome, as well.

In the 2008 presidential election, Barack Obama won by 9,529,918 votes. Only four presidential elections in the last 100 years have had a popular vote margin less than the current population of Montana (Wilson v Hughes in 1916, Kennedy v Nixon in 1960, Nixon v Humphrey in 1968, and Bush v Gore in 2000).

By contrast, in last November's local election Judith Swan became Joliet's mayor by a margin of 28 votes. Richard Anderson won as Fromberg's mayor by 16. And Pits DeArmond took Bearcreek by only 7. Even in Red Lodge, the margins are small. Jason Priest only beat his City Council runner-up by 27 votes, and Brian Roat became mayor by a margin of 142.

In small communities like ours, every vote counts. It *really* counts.

If you and a group of like-minded friends choose to go out for a beer instead of going to the polls, it could very likely change the outcome of a local election.

Our selection of presidents, senators, and representatives obviously affects our lives. But it's your commissioners, mayors, city councils, and school boards that determine whether you get the stop sign at your intersection; when the pothole in front of your house gets filled; whether your neighbor can build a gravel pit or a house that blocks your view. Local government decides whether your dog needs a leash, your cat needs a license, or your child gets a new math book. Local politics affects your life directly and personally, every day.

As I've said in the past, politics in states like Montana and Wyoming are different from the rest of the country. If you're having trouble deciding between two candidates for state Senate, you can just pick up the phone and call them. They'll be happy to chat with you. Candidates for city and county offices would probably meet you for a cup of coffee. There's simply no excuse for not knowing where candidates stand on issues.

People around here don't vote so much by party as they vote by individual. You look the candidate in the eye, shake his or her hand, and decide whether this is someone you can trust in public office. Politics are personal.

So do your homework. Become an informed voter. And then cast your ballot next month. It matters.

---

chat room

Why, yes, this did come from the April Fool issue. Why do you ask?

Teini for Prez, '08

Within hours of receiving news that Tom Vilsack dropped out of the '08 Presidential race, Red Lodge's own Tom Teini decided he needed to step up and throw his…plunger…as it were, into the ring.

So Tom, this is exciting news: A Presidential bid! Tell me about your platform.

Well, it's still pending approval from the bank—I need a loan to get it built—and bids are still out to contractors. But it's going to be pretty high, I think. And we're planning on painting it yellow.

On to the war in Iraq. What are your thoughts on early withdrawal?

Well, I believe that in most cases, early withdrawal is the best protection. It could help solve those problems with spontaneous explosions, but on the whole, I have to say I'm against it.

Are you running on the Republican or Democratic ticket?

Yes.

Who do you see as your biggest competitor in the race to the White House?

I'm thinking Pat Paulsen*, I've been pulling for him since the 1968.

What qualifications will you bring to the Presidency?

Plumbing. And theater productions, which involve total fabrication of the truth.

Yes…. Just what is the status of the White House plumbing?

I haven't actually checked out the plumbing, since I snuck into the building back in '68. But I know it needs updating. I'm planning on doing it myself. Enlisting the help of aides.

And pages?

I'll leave that to Mark Foley.

So who is your running mate?

Gus. *[pictured with Tom]* Though he does a lot more running than I do. Especially when it involves sneaking through the fence.

How important do you think integrity and pride in the job will be in this new position?

I have none. I just sold them to a rich California couple.

And I guess we need to talk about the big issues: what is your stance on gay marriage and abortion?

I say no abortions for gay couples.

And what about the rumor that you might actually be the real father of Anna Nicole Smith's baby?

Despite the logistical improbabilities, and the fact that my wife would kill me—which would put a damper on my political ambitions—I maintain that little Danielynn is indeed the fruit of my loins.

*Pat Paulsen died in 1997. Ed.

UNOFFICIAL PRIMARY ELECTION BALLOT – JUNE 8, 2010
CARBON COUNTY, MT

Justice of the Peace

Political coverage often focuses on the highest-level races, or the ones where some scandal is involved. Rarely do we read much about the Justice of the Peace. This year, however, we have three qualified candidates facing off over the position, and we felt that our readers might want to get to know them better.

Johnny Seiffert is the incumbent. He's held the position of Justice of the Peace here since the early 1990s.

Lou ("Skip") Aleksich is a retired court clerk who has been working part-time as a Judge Pro-tem and substitute judge in Carbon County.

Kevin Nichols is the Montana Department of Fish, Wildlife and Parks Game Warden in Red Lodge.

We asked each of them the same questions in separate live interviews. None of the candidates saw the questions in advance, and they weren't given time to prepare and write out answers. They all had an opportunity to review our transcript of their answers to make sure we hadn't made any mistakes, but none of them had a chance to see each other's answers.

As always, we mixed up serious job-related questions with some Local Rag-style "getting to know you better" questions. Their answers here are presented (in alphabetical order by last name) just as they gave them.

RAG: Why do you want to be Justice of the Peace?

ALEKSICH: When I moved here I wanted to become involved in the community. Red Lodge was going to be my new hometown, so I needed to be involved. I've been president of the Historical Society, I'm currently president of the Inquiry Club, and I'm involved in the Elks and Rotary. This is a natural extension of my community involvement.

NICHOLS: I think the job needs a new perspective, and I want to increase people's respect for the job in the county. I think my temperament and values are a good fit for this job.

SEIFFERT: I've been Justice of the Peace for over 17 years. I enjoy the job; I enjoy the people. I love Carbon County and Red Lodge.

RAG: What expertise do you bring to the job?

ALEKSICH: My career was 25 years as Clerk of the United States District Court for the State of Montana. For the past 2 years, I've been Judge Pro-tem for the Justice Court and the City of Red Lodge, and I've subbed for the cities of Bridger and Joliet.

NICHOLS: Thirty years of law enforcement experience as a Montana Game Warden. I've dealt with Justice Courts my whole career, all over the state, in small towns with part-time Justices of the Peace that work a few hours a week, up to Yellowstone County, with two full-time Justices of the Peace. I'm familiar with the job at all levels. I've had lots of law-enforcement related training, including domestic violence, DUI detection, search and seizure, and defendant's constitutional rights. I am a Montana Law Enforcement Academy graduate and hold an advanced certificate from Montana Peace Officers Standards & Training.

SEIFFERT: Over 17 years of experience as Justice of the Peace. I'm a graduate of University of Montana School of Law, Judicial Institute, and the National Judicial College in Reno, Nevada. I'm also a graduate of the Montana Law Enforcement Academy, with honors. Lots of people don't know this, but limited-jurisdiction judges in Montana are required to attend week-long training conferences twice a year. I'm attending my 35th conference right now. We're also required to take a comprehensive law exam

UNOFFICIAL PRIMARY ELECTION BALLOT – JUNE 8, 2010
CARBON COUNTY, MT

Justice of the Peace

once every four years, after the election cycle. We get extensive training for a week, and then take the exam. I have taken and passed the exam five times. Judges who do not pass can be removed from office and a replacement appointed.

RAG: Are you a catch & release kind of guy, or do you eat the fish you catch?

ALEKSICH: I love to fish, but I do not like to eat them, so I don't keep them. I don't even carry a creel.

NICHOLS: I'm a catch-and-release type if it's trout. I keep walleyes unless they're spawners.

SEIFFERT: Depends on the fish. Trout would be catch and release, but if I hook into a walleye, that one's getting eaten.

RAG: How long have you lived in this area?

ALEKSICH: We moved here permanently in May of 2002.

NICHOLS: I've lived in the Red Lodge area for 15 years.

SEIFFERT: Twenty years, and I came to Red Lodge from Billings. I was a detention officer and reserve deputy sheriff in Yellowstone County and came to Red Lodge as a police officer.

RAG: Our judiciary is making increasing use of technology, from video arraignments to use of GPS devices and cell phones in evidence. Are you comfortable with new technology?

ALEKSICH: I was responsible for the automation of the Federal Courts in Montana beginning in about 1990. I hired automation staff, we automated five divisional offices where my 30 deputies worked, and it was my job to manage and oversee—and educate myself—on technology. So for about 20 years I've been involved in court automation.

NICHOLS: Yes. We use a lot of it in my job as a Montana Game Warden. We use GPS, computers, and other technology.

SEIFFERT: I am very comfortable with new technology. I brought some of that technology to Justice Court in Red Lodge. When I started as Justice of the Peace, everything was done by hand, from receipts to docketing. Within a year of taking over, I started automating the office, and through my involvement with the Montana Supreme Court's automation committee, my office is now one of the first places to get new technology. Mine is one of the most automated courts in the state since I was appointed to the automation committee in 1996.

RAG: What's the last good book you read?

ALEKSICH: *River of Doubt*, by Candice Millard.

NICHOLS: Recently finished a book called *We Die Alone*, by David Howarth. It's a survival book about a World War II Norwegian commando who endures incredible hardship.

SEIFFERT: Joel Osteen, *It's Your Time*.

RAG: How do you feel about not having a jail in Carbon County?

ALEKSICH: It would be really convenient for our law enforcement officers, but I fully understand that jails are very expensive to build and very expensive to maintain. I don't think we could afford it right now. When they did a jail study in Billings many years ago, I read that jails cost about $100,000 per cell to build.

NICHOLS: I think it's a huge problem. It's a lot of time and resources spent by local law enforcement transporting people back and forth to Billings. The county has a real, but small, liability if there was an accident while transporting people. The biggest problems are the inconvenience to law enforcement people, the expense to the County, and the liability. We pay Yellowstone County Detention Facility about $65 per day per prisoner.

SEIFFERT: It's been a difficult transition. When I first started as Justice of the Peace, we did have a jail, and the commissioners decided it was in the County's best interest not to rebuild it. It was a learning process, but over time it has worked out very well. We house all of our prisoners in Billings, which used to require officers to transport prisoners back and forth. With the video system that I had installed, they just bring prisoners to the secure video facility in the jail, and I can work with them from Red Lodge. It works well now, and it's a lot less burden on the taxpayers.

RAG: Briefly, what do you think is the most important job of our Justice of the Peace?

ALEKSICH: I think maintaining the high standard that the office demands, while handling the myriad of legal matters that come before the

Justice of the Peace

judge.

NICHOLS: Being a fair member of the judicial branch of government. Justice Courts in this state handle about ten times more people than District courts do. They are the first taste most people get of the Justice system, and so it's important to be fair and accessible.

SEIFFERT: Administering justice. Fair and consistent. Making sure that people know, no matter how small or how big the case is, it's as important to me as it is to them.

RAG: If you could bring any one musician or band to Red Lodge for a concert, who would it be?

ALEKSICH: Simon & Garfunkel.

NICHOLS: Bruce Springsteen.

SEIFFERT: Jimmy Buffett.

RAG: What is the biggest problem in Red Lodge right now?

ALEKSICH: I guess regulated growth.

NICHOLS: I think it's probably the economy, like everywhere. A lot of people are out of work and having a hard time.

SEIFFERT: I would say money. That's the way it is with everybody. Businesses are struggling. I don't know if we've been hit as hard as some of the rest of the country. When the businesses are in a fruitful environment, the whole town prospers. When they're not, the whole town suffers.

RAG: What do you foresee will be the biggest changes in the way our local legal system works in the next 5-10 years?

ALEKSICH: I think that the hue and cry of Montanans who are concerned about the DUI laws is going to precipitate a change in our local customs. Montana has a long culture of drinking and driving and I think those days are going to be over and the courts are going to have to help change that.

NICHOLS: Probably the increasing demands in resources due to population growth, which will most likely take off again when the economy heals up.

SEIFFERT: I don't foresee any huge changes. We have a very, very good set of people on all sides. As a judge, I look at the legal system from the center. We have good people representing the State and defendants on the criminal side; and the plaintiffs and defendants on the civil side.

RAG: You are entertaining friends that have never been to Montana. What do you serve them for dinner?

ALEKSICH: We had two Irish ladies visit us in September of 2007, and the menu was entitled, "The All-American Dinner." We had ribs, Don Kinney's world-famous fried chicken, corn on the cob, Karen Hoiness' famous deep-dish apple pie. Those were the highlights of the menu.

NICHOLS: Buffalo.

SEIFFERT: Tri-tip steak or roast that I barbecue, green beans, and baked potato.

RAG: The American Bar Association is making efforts to do away with the office of Justice of the Peace because a law degree is not required. How do you feel about that?

ALEKSICH: With the extensive training that the state Bar Association puts each Justice of the Peace through, plus the testing that they require, I don't think that it's a real issue. I believe that the Justice of the Peace in small rural communities gives everybody an opportunity to have their grievances adjudicated on a local level.

NICHOLS: I don't agree with that. I think the Justice of the Peace job, with my 30 years of experience with Justices of the Peace all over the state is mainly about common sense, values, fairness, and following guidelines set for you by higher courts.

SEIFFERT: I think that's a big mistake. JP Court is a Constitutional Court. When the framers of the Montana constitution came up with our latest constitution, they made JP courts non-attorney courts on purpose; 80% of the people who interact with the courts in Montana interact with either a JP court or City Court, neither of which are attorney courts. Our courts are supposed to be—for lack of a better term—the people's court. Our cases are very important, and that's one of the reasons we're required to attend these trainings, so we know what we're doing and that we're doing it the correct way, even if you're not an attorney. I am against having lawyer-only courts.

County Commissioner: Doug Tucker vs Pits DeArmond vs a bear?

The rules for our county commissioners were the same as for the other candidates (see the introduction on page 20). For this race, however, we had a write-in candidate that required just a bit of extra help with his answers. Given that Pandolph the Black Bear was featured in last month's paper and had some important things to say about his home, we decided to include him in our interview.

Don't let his presence fool you, though. The other candidates answers are still perfectly serious!

RAG: You have VIPs visiting who have never been to Montana. What do you serve them for dinner?

DEARMOND: Meat and potatoes. I'm a meat & potatoes guy.

TUCKER: Got to serve them steak. It's Montana.

PANDOLPH: Chokecherry pie, whitebark pine nuts, fresh trout, a few termites, and maybe some trash from my favorite alley. Just kidding on the trash. Really.

RAG: Do you feel that future growth in our county should stay within the various city limits or spread out?

DEARMOND: The city limits won't hold it. I feel that any future growth in our county should be well thought out. I'm not anti-growth or pro-growth; I just think it should be smart.

TUCKER: I don't think we have a choice in that, with the subdivisions that are being built every day. We can't stop it; we just need to manage it and be fair about it. Whether we like it or not, it's going to happen—especially with the new owners of Red Lodge Mountain.

PANDOLPH: As we add more bears, I think they should stay outside the city limits. And the cute sows can move in near me.

RAG: What's your favorite gun?

DEARMOND: I just have a .17 caliber varmint rifle and an 8-weight streamer fly rod.

TUCKER: My Ruger .270.

PANDOLPH: Gun? You're asking a *bear* about his favorite *gun*? What kind of sicko are you?

RAG: How do you feel about school consolidations?

DEARMOND: I want the best education for the kids, no matter what direction the Office of Public Instruction takes.

TUCKER: Right now in the Clarks Fork Valley there's a lot of talk that's been going on. Economically, it would be advantageous. We wouldn't save money, but we'd be able to provide a better education for our kids with the lessening tax dollars we have to spend. But we have to leave it to the people. When you lose the school in your small town, many people feel you lose your identity.

PANDOLPH: I'm for them! The more consolidated the school is, the easier it is to catch the individual fish.

RAG: What's the biggest danger facing agriculture in Carbon County?

DEARMOND: The quality and quantity of the water that's available.

TUCKER: Right now, I would say brucellosis in the cattle industry. It's pretty scary right now. And the rising fuel costs.

PANDOLPH: Grizzlies. They're all up in your face all the time: "I think I'll be taking your lunch there, little dude." Can't stand 'em. Oh. Agriculture? Well, I'd still say grizzlies. Big danger.

RAG: If you could bring one band to Carbon County for a concert, who would it be?

DEARMOND: John Prine, or you can't go wrong with Hall & Oates.

TUCKER: I'd have to say the Eagles.

PANDOLPH: I'm a big fan of the Bear Naked Ladies, but Beary Manilow would be good, too. My favorite album is *A Taste of Honey*.

RAG: Where do you go to get away?

DEARMOND: Floating a river somewhere.

TUCKER: Camping in the Beartooths—as much as I can.

PANDOLPH: Depends on what I'm getting away from. If it's a grizzly, I go straight up a tree. Big old clumsy things don't climb so well. If it's people, I just run away—no place in particular. I don't tend to plan these things out much.

RAG: Describe why you'd be the perfect Carbon County Commissioner, in 25 words or less.

DEARMOND: I look at both sides of the issue, and when I make a stand I stick with it. But I have the capacity to change.

TUCKER: Nobody is perfect, but I'm a well experienced, dedicated, open-minded person who enjoys working with the public. Serving Carbon County would be my honor.

PANDOLPH: I'll hibernate all winter and leave you alone.

CHAPTER 14
The Best of Red Lodge

BEST OF RED LODGE SHOW

Booty Awards

Monday, Jan 29
Roman Theater
7:00pm

$8 or 2/$15

PLUS: *Best Dressed!*

Vote online @ www.localrag.com

Best of Red Lodge 2006 nominees

Best locals' hangout: Foster & Logan's • Front Bar • Sam's Taproom
Best volunteer organization: RLACF Fun Run • Beartooth Nature Center • Fire Dept/EMS
Best place to stop at Christmas Stroll: Kibler & Kirch • Sylvan Peak • the Snow Creek
Best soccer mom: Rena Beck • Dana Castellani • Anne Christ
Best phone voice: Quincy Zahn • LaVonne Ervin • Melissa Rickbeil
Best medical professional: Dr. Billy Oley • Dr. Bill George • Gretchen Schuck
Best local fashion icon: Crazy Carl • Libby Lane • Heather Drake
Best dog: Freddy • Jackson • Kona & Kiko
Most eligible single: Brad Hauge • Karen Saint • Tom Doddy, Jr.
Easiest Boss to work for: Tom Kuntz • Judy Christensen • Tom Doddy
Best event at RLM: Town Series • Winter carnival • Ullr Party
Best contractor: Beartooth Custom Builders • Malin Construction • L&L Builders
Best unsung hero: Sarah Ewald • Les Dimich • Chuck Murphy
Best burger: Foster & Logan's • Front Bar • the Snag
Best new business: Beijing Garden • Rock Dodge Longboards • Foster & Logan's
Best waiter/waitress: Janice Williams • Denise Howard • Piney Hardiman
Most relaxing place to shop: True Value • Glass Rabbit • Boomerang Beads
Best local activist: Martha Young • Marisa Godoy • Tera Reynolds
Best cashier at the IGA: Evie • Mona • Brad
Friendliest face: Judy Christensen • Bill Temple • Jodie Moore

Check out the full list of Nominees online! @ www.localrag.com

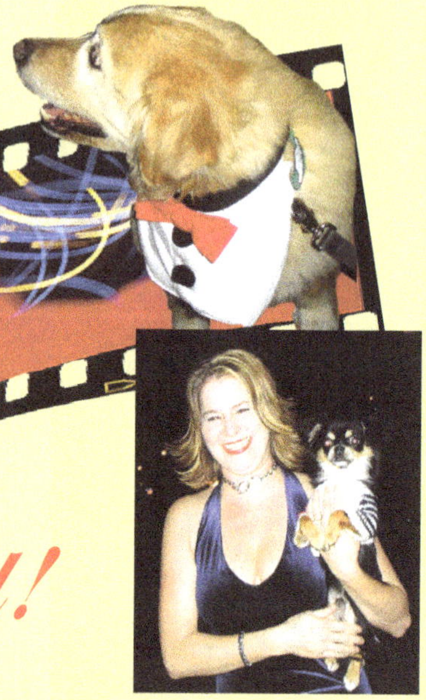

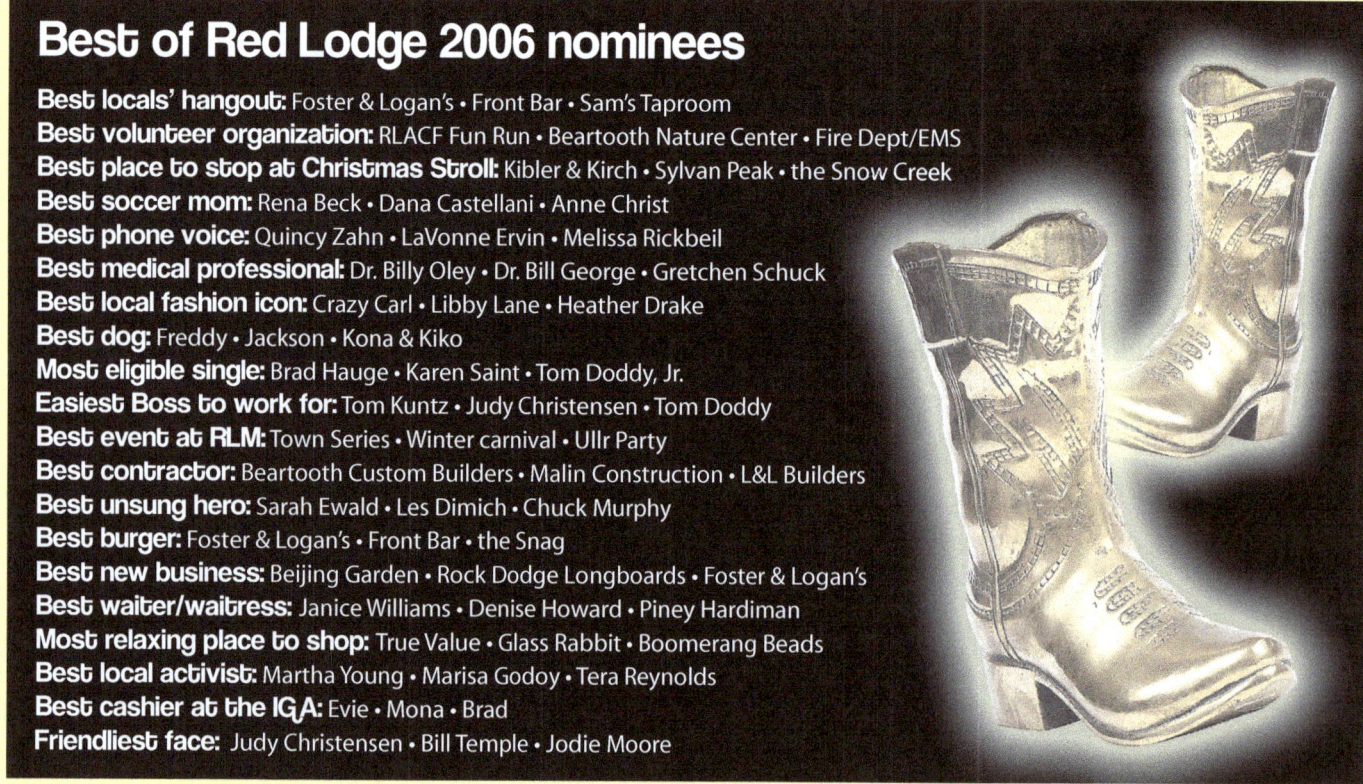

Best of Red Lodge

All of us who live in Red Lodge know that it's the best place to be. But what is it about Red Lodge that makes it such a special place? We asked the locals, (and those people who wish they were locals), to vote for what they consider to be the Best of Red Lodge. Some of the answers surprised us, some made us laugh, some made us queasy, but of the hundreds of ballots we received, the following people, places and things are what our readers consider to be **The Best of Red Lodge**.

Best place to have a drink
Front Bar. Eight different beers on tap, food from the Pizza Co., free peanuts and you get to throw the shells on the floor, cool. Our favorite answer, "In your hand".

Best public bathroom
The Pollard won. But for pure entertainment value, we like Sam's Tap Room. Where else in Red Lodge will you find a disco ball or "Welcome Back, Kotter" posters?

Best place to take the kids to eat
The Pizza Co. won. They have kid friendly atmosphere, menu items that kids love and good video games.

Best dance floor
Snow Creek, however, we're not quite sure if the railings and bar tops count as "floor".

Best restaurant to go when someone else is paying
Carbon County Steakhouse, specializing in steaks, pasta and fresh seafood and to our knowledge it is the only place in Red Lodge with Rocky Mountain Oysters on the menu.

Best place to shoot pool
The Silver Strike won this one. A couple of tables and plenty of room to take your shot. For a different approach try the right angle table at the Red Lodge Lounge.

Best local band
Hounddogs From Outer Space in all their various forms, is the winner of what turned out to be one of the biggest categories. The musical talent pool in Red Lodge is deep. From chamber music to rock, we certainly enjoy a variety of musical talent.

Best place to take your friends from out of town
Snow Creek again, with Bridge Creek a close second. If you really want to impress your friends, take them out to dinner at the Bridge Creek and then for drinks and dancing at the Snow Creek. Or you could always take them "back out of town".

Best place to spend New Year's Eve
Two completely different places got the most votes, the Snow Creek edged out Home. Of course "under a party hat" whether at the Snow Creek or at home is a good answer.

Sometimes the "Booty Award" winners from Best of Red Lodge were announced in the paper. Other times, as you can see in this ad from January 2007, the Local Rag made an event out of it, with everybody dressing up and making it quite the evening!

Best of Red Lodge 2002

Best Red Lodge Ale
The race was tight between Glacier and Hefeweizen, so since those of us here at the Local Rag prefer Glacier, that's the one we're announcing as the winner.

Best annual event in Red Lodge
The Beartooth Rally won this category. The three day event features a golf tournament, poker run, street dance and the Iron Horse Rodeo.

Best lunch
Bridge Creek ran away with this one. Check out the daily lunch specials, pasta salads and of course, their clam chowder, all served in plenty of time to make it back to work.

Best storefront
Mountain People won this category even though almost every business in town got at least one vote, even us. Wow.

Best place to satisfy your sweet tooth
Montana Candy Emporium by a landslide, or should we say fudgeslide.

Best way to spend Sunday afternoon
Skiing and hiking were neck and neck, obviously we love to spend time in the mountains, snow covered or not.

Best coffee spot
Coffee Factory Roasters, now under new ownership. Best answer "The one on my shirt."

Best place to hang out with your dog
Snow Creek won, but this was one of those categories with lots of individual answers. Seems most of Red Lodge is dog friendly, as long as they are on a leash, Bridget.

Best excuse to play hookey
Powder Day. 'nuff said.

Best locally made product
Very close between Red Lodge Ales and King's Cupboard Chocolates. Both of these major food groups are necessary for a healthy existence, but Sam's won by a nose.

Best place to do something you'll regret in the morning
Snow Creek. We liked the answer "cooking dinner in the kitchen."

Best place to get stuck
Close between Red Lodge in general or the Snow Creek. "In the middle with you" got one vote.

Best place to read graffiti
Snow Creek bathrooms. Truly some good stuff there, it's where we do our research.

Best annual parade
4th of July. Stop by to sign our petition to legalize candy throwing.

Best camping spot
Secretive group we are, "Not Telling" is the best camping spot. Tip for the person who said "Main Street" there is a nice flat spot near Pride Park.

Best place to work up a sweat
The Pollard won by a large margin. All the outdoor activities ranked high and there was even one vote for "City Council Meetings." Might be a workout book in there somewhere.

March History in Montana
Mar 1, 1872—Congress passes the law authorizing the creation of the country's first National Park (Yellowstone)
Mar 9, 1880—Montana's first railroad (the Utah & Northern) arrives
Mar 13, 1889—The Montana Territorial Legislature adjourns for the last time
Mar 10, 1902—Dean Post Office established: Bessie Haskin, Postmaster
Mar 12, 1902—Linley Post Office established: Walter R. Linley, Postmaster
Mar 21, 1903—Fromberg Post Office established: Abraham Pierson, Postmaster
Mar 4, 1907—Linley, MT Post Office changes its name to Luther; Grace R. Luther named Postmaster
Mar 12, 1909—Boyd Post Office established: Roland N. Doughty, Postmaster
Mar 4, 1932—Death of Plenty Coups, Chief of the Crow (Apsáalooke)
Mar 24, 1978—Congress passes a bill creating the Absaroka-Beartooth Wilderness, those 944,000 acres we all love so much!

March is one of seven months containing 31 days. Originally the first month of the year according to the Roman Calendar, March was called Martius, for Mars, the Roman god of war. Many countries still use March 1 as the first day of the new year, owing to spring beginning in this month. The March birthstone is aquamarine and the flower is the daffodil.

The Very Best of the Red Lodge Local Rag

Best of Red Lodge 2002

Best appetizers
Bridge Creek - Eric's favorite? Fried Artichoke Hearts, dipped in a house-made batter and served with a chipotle aioli. (whatever the heck a chipotle aioli is.)

Best ski run
Lazy M by an avalanche. Our favorite? "From the Ski Patrol."

Best breakfast
Very, very close between Hank's and Regis, with Hank's emerging victorious in the last days. Both restaurants offer great meals. You can't beat Eggs Bene at Hank's. Try The Regis (pronounced ree-jus) for fresh vegetables and wonderful marmalades. The Regis is also the only place you can order crumpets, that's important stuff for those of us who like to use the word crumpet in a sentence.

Best restaurant if you are paying
The Pizza Co. won by a slim margin over Bogarts. Reasonable prices and great menus with lots of variety.

Best food if you're in a hurry
Subway came out on top by a very narrow margin, followed by Red Box Car, The Lucky Dog and Taco Time. What we need is a "Top Ramen" restaurant.

Best local controversy
New airport. Lots of "controversies" that we weren't even aware of. One of our favorite answers was "Senior Center Lunch - Sloppy Joes or ?"

Best place to crash on Red Lodge Mountain
The Bierstube won hands down. I guess if you must crash it may as well be in a warm, carpeted place that serves beer.

Best place to pamper yourself
The Body Lodge. Let Kim and the crew pamper you with a pedicure, manicure, facial or a massage. Men welcome too.

Best local photographer or artist
Merv Coleman! We'd have to agree, his pictures grace the Local Rag every month. No need to go back to your singing career "Mac".

Best Bed & Breakfast
Willows Inn. Of course who could argue with "my bed and shredded wheat with milk."

Best hotel hot tub or pool

The Super 8 of Red Lodge won this one with indoor and outdoor hot tubs and a big pool. Open to locals for a small fee.

Best place to buy souvenirs
"A gift shop" was a good suggestion but for more direction try our winner, The Glass Rabbit.

Best antique shop
Twice Touched. One of the newer stores in Red Lodge and filled with great antiques and unique items. Stop in, we did, we like it.

Best place to meet someone special
Snow Creek won, Bridge Creek was second. You can't beat the Bridge Creek, Snow Creek combo for a memorable evening with that someone special.

Best place for family fun
Red Lodge Mountain. Bridge the generation gap, pile them all in the car and head up the hill.

Best ski shop
Sylvan Peak was the top vote getter and specializes in Nordic skiing, The Edge was not far back and specializes in alpine skiing and snowboarding. Pick your sport, pick your shop but don't pick at that.

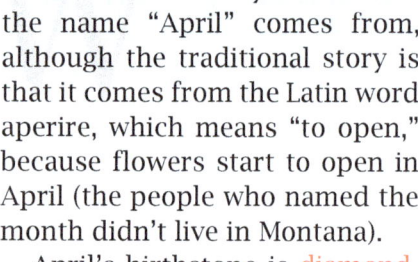

April History in Montana

Apr 3, 1996—The FBI arrests Ted Kaczynski (the Unabomber)
Apr 6, 1854—Death of Etsowish Semmegee-itshin ("Grizzly Bear Erect"), Chief of the Flatheads
Apr 10, 1866—Montana's first Constitutional Convention meets in Helena
Apr 11, 1867—The Pony Express run from Minneapolis to Helena begins
Apr 15, 1914—Dean Post Office closed
Apr 16, 1891—Nye Post Office reopens after being shut down for about a month
Apr 16, 1906—Rockvale Post Office reopens after being shut down for seven months
Apr 22, 1898—Carbonado Post Office established between Boyd & Joliet: Lucius Whitney, Postmaster
Apr 22, 1938—Lewis & Clark Caverns (then called "Morrison Cave") becomes Montana's first State Park
Apr 26, 1991—Montana writer A.B. Guthrie dies
Apr 28, 1805—Lewis & Clark first enter Montana
Apr 30, 1803—The Louisiana Purchase is completed
Apr 30, 1906—Riverview Post Office (south of Belfry) closed
Apr 30, 1914—Rockvale Post Office closed

We're not entirely sure where the name "April" comes from, although the traditional story is that it comes from the Latin word aperire, which means "to open," because flowers start to open in April (the people who named the month didn't live in Montana).

April's birthstone is diamond, and the flower is the daisy. April is Jazz Appreciation Month, National Poetry Month, and Be Vigilant Against Child Abuse Month.

Best of Red Lodge 2002

Best place to catch the big one
The true fishermen voted for Rock Creek, Snow Creek took second....

Best place for aprés ski
The Bierstube on Red Lodge Mountain. And to answer the question many of you asked, "aprés" means "following."

Best place to get away from it all
Home was the winner although we're not really sure about "The bedroom closet" or "a bottle of Black Velvet"?!

Best extreme sport
Skiing and snowboarding won, but both seem tame next to "naked ski-joring" or "keeping up with the Local staff on paper day." But the "freelance writing" guy, whew, now that's extreme checkbook balancing.

Best place to take a walk or hike
Silver Run was the favorite but there were many, many answers. Obviously we live in an area with plenty of outdoor recreation possibilities.

Best place for a picnic
City Park by Rock Creek is the winner.

Best place to spend a romantic evening
Home, followed closely by the Pollard. And to the guy (yes, you can be sure that it was a guy) who wrote in "outhouse", don't count on that second date.

Best place to find out what's up
The Local Rag. Hey, thanks Red Lodge. 50 categories, we were bound to win one!

Best thing about Red Lodge – The People/

Locals was by far the number one answer. But we already knew that. Where else can you find such an accepting, eclectic group of people? There seems to be a never ending stream of talented and interesting people to write about. *Thank you Red Lodge, you make our job rewarding and fun.*

May History in Montana

May 3, 1863 — Crow Indians capture Henry Edgar and five companions. They were later released.
May 6, 1877 — Crazy Horse, along with 1,100 Oglalas and Cheyennes, surrenders at Fort Robinson, Nebraska.
May 9, 1879 — Fort Assiniboine established on the Milk River near Havre
May 11, 1906 — Fairbanks Post Office (near Luther) closed
May 11, 1910 — President Taft signs bill creating Glacier National Park
May 12, 1894 — Rockvale Post Office established: Orren Clawson, Postmaster
May 15, 1912 — Coalville Post Office (formerly Gebo; west of Fromberg) closed
May 18, 1900 — Silesia Post Office established: Charles Buzzetti, Postmaster
May 19, 1922 — Montana's first radio station (KDYS) goes on the air
May 20, 1862 — Congress passes the Homestead Act. Get your 160 acres
May 24, 1863 — Henry Plummer elected sheriff of Bannack
May 28, 1909 — Edgar Post Office established: John J. Thornton, Postmaster

The month of May might have been named for the Greek goddess Maia. In common (non-leap-year) years, no other month starts with the same day of the week as May.

May's birthstone is emerald, and the flower is the sunflower or lily of the valley.

May is Mental Health Awareness Month, Asian Pacific American Heritage Month, and Celebrate Older Adults Month.

The Best of Red Lodge 2005

It's amazing who shows up when you're handing out booty! The response to our 4th annual Best of Red Lodge survey was three times greater than last year. As usual, the answers made us laugh, and cry, and often scratch our collective... body part...that Craig Beam apparently only has one of.

But enough of that. On to this year's Booty Award Winners!

Best Place for a Drink
Natali's Front Bar

Though the perennial favorite of "in my hand" received three votes, it appears we've all adjusted to the "new" Front Bar, with its copper-top tables and schmantzy new bar.

Best Annual Event
Beartooth Rally

It's the biggest, baddest, & loudest weekend of the year. And by your votes, Red Lodge, you love it. We all owe Leo & Jerry Wilson thanks for putting on a party that people drive across the country for.

Hats off Answer: Best of Red Lodge Awards. You know it, baby!!

Best Annual Fundraiser
Red Lodge Fun Run for Charities

This year's 800 runners or walkers and 100 volunteers, mean that practically half of Red Lodge participated in this event. No wonder you were able to raise $71,000! And while it seems everything that goes on in this town is a fundraiser for one cause or another, can you imagine if we'd have had to raise the money for the Beartooth Highway? $14 Million would've been one BIG Bake sale!!

Best Rumor
Sandra Bullock & Jesse James got married at Rock Creek Resort

Beartooth Highway reconstruction, June-October '05

Which beat by only one vote the...number of... dangling participles belonging to a local fishing scribe.... Ahem, ask a stupid question. We received more entertaining, bizarre, and Witness Protection-oriented answers this year than we care to acknowledge. The trauma keeps us awake nights. There's one thing we'd definitely like to dispel right now, though: we have it from a good source that Dr. Dan is not pregnant.

Best Excuse for a Really Stupid Act
"One liquor, One Shot, and One Beer"

This was one of those categories where we're not really interested in who wins, but more in finding out how funny you are. And funny you were, with answers like "I am Chuck Sallade," "Martha Young did it too," "You must be confusing me with someone else," "If I do this it will snow," "I've run out of these," "Libby made me do it," and "My president/mom/dog said I should." There were also the ubiquitous political answers that we don't feel w should get into here. (such as "RLPD," or "WMD")

🎩 Hats off Answer: "I left my garbage out on the deck during bear season"

Best Place to Take Your Friends from Out of Town
Bearcreek Saloon

It's been perhaps 16 years that Pits has been turning Bearcreek into a porcine Pamplona, but there are still people who haven't yet bet on the little piggers. And by your votes, Red Lodge, they certainly need to.

St. Olaf's Church

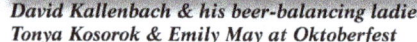
David Kallenbach & his beer-balancing ladies Tonya Kosorok & Emily May at Oktoberfest

🎩 Hats off Answer: the Post Office. "...and here's where we put the letter in the little hole! It can go anywhere in the country for only 37...make that...39 cents!"

Best Locally Made Product
Red Lodge Ales

We live in a town that makes BOTH chocolate and beer...now there's a slogan for the Chamber of Commerce! However, until Kings Cupboard opens a tasting room (48 oz daily limit, Hint! Hint!), Sam's reign looks secure.

🎩 Hats off Answer: "ME!"

Best Bartender
Heather Drake

Heather at the Front Bar may have gotten married and changed her name. She may even be job-sharing with another bartender named Heather, but you, dear voters, made yourselves clear: Heather Drake neé Shannon is our girl. Though she never writes anything down, she never gets your order wrong. Also strong in this category were Richie at the Snow Creek, Jason & Tom at FoLo's & Yvonne at the Tap Room. In fact, 30 bartenders made their mark this year.

Kris Thomas & Susie Hoffmann vamp it up 70s-style.

Best Local Dog
Buddy Irish

Mayor? Nah... County Commissioner? Nope. Dog! This is the most hotly contested race in Red Lodge. Buddy's campaign manager Dan Upton printed t-shirts, put up posters, and (we're sure this one put him over the top) even bought an ad in

The Best of Red Lodge • The Best of Red Lodge • The Best of Red Lodge

Lions' Park hockey rink waits for skaters.

this esteemed publication! Buddy is a mutt who actually belongs to Russ Irish. For great stories about Buddy's exploits, including tips on how he picks up girls, buy Russ a beer.

Hats off Answer: "The one that doesn't eat the garbage or poop on my lawn." Or "the chili dog at Foster & Logan's."

Best Time of Day to Go to the Post Office
Either "When it's open," or "When it's closed."

There was no a winner in this category—we just knew you'd all have an opinion on it. To that person who said "All day, great place to get a date," come talk to us—we've got a list of 50 most eligible singles.

Best Bloody Marys
Bogart's

We changed this category from Best Margaritas last year because Bogart's never had any competition. But since they insist on winning, next year we may change it to "Best person to clean my house this Saturday?" Meanwhile, you now know where to head for a little hair of the dog.

We had been feeling compelled to write something here about how Greg Shanks came in a strong third, but Maryvette informed us that "he's a plumber, he doesn't read." So we won't bother.

Best Steak
Carbon County Steakhouse

The Steakhouse received the most votes of any contender, in any category, ever, in the history of the Best of Red Lodge contest. Weird, but there it is. Rare, medium or well-done, Red Lodgers know their favorite haunt when it comes to beef.

Best Coffee
Coffee Factory Roasters

In a race with a lot of votes, the Coffee Factory edged out the Bikery and Buckin' Bronc for the best cup of smooth java to

brighten up your morning. Somebody nominated the First Interstate Bank in this category, saying "It's Free!" Now, we would hate to mess with anyone's financial planning, but we feel obliged to note that at Rock Creek Lumber, not only is the coffee free, but there's also popcorn for the taking.

Best Volunteer Organization
RL Volunteer Fire Dept

It was a runaway! These guys smoked the competition! The torrent of votes for the Fire Department this year was like when a really big truck backs over a hydrant and all the water spurts up really really high. Wheee!!!

Most Eligible Single
Lonnie Bradshaw

Talk about eligible! This guy has had the same job for twenty years. Hell, he's had a job for 20 years! Hell, he has a job! So, to whomever it was trolling for dates at the Post Office,….

Hats off Answers: "Francis the cat—she's fixed!" or "Father Keane."

Best Artist/Artisan
Dale Marie Muller

Three years in a row, Dale's heartfelt paintings of our wild animal neighbors reminds us of why we love Red Lodge. We're anticipating a possible upset next year, however, with Kevin Red Star moving back to town. Looks like it might be a face-off!

Best Teacher
Joe LeFebvre

Now, Anner and Guynema both insisted that they voted for one another in this category (yeah, watever!) Regardless, no amount of ballot-stuffing could overcome everyone's love for this quiet Environmental Sciences teacher who relates to his students in an extraordinary way. (And we're not just giving this to him because he's recovering from cancer. But we are all very relieved to hear he's doing so well. God Bless, Joe!)

Best Place to Spend Your Allowance
Candy Emporium

Our intention was to make the Best Of survey more kid-friendly this year.

So we're grateful that "Shotgun Willie's" got only one vote in this category. However, every bar in town received at least a dozen. Shows where people are when they're filling out our survey, I guess. Luckily, the Candy Emporium appeals to allowance earners of any age.

Best Kids' Hangout
the Skatepark

Turns out, kids in this town do know what they want! The skate park could also win Best Dream Come True in Red Lodge, since the kids dreamed it up, and with a lot of hard work and planning, made it happen. These days, it's the first place to look when your kids aren't home from school right away.

Hats off Answer: "Apparently in front of my fridge."

Best Breakfast
Cafe Regis

It's their third win in a row, which has the potential to make this category a little boring, unless next year we separate out the people voting for "Reggis" versus those who prefer the "Reejus."

Hats off Answer: "In Bed." (I want to live at your house!) Or "Blue Burger." (not so much). Note to the person who voted "oatmeal": Live a little! Your doctor is not grading this test.

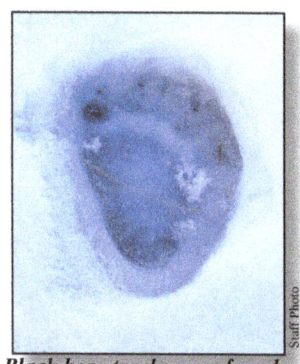
Black bear tracks were found in many alleys this fall.

Best Lunch
Foster & Logan's

Quick, convenient, healthy and really, really tasty? How can you go wrong? These guys came to town just over a year ago, and they've made some serious fans out of us.

Best Vegetarian Menu Item
Cafe Regis Tofu Scramble

We expected a lot more answers like

The Very Best of the Red Lodge Local Rag

The Best of Red Lodge • The Best of Red Lodge • The Best of Red Lodge

"grilled Kallenbach," or "Martha du jour." But luckily, you took us generally seriously, voting for three dozen different items in town, including such unusual vegetarian fare as "swizzle sticks," "Kings Cupboard chocolate," and "Beer." ...do you think if we got those all in the same meal, they'd make up a complete protein? The winning entry, however, really is one of the Regis' best dishes, even if you're not vegetarian.

Best Red Lodge Ale
Hefeweizen
ONE MORE TIME: "Moose Drool" is not a Red Lodge Ale!

Best Pat's Plumbing Ad
Cosmo Plumber
It's not every day you get to see your plumber in glamour mode. Unless he's Tom Teini. And Maryvette is calling the shots. These guys are a big reason we love our job here at the Local Rag, and we sincerely apologize to Gina. Again and Again.

Best Place To Pamper Yourself
Appearance Plus
This writer is forced to wonder if there's any correlation between the fact that these ladies won this category, and that they had at least one vote under Best Place to Have a Drink. It makes us wonder how you all define "pamper." I plan to find out next time I go in for a cut. Or a color. Or a massage. Or facial. Or mani/pedi. These girls do it all!

Hats off Answer: This category also gives us our favorite answer of the entire survey. Last year it was "the diaper aisle at IGA"; this year it's "On your Buttocks!"

Best Lifty
Fitzy
Sadly, the only lifty whose name people could remember is now working somewhere in New Hampshire. But to the person who asked "what's a lifty?" we must know: what do you do in the winter???

Hats off Answer: My wife's WonderBra.

Best Postal Worker
Sue Pitts
We phrased this one intentionally so you could answer things like "the unarmed one," or "glock 20." But luckily, lots of you voted for Sue, Arnetta, DeeDee, and all those wonderful folks who, for at least one person, can hook you up with a date when you're really desperate.

American History Teacher Hats off Answer: Ben Franklin

Best Reason to Buy a Season Pass at RLM
This was another question that doesn't have a meaningful winner—it's just that we were writing the survey in September and were really anxious to get on our skis.

Hats off Answer: "To stay out of The Blue before Noon."

Best Place to Gear Up
Sylvan Peak
It's Toys R Us for grownups! How often do you wander through that door dreaming about how much more fun you'd have in these Great Outdoors if only you had the newest...skis, or backpack, or lightweight tent, or bottle water purifier, or shoes, or intsy-bintsy camp stove? Luckily, they're right here in town, and if you need ANY information, Mike can talk your ear off about it.

Best Getaway
Chico Hot Springs
We may live in heaven, but every now and then we have to get away to Paradise. Valley, that is.

Hats off Answer: "the meth couple's high-speed chase."

Best Place to Find a Halloween Costume
ECHO Clothing
Some people apparently misunderstood the category and listed the best place to find inspiration: ex-wife's mother, Jon Philipsborn's rodeo outfit, the Snow Creek. But in the end, our second-hand clothing store beat out the Senior's Center as the source for Red Lodge's favorite night.

Best Auto Repair
RATTS
In this country, in any time of year, your tow truck driver ought to be your best friend. And who better than the Ronnings, who will tow you in and fix you up so they don't have to do it again?

Best Job to Have in Red Lodge
Bartender
...I'm sensing a pattern here... Maybe bartending is the only job that gives you enough free time and access to Best of Red Lodge ballots—were the bars really that dead last month???

Hats off Answer: the Local Rag. (I don't know who you are, but I like the way you think!)

Best 3rd Job
Bartender
Once again, we just thought we were funny. Though gigolo/man-slut was neither funny nor encouraging.

Hats off answer: None, the one that allows you to get rid of numbers 1 & 2.

Best Reason to Be a Local
We actually got some fun answers to this one: "We understand the jokes," "To tell visitors to look out for the Yeti," "Permanent Vacation," "3 cents off on gas," and our personal favorite: "Wahoo!!" But by far, most of you said you liked living here because of the people. Hard to argue with that.

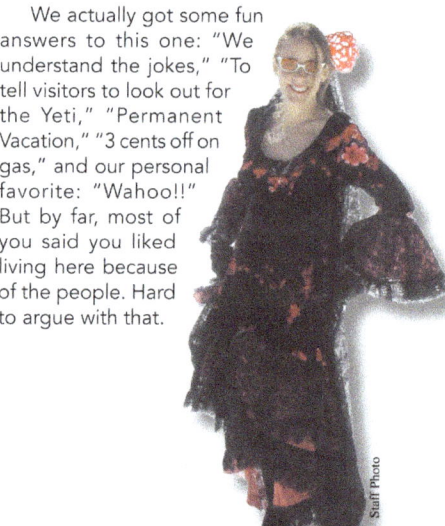

Tera Reynolds gets into the spirit of a Mexican Fiesta Winter Carnival.

Best of Red Lodge 2006 Winners

Okay. So I had no idea just how competitive Dr. George really is until we unveiled the survey this year. Really, the number of times he tried to get me to tell him who won Best Doc…Sad. Really. Thing is, I never figured out whether he was hoping he'd lose, or win.

Well, the wait is over, Dr. George. And for the rest of you competitive-types as well. Read on. And if you're disappointed that you didn't win this year, maybe you can take a page out of the Best Dog winner's book: campaign promises. That's what it's all about. I'm telling you.

Best locals' hangout
Sam's Taproom

When Playboy magazine was here six or eight years ago, they said the way to be a local was to wear your waders into the bar. Contrary to that advice, we've never seen anybody (except maybe Bucky…) wearing waders at any of the top three nominees in this category: the Front Bar, Foster & Logans, or Sam's Taproom. So much for reading that magazine for its articles…! However, the real locals know, when you want to go where everybody knows your name,…head to one of these fine watering holes.

Most anticipated *unadvertised* event
Burning Dog

The real Burning Man is in Nevada somewhere, but our own local knock-off, disorganized by a group including David Rivers, Russ Irish, Yvonne Proeller, and Dan Hogan, Mike Holmen, makes a pretty cool bonfire out of a man or dog or some constructable object every October. And the invite list is always the same: if you've heard about it, you're invited. Hard to beat.

Hats off answers: "Dollar-a-bag day"; "March powder"; "Kate Scott's rum punch."

Person most likely to keep a secret
Ya' think we'd tell?

Best volunteer organization
RL Fire/EMS

Whether it's a pilot light gone out in the basement, or a turkey fire blazing on the ridge, you can always count on these strapping lads and lasses to get you out of a jam.

Hats off answer: "Vol-Anon: The 12-Step Program for compulsive volunteers."

Best place to stop at Christmas Stroll
Kibler & Kirch

Wasn't Stroll picture-perfect this year? If you were there, you recall the perfect snowstorm, festive cheer, and as always, the phenomenal treats at Kibler and Kirch. Besides being a great time to do your holiday shopping, the treats these ladies offer make them your Number 1 fave.

Best soccer mom
Anne Christ

Will soccer ever be same? We can just see it now: next year, all the action moves to the sidelines as the moms (along with Nate Davis) bake cookies, dress in cheerleader outfits, and elbow each other to get the best position to be photographed in. We're sorry we ever brought it up, but just for the record, Anne was your golden girl.

Best phone voice
LaVonne Ervin

Stop reading right now. Take this paper up to Red Lodge Mountain and have LaVonne read the answer out loud to you. With that sweet, happy voice, she makes you just want to call up and chat. Not that you should do so right now. I'm sure poor girl has plenty of other things to do, than spend all day answering our dumb questions.

Hats off answer: "The person from City Hall on the recording who says, 'The trial has been cancelled.'"

Best medical professional
Dr. Billy Oley

It's tempting to prolong Dr. George's agony by not printing the answer here… but we love Billy Oley, and by your votes, so do you. He takes home this year's prize. We do have to mention here that all of the veterinarians in town received votes, as did Richie at the Snow Creek and "Goodtimes" Gessling. So just remember: whatever ails you, Red Lodge medical professionals can get you back in the game.

Best person to star in a "Visit Red Lodge" commercial
Eliza Kuntz

One of the things everybody says about this town is that people are so friendly. So who better to represent Red Lodge than the always-smiling, always-energetic Eliza Kuntz?

Hats off answer: "Mac Davis." We just can't get away from the guy.

Best local fashion icon
Heather Drake

Red Lodge fashion usually incorporates everything from "Sorels on the dance floor," to "Sorels in church." And when we need to know how to best accessorize those Sorels, we turn straight to Heather Drake. This woman is proof positive that you can take the girl out of New York, but you can't take the New York out of the girl. And Red Lodge fashion is the better for it.

Best Dog
Kona & Kiko

Only in Red Lodge can the most hotly contested race of the year be the Best Dog Booty Award. Again this year, the winner took to the streets with a well-thought-out campaign, complete with sandwich boards, posters, and a platform promising "honest government for the dogs by the dogs." Kona & Kiko, remember, we're going to hold you to that!

Best of Red Lodge ★ Best of Red Lodge ★ Best of Red Lodge

Most needed local ordinance

There are times when everybody in this town seems to have an opinion, and we're almost sorry we asked with this question! But here are seven of our favorite answers: "All dogs should be the size of dachsunds or smaller"; "No driving on the sidewalks while intoxicated"; "Open big game season in town"; "Lynchings for gossiping"; "Wild animal poop scoop"; "Turkey crossings"; and "Stop dogs from crapping on my lawn."

Local ordinance that should be repealed

...What struck us, though, was how many answers appeared in both of these categories. Open containers: impose or repeal? DUI: good or bad? Dogs in bars: should that be legal or not? Hunting in city limits: do we need it, need to enforce it, need to promote it? Leash law: do we have one? Do we need one? Sigh. Those City Council folks have a lot tougher job than you might think.

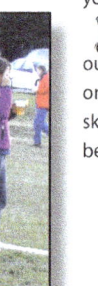

Best local controversy
ElkGate

Any award-winning controversy needs a catchy nickname. And, since 1973, that nickname has had to include the suffix "-gate." So when our esteemed local news outlet applied the "ElkGate" moniker to a controversy we'd rather not get into here, it was a shoo-in.

Most eligible single
Tom Doddy, Jr.

We've never quite figured out whether it's a good or a bad thing to win this category. But we must say that Tom's certainly a winner.

Easiest boss to work for
Judy Christensen

Maybe it's the margaritas. Maybe it's the staff parties. Maybe it's the memories of those trips to Mexico. But whatever she does, however she does it, Judy has always got a great relationship with her staff, and treats them right. Wonder if there are any openings...?

Best potluck cook
Jay West & John Overton...TIE!!

It's winter entertainment around here, something many people invest heavily in. Still, we have to wonder at one of the respondents in this category, who voted for "Jeannie - East Bench Road." Now how, exactly, am I going get Jeannie to come to my next potluck? Come on, voters, there are great dinners depending on this! I need Jeannie's last name! I intend to invite her to a potluck with this year's co-winners, so I can do a recount myself. (Stay tuned for details....)

Best free activity
Christmas Stroll

I'm really surprised and somewhat proud of this town for its answer here. It warms my heart. Though "sex" did come in a close second, Christmas Stroll actually pulled through as your favorite free activity. Good for you.

🎩 Among our favorite answers were "Drinking on someone else's tab"; "Over-70 skiing"; "Walking to the bar"; "Deadbeat pizza"; and "Loitering."

Best drink
Bogart's Margaritas

First, they won the Margarita category without any competition. Then, they ran away with the Bloody Mary category. Now, they're going for World Domination by being the best overall drink in town. These people are unstoppable! The bottom line is, in a town with 13 bars, that ought to tell you where to go the next time you need to let off a little steam.

Best neighbor
Bill Temple

There's something sweet, though odd, about a homeless guy being the town's best neighbor. Not that Mr. Bill is a regular homeless guy,...just that he's a guy who doesn't have a home. Then again, Mr. Bill's not a regular anything. It looks like we might have to add a new line to next year's survey, though: "Person Receiving Votes in the Most Categories." Your favorite neighbor was also nominated for: Best person to keep a secret, Star in a "Visit Red Lodge" commercial, Most eligible single, Best unsung hero, and Friendliest face. Just goes to show you: it's not what you do, but who you are that matters in this little town.

🎩 Hats off answers: "Canada"; "Mexico"; "The one who lives near me"; "the Snow Creek—you can walk home"; and "Roberts."

Most likely to become World Famous
Bogart's Margaritas

Now what was I just saying about World Domination?

🎩 Hats off answer: "Mark (author)"—yeah, we don't remember the guy's name either, but dammit, he oughtta be famous!

Most kid-friendly business
Pizza Company

We keep trying to add more kid-friendly categories to this survey. And you keep giving us answers like this year's "county jail." Well at least the Pizza Company is still a great place to keep your kids entertained.

Best event at RLM
Winter carnival

With the snowmobile hillclimb, Fat Tire Frenzy, and the Bluegrass Festival, there are more and more destination events at the Mountain, even for people who don't ski. But our favorite remains the always-fun Winter Carnival where everyone can do something—building a Cardboard Classic, racing it down the hill, or dressing in costume and eating jalapenos til your hair turns red. What says "Red Lodge winter" better than that?

Best contractor
Beartooth Custom Builders

With all of the new construction in this area, this category had a lot of competition. We were impressed that the top three nominees (Peder Nees, Dave Malin, and Albert Loeffen & Bob Lee) have all been around a long time. They run their own small businesses, keep as much business as they can right here in town, and they're all nice guys to boot—no wonder they're always so busy.

Best place to work for minimum wage
Red Lodge Mountain

We chuckled at the answer "People should receive more than minimum wage for working!" We chuckled not only because we hadn't asked for political commentary, but because the Mountain does give you more than minimum wage. With the free ski pass,

Best of Red Lodge

flexible schedule, and fun atmosphere, it's no wonder they've always got a great staff.

Best place to work for cash under the table

It's scary how many people answered this question. We did appreciate the person who said "Boycott!!"; and of course "The IRS" was a funny answer. But we've burned all the ballots, people, so don't worry: there's no tracing the rest of you, doling out a little pre-tax income.

Best unsung hero
Les Dimich

There are people in this town—not that we're related to any of them—who know absolutely nothing about car repair, but somehow when they buy a $2 part at NAPA, they get the expertise (and, well, sometimes even the labor) to install it. That spirit must have been what voters had in mind when they filled out this category, because it certainly gives Les our vote.

 Hats off answer: Best unhung hero: Nip & Tuck.

Best burger
FoLo's/F&L
(That's Foster & Logan's, for the uninitiated)

By our most recent count, you can get a burger at no less than 13 establishments in this town, not to mention your own backyard grill. From last year's Best Lunch to this year's Best Burger, FoLo's is coming in strong as your favorite place to eat.

Best new business
Beijing Garden

You had to pity their staff, being completely, totally, unbelievably, slammed with business those first few weeks. But they came through in a big way. Do you think maybe we were hungry for Chinese food? Steve & company ran away with this win. But maybe it's actually all of us Chinese-food-lovers who are the real winners in the deal.

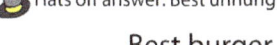 Hats off answer: "I don't know, they closed before I got there."

Best waiter/waitress
Denise Howard

After last year, we had lots of people telling us we needed to add this category to our survey. And

we agreed with them: With all the hard work they do, waitstaffs in this town certainly deserve some credit. And Denise is one of the pros. You always know your visit to the Steakhouse is gonna be a good experience.

Most relaxing place to shop
Boomerang Beads

Is it the waft of incense that greets you as you walk in the door? The funky World Music playing overhead? Or just the fact that Kate's never in a rush: she's happy to stop and chat with you, or get you started on your beads, or show you the new cool stuff she just got in. Kinda makes you want to be Australian.

Best local activist
Martha Young

She's been wearing a piece of masking tape to her job at the Regis for the last three-plus years. You notice it, though she won't call your attention to it. She tells you what she thinks, and acts on what she believes. All that added up to a win for her in this category.

Shortest parade
St Patrick's day

Were it not for Brad Logan and his kids, we would not have a St. Patrick's day parade each year. And for that we're grateful. However, our favorite answer in this category was: "The turkeys crossing Broadway." We assume you were talking about the fowl, not the human, pedestrians.

Hats off answers: "Tamara's piano-moving"; or "Kris Thomas' house going down Broadway."

Best place to catch up on local gossip
Sam's Taproom

Okay, so it also won Best Locals' Hangout. ...we're thinking maybe there's a connection. Just watch out, though, for when the new city ordinance requires all those lynchings. PS: I suspect that whomever's gossiping during those morning aerobics needs to be working just a little bit harder.

Best cashier at the IGA
Evie

Awwwww....Evie! Have you ever noticed that her line is often the longest? It's certainly not because she's inefficient - it has to be 'cause everyone likes her so much. She's quick, she's sweet, she's been there forever. We're lucky to have Evie as such a prominent face in this community.

Best place to see a nude or lewd act
The Snow Creek

We swear, it was just coincidence, we did not know when we put our survey together in this order that the girl on the IGA self-checkout screen was naked from the waist up. (Hey! You said it, not us!) We've never even been to the self-checkout. We're always in Evie's line.

Best vehicle never meant to be on the road
Hummers

Some of the answers in this category included "Jacob (son of Judge) Seiffert's Dodge pickup"; "Jacob (son of Judge) Seiffert's Subaru"; and "Jacob (son of Judge) Seiffert's dune buggy." Poor Jacob. We are interested in "Craig Abbey's pewter commuter" though; and we haven't met "Marilyn the '59 Nash Metropolitan" or "Griffin's yellow truck," but we're pretty sure it's a good thing that a certain golf cart is no longer out there on the streets.

Friendliest face
Judy Christensen

I'm telling you: WORLD Domination. Friendly World Domination. She's like a smiling, margarita-wielding Genghis Khan. There's no stopping her. And you've just got to love her to bits.

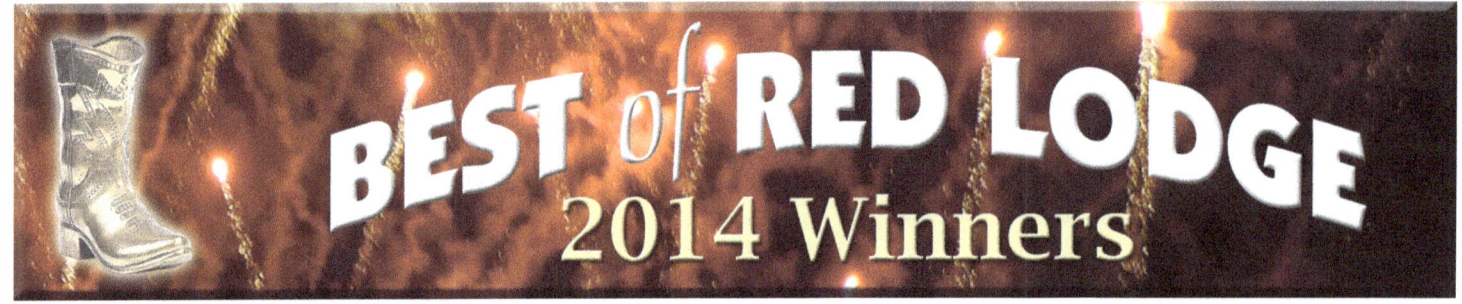

Best of Red Lodge 2014 Winners

Most kid-friendly business

This was a close race, with **Red Lodge Pizza Co.** barely edging out Honey's Café for first place. Third goes to Kids Corner.

Best place (or way) to cure your hangover

This category was sewed up by the only place in town that has both breakfast and bloody marys: **The Knotty Casino.** Biscuits and gravy at the Regis Café came in second.

Our favorite answer: Beartooth Clinic. That must be one helluva hangover!

Most awesome teacher

Fifteen different teachers received votes in this category, but the winner was clear: 3rd grade teacher **Robb Sager** is Red Lodge's most awesome teacher!

Honorable mentions to Karla Moos, Libby Johnson, Jennifer Collins, Kay Kovach, Bobbie Wooldridge, and Sheila Riches. We fully expect all of them to get raises now!

Best 3rd job in Red Lodge

Oh, this was fun. We got everything from housesitting to dealing drugs (we should have seen that coming). The winner, however, was **Red Lodge Mountain**, with "tending bar" coming in a close second.

Most people-friendly law enforcement officer

Six officers got votes in this category, plus the crossing guards at the school. The winner is **Joe Enos**, followed by Acting Chief Scott Cope and Greg Srock.

Don't feel too bad for Greg getting third place, though. Keep reading and you'll see his name again!

Best fancy-schmancy cocktail

The "Governor's Mule" from **The Pollard Pub** took this category by storm; nobody else got more than two votes.

Most pet-friendly business

As we counted up votes, this category was a tight race between two veterinarians. In the end, **Silver Run Veterinary Associates** squeezed out Grizzly Peak Animal Hospital for the win.

Favorite local character

He may not have won the race for the Mayor's job, but **"Walking Tom" Weaver** handily clinched the race for favorite local character! He was followed by Brad "Bradley" Evans, "Mr. Bill" Temple, and Norm.

Our favorite answer on this one was the Pollard Ghost.

Best beard

Doug Bailey has been working on this one for two years, so it's only fitting that he win it. Second place goes to "Jason Priest's mugshot," and third is a tie between "Mr. Bill" Temple and Harry Hollman.

Best boss

This was a close race, with 20 (!) different bosses getting votes. You have chosen **Kelly Heaton** from DSVS as the best boss in Red Lodge, and second place is a tie between "Papa Z" (Greg Zeiler) and Jim Noe. Our favorite answers were "myself" and "my wife."

Most bitchin' ski run

This one is a tie between **Miami Beach** and **Drainage**. You folks had a hard time reaching consensus, giving votes to 14 different runs!

Best place to get warm

We should have seen this coming, too. The number one answer was variants on "bed" including "my bed," "your bed," and "your mom's bed." Once we trimmed those out, we ended up with **The Pollard Pub** at number one, followed by a tie between the Coffee Factory Roasters and Honey's Café.

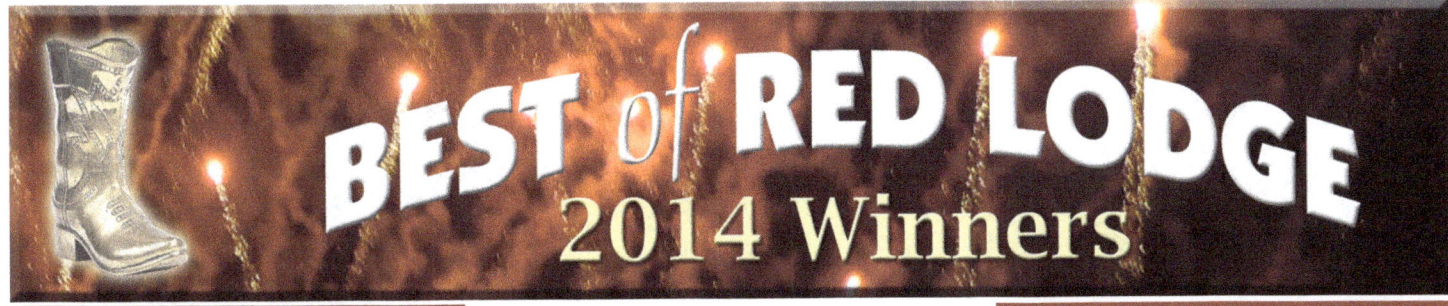

Best of Red Lodge 2014 Winners

Best Fest

So many good festivals in Red Lodge that it's hard to know where to start.

Of the dozen events that got votes, the Red Lodge Festival of Nations barely beat out Oktoberfest and the Home of Champions Rodeo.

Best place to watch drunk people fall over

The Snow Creek Saloon absolutely ran away with this one, gathering 60% of the total votes. Some of the other bars got votes, too, as did the Beartooth Rally and the Catholic Church.

Most talented local musician

We have a *lot* of musical talent in this town! Votes went to 16 different musicians (and a few groups). The winner is Travis Burdick – perhaps because he plays in 415 different bands – followed by Charlie Brandine in second place and Shannon Patchen in third.

Best burrito

The people have spoken, and they have selected Más Taco as the best burrito in town.

It looks like you can't go wrong with Las Palmitas (a.k.a. the "Burrito Not-A-Bus-Anymore") either, as they pulled in 16 votes to get second place.

Favorite Bloody Mary maker

Callie Stewart from the Pollard Pub won this one, barely edging out Luke Tolle of Foster & Logan's. Third place went to the Blue Ribbon Bar.

Best place to take your friends from out of town

The Red Lodge area is filled with wonderful places to hang out with your friends, and lots of votes in this category went to restaurants, bars, and other hangouts. The clear winner, however, was the Beartooth Pass. We're not quite sure who to hand the certificate to!

Second place went to the Bearcreek Saloon (love those pig races!), and third was a tie between Red Lodge Mountain and Sam's Taproom.

Best "Big Fish" storyteller

The winner is Jake Barton, followed closely by Don Coutts. Thirteen other people got votes in this category.

Best waiter or waitress

Laurel Hunter at Old Piney Dell handily took first place, with twice as many votes as second place winner Callie Stewart from the Pollard Pub. Anna Drew (also at the Pollard Pub) took third.

Best place to learn something

We're just going to have to call this a three-way tie between the Carbon County Historical Society & Museum, the Red Lodge Carnegie Library, and Appearance Plus (no telling what you'll learn there)!

Hottest bartender

Votes were cast for 19 different bartenders, and we ended up with a three-way tie for first place between Erin Priest, Callie Stewart, and Luke Tolle. Erin and Luke both work at Foster & Logan's, so that's where you look for hot bartenders in this town!

Favorite Medical Professional

Erin Oley won this handily, and second place was a tie between her husband, Dr. Billy Oley, and Dr. Brad Fouts. It wasn't just Beartooth Clinic staff, though. Votes also went to an EMT (Aaron McDowell), a chiropractor (Dan Upton), and a vet (Jane Nibler).

Best customer

We're not sure what we expected for this category, but what we got was a tie between "locals" and Tim Buckstead.

Tastiest vegetarian menu item

This was intended to go for a specific dish, but so many people just wrote "Regis Café" that we have to give the prize to the restaurant itself. Second place goes to Más Taco's carrot chipotle soup, and third goes to the

The Very Best of the Red Lodge Local Rag

Best of Red Lodge 2014 Winners

portobello sandwich at the Pollard Pub. Six other restaurants got votes, so vegetarians shouldn't have any trouble finding something to eat in Red Lodge!

Our favorite answer: A buffalo burger with *LOTS* of lettuce and tomato.

Favorite shop owner

Amber Enos of Sagebrush Sirens took first place, with Gary Robson of Red Lodge Books & Tea in 2nd and Kerri Wolfson of Honey's Café in 3rd.

Best Burger

There are plenty of places in town to get a burger, and nine of them got votes in this category. None, however, came close to the votes that the Snag Burger got.

Second place went to Foster and Logans, and Bridge Creek tied with the Pollard Pub for third. Our favorite answer: "Whatever comes with a beer at the Front Bar."

Best Restrooms

The Pollard Pub won this category, with Knotty Casino and Honey's Café taking second and third.

Best place to spend your allowance

Oh, there are a lot of places to spend your allowance in Red Lodge, but it looks like the best is Sylvan Peak Mountain Shop. The Candy Emporium took second, followed by the Snag Bar.

Our favorite answer: "on your wife."

EMT you'd want in an emergency

Votes went to 18 different people, but it looks like your favorite is Sarah Ewald. Second place goes to George Clow and third to Kristen Hobson.

Our favorite answer: God.

Person most likely to be a superhero in disguise

It looks like Batman's secret identity is blown: it's RLPD officer Greg Srock! Second place goes to Travis Burdick, with Cody Nelson right behind. Fourth place was a tie between "Mr. Bill" Temple and Kevin Brady.

Yummiest dessert

"Anything by Mel Davis at the Pollard" came in first, followed closely by the Crazy Cookie at Red Lodge Pizza Co.

Best person to have on your zombie apocalypse team

RLPD officer Joe Enos is the most popular pick to fight off zombies with you. At his side will be Doug Robson and Callie Stewart, who tied for second place.

Best person to star in a Visit Red Lodge commercial

For town ambassador, you've chosen Donna Madson from the Carbon County Historical Society & Museum. Second place went to "Walking Tom" Weaver and third is Sarah Ewald.

Classiest drunk

Boone Buckmiller won this, with 14 other people receiving votes, including Wells Reitz and our own editor-in-chief, Heather Robson.

Best breakfast

This was an absolute runaway win for the Regis Café, which took 64% of the votes! Second place was a tie between the Red Lodge Café and the Roberts Café.

Red Lodge's unsung hero

The winner is Brad "Bradley" Evans, with Patty Davis from the Chamber of Commerce coming in second.

Red Lodge Local

INSIDE: Mountain Man Rendezvous Schedule

FREE Local Event Information

VOLUME II • JULY 1992 • ISSUE 7

The Fourth of July guarantees to be the best in years as it falls this year on a Saturday... look out!

The following is a summary of events to be held over the Fourth weekend, though there are still many other happenings besides those listed here.

PARADE

The 63rd Annual Home of Champions Rodeo Parade will be held on the 2nd, 3rd and 4th. The theme this year is "Montana Recreation," which includes indoor and outdoor fun (hunting, fishing, poker, bar-flying, and just about anything we Montanans do for fun).

Joining the parade this year will be the 7th Cavalry Drum & Bugle Corps from Sheridan Wyoming and the Black Horse Patrol...

The **CHILDREN'S ENTRIES** will be judged on July 2nd, and the categories are:
1. Best Costume
2. Best Comic Entry
3. Best Bicycle Entry

Each of the three winners will receive a $10 prize, and all entrants will receive a free family pass to the rodeo for the 2nd and 3rd.

The parade on the 3rd is not judged and is open for anyone and everyone to have fun with.

The **ADULT ENTRIES** will be judged on July 4th according to the following categories: (prizes listed after each)
1. Best Float - $50
2. Best Theme Float - $50
3. Best Mounted Group - $50
4. Best Harness Team - $50
5. Best Musical Entry - $50
6. Best Motorized Entry - $50
7. Best Dressed Cowboy - Belt Buckle
8. Best Dressed Cowgirl - Belt Buckle

The parade line-up will commence at 10:30 a.m. on the 2nd and 4th, with registration on site at the Civic Center parking lot. The parades begin at high Noon. (Notify parade officials on site if you'll be throwing candy from your entry so they can place your entry accordingly.)

If you'd like more information, contact Marlene Donelson at 446-2852.

63rd Annual HOME OF CHAMPIONS RODEO

Born in the hard times of the late '20s when attendance numbered 20,000 spectators and a $5,000 purse; this year's rodeo promises to be one of the biggest in the country. As a part of the Professional Rodeo Cowboys of America circuit, you can expect to see nearly all of the national champions competing.

The rodeo is also open to young cowpokes in the Sheep Riding contests...

...but the main event so far is the Wild Horse Race, where the mad man climbs on an unwilling horse. The horses usually win but at least our team of humans wins...

SNOW CREEK SALOON
Johnny Quest will be playing on the 2nd, 3rd and 4th from 9 p.m. to 2 a.m. each night.

TIN PIN ALLEY & CASINO
Billy Waldo & The Flyin' Grizzleys will be playing on the 1st through the 4th from 9 p.m. to 1:30 a.m.

SNAG BAR
Yogo (Ron & Kim Hardin) will play on the 2nd, 3rd and 4th from 8:30 p.m. to 1:30 a.m. nightly.

RED LODGE LOUNGE
Verlyn & Friends will perform on the 3rd and 4th from 9 p.m. to 1:30 a.m.

BULL AND BEAR SALOON
Overland Stage will play on the 2nd (downstairs saloon), and on the 3rd and 4th (upstairs ballroom) from 8 p.m. to 1 a.m.

ELK'S LODGE
Midnight Rider will play from 9 p.m. to 1 a.m. on the nights of the 3rd and 4th.

July 1st through 4th will find the Past Exalted Rulers of the Elk's hosting a hamburger cook-out in front of the Lodge during the day.

The Red Lodge Police Department would like to welcome all hearty party-ers to Red Lodge on the Fourth of July weekend. Have a good time, wine, dine, 69, drink, dance, party, puck your guts out if you have to... but please don't drink and drive. You don't want to spend the Fourth in jail, or in the hospital, or in the morgue, and the officers don't want to spend it doing paperwork on you! Have fun and be safe. And for those who've taken a liking to being mouthy toward the cops... it's not a good idea to push your luck.

GUNFIGHTERS

The National Association of Old West Gunfighter teams will perform at the football field on the 2nd and 3rd at 1:30 p.m. and on the Fourth at 1 p.m. They will also perform each night at the Home of Champions Rodeo just before the Wild Horse Race.

On the night of the 2nd at 7 p.m. they will be celebrating their Decade Anniversary with a social hour at the Carbon County Coal Company Casino. Everyone is invited to come and meet the out-of-state... decade-arians... and to party with them.

The Red Lodge Gunfighters will host an exhibition shootout at the O K Corral downtown at 4 p.m. on the Fourth. After the rodeo that evening, they'll have a weenie roast (BYOW - bring yer own weener) at the barbecue. Everyone's welcome to join in the fun... bring your musical instrument of choice to the sing-along and jam.

NO FIREWORKS DISPLAY

Due to a lack of interest, manpower, organization, and fifty other excuses, there will not be a fireworks display on the Fourth this year unless someone pulls something really tricky and impressive out of their hat in the next few days... hint, hint.

HELLO, Red Lodge!

New format again... fickle editor (women reserve the right to change their minds often, and blondes wrote the book on unpredictable - so, I'm covered). I won't swear to it, but I think this might actually be the format I've been looking for. Come now, it's only the third one!

This will be the last issue to appear as an insert in The Carbon County News. The Local will again be out in local stores at no cost to readers. Subscriptions are available for $10 a year in the USA (foreign rates depend on postage; our address is on page 12.

In closing, a note of thanks to the crew at the Carbon County News: Jim, Burt, Mean Jean, Danielleee, Patti, Mary, Sally and Pam; thanks for the fun, guys, and for all the valuable instruction I wax first, then cut... and always SAVE text when the phone is on the blink! It was great working with you all and my paper will be easier because of you. Remember, friends; it's not that the world has gotten worse, just that the media coverage has gotten so much better! Carry on, ye wild and wacky wizards of word. I'll think of you every Tuesday night... and smile. Cheers! —from Lou

A

Abbey, Craig 235
Adams, Ken 56
Aga, Augie 109
Albus, Jean 32
Ale House 121
Aleksich, Kandy 42
Aleksich, Skip 42, 219–221
Allen, Mary 63
All Nations Garden Club 150
Alsager, David 202
Andersen, "Stormin Norman" 179, 236
Anderson, Richard 218
Annighofer, Frank 66
Appearance Plus 232, 237
Arthun, Erik 45
Arthun, Kirsten. *See* Wilson, Kirsten
Arthun, Peggy 45
Arthur's Grill 130
Ashby, Lola 49
Aspen Ridge Ranch 208
Atherly, Jean 12, 13–15, 30
Aukema, Kevin 208
Ayre, Becky 63

B

Bailey, Doug 135, 208, 236
Bailey, Suzanna 167
Baker, Alastair 13
Barnes, Bill 64
Barton, Jake 237
Battles, Jenn 69
Battles, Jeremy 69
Beach, Dave 31, 33
Beam, Craig 25, 34, 138–139, 142–143, 190, 230
Beam, Vivian 25, 138–139, 191
Bear Creek Saloon & Steakhouse 121, 230, 237
Beartooth Bar 128
Beartooth Billings Clinic 237
Beartooth Clinic 236
Beartooth Custom Builders 111, 121, 224, 234
Beartooth Highway
  mudslides 86
Beartooth Nature Center 224
Beartooth Rally 7, 111, 208, 227, 230, 237
Beck, Barb 38
Becker, Angie 125
Becker, Gary 125
Becker's Kitchen & Steak House 125
Beck, Paul 50, 160
Beck, Rena 224
Beer Snob 146
Beijing Garden 224, 235
Belfry, William 89
Bierstube 126, 228, 229. *See also* Red Lodge Mountain
Bikery 231

Binando, Erika 31
Blake, Lincoln 160
Bloomer, Al 70
Bloomer, Carol 70
Bloom, Walter 108
Blue Ribbon Bar 237
Body Lodge 228
Bogart's 117, 128, 231, 234
Boggio, Tamara. *See* Upton, Tamara
Bone Daddy's 121, 150, 157
Boomerang Beads 224, 235
Bosworth, Grace 90
Bowler, John 89
Boyd, John 89
Boyer, Monja 63
Bradshaw, Lonnie 231
Brady, Kevin 238
Brajcich, Sandy 63
Brandine, Charlie 97, 237
Bridge Creek Backcountry Kitchen 3, 120, 226, 227, 238
Buckin' Bronc 160, 231
Buckmiller, Boone 238
Buckstead, Tim 150, 237
Bucky 177, 233
Bull Moose Bistro 22
Bullock, Jean Anne 33
Bullock, Richard 33
Burdick, Travis 237, 238
Burgener, Kathy 214
Burns, Kerry 53
Burton's Cafe 129
Bury, Susan 30, 32
Bustos, Stan 97

C

Café Regis. *See* Regis Café
Camp Senia 102
Caporali, Bill 66
Carbon County Historical Society 237, 238
Carbon County News 13
Carbon County Steakhouse 128, 226, 231
Cardoza, Mike 31, 34
Carpenter, Doug 214
Carter, Charla 33
Castagne, Frank 89
Castellani, Dana 224
Cestnik, Terry 92
Chamber of Commerce 238
Chance, Nathan 89
Charles, Josh 154
Chatlain, Jane 121
Chatwood, Cobe 43
Christ, Anne 120, 224, 233
Christ, Dennis 39
Christ, Peter 120, 130
Christensen, Jodie 30, 128
Christensen, Judy 30, 128, 224, 234, 235
Christmas Stroll 234

Chupp, Karen 60, 63
Chupp, Kylie 33
Clark, Audrey 39
Clawson, Orren 229
Clayton, John 20, 40, 41, 192
Clayton, Kari 15, 18, 20, 24, 25, 30, 40, 86, 193
Cline, Joan 31, 60, 231
Clow, George 33, 238
Clow, Paula 33
Cobetto, Della 108
Coffee Factory Roasters 127, 227, 231, 236
Coleman, Merv 78, 106, 228
Collar, Marian 61
Collins, Jennifer 98, 236
Conis, Patricia 214
Conlee, Craig 27
Cope, Scott 35, 236
Coutts, Don 7, 100, 237
Coutts, Gloria 100
Cowboy Coffin & Pine Box Co 94
Crazy Carl 224
Crazy Creek 111
Critelli, Nancy 212
Cross, Dan 40
Cross, Melissa 28, 122
Culp, Carrie 40

D

Dandy Cakes 147
Daniel, Art 48
Daniel, Bonnie 48
Davidson, Kathy 47, 64
Davis, Frankie 6, 9, 32
Davis, Melissa 124, 238
Davis, Nate 233
Davis, Patty 238
Day, Doris 129
Day, Ted 129
Dayton, Abbi 33
DeArmond, Lynn 121
DeArmond, Pits 121, 218, 222, 230
Densmore, Jon 121
DeRosiers, Nancy 25
DeShano, Lisa 94
DeVries, Wyatt 63
Dewi Shinta 147
Dillon family 13, 14
Dimich, Les 224, 235
Doddy, Tom 23, 224
Doddy, Tom Jr. 224, 234
Doughty, Roland N. 227
Drake, Heather 224, 230, 233
Drake, Jacob 34
Drake, Robert 32, 34
Draper School 102
Drew, Anna 237
Duncan, Marilee 210
Dye, Marci 25, 140
Dye, Noah 140

E

Eder, JoAnn 49
Edgar, Henry 89, 229
Edge of Red Lodge 41, 228
Egenes, Tom 78
Ehlers, Thomas 43
Enos, Amber 148, 238
Enos, Joe 236, 238
Entenmann, Quinn 214
Erkens, Carol 59
Erkens, Jim 59
Ervin, LaVonne 224, 233
Estelle, Graham 51
Estelle, Steve 51
Evans, Brad "Bradley" 236, 238
Evenson, Emma 40
Ewald, Sarah 224, 238
Ewelt, Jeff 61, 152
Eyden, Brodie 48
Eyden, Heather. See Robson, Heather

F

Fahrenthold, Jerry 88
Fake ads 10, 51, 52, 133, 174–175
Farley, Mike 7
Farnham, Gina 63
Farnham, Stan 63
Faygal, Mark 102
Faygal, Mary 102
Ferguson, Gary 79, 115, 162
Festival of Nations 3, 150, 210–211, 237
Filkin, Rose 60
First Interstate Bank 231
Flaherty, Dorothea 150
Flaherty, Tom 115, 150
Flash's 150
Flockhart, Bill 210
Food Farm 121
Forney, George "Doc" 92
Fosdal, Scott 56
Foster & Logan's 23, 224, 231, 233, 235, 237, 238
Fourth of July 3, 17, 227
Fouts, Brad 237
Fox, J.M. 89
Frerichs, Dolly. See Stuber, Dolly
Front Bar. See Natali's Front Bar
Fuchs, Threse 158
Fun Run 224, 230
Fusaro, Jenn. See Battles, Jenn

G

Gale, Janet 38
Garritson, Bob 88
Garritson, Ron 88
G-Dawg. See Kisthard, Gary
Gebo, Mose 89
George, Bethany 27
George, Bill 224, 233
George, "Yankee Jim" 92
Gessling, Richard 31, 99, 157, 214, 233
Gilbertson, Vanessa 160
Gildehaus Family 57
Gildehaus, Jeff 70
Gildehaus, Liam 70
Gillet, Benny 164
Glass Rabbit 224, 228
Godoy, Marisa 224
Goldberg, Debbie 40
Graham, Joseph, H. 104
Greathouse, Mariah 166
Green, Emma 63
Greenough, Deb 96, 209
Greenough, Quinn 96
Greenough, Turk 96
Griz 154
Grizzly Peak Animal Hospital 236
Gumper, Diny 50
Gumper, Lew 50

H

Hamilton, Don 32, 67
Hamilton, Nancy 67
Hancock, Kenny 126
Hank's Place 22, 86
Hansen, Chad 137, 188
Hansen, Cindy 121
Hansen, Tory Host 31, 35, 37, 38, 44, 48, 53, 54, 55, 56, 59, 62, 65
Hardiman, Piney 224
Hardy, Becky 48, 72–77
Hardy, Don 48, 74
Hardy, Gloria 181
Hardy, Joel 181
Hardy, Molly 40
Harsha, D.G. 108
Haskin, Bessie 227
Hauge, Brad 224
Hauge, Lee 44
Hauge, Teresa 44
Haugen, Buster 43
Haugen, Carly 43, 44
Haugen, Clay 43, 44
Haugen, Laurie 43, 44
Hawthorne, Alex 90
Heaton, Kelly 236
Heinzen, David 31
Herbert, Barbara 60
Herbert, Sid 60
Herzberg, Rand 38, 94, 154
Highburger, Ceily Rae 214
Hill, Becky. See Hardy, Becky
Hobson, Kristen 238
Hodges, Gregg 32, 35
Hodges, Pat 35
Hoffmann, Susie 230
Hoffman, Sam 110
Hoffman's Department Store 110
Hogan, Dan 233
Hogg, Jodee 53
Hoiness, Karen 221
Holbrook, Zane 63
Hollman, Harry 236
Holmen, Mike 233
Home of Champions Rodeo 208, 237
Honey's Café 236, 238
Hound Dogs From Outer Space 97, 226
Houtonen, Eli 90
Hovde, Susan 43
Howard, Denise 224, 235
Howard, Jimmy 127
Howell's Camp. See Mountain Man Rendezvous
Hunter, Laurel 237

I

Irish, Buddy 230
Irish, Russ 231, 233
Iron Horse Rodeo. See Beartooth Rally

J

Jacks, Larry 171
Janskovitch, Frank 92
Janskovitch, Leopold 92
Jelley, Jessica 69
Johnson, Gary 88
Johnson, Libby 236
Johnson, Louella 88
Johnson, Paul 27
Jorgenson, Bob 46, 65
Jorgenson, Laurie 64

K

Kaiser, Peter 53
Kaiser, Roberta 53
Kalico Kitchen 11
Kallenbach, David 55, 93, 178, 230
Kampfe, Aaron 30, 34, 41
Karas, Bill 94
Karas, Margaret 94
Karina, Jewel 157
Kennen, Shelly 31
Kennicott, Wanda 47
Khatchikian, Gerry 61
Kibler & Kirch 121, 224, 233
Kids Corner 236
King's Cupboard Chocolate 179, 227, 230, 232
Kinney, Don 221
Kirkpatrick, Jay 88
Kisthard, Gary 17
Knotty Casino 236, 238
Kohley, Tom 110
Kosorok, Joe "JK" 108, 175
Kosorok, Judy 108
Kosorok, Mary Anne 108
Kosorok, Mike 98, 99, 108, 166
Kosorok, Nick 99, 108
Kosorok, Tonya 33, 210–211, 230
Kotar, Mark 17
Kovach, Kay 236
Kramsky, Barb 63
Kriner, Nancy 45, 47

Krumheuer, Tony 11, 101
Kuhlman, Fay 91, 115
Kujala, Jim 97, 101, 117, 155, 171
Kuntz, Eliza 78, 128, 233
Kuntz, Ray 112
Kuntz, Tom 128, 224

L

Labrie, Maryvette 114, 186, 231, 232
Laird, Anne 109
LaMonaca, Mary Critelli 212
Lane, Libby 224
Larkin, Grace 150
Las Palmitas 237
Lauritzen, Carl Jr. 158
LeFebvre, Joe 231
LeFore, Kimberly 50, 70, 177
Lehnherr, David 41, 67
Lehrkind, Julius 89, 90
Levi the Coyote 58
Lindgren, Julie 63
Linley, Walter 89, 227
Lions Park 231
L&L Builders 224
Logan, Brad 23, 93, 182, 235
Logan, Sue 182, 212
Lohof, Nicole 22
Lombard, Earl E. 92
Lost Village Saloon 127
Loughrie, Todd 97
Lubbers, April 60
Lubbers, Beverly 60
Lubbers, Bruce 60
Lucky Dog 125, 228
Luff, Terence 88
Luther, Grace R. 227
Lyall, Susan 39
Lynch, Jack 57
Lynn, Adam 33

M

Madson, Donna 238
Magida, Cathy 37
Magida, Jason 37, 137, 230
Magpie Toys 181
Mahan, Glory 103, 108, 214
Majerus, Mike 89–91
Malin Construction 224
Malin, Dave 37
Manderscheid, Jim 65
Mangus, MaryEllen 47
Manuel, Tom 33
Marble, Anner 34, 98, 231
Martin, Becky 214
Martin, Janal 31
Martin, Scott 34
Más Taco 237
Mattraw, Chuck 52
May, Emily 230
McAlpine, Rosemary 45, 47
McCafferty, Edmund 39

McCampbell, Jody 121
McCarty, Marge 110
McClelland, Doug 33
McClelland, Liza 33
McCloud, Whispy 199
McDowell, Aaron 237
McDowell, Ethan 201
McDowell, Tam 200
McKown, Bonnie 53, 54, 57
McKown, Terry 53
McNamara, Erin 94
McQuillan, Rosalie 158
Meier, Pius 128, 210
Mennenga, Jay 51
Metcalf, Jon 99, 108
Mignon's Gifts & Flowers 115
Miller, George 100
Miller, Jacob 63
Miller, Kasi 63
Mills, Patty 79–85
Minecraft 19
Mitchell, Charles 196
Mitchell, Kari. *See* Clayton, Kari
Montana Candy Emporium 227, 231, 238
Montana Chinook 45
Montana Coal & Iron Company 90
Montana Reds 129
Montana Trout Scout. *See* Beam, Craig
Moore, Jodie 107, 224
Moos, Karla 236
Moran, Bob 210
Morgan, Steve 52
Morgan, Theresa 52
Morris, Robert 89
Mountain Man Rendezvous 88
Mountain People 42, 227
Mourich, Mary 92
Mr. Bill. *See* Temple, Bill
Muller, Dale Marie 231
Murphy, Chuck 115, 224

N

NAPA 235
Natali's Front Bar 101, 128, 224, 226, 230, 233, 238
Nees, Peder & Maren 111
Neff, David 69
Neff, Priscilla 69
Nelson, Cody 238
Nelson, Gunnar 214
Nelson, Jamie 214
Nelson, Taylor 63
Newton, Bill 88
Nibler, Jane 237
Nichols, Kevin 219–221
Nix, Sharon 130
Noe, Jim 44, 236
Noe, Mary Beth 44
Nolan, Gretchen 36, 47
Nolan, Richard 36, 47

Nordstrom, Mike 182
Nordstrom, Tim 182
Northern Lights 9, 17

O

O'Brien, James 212
Oktoberfest 237
Olczak, Ted 68
Old Piney Dell 122, 237
Oley, Billy 93, 224, 233, 237
Oley, Erin 93, 237
Oliphant, Brent 66
Ostrum, Barb 41, 64
Otsu, Paul 18, 27
Overton, John 22, 25, 39, 45, 234
Overton, Shirley 25
Owen, C.R. "Smokey" 214

P

Page, Lea 112
Pandolph the Bear 222
Papez, Doreen 103
Papez, Frank 102–103
Papez, Joe 102–103, 108
Papez, John 102
Papez, Mary 102
Parker, Beverly 63
Patchen, Shannon 237
Pat's Plumbing 34, 77, 112, 114, 116, 118, 129, 232
Perkins, Terry 37
Peters, John 101
Peterson, Carl 214
Philipsborn, Jon 187, 232
Pierson, Abraham 227
Pig Races. *See* Bear Creek Saloon & Steakhouse
Pippi the Clown. *See* Thomas, Jeanne
Pirtz, Frank 37, 97
Pitts, Sue 232
Planichek, Frank 92
Plumb, Kathy 3, 17
Pollard Hotel 124, 130, 226, 227, 229, 238
Pollard Pub 236, 237, 238
Pony Express Stop 32
Poore, Lila 33
Pride Park 150
Priest, Erin 237
Priest, Jason 218, 236
Priest, Paula 36, 52
Proeller, Yvonne 233
Prudden, Curt 46

Q

Quinn, Shirlee 45, 55
Quirk, Dari 94

R

Radio Shack 157
RATTS 232

Red Lodge Ales 110, 126, 146, 179, 224, 226, 227, 230, 232, 233, 235, 237
Red Lodge Area Chamber of Commerce 78
Red Lodge Books & Tea 115, 238
Red Lodge Café 2, 7, 129, 238
Red Lodge Carnegie Library 107, 237
Red Lodge Fire Rescue 231, 233
Red Lodge Lounge 226
Red Lodge Mountain 6, 15, 78, 126, 160, 228, 233, 236, 237
Red Lodge Music Festival 212
Red Lodge Pizza Co 3, 128, 226, 234, 236, 238
Red Star, Kevin 231
Reed, Andy 63
Regis Café 102, 231, 236, 237, 238
Regis Grocery 102
Reid, Willard 90
Reitz, Wells 238
Reko, Jesse 27
Reseland, Joe 63
Restani, Marco 43
Reynolds, Tera 214, 215–217, 224, 232
Rice, Charlotte 158
Richards, Betsy 59
Richards, Jim 59
Richards, Kit 38
Riches, Sheila 236
Rickbeil, Melissa 224
Ringer, Charlie 104, 231
Ringer, Emily 104, 231
Ringer, Mary 125
Ringer, Robby 33
Ritter, David 36, 106
Ritter, Donna 36
Rivard, Rick 88
Rivers, David 93, 233
Rivers, Robyn 18, 20, 24, 25, 27
Roat, Brian 159, 178, 215–217, 218
Roat, Shirley 103
Roat, Steven 122
Robert Burns Night 7
Roberts Café 238
Robertson, Phil 36
Roberts, W. Milner 89
Robichaud, Sean 154
Robinson, Emory 141
Robson, Doug 27, 149, 204, 238
Robson, Gary 2, 23, 25, 48, 55, 91, 115, 118, 136–137, 146, 171, 176, 195, 210, 238
Robson, Heather 15, 27, 28, 48, 124, 127, 238
Robson, Kathy 2, 25, 27, 55, 57, 169, 171, 181, 210
Robson, Keith 53
Rock Dodge Longboards 138, 224
Rodman, Gene 25, 123, 144–145
Roemmich, Eileen 40
Roemmich, Harvey 40

Rogers, Linda 106
Rolshoven, Evelyn 45, 47, 55
Romeijn, Bryan 39
Rood, Anne 18, 20, 21, 24, 60
Ropp, Macy 63
Ropp, McKenzie 63
Roscoe the dog. See Young, Roscoe
Rosin, Marek 47, 106
Round Man. See Kujala, Jim
Rudy's 127
Rylands, Ann 212

S

Sacks, Bobbie 39, 61, 130, 133
Sagebrush Sirens 238
Sager, Robb 236
Saint, Karen 37, 224
Sallade, Chuck 103, 109, 185, 230
Sam's Tap Room. See Red Lodge Ales
Sandretto, Anita 34
Sandretto, Laure 34
Sankey, Ryan 152
Savsek, Wally 102
Scanlin, Betsy 109, 159, 215–217
Scanlin, Carolyn 109
Scanlin, Don 109
Scanlin, Millicent 109
Scanlin, Steve 109
Scanlin, Tom 109
Scheidecker, Norma 41
Schilz, Angela 33, 197
Schuck, Gretchen 224
Schulyer, Alan 67
Scott, Kate 106, 170, 233, 235
Seiffert, Eliza 61
Seiffert, Jacob 235
Seiffert, Johnny 219–221
Seymour, Dan 58
Seymour, Martha 58
Shades & Specs 54
Shanks, Greg 231
Shaw, Tracy 62, 123–124, 144–145
Sheller, Ruth 36, 52
Shenk, Chuck 64
Shiver, Anita 53, 54, 57, 60
Shiver, Don 53, 60
Shriver, Nettie 89
Silver Run Veterinary 236
Silver Strike 226
Simpson, Tim 57
Skate Park 231
Smith, Doug 105
Smith-Estelle, Allison 51
Smith, Maud 104
Smith Mine 90–91
Snag Bar 111, 150, 224, 238
Snow Creek Saloon 6, 111, 157, 161, 224, 226, 227, 228, 232, 234, 235, 237
Sobral, Martha 36
Sokoloski, Linda 67

Sommerfeld, Stephen 33
Spicy McHaggis. See Hansen, Chad
Spragg, Mark 234
Squirrel Appreciation Day 133
Srock, Greg 236, 238
Stanhope, Charles 62
Stanhope, Virginia 62
Steen, Beth 110
Steinmasel, Lou. See Ward, Lou
Stevens, Dennis 64
Stevens, Jamie 64
Stevens, Nancy 63
Stewart, Callie 237, 238
Stifya, Wil 101
Storm, Marguerite 44
Stratton, Bill 54
S&T Ready Mix 18
Strum, Ernie 39
Strum, Marge 39
Stuber, Dolly 165
Subway 228
Super 8 228
Sutherland, Doug "Rabbit" 177
Swan, Judith 218
Swinging Door Saloon 150
Sylvan Peak 157, 224, 228, 232, 238

T

Table, Stylus T. 25, 101, 189
Taco Time 228
Tafoya, Estelle 150
Tate, Pat 37
Taylor, Mike 53, 57
Teini, Gina 232
Teini, Tom 114, 129, 218, 232
Temple, Bill 65, 224, 234, 236, 238
Terry, Edward 198
Terry, Guynema 98, 231
Tetrault, Marlene 38, 49, 55, 64
Theatorium 103
Thomas, Jeanne 98, 105, 212
Thomas, Kris 39, 126, 230, 235
Thompson, Candis 13
Thompson, Corey 134
Thormalen, Barb 128
Thornton, John J. 229
Toler, John 158
Tolle, Luke 237
Tower, Cheryl 14
Town Series 224
Tracy, Randy 10, 88, 151, 159, 182, 212
Trager, Eric 120
Trammel, Pam 59
Trammel, Troy 59
Trapp, Jon 38
Trapp, Katelyn 58
True Value Hardware 224
Tucker, Bridgett 40
Tucker, Doug 222
Tucker, Linda 40
Tucker, Mark 40

The Very Best of the Red Lodge Local Rag

Tucker, Pam 40
Tucker, Scott 40
Twice Touched 228

U

Ullr Fest 224
Upton, Dan 25, 32, 184, 230, 237
Upton, Tamara 232, 235
Upton, Taylor 35

V

Village Shoppe 110
Villard, Henry 89
Vinyl, Viv 101
Von Fossen, Ruth Pitcher 150

W

Ward, Lou 2–3, 6–9, 13, 23, 32, 48, 78, 109
Warner, Jeff 54
Warrington, Melissa 124
Waters, Betty 101
Waters, Wesley 101
Weamer, Tim 14, 78, 109
Weaver, John 102
Weaver's Livery Stable 102
Weaver, "Walking Tom" 236, 238

Weimer, Bud 126
West, Jay 132, 234
Weydt, Eddy 108
Whiteside, Shari 37
Whitney, Lucius 228
Williams, Don 42, 44
Williams, Gwen 159
Williams, Janis 42, 44, 224
Williamson, Kate 88
Willie Fire 86
Willows Inn 228
Wilson, Jarl 45
Wilson, Jerry 121
Wilson, Joan 111
Wilson, Kirsten 45
Wilson, Leo 111, 121, 209
Winter Carnival 224, 234
Witcomb, Clare 40, 150
Wolfson, Kerri 238
Wollenburg, Callie 214
Wollenburg, Hannah 214
Wooldridge, Bobbie 236
Wright, Harry 92
Wright, Myrna 156

Y

Yellowstone National Park 79–85
Yellowstone Wildlife Sanctuary. *See* Beartooth Nature Center
Young, Dianne 40
Young, Kent 40, 106, 162
Young, Martha 215, 224, 230, 235
Young, Matt 40
Young, Roscoe 215–217
Young, Tracy 40

Z

Zahn, Quincy 224
Zeiler, Greg 11, 111, 150, 236
Zimmerman, Jenny 14

www.ingramcontent.com/pod-product-compliance
Lightning Source LLC
Chambersburg PA
CBHW080519300426
44112CB00018B/2786